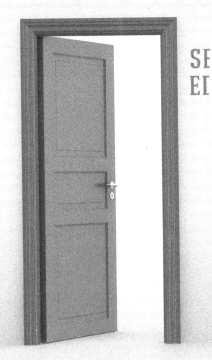

PEER-TO-PEER LEADERSHIP

Research-Based Strategies for Peer Mentors and Peer Educators

Gregory Metz ‖ Joseph B. Cuseo ‖ Aaron Thompson

Kendall Hunt
publishing company

Cover image © Shutterstock, Inc.

Kendall Hunt
publishing company

www.kendallhunt.com
Send all inquiries to:
4050 Westmark Drive
Dubuque, IA 52004-1840

Copyright © 2013, 2019 by Kendall Hunt Publishing Company

ISBN 978-1-5249-7671-2

Published in the United States of America

BRIEF CONTENTS

CONTENTS

Chapter 4: Social and Emotional Intelligence: The Foundation of Effective Leadership   107

Chapter 5: Setting Goals and Maintaining Motivation   139

Chapter 6: Managing Time and Tasks   171

Chapter 7: Academic Coaching: Helping Students Learn Deeply and Think Critically   197

Chapter 8: Holistic Leadership: Mentoring and Developing the Whole Person 235

Chapter 9: Leadership for Diversity: Appreciating and Harnessing the Power of Human Differences 277

Chapter 10: Leading Groups: Understanding Group Dynamics and Facilitating Teamwork 319

Chapter 11: Organizational Leadership: Leading Student Organizations and Catalyzing Campus-Wide Change　359

Chapter 12: Civic Leadership: Promoting Change at the Local, National, and Global Level　395

Appendix A: Key Campus Resources and Why Students Should Use Them　427

Appendix B: Leadership Self-Assessment Instrument: Assessing Your Leadership Skills and Attributes　431

Index　441

PREFACE

If you're reading this book, you are currently, or soon will be, a peer leader. Congratulations! Don't underestimate the impact of your leadership role. Changing the world starts with changing your piece of the world. As you will learn in the very first chapter of this book, research points resoundingly to the power of peer leaders and mentors. Working from the ground up, you have the potential to exert positive and significant impact on your peers, your campus, and its surrounding community.

Plan and Purpose of This Book

Outstanding leadership involves integration of knowledge from multiple fields of study and utilization of multiple skill sets. Nobody could or should expect to acquire this knowledge and skill set in a day, a week, a year, or even a lifetime. The best you can do is to make a commitment to leadership development that involves: (a) gaining knowledge about what constitutes effective leadership, (b) building on that knowledge to develop an intentional leadership plan, (c) putting your plan into action, (d) seeking feedback regularly on how well you're executing the plan, and (e) using the feedback you receive to continue growing as a leader.

This book will help you navigate each step in the leadership development process. It's designed to touch all the bases of effective leadership and equip you with the most powerful leadership practices and principles. If you haven't been a leader in the past, this book will help you become a future leader. If you've already had leadership experience, this book will help you build on that experience to become an even better leader.

Specific, action-oriented strategies make up the heart of this book. You will find that these strategies are not presented simply as a laundry list of leadership "tips." Instead, the recommended practices are accompanied by research-based evidence supporting their effectiveness. While it's certainly important to know *what* practices constitute effective leadership, it's equally important to know *why* the practices are effective. If you know the principle that underlies an effective practice, you can develop additional practices that implement the same principle and apply them to a variety of leadership settings and challenges—in college and beyond.

Since the strategies recommended in this book are grounded in leadership theory and research, you will find references cited throughout each chapter and a sizable reference section at the end of every chapter. Notice that the references cited represent a balanced blend of older, "classic" studies and more recent, "cutting edge" research. The wide time span of research cited, and the wide range of fields in which the research has been conducted, underscores the fact that the leadership strategies recommended in this book are timeless and transferable across different leadership roles and positions.

> *The man who knows <u>how</u> will always have a job. The man who also knows <u>why</u> will always be his boss.*
>
> —Ralph Waldo Emerson, influential 19th-century American essayist, poet, and champion of personal freedom

Since the strategies recommended in this book are research-based, you will see references cited throughout all the chapters and will find a sizable reference section at the end of the book. The references cited represent a balanced blend of older classic studies and more recent cutting-edge findings from a wide variety of fields. This range of research underscores the fact that the subject of leadership, like any other subject in the college curriculum, is a scholarly field that is supported by a solid body of knowledge that spans many decades.

Author's Experience I've had the opportunity to work with peer leaders and mentors throughout my professional career, including the privilege of coordinating an extensive peer-led Learning Communities program at the University of Cincinnati. I have learned from each peer leader and every leader of peer leaders. I have read and been inspired by numerous books on peer leadership, but have not found one source that has systematically pulled together a complete set specific, practical strategies for the full range of roles peer leaders play on college campuses, including personal mentoring, academic coaching, small-group facilitation, leading student organizations, and civic leadership. So, along with my colleagues, I humbly but excitedly accepted this challenge of creating a comprehensive resource to help peer leaders and mentors thrive in their varied and challenging roles. Writing this book has given me the opportunity to share what I've learned from my experiences with students, my professional colleagues, and the many peer leaders I've worked with over the course of my career.

— *Greg Metz*

Preview of Content

Chapter 1

The Purpose and Power of Peer Leadership

In this chapter, you will discover what leadership actually means and why it really matters. You will learn about the variety of leadership roles and positions that peer leaders occupy in higher education and the extraordinary impact they have on the students they lead. You will also gain insight into your leadership values, interests, and talents, enabling you to identify leadership roles that best match or "fit" your personal strengths.

Chapter 2

The Essence of Leadership: Essential Attributes, Foundational Theories, and Powerful Practices

This chapter provides a "big picture" overview of effective leadership principles and processes, as well as a summary of the key qualities and characteristics of successful leaders. You will learn about the myths and realities of effective leadership and discover that being a peer leader involves more than simply showing students "the ropes" or supplying them with a laundry list of college success "tips." Outstanding leadership requires deep knowledge of research-based leadership principles and theories, such as those discussed in this chapter.

Chapter 3
The College Experience: Applying Student Development Research and Theory to Promote Student Success

During the 1960s, record numbers of baby-boom children attended college. It was at this time that research on the college student experience began to explode. Studies continued over the next four decades, leaving us now with more than 50 years of research on how students learn and develop in college. The purpose of this chapter is to synthesize the major findings of this research and help you apply them to promote the success of the students you lead and mentor.

Chapter 4
Social and Emotional Intelligence: The Foundation of Effective Leadership

Relating well to others, and communicating effectively with them, is a key leadership skill and an essential element of "social intelligence." Similarly, "emotional intelligence"—the ability to be aware of and manage our own emotions and the emotions of others—is critical for effective leadership. This chapter identifies specific ways in which you can exhibit social and emotional intelligence. It also supplies you with interpersonal communication and human relations strategies that will help you develop positive relationships with students, which, in turn, will enhance your effectiveness as a peer leader and mentor.

Chapter 5
Setting Goals and Maintaining Motivation

One of the goals of peer leadership is to help students be successful, and since success is often defined as achieving one's goals, a key role of peer leaders is to help students identify their goals and the means (succession of steps) needed to reach their goals. Studies show that people are more likely to be successful when they set specific goals for themselves rather than simply telling themselves they're going to "try hard" or "do their best." This chapter supplies you with practical leadership strategies for helping students set specific, realistic goals and maintain their motivation until their goals are reached.

Chapter 6
Managing Time and Tasks

Setting goals may be the first step in the process of achieving success, but managing time and completing the tasks required to reach those goals is the critical second step. This chapter supplies you with a comprehensive set of mentoring strategies to help students establish personal priorities, manage time, combat procrastination, and complete tasks.

Chapter 7
Academic Coaching: Helping Students Learn Deeply and Think Critically

This chapter prepares you to be a "learning coach"—a peer educator who helps students learn deeply, think at a higher level, and achieve peak levels of academic performance. The chapter provides specific, research-based strategies you can share with and model for students to handle the key academic tasks they're expected to perform in college, such as: taking lecture notes, completing reading assignments, studying, and test-taking. Equipping students with these strategies will help them acquire learning and thinking habits that they can apply across the curriculum and throughout life.

Chapter 8

Holistic Leadership: Mentoring and Developing the Whole Person

Learning and development in college is maximized when students maintain physical wellness, are mindful of what they put into their body (healthy food), what they keep out of it (unhealthy substances), and how well they restore it (quality sleep). Students' academic performance in college and their ability to persist to college completion also depend on how well they maintain their mental health and cope with emotional stressors, particularly anxiety and depression. This chapter supplies you with leadership and mentoring strategies for helping students deal with the stress of college life, attain optimal physical and mental wellness, and develop holistically—as full ("whole") human beings.

Chapter 9

Leadership for Diversity: Appreciating and Harnessing the Power of Human Differences

This chapter explains what "diversity" truly means and documents how experiencing diversity deepens learning, strengthens critical and creative thinking, and enhances career development. The chapter arms you with specific strategies to help students break down barriers and biases that can block them from developing rewarding relationships with members of diverse groups. It also supplies inclusive leadership practices that you can use to foster collaboration among diverse groups of students and mentor students from diverse backgrounds.

Chapter 10

Leading Groups: Understanding Group Dynamics and Facilitating Teamwork

Leadership can go beyond mentoring individuals on a one-to-one basis to leading groups, both small and large. High-impact leaders understand how groups function and how to transform a group of individuals into a unified, high-performing team. This chapter equips you with specific strategies for building team vision and developing team commitment to that vision. You will also acquire practical strategies for delivering presentations to groups, managing group dynamics, and empowering groups to make consensus-based decisions.

Chapter 11

Organizational Leadership: Leading Student Organizations and Catalyzing Campus-Wide Change

Leadership can extend beyond influencing individuals and groups to producing positive change in entire organizations. Leadership in this wider arena requires knowledge of how organizational systems work and how to "work the system" to advance your leadership purpose and cause. This chapter discusses strategies for leading organizations effectively, employing your positional power ethically, and collecting committee input and assessment data to improve organizational performance and mobilize campus-wide change.

Chapter 12
Civic Leadership: Promoting Change at the Local, National, and Global Level

The mission of colleges and universities goes beyond that of helping students better themselves individually to helping students better their communities, their nation, and the world in which they live. You can contribute to this larger mission of higher education by engaging students in change efforts that go beyond the boundaries of your campus. This chapter provides you with peer-leadership strategies for promoting students' civic engagement, community service, participation in local and national elections, and involvement with worthy societal and global causes.

Appendix A
Key Campus Resources and Why Students Should Use Them

This appendix describes the key campus resources offered on most college campuses and, more importantly, the key reasons why students should take advantage of them. The specific names given to these resource centers or offices vary from campus to campus, but their purposes are similar, as are their benefits for students who capitalize on them.

One of your key roles as a peer leader and mentor is to connect students with campus resources that can promote their college success. It's probably safe to say that, after college, students will never again be part of another organization or community with so many resources and services at their fingertips that have been intentionally designed to promote their personal development and future success. By helping students take advantage of the campus resources available to them, you're helping them capitalize on a once-in-a-lifetime opportunity.

Appendix B
Leadership Self-Assessment Instrument: Assessing Your Leadership Skills and Attributes

Effective leaders continually assess how well they are leading and use the assessment results to become better leaders. The self-assessment instrument included in this Appendix is designed to help you engage in the process of continuous leadership improvement. It's not meant to be a test of your leadership competence or potential; it's simply a tool to help you recognize and accentuate your strengths and identify areas for self-improvement and future growth.

The instrument's 12 sections correspond to the 12 chapters of the book. You could complete the instrument one section at a time—right after you've read the corresponding chapter and completed its reflections and exercises. Using the instrument in this way would enable you to get feedback on whether you acquired the leadership knowledge covered in each chapter immediately after completing the chapter. You could also use the instrument to assess your overall leadership development. For example, you could complete the entire instrument *before* and *after* experiencing a leadership development course or program to assess how much you've changed or improved.

Lastly, you may use the instrument as a tool for "360 degree" assessment—a full-circle assessment process that involves not only assessing yourself, but also assessments you receive from your students and your supervisor(s). Comparing your self-assessment with the assessment of other parties can help you uncover personal leadership strengths you may have underestimated and discover leadership weaknesses you may have overlooked.

Sequencing of Chapters

The book's chapters are arranged in an order that addresses the following sequence of questions:

1. *Why* is peer leadership important?
2. *What* are the attributes, skills, and practices of effective leaders?
3. *How* do I become an effective leader in different leadership situations, both on and off campus?

The early chapters are intended to reinforce your decision to become a peer leader and help you discover what leadership roles and positions best "fit" your leadership talents, interests, and values. These chapters are designed to supply you with a blueprint or mental map for developing leadership self-awareness and leadership role-awareness. The middle chapters are devoted to preparing you for the practical, day-to-day realities and responsibilities of peer leadership in college. The final chapters focus on leadership in a larger context, demonstrating how leadership can be practiced in organizations and communities, and applied to societal, national, and global issues.

Process and Style of Presentation

The effectiveness of a book not only depends on what information it contains (the content); it also depends on how the information is delivered (the process). In this book, the following key learning processes have been built into the content-delivery process.

Reflections

At the *start* of each chapter, a question is posed to activate your thoughts and feelings about the chapter topic. This pre-reading exercise is designed to "warm up" or "tune up" your brain, preparing it to connect the ideas you will encounter in the upcoming chapter with the ideas you already have in your mind. This practice implements one of the most powerful principles of learning: Humans learn more deeply when they activate their prior knowledge relating to what they're about to learn and connect it to what they're about to learn. (This principle is referred to as "constructivism," meaning that deep learning occurs when the learner actively "constructs" or builds new knowledge onto previously acquired knowledge.)

Reflective questions are also interspersed throughout each chapter to give you time to think about the material you've just read. These timely pauses keep you mentally active throughout the reading process, breaking it up with opportunities to think, and breaking down "attention drift" that typically takes place when the brain continually processes information for an extended period—as it does when reading for a stretch of time.

Another way in which these reflective questions strengthen your understanding of the material is by prompting you to respond *in writing* to what you are reading. Compared with simply highlighting what you read, writing about what you read promotes personal reflection, deepens learning, and stimulates higher-level thinking.

Multiple Modes of Information Input

The information contained in this book is delivered through a variety of formats, including visual images, advice shared by current and former peer mentors, words of wisdom from famous and successful leaders, and personal stories drawn from the authors' experiences. Infusing variety and change of pace into the learning process improves concentration and motivation by combating "habituation"—the tendency for humans to lose interest in (and attention to) information that's delivered repeatedly through the same perceptual modality or that involves repetition of the same mental task.

Concept Maps

Contained in most chapters are concept maps designed to organize ideas presented verbally (in writing) into visual formats (diagrams and figures). When ideas are organized and depicted in a visual-spatial format, they're more likely to be retained because two different memory traces (tracks) are recorded in the brain: a verbal memory trace and a visual memory trace. (This memory improvement principle is known as "dual coding.")

Summary Boxes

Boxes containing summaries of key leadership concepts and strategies appear at different points in the text. These boxed summaries are designed to pull together the major ideas relating to the same concept and get them organized in the same place. When ideas that should be connected mentally are connected in the same place on a page, they're more likely to get connected in the same place in your brain.

Highlighted Passages

Within each chapter of the book, certain passages are highlighted to emphasize that the passage contains a high-impact, high-priority idea worthy of special attention and retention. Research on human memory indicates that information which is highlighted or stands out in some way is more likely to be attended to and remembered. (This memory principle is known as the "Von Restorff effect.")

Sidebar Quotes

Quotes from successful and influential people appear in the side margins; these quotes relate to and reinforce nearby ideas discussed in the body of the chapter. You will find quotes from accomplished leaders living in different historical periods and from notable leaders in a wide variety of fields, such as politics, philosophy, religion, science, business, music, art, and athletics. The wide-ranging timeframes, cultures, and vocations of the successful leaders quoted in this book

We do not learn from experience. We learn from reflecting on our experiences.

—John Dewey, American philosopher, psychologist, and educational reformer

I write to understand as much as to be understood.

—Elie Wiesel, Nobel prize winner and Holocaust survivor

suggest that their words of wisdom are timeless and universal. Their words can serve as both a resource for learning and a source of inspiration.

Tips and Tales from the Trenches

Throughout the book, you will find insights from students and advice from peer leaders at different stages of the college experience and college alumni. Studies show that students can learn a great deal from their peers, especially from peers "who've been there, done that." You, too, can learn much from the experiences of other peer mentors and from the students who benefited from the mentorship they provided.

Authors' Experiences

Each chapter contains personal stories drawn from the authors' experiences. We've learned many lessons from years of work with peer leaders, as college instructors, as student advisors, and as college students ourselves. We share these experiences with you to personalize the book and with the hope that you will learn from our experiences, including the mentoring and leadership mistakes we made!

Internet Resources

At the conclusion of each chapter, you will find recommended websites for additional information relating to the chapter's major ideas. If the material contained in the chapter ignites your interest and motivation to learn more about it, you can use these online resources to access additional information.

Exercises

At the end of each chapter are leadership exercises designed to help you think more deeply about the material and apply it to your leadership role or position on campus. Acquiring knowledge is just the first step to effective performance. Knowledge acquisition needs to be followed by knowledge application—taking the knowledge acquired and putting it into practice.

A Few Final Words

Keep in mind that it takes time for any effective skill to take hold and take effect; the same is true for leadership. At first, exhibiting the behaviors associated with excellent leadership is likely to require effortful concentration and intentional practice because many of these behaviors may not be familiar to you. However, by engaging in effective leadership practices repeatedly and reflectively, they will eventually morph into natural habits.

Furthermore, when leadership skills develop into enduring habits, they become integral elements of yourself—your leadership character. By continually applying the knowledge you acquired from this book, intentionally practicing the skills of excellent leadership, and consistently exhibiting the virtuous traits of a leader with character, you will make a real difference in the quality of life of those you lead, including your own.

Sincerely,

Greg Metz, Joe Cuseo, and Aaron Thompson

> One must learn by doing. For though you think you know, you have no certainty until you try.
>
> —Sophocles, ancient Greek philosopher

> We are what we repeatedly do. Excellence, then, is not an act, but a habit.
>
> —Aristotle, ancient Greek philosopher

> Sow an act and you reap a habit; sow a habit and you reap a character; sow a character and you reap a destiny.
>
> —Frances E. Willard, 19th-century American educator and women's rights activist

ACKNOWLEDGMENTS

I am grateful for great friends, great colleagues, great professional networks, a great wife and daughter and the hundreds of incredible peer educators whom I've worked with over the years at the University of Cincinnati. I thank you Paul Carty of Kendall Hunt for having the vision for this book, seeking my participation, and being persistent and patient during its ebbs and flows. I thank you Pam Person for your imagination, ingenuity, and artfulness in cultivating UC's First Year Experience and Learning Communities Program, placing your faith in me to lead the peer educator program, and heartily supporting my involvement in this book and similar efforts. You are a colleague and friend. Thanks to co-authors Joe Cuseo and Aaron Thompson—amazingly engaged educators, difference makers, and fine human beings. I thank my wife Sharon and daughter Lauren for your understanding as I toiled many a weekend with drafts of these manuscripts. You are my lights. Most of all, thank you to hundreds and hundreds of peer educators whom I have worked directly with at the University of Cincinnati and thousands of others who I have yet to meet. Your care for, concern for, and commitment to fellow students is truly laudable and remarkable. You make a profound difference each day in students' lives. We must transform learning and teaching in higher education. You have the power and potential to play integral roles. I hope this is just the beginning.

Greg Metz

Peers have made a major difference in my life, starting with two of my best childhood friends (Brian and Michael McMahon) who welcomed me into their neighborhood and valued me for the person I was, rather than attempting to persuade or pressure me to be someone I wasn't. I also owe a lot to my unofficial peer mentor in graduate school, Jim Cooper, who took interest in me as a whole human being and took as much pride in my accomplishments as he did in his own. Lastly, I'd like to thank the peer leaders who did so much for my son while he was in college, helping to transform him from a self-conscious, cancer-stricken high school student into a peer leader himself in college; they changed his life. My contribution to this book reflects my appreciation of them and my desire to give something back to current and future peer leaders.

Joe Cuseo

There were many peers in my life who have had powerful influence on my professional and personal development. They include peers who protected me from bullies and those who helped guide me through some rough waters in high school, college, and graduate school. They also include peers who were my coworkers, and friends who "had my back" and helped me get back on track when I sometimes got off track. I want to thank all of these peers for being my friends, mentors, and leaders.

Aaron Thompson

ABOUT THE AUTHORS

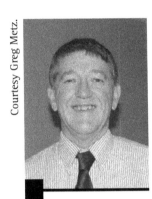

Greg Metz has served as the Assistant Director of the University of Cincinnati First-Year Experience and Learning Communities Program. He oversaw UC's extensive Learning Community Peer Educator Program, which trained and supported 80 to 100 peer educators each year and typically served more than 1,500 first-year students annually.

Greg has over 20 years of teaching experience at the graduate, undergraduate, and high school level. He also coordinated K-12 school change efforts, designed and taught first-year seminars, and has served as a faculty member for the Peer Educator Institute sponsored by The National Resource Center for The First Year Experience and Students in Transition.

Greg is a wholehearted music aficionado and basketball fanatic. He still plays hoops and will continue to do so for as long as he can.

Joe Cuseo holds a doctoral degree in Educational Psychology and Assessment from the University of Iowa and is Professor Emeritus of Psychology. He's a 14-time recipient of the "faculty member of the year award" on his home campus—a student-driven award based on effective teaching and academic advising, a recipient of the "Outstanding First-Year Student Advocate Award" from the National Resource Center for The First-Year Experience and Students in Transition, and a recipient of the "Diamond Honoree Award" from the American College Personnel Association (ACPA) for contributions made to field of student development and profession of Student Affairs.

Currently, Joe serves as a workshop facilitator and educational consultant for colleges and universities, including AVID for Higher Education—a non-profit organization whose mission is to promote the college access and success of underserved student populations. He has delivered hundreds of campus workshops and conference presentations across North America, as well as in Europe, Asia, Australia, and the Middle East. He has authored numerous articles and books on student learning, student retention, college teaching, and academic advising.

Aaron Thompson, Ph.D., is Executive Vice President and Chief Academic Officer at the Kentucky Council on Post-secondary Education and a professor of sociology in the Department of Educational Leadership and Policy Studies at Eastern Kentucky University. Thompson has a Ph.D. in sociology in the areas of organizational behavior and race and gender relations. Thompson has researched, taught, and/or consulted in the areas of assessment, diversity, leadership, ethics, research methodology and social statistics, multicultural families, race and ethnic relations, student success, first-year students, retention, and organizational design. He is nationally recognized in the areas of educational attainment, academic success, and cultural competence.

Dr. Thompson has worked in a variety of capacities within two-year and four-year institutions. He got his start in college teaching at a community college. His latest co-authored books are *The Sociological Outlook; Infusing Diversity and Cultural Competence Into Teacher Education; Diversity and the College Experience; Thriving in the Community College and Beyond: Research-Based Strategies for Academic Success and Personal Development; Humanity, Diversity, and the Liberal Arts: The Foundation of a College Education; Focus on Success;* and *Black Men and Divorce.* His upcoming book is entitled The Sociological Outlook. He has more than 30 publications and numerous research and peer-reviewed presentations. Thompson has traveled over the United States and internationally, giving more than 800 workshops, seminars, and invited lectures in the areas of race and gender diversity, living an unbiased life, overcoming obstacles to gain success, creating a school environment for academic success, cultural competence, workplace interaction, organizational goal setting, building relationships, the first-year seminar, and a variety of other topics. He has been or is a consultant to educational institutions, corporations, nonprofit organizations, police departments, and other governmental agencies.

CHAPTER 1

The Purpose and Power of Peer Leadership

Reflection 1.1

When you hear the word "leadership," what are the first words that come to mind?

Chapter Purpose and Preview

In this chapter, you will discover what leadership actually means and why it really matters. You will learn about the variety of leadership roles and positions that peer leaders occupy in higher education and the extraordinary impact they have on the students they lead. You will also gain insight into your leadership values, interests, and talents, enabling you to identify leadership roles that best match or "fit" your personal strengths.

What Is Leadership?

As you progress through this book, you will encounter different models, theories, and styles of leadership. Despite these variations, the common denominator that defines all forms of leadership is that it's a process of exerting positive *influence* or *change* (Northouse, 2016). Effective leaders are *change agents* who positively influence: (a) individuals, (b) groups, (c) organizations, (d) communities, or (e) society (Heifetz, Grashow, & Linsky, 2009; Higher Education Institute, 1996; Komives, Lucas, & McMahon, 2013).

> Influence is the sine qua non of leadership. Without influence, leadership does not exist.
>
> —Peter Northouse, *Leadership: Theory and Practice*

The Range and Scope of Leadership

As illustrated in Box 1.1, leadership can take place at different points along a spectrum or continuum, ranging from micro (changing an individual) to macro (changing society).

> The work of leaders is change. And all change requires that leaders seek ways to make things better.
>
> —Kouzes & Posner, *The Student Leadership Challenge*

Box 1.1

The Leadership Spectrum: Micro to Macro

Macro

Society: promoting positive change at a community level (e.g., providing leadership in local, regional, or national communities)

Organization: promoting positive change in an organization's policies, programs, practices, or procedures (e.g., student government, clubs, or associations)

Group: promoting positive change in small-group settings (e.g., orientation group leader or peer co-educator for a first-year experience class)

Individual: promoting positive change on a personal level (e.g., helping students individually as a peer tutor or peer mentor)

Micro

Reflection 1.2

As a peer leader, which of the micro-to-macro leadership opportunities along the leadership spectrum described in Box 1.1 do you have the most interest in? Why?

What Is Peer Leadership?

Helping students develop the integrity and strength of character that prepares them for leadership may be one of the most challenging and important goals of higher education.

—Patricia King, *Character and Civic Education: What Does it Take?*

Colleges are intentionally developing and deploying peers as student-support agents at a growing rate. The increasing use of peer support has been accompanied by an increasing number of terms used to describe who these peer-support agents are and what they do. Most commonly, they are referred to as "peer leaders" (Kouzes & Posner, 2012), "peer mentors" (Beltman & Schaeben, 2012), or "peer educators" (Ender & Newton, 2010). The term *peer leaders* will be used primarily in this book because it's an inclusive and comprehensive term that best captures the wide range of roles peers are now performing on college campuses across the nation. The term peer "leader" also accurately captures a common goal of colleges and universities: The development of future leaders (Astin & Astin, 2000; Zimmerman-Oster & Burkhardt, 1999). In fact, the primary mission of the original American colleges (the colonial colleges) was to prepare students to fulfill future leadership roles in our new country (Conley, 2005). According to many leadership scholars, America is currently in the midst of a leadership crisis and our colleges and universities need to renew their original commitment to preparing future leaders (Ehrlich, 1999; Korten, 1998; Lappe & DuBois, 1994; Lipman-Blumen, 2005).

What Is Peer Mentoring?

Although the term "peer leader" will be used primarily in this book, *peer mentor* is also a term frequently used to describe peer-support agents on college campuses. Mentoring has been defined in multiple ways (D'Abate, 2009); one comprehensive review of the literature on mentoring revealed that there were over 50 definitions of the term (Crisp & Cruz, 2009). However, there is a common thread that unites all definitions of mentoring: it involves a close interpersonal relationship in which a more experienced person (mentor) provides personal and practical support to a less experienced person (mentee or protégée) (Beltman & Schaben, 2012; Karcher et al., 2006).

The origin of the term "mentor" can be traced to the 8th century BC when it appeared in the *Odyssey*—an epic poem in which King Odysseus left home to fight in the Trojan War, leaving his son in the care of his most trusted friend and advisor—a gentleman by the name of Mentor. Thus, the meaning of mentoring is rooted in the idea of a close, ongoing, one-on-one relationship between a mentor and a mentee (a.k.a. protégée). In one of the earliest formal definitions of mentoring to appear in the peer leadership literature, Lester and Johnson (1981) define it as a "one-to-one learning relationship between an older person and a younger person that is based on extended dialogue between them. [It is] a way of individualizing a student's education" (p. 50).

Both peer mentoring and peer leadership involve promoting positive change (Johnson & Ridley, 2015). Peer mentoring may be viewed as a special and important form of peer leadership. What distinguishes peer mentoring is that it's a more personalized, relationship-based form of peer leadership that takes place over an extended period of time. The best peer mentors don't sit back and wait for personal relationships to happen by chance; they make them happen intentionally. They are social catalysts who initiate, facilitate, and cultivate relationships with others.

> *Mentorships first and foremost are relationships.*
> —W. Brad Johnson & Charles R. Ridley, *The Elements of Mentoring*

Author's Experience
Over the past few years, I have spoken personally to hundreds of student leaders and read thousands of reflections on their work. Over and over again, leaders report that the establishment of relationships was fundamental to effective leadership, whereby the leader was first and foremost a "peer" and then a source of expertise or guidance.

— *Greg Metz*

When a peer serves as a mentor, the boundaries between mentor and friend can often become delicate and blurred. Although peer mentors may have lots of experience and wisdom to impart to their student protégées, their primary role is to be a trusted friend. That being said, it's important for peer mentors to help students realize that they are also friends of a different type—friends with a vision and mission; they support students in their quest to achieve their academic and personal goals, have experience and wisdom to share with students to help them reach their goals, and serve as role models for students to emulate. By forming this type of relationship with students, the peer mentor becomes a special type of friend and provides a special type of peer leadership.

> *Mentoring [is] friendship with a vision.*
> —Evan Griffin, Professor of Communication, University of Cincinnati

Tale FROM THE Trenches
The most significant change I have dealt with was the transition from my students viewing me as a teacher/stranger to my students viewing me as a mentor/friend. I found a comfortable way to handle myself so that my students felt secure enough to come to me with personal problems while continuing to view me as a mentor and someone to look up to.

—PEER LEADER

Reflection 1.3

Has anyone ever served as a mentor to you? If yes, what did that person do for (and with) you?

Arenas of Peer Leadership in College

On college campuses across the country, peers serve as leaders in multiple roles and positions. The ways in which peers can demonstrate leadership on campus are almost limitless. However, most formal peer-leadership positions fall into the following three general arenas or categories.

1. **Academic Leadership.** Peer leaders can engage in a variety of academic leadership roles, including: (1) leading study groups and group projects, (2) providing peer tutoring, and (3) serving as co-educators in college courses (e.g., first-year seminars). Peer leaders can provide effective academic leadership in any of these roles without being intellectually gifted or brilliant, but simply by being serving as a learning resource for students who may be struggling academically and by modeling effective learning strategies, such as exhibiting intellectual curiosity, engaging in active note-takers in class, and contributing insightful questions and informed comments during class discussions.
2. **Social and Emotional Leadership.** Peer leadership and mentoring can be provided in ways that are more personal than academic in nature, such as making minority students feel welcome, reaching out to shy or bashful students, being an empathic listener, and supporting students who are experiencing setbacks or crises.
3. **Organizational and Civic Leadership.** Peers can serve as leaders on a broader scale, such as leading student clubs, campus organizations, fraternities, sororities, and athletic teams, as well as organizing community-outreach efforts and political campaigns.

Formal Peer Leadership Positions at Colleges and Universities

Colleges first began using peers to support and promote student development during America's colonial period when they were used exclusively as tutors (Winston & Ender, 1988). Since then, the formal roles played by peer leaders have steadily grown. By the 1950s, peer leaders were providing leadership in new-student orientation programs and residence halls (Powell, 1959). By the 1980s, peer leadership expanded to other positions, including judiciary programs, student activities, advising, counseling, study skills, and crisis intervention (Ender, 1984).

During the 1990s, the scope of peer leadership expanded dramatically (Dugan & Komives, 2007). One national survey conducted during that decade revealed that more than 85% of all colleges and universities reported they had students employed in peer leadership positions on campus (Carns, Carns, & Wright, 1993). This upward trend continued into the 21st century, as evidenced by the growing number of national conferences on peer leadership (College Summit, 2011;

Institute on Peer Educators, 2010; Inside Higher Education, 2017) and by the expanding number of peer-leadership positions occupied by college students. When you accepted the challenge of becoming a peer leader, you joined a major movement that's spreading rapidly across the United States and around the world (Keup, 2012).

Some of the key positions now being held by peer leaders are listed in Box 1.2. The wide variety of positions that appear on the list is testimony to the diversity and versatility of peer leadership. The list is long, but not exhaustive. It's likely that peers occupy additional leadership positions on college campuses that do not appear on this list. As you read the leadership positions and descriptions listed in the box, place a checkmark next to those that you think best "fit" your personal talents, interests, and values.

Box 1.2

Peer Leadership Positions in Higher Education

1. **Student Leaders of Campus Clubs and Organizations**—provide leadership for student government and student groups who share common interests or goals.
2. **Student Ambassadors**—work with college admissions offices to represent the college, recruit new students, and facilitate campus visits from prospective students and their families.
3. **Peer Orientation-Week Leaders**—welcome new students to campus and facilitate their transition to college life.
4. **Peer Resident Advisors (a.k.a. Community Assistants)**—provide advice, support, and guidance to students living in campus residences.
5. **Peer Mentors**—serve as role models and success coaches for new students.
6. **Peer Tutors**—provide learning assistance to students on an individual or group basis.
7. **Supplemental Instruction (SI) Leaders**—provide learning assistance for students enrolled in difficult courses (e.g., courses with high rates of Ds, Fs, or Ws) by leading supplementary group-study sessions regularly scheduled outside of class time.
8. **Peer Leaders for Learning Communities**—meet regularly to support students who enroll in two or more courses together (a learning community), helping these students connect with one another, their course instructors, and learning-support professionals.
9. **Peer Co-Educators/Co-Facilitators for First-Year Seminars**—work with instructors in first-year experience courses, serving as a liaison between instructor and students, providing a student perspective on course topics, and promoting student involvement in class and on campus.
10. **Peer Academic Advisors**—help students schedule classes and register for courses.
11. **Peer Counselors**—provide personal support for students relating to social or emotional issues and mental health.
12. **Peer Wellness Counselors**—assist students on matters relating to physical health and well-being.
13. **Peer Ministers**—support students' spiritual development and organize faith-based experiences.
14. **Peer Community-Service Leaders**—facilitate volunteerism and service to the community by organizing, publicizing, and encouraging student involvement in community-based experiences.
15. **Team Captains**—provide leadership for teammates participating in college and university athletic programs.

Reflection 1.4

Review the checkmarks you placed next to the leadership positions listed in Box 1.2. Why did you think those positions best matched your personal talents, interests, and values? Are there any leadership positions not listed in the box that are offered on your campus, or that you think should be offered on your campus?

Specific Peer-Leadership Roles and Functions

When formal peer-leadership positions are analyzed and examined at a more molecular level, it becomes clear that they involve a variety of informal yet influential roles—such as those summarized in Box 1.3. The long list of roles in the box illustrates the many subtle, yet powerful, ways in which peer leaders contribute to students' educational and personal development.

As you read through the alphabetized list of leadership roles described in Box 1.3, circle those that you think most closely match your talents, and underline those that you think will require the most preparation and practice on your part.

Box 1.3

Specific Roles and Functions Performed by Peer Leaders

Coach: provides guidance and feedback to improve students' personal performance.

Communicator: delivers information and shares knowledge in a clear, concise, and convincing manner.

Community Builder: promotes relationship building and a sense of belonging among students on campus or between students and people in the local community.

Confidante: serves as a sounding board for students to confide in, and as someone with whom students feel comfortable sharing their personal values, beliefs, concerns, and issues.

Educator: helps students learn how to learn and serves as a knowledgeable source of information about the curriculum, co-curriculum, college policies, and administrative procedures.

Group Facilitator: stimulates interaction, discussion, collaboration, and teamwork among students working in groups.

Guide: helps students stay on course, navigate the system, and circumvent potential obstacles or stumbling blocks that they typically encounter at different stages of the college experience.

Campus Catalyst: mobilizes the campus to make positive changes in practices, procedures, or policies.

Meaning Maker: helps students make sense of (find meaning in) the college experience, enabling them to see the "connection" between their present academic experience and their future life plans.

Motivator: challenges students to set personal goals and inspires them to reach the goals they set.

Organizer: plans and designs group functions, projects, and activities.

Problem Solver: helps students recognize and resolve academic and personal problems.

Referral Agent: connects (refers) students to campus resources in a sensitive and timely manner.

Role Model: serves as an example setter whom students can identify with, emulate, and aspire to be like.

Reflection 1.5

Look back at the leadership roles and functions you circled in Box 1.3 as those that best matched your personal talents, interests, and values. Why did you think these roles and functions match up well with your personal attributes?

The Importance of Self-Awareness and Self-Knowledge for Effective Leadership

A cardinal characteristic shared by all effective leaders is self-awareness and self-knowledge (Bennis, 2009; Bennis & Nanus, 1985; Wagner, 2006). Leadership starts with introspection—an internal search for and discovery of one's leadership identity. Leaders must first know who they are before they can become the leaders they want to be.

Self-awareness includes awareness of one's values. Leaders are more likely to promote positive change in others when they have deep knowledge of their personal values and act in ways that reflect and enact those values (Higher Education Research Institute, 1996). When leaders know themselves well, know what they stand for, and act in ways that are consistent with who they are, they become "authentic" leaders (George, 2003; George & Sims, 2007)—they lead in a way that's genuine and "real" (Shamir & Eilam, 2005).

Leaders who take on leadership roles that align with their personal values are more likely to develop the drive, passion, and commitment to become the best leader they can be. When leaders do what they value, they do it with greater strength, energy, and intensity. (Note that the word "value" derives from two roots: "valor"—to be strong, and "valence"—to be strongly attracted to.)

In addition to being aware of their values, effective leaders are aware of their *strengths* and *talents*. Research indicates that when people do what they have a talent for doing, they find it more interesting, meaningful, and fulfilling, and they also do it more successfully (Buckingham & Clifton, 2001; Kouzes & Posner, 2003). (See Exercise 1.3 at the end of this chapter for a self-assessment questionnaire that is designed to help you gain greater self-insight into your values, talents, and interests.) Once you have gained deeper insight into your leadership attributes, you are ready to take on a leadership role or position that best "fits" you and best capitalizes on your attributes (Haas & Tamarkin, 1992).

There's another benefit associated with choosing a leadership position that aligns with your personal values, talents, and interests: It helps you dodge the danger of spreading yourself too thin by taking on too many different leadership roles or responsibilities. One national survey revealed that close to 50% of peer leaders on college campuses held more than one peer leadership position at the same time, and almost 10% held four or more positions (Keup, 2010). Ambitious leaders sometimes take on too much, which can quickly lead to stress, burn out, and poor leadership results (Dugan & Komives, 2007).

> *Leadership development is fundamentally self-development, and it begins with an exploration of your inner territory.*
> —Kouzes & Posner, *The Student Leadership Challenge*

> *Perhaps the most basic life trait that translates to leadership effectiveness is honest, authentic self-awareness.*
> —Komives, Lucas, & McMahon, *Exploring Leadership: For College Students Who Want to Make a Difference*

> *Open your arms to change, but don't let go of your values.*
> —Dalai Lama, Tibetan Buddhist guru

> *I learned that everything I wanted to do, I can't do at one time . . . my plate's not big enough. That [being a peer mentor] taught me a lot about my limits . . . that if I spread myself too thin, I won't do a good job at everything.*
> —Peer leader

Be careful not to overextend yourself. Successful leaders focus their efforts on leadership roles that most closely reflect who they are, what they believe in, and what they do well. They go for quality, not quantity!

Positive Outcomes of Peer Leadership

Contrary to how peers are portrayed in the popular media, they are less often a source of negative "peer pressure" and more often a source of positive "peer power," serving as collaborators, teammates, and role models. Research repeatedly shows that peer leaders make significant contributions to the educational and personal development of the students they lead and mentor (Astin, 1993; Feldman & Newcomb, 1997; Pascarella & Terenzini, 2005; Mayhew et al., 2016). In particular, students involved in peer leadership have been found to exert positive influence on four key college outcomes: (1) student retention and persistence to graduation, (2) learning and academic performance, (3) social and emotional development, and (4) career readiness.

1. The Impact of Peers on Student Retention (Persistence to Graduation)

A college degree has always been a stepping-stone to personal growth, career success, and advancement to leadership positions in society. However, in today's knowledge-based, communication-driven world, a college education is more critical than ever. It's now essential that all high school graduates continue their formal education after high school in order to succeed in today's workforce and help our nation meet the economic challenges of the 21st century (College Board, 2008; McCabe, 2000). By 2020, more than six out of every ten jobs will require education beyond high school (Carnevale & Rose, 2014). In this competitive labor market, college students must complete in order to compete; if they withdraw without earning a credential or degree, their prospects for finding gainful employment will be seriously jeopardized (Collins, 2009). Furthermore, 3 out of 10 students who leave college before graduating will leave with loan debt (Johnson et al., 2009). Consequently, students who start college but don't finish typically end up paying a double penalty: They accrue immediate debt and forfeit future income (and other benefits) they would have earned if they had completed their college education.

Research consistently shows that student persistence to graduation is enhanced by peer support and peer mentoring (Pascarella & Terenzini, 2005; Mayhew et al., 2016; Ward, Thomas, & Disch, 2010). Campus studies indicate that students who receive support from peer mentors remain in college at higher rates than students who do not (Black & Voelker, 2008; Schwitzer & Thomas, 1998). One national study revealed that peers exerted more influence on student retention than all other social agents on campus, including faculty (Bean, 1985). Peer leaders can help create a sense of community among students, bind them to their college, and increase the likelihood that they will remain in college until they complete their degree (Braxton, Sullivan, & Johnson, 1997; Tinto, 1987, 1993, 2012).

Author's Perspective I believe in the power of social networks and that peers are vital for weaving those networks. Peers can support, emulate, and motivate one another. When colleges make a firm commitment to develop, mobilize, and honor the potential of peer leadership, the sky's the limit.

— *Greg Metz*

Ultimately, students are responsible for their own success. However, peer leaders can play a key supporting role by helping them navigate the adjustments, challenges, and choices they face in college. Many students begin college with significant gaps between their existing learning habits and the habits needed to achieve academic success. Other students enter college with productive habits, but lack motivation and direction. Peer leaders can play a pivotal support role, both helping underprepared and under-motivated students persist to degree completion and make the most out of their college experience.

2. The Impact of Peers on Student Learning and Academic Achievement

In addition to enhancing student retention, peers can exert powerful impact on student learning and academic performance. In a national study of almost 500,000 students at colleges and universities of all types, it was found that when peers interact with each other while learning, they achieve higher levels of academic performance. Peer mentoring programs, in particular, have been found to improve the academic achievement of college students (Leidenfrost et al., 2011; Rodger & Tremblay, 2003), particularly those who struggle academically during their first year (Salinitri, 2005). Furthermore, the learning benefits achieved through peer interaction are not restricted to formal, academic settings. College graduates often report that their most significant learning experiences occurred *outside the classroom* and were strongly influenced by interactions with their peers (Gallup-Purdue Index Report, 2014; Marchese, 1990; Murphy, 1989).

The best answer to the question of what is the most effective method of teaching is that it depends on the goal, the student, the content and the teachers. But the next best answer is students teaching other students.
—Wilbert McKeachie, *Teaching and Learning in the College Classroom*

Research also reveals that students' brains are much more active when they explain concepts to one another than when learning alone (Willis, 2006); both the explainer (peer teacher) and listener (peer learner) experience significant gains in learning (Mayhew et al., 2016; Pascarella & Terenzini, 2005; Whitman, 1988). In addition, studies show that when peers tutor other students, they experience gains in self-concept and achieve higher scores on graduate-school admissions tests (Astin, 1993).

I have been able to gain a better understanding of my own learning by actively engaging in the learning process of others.
—Peer leader

3. The Impact of Peers on Students' Social and Emotional Development

Research indicates that peer mentors can provide students with more effective social and emotional support than older mentors (Barrow & Hetherington, 1981; Grant-Vallone & Ensher, 2000) and are able to contribute to the development of students' social and emotional skills (Cross, 1985; Feldman & Newcomb, 1997; Goleman, Boyatzis, & McKee, 2002). In addition, students who serve as peer mentors make gains in their own social and emotional development—such as improved interpersonal skills, self-confidence, self-esteem, sense of purpose, and personal identity (Astin & Kent, 1983; Harmon, 2006; Schuh & Laverty, 1983). Lastly, it's been found that when students become involved in peer leadership and mentoring activities, they experience gains in social concern, development of altruistic values, civic engagement, and character development (Bennis, 2009; Komives & Wagner, 2009; Pascarella, Ethington, & Smart, 1988). In fact, many peer mentors report that their motive for getting involved in peer mentoring in the first place was to give back to other students the same type of support they received from others when they were new students transitioning to college (Bunting et al., 2012).

I enjoy it when my former students return [and] express to me the impact I have had on their lives. This is one of the best jobs I ever had.
—Peer leader

> Not only was I able to use the [peer leadership] experience as a resume builder, it actually became the center of my discussion in an interview. My interviewer spent 20 minutes during a one-hour interview discussing the responsibilities of being a peer leader. He was impressed that I was chosen for such a program.
>
> —Peer leader

> Education is the most powerful weapon which you can use to change the world.
>
> —Nelson Mandela, anti-apartheid activist, Nobel Peace Prize winner, and first democratically elected president of South Africa

> It is one of the beautiful compensations of this life that no one can sincerely try to help another without helping himself.
>
> —Ralph Waldo Emerson, 19th-century American essayist, poet, and leader of Transcendentalism (a philosophical movement founded on the principle of the inherent goodness of people and nature)

4. The Impact of Peer Leadership on Students' Career Readiness

College graduates consistently report that they developed career-relevant leadership skills and attributes as a result of their peer leadership experiences in college (Pascarella & Terenzini, 1991; Peter D. Hart Research Associates, 2006). These alumni reports are supported by studies of employers' job-performance evaluations of college graduates; these studies indicate that the best predictor of college graduates' successful performance in managerial positions in the workplace is their prior involvement in leadership positions while in college (American Telephone & Telegraph, 1984; Howard, 1986). In a multi-campus study that tracked students throughout their college experience, it was discovered that peer-to-peer interaction had the strongest effect on students' leadership development. In other words, students who interacted most frequently with peers while engaging in their academic and co-curricular experiences in college were most likely to acquire career-relevant leadership qualities and qualifications by the time they graduated from college (Astin, 1993).

In addition to these national findings, campus-specific studies indicate that peer leaders and mentors exert positive influence on students in other areas, including: (a) academic advising (Carns, Carns, & Wright, 1993), (b) health and wellness (Burke, 1989; Lenihan & Kirk, 1990), (c) interpersonal relationships (Waldo, 1989), and (d) intercultural interaction (Berg & Wright-Buckley, 1988; Keup, 2010).

Not only do peer leaders help other students, they help promote positive change on campus. Working "from the ground up," student leaders can serve as architects and artisans who shape and create better college communities. By becoming an educated peer leader, and by collaborating with faculty, advisors, student development professionals, and campus administrators, you can change the lives of students and make your campus a better place for both current and future students.

In short, when all the research on the positive impact of peer leadership is viewed together, it points strongly to the conclusion that peer leaders create a "win-win-win" scenario for three parties:

1. Their *peers*—who experience academic and personal benefits from interacting with peer leaders.
2. Their *campus*—where peer leaders can help build a campus culture characterized by higher college-completion rates for current and future students.
3. *Themselves*—when contributing to the development of other students, peer leaders simultaneously acquire knowledge and skills that contribute to their own college and career success.

Reflection 1.6

Which of the above three benefits of peer leadership were you least aware of? Now that you're more aware of it, what might you intentionally do to achieve it?

The bottom line: Research shows that peer leaders promote positive change in other *students*, in *themselves*, and in the *college or university* where their leadership takes place. That's a perfect trifecta!

Why Peer Leadership Matters

Research clearly shows that peer leadership matters, but why does it matter? One reason is that humans are inescapably connected to other humans, particularly those in their immediate social environment. We construct our own destinies, but we do so in a web of interpersonal relationships. Those relationships have a profound impact on our development and make a huge difference on the outcomes of our lives. Just as investors invest economic capital in businesses to promote financial growth, we invest in each other to create "social capital" for personal growth.

Social capital may be viewed as "sociological superglue" (Putnam, 2000)—it binds people together. To a significant extent, each of us owes a good deal of our individual success to social-capital networks. The people who have encouraged us, guided us, stayed with us through thick and thin, and kept us on course have contributed to our past accomplishments and our future aspirations. New college students, in particular, are likely to have strong needs for networking and social capital. They need support and direction from peers who have already successfully transitioned to college, who have a "feel for the game" and know how to navigate the system.

> Social capital refers to the collective value of all social networks [who people know] and the inclinations that arise from these networks to do things for each other. Social capital creates value for the people who are connected.
>
> —Harvard Kennedy School

Author's Experience I was the first in my family to go to college and didn't know anyone who knew how to "do college." My parents told me that if I could find a group of peers who seemed to understand the lay of the land, I'd be able to use their knowledge to help myself. So, I spent my first semester identifying students who made good grades and I joined organizations where motivated students were likely to be found. These peer connections also helped me make connections with supportive faculty and staff.

Because of the initiative I took to identify successful peers and because of their leadership skills and willingness to share their knowledge with me, instead of feeling like I was a stranger in a strange land, I found myself being part of a positive, socially supportive community.

———— Aaron Thompson

Peer leaders provide a particularly potent source of social capital because students are likely to see them as more approachable and less threatening than older professionals and authority figures (Gross & McMullen, 1983; Rice & Brown, 1990). Research indicates that students often prefer to receive personal support from experienced peers than from administrators or faculty (Rice & Brown, 1990). Since peer leaders are at a slightly more advanced stage of development than the students they are leading, students more readily relate to them and identify with them (Bandura, 1986; Ender & Newton, 2010; Vygotsky, 1978). In addition, the power of peer leadership is magnified by the fact that it can take place in settings beyond classrooms or campus offices where faculty and staff are not found, and at times when faculty and professional staff are not available.

Peer leaders also provide students with valuable social capital at a critical stage of student development—when new students are transitioning to college—a life-changing experience. Moreover, this transition takes place in an unfamiliar environment in which beginning college students have considerably more individual freedom, more personal choices, and more decision-making responsibilities than at any other time in their lives. When humans find themselves in unfamiliar, challenging, and stressful situations, they often look to others for cues on how to act (Conger, 1999; House, 1976). Particularly during times of social change and upheaval, people hunger for a leader (Parks, 2008)—they look for support and direction from others whom they see as successful and similar to themselves (Bandura, 1997)—someone like a peer leader. Your peers are watching you; the behavior you model matters.

As a peer leader, you can help students adjust to and navigate their new social environment by:

- Sharing your understanding of the rules of the road and strategies for navigating the transition to college
- Directing them to learning opportunities and campus resources
- Helping them acquire and refine skills needed to succeed in college
- Supporting them during setbacks and crises
- Working with them to create social-support networks.

Author's Experience

I have benefitted from the power of positive peer influence twice in my life. First, as a new graduate student with serious doubts about whether I could "cut it" at the graduate level, a student two years older than me took me under his wing, advised me, and instilled in me the confidence I needed to survive my first year. He also helped me change direction and find a graduate program that better matched my interests, talents, and values.

The second time I witnessed the power of positive peer influence came as a parent of a teenage boy who spent his entire high school years fighting a very serious form of cancer and suffering from severe side effects of chemotherapy (baldness, anorexia, stroke, and loss of social self-confidence). My son entered college with extreme self-doubt and trepidation. During his first term on campus, peers in a leadership fraternity (Delta Tau International) persuaded him to join their organization; it changed his life. He was transformed from a scared, self-conscious freshman into an optimistic, altruistic and gregarious student leader himself—who served as an orientation-week leader for three years and vice-president of student government during his senior year.

Thus, peers have played a major role in shaping my own life and the life of my only son. I will never forget these experiences and will forever be grateful for the power of peer leaders. In fact, one of my primary motives for co-authoring this book is to return the favor by contributing to the development of future peer leaders.

— Joe Cuseo

Reflection 1.7

Has a peer made a difference in your life? If yes, in what way(s) did that person contribute to your personal growth or development?

Internet Resources

For additional information on leadership and mentoring, consult the following websites:

Peer-to-Peer Leadership: A Sea Change, Starting With You
https://www.psychologytoday.com/blog/self-promotion-introverts/201402/
peer-peer-leadership-sea-change-starting-you

MY-PEER Toolkit: Peer Leadership
http://mypeer.org.au/planning/what-are-peer-based-programs/program-types/
peer-leadership/

Strengths Based Leadership—A Synopsis
http://www.harshman.com/assets/files/Strengths%20Based%20Leadership%20-
%20A%20Synopsis.pdf

National Resource Mentoring Center
https://nationalmentoringresourcecenter.org/

National Mentoring Month
www.nationalmentoringmonth.org

The Mentoring Group
https://mentoringgroup.com

References

American Telephone & Telegraph. (1984). *College experiences and managerial performance.* New York: AT&T Human Resource Study Group.

Astin, A. W. (1993). *What matters in college?* San Francisco: Jossey-Bass.

Astin, A. W., & Astin, H. S. (2000). *Leadership reconsidered: Engaging higher education in social change.* Battle Creek, MI: W. K. Kellogg Foundation.

Astin, H. S., & Kent, L. (1983). Gender roles in transition: Research and policy implications for higher education. *Journal of Higher Education, 54,* 309-324.

Bandura, A. (1986). *Social foundations of thought and action: A social cognitive theory.* Englewood Cliffs, NJ: Prentice-Hall.

Bandura, A. (1997). *Self-efficacy: The exercise of control.* New York: Freeman & Co.

Barrow, J., & Hetherington, C. (1981). Training paraprofessionals to lead social anxiety management groups. *Journal of College Student Personnel, 22*(3), 269-273.

Bean, J. P. (1985). Interaction effects based on class level in an explanatory model of college student dropout syndrome. *American Educational Research Journal, 22*(1), 35-64.

Beltman, S., & Schaben, M. (2012). Institution-wide peer mentoring: Benefits for mentors. *The International Journal of the First Year in Higher Education, 3*(2), 33-44.

Bennis, W. (2009). *On becoming a leader.* Philadelphia: Basic Books.

Bennis, W. G., & Nanus, B. (1985). *Leaders: The strategies of taking charge.* New York: Harper & Row.

Berg, H. H., & Wright-Buckley, C. (1988). Effects of racial similarity and interview intimacy in a peer counseling analogue. *Journal of Counseling Psychology, 35,* 377-384.

Black, K. A., & Voelker, J. C. (2008). The role of preceptors in first-year student engagement in introductory courses. *Journal of The First-Year Experience & Students in Transition, 20*(2), 25-43.

Braxton, J. M., Sullivan, A. S., & Johnson, R. M. (1997). Appraising Tinto's theory of college student departure. In J. C. Smart (Ed.), *Higher education: Handbook of theory and research, volume 12* (pp. 107-164). New York: Agathon.

Buckingham, M., & Clifton, C. (2001). *Now, discover your strengths.* New York: Free Press.

Bunting, B., Dye, B., Pinnegar, S., & Robinson, K. (2012). Understanding the dynamics of peer mentor learning: A narrative study. *Journal of the First Year Experience & Students in Transition, 24*(1), 61-78.

Burke, C. (1989). Developing a program for student peer educators. *Journal of College Student Development, 30,* 368-369.

Carnevale, A. P., & Rose, S. J. (2014). *The undereducated American.* Georgetown University: Center on Education and the Workforce. Retrieved from http://cew.georgetown.edu/undereducated

Carns, A. W., Carns, M. R., & Wright, J. (1993). Students as paraprofessionals in four-year colleges and universities: Current practice compared to prior practice. *Journal of College Student Development, 34,* 358-363.

College Board (2008). Winning the skills race and strengthening America's middle class: An action agenda for community colleges. *A Report of the National Commission on Community Colleges.* Retrieved from http://professionals.collegeboard.com/.../winning_the_skills_race.pdf

College Summit. (2011). *College summit: New York's fifth annual peer leadership conference.* Retrieved from www.collegesummit.org/.../csny-2011-peer-leadership-conference

Collins, M. L. (2009). Setting up success in developmental education: How state policy can help community colleges improve student outcomes. In *Achieving the dream: Community colleges count,* Boston: Jobs for the Future.

Conger, J. A., & Kanungo, R. N. (1998). *Charismatic leadership in organizations.* Thousand Oaks, CA: SAGE.

Conley, D. T. (2005). *College knowledge: What it really takes for students to succeed and what we can do to get them ready.* San Francisco: Jossey-Bass.

Crisp, G., & Cruz, I. (2009). Mentoring college students: A critical review of the literature between 1990 and 2007. *Research in Higher Education, 50*(6), 525-545.

Cross, P. K. (1985). Education for the 21st century. *NASPA Journal, 23*(1), 7-18.

Cuseo, J. (2010, March). Empirical evidence for the positive impact of peer interaction, support, and leadership. *E-Source for College Transitions* (Electronic Newsletter published by the National Resource Center for the First-Year Experience), 7(4), pp. 4-6.

D'Abate, C. (2009). Defining mentoring in the first-year experience: One institution's approach to clarifying the meaning of mentoring first-year students. *Journal of the First-Year Experience & Students in Transition, 21*(1), 65-91.

Dugan, J. P., & Komives, S. R. (2007). *Developing leadership capacity in college students: Findings from a national study. A Report from the Multi-Institutional Study of Leadership.* College Park, MD: National Clearinghouse for Leadership Programs.

Ehrlich, T. (1999). Civic engagement and moral learning. *About Campus, 4*(4), 5-9.

Ender, S. C. (1984). Student paraprofessionals within student affairs: The state of the art. In S. C. Ender & R. B. Winston, Jr. (Eds.), *Using students as paraprofessional staff.* New Directions for Student Services, No. 27 (pp. 3-21). San Francisco: Jossey-Bass.

Ender, S. C., & Newton, F. B. (2010). *Students helping students: A guide for peer educators on college campuses* (2nd ed.). San Francisco: Jossey-Bass.

Feldman, K. A., & Newcomb, T. M. (1997). *The impact of college on students.* New Brunswick, NJ: Transaction Publishers (originally published in 1969 by Jossey-Bass).

Gallup-Purdue Index Report. (2014). *Great jobs, great lives: A study of more than 30,000 college graduates across the U.S.* Retrieved from https://www.luminafoundation.org/files/resources/galluppurdueindex-report-2014.pdf

Gardner, H. (2006). *Five minds for the future.* Cambridge, MA: Harvard Business School Press.

George, B. (2003). *Authentic leadership: Rediscovering the secrets of creating lasting value.* San Francisco: Jossey Bass.

George, B., & Sims, P. (2007). *True north: Discover your authentic leadership.* San Francisco: Jossey-Bass.

Goleman, D., Boyatzis, R., & McKee, A. (2002). *Primal leadership: Realizing the potential of emotional intelligence.* Boston: Harvard Business School Press.

Grant-Vallone, E. and Ensher, E. (2000). Effects of peer mentoring on types of mentor support, program satisfaction and graduate student stress: A dyadic perspective. *Journal of College Student Development, 41*(6), 637-642.

Gross, A. E., & McMullen, P. A. (1983). Models of help-seeking process. In F. D. Fisher, A. Naples, & B. M. DePaul (Eds.), *New directions in helping and help-seeking,* Volume 2. New York: Academic Press.

Haas, H. G., & Tamarkin, B. (1992). *The leader within.* New York: Harper-Collins.

Harmon, B. V. (2006). A qualitative study of the learning processes and outcomes associated with students who serve as peer mentors. *Journal of The First-Year Experience & Students in Transition, 18*(2), 53-82.

Heifetz, R. A., Grashow, A., & Linsky, M. (2009). *The practice of adaptive leadership: Tools and tactics for changing your organization and the world.* Boston: Harvard Business School Press.

Higher Education Research Institute (HERI). (1996). *A social change model of leadership development: Guidebook version III.* Los Angeles: University of California Los Angeles Higher Education Research Institute.

House, R. J. (1976). A 1976 theory of charismatic leadership. In J. G. Hunt & L. I. Larson (Eds.), *Leadership: The cutting edge* (pp. 189-207). Carbondale: Southern Illinois University Press.

Howard, A. (1986). College experiences and managerial performance. *Journal of Applied Psychology, 71*(3), 530-552.

Inside Higher Education. (2017). "2017 national conference on student leadership." Retrieved from https://www.insidehighered.com/events/2016/07/25/2017-national-conference-student-leadership

Institute on Peer Educators. (2010). Indianapolis, Indiana. Retrieved from www.sc.edu/fye/ipe/faculty.html

Johnson, W. B., & Ridley, C. R. (2015). *The elements of mentoring.* New York: St. Martin's Press.

Johnson, J., Rochkind, J., Ott, A. N., & DuPoint, S. (2009). *With their whole lives ahead of them: Myths and realities about why so many students fail to finish college.* A public agenda report for the Bill & Melinda Gates Foundation. New York: Public Agenda.

Karcher, M. J., Kuperminc, G. P., Portwood, S. G., Sipe, C. L., & Taylor, A. S. (2006). Mentoring programs: A framework to inform program development, research, and evaluation. *Journal of Community Psychology, 34*(6), 709-725.

Keup, J. R. (2010, October). *National context and institutional practice: Findings from a national survey of peer leadership experiences and outcomes.* Presentation at the Institute on Peer Educators, Indianapolis, IN.

Keup, J. R. (2012). Editor's notes. In J. R. Keup (Ed.), *Peer leadership in higher education* (pp. 1-3). New Directions for Higher Education, no. 157. San Francisco: Jossey-Bass.

Komives, S. R., Lucas, N. & McMahon, T. R. (2013). *Exploring leadership: For college students who want to make a difference* (3rd ed.). San Francisco: Jossey Bass.

Komives, S., & Wagner, W. (2009). *Leadership for a better world: Understanding the social change model of leadership development.* San Francisco: Jossey-Bass.

Korten, D. C. (1998). *Globalizing civil society: Reclaiming our right to power.* New York: Seven Stories Press.

Kouzes, M. M., & Posner, B. Z. (2003). *Encouraging the heart: A leader's guide to rewarding and recognizing others.* San Francisco: Jossey-Bass.

Kouzes, M. M., & Posner, B. Z. (2008). *The student leadership challenge: Five practices for exemplary leaders.* San Francisco: Jossey-Bass.

Kouzes, M. M., & Posner, B. Z. (2012). *The leadership challenge* (5th ed.) San Francisco: Jossey-Bass.

Lappe, F. M., & DuBois, P. M. (1994). *The quickening of America: Rebuilding our nation, remaking our lives.* San Francisco: Jossey-Bass.

Leidenfrost, B., Strassnig, B., Schabmann, A., Spiel, C., & Carbon, C. (2011). Peer mentoring styles and their contribution to academic success among mentees: A person oriented study in higher education. *Mentoring and Tutoring: Partners in Learning, 19*(3), 347-364.

Lenihan, G., & Kirk, W. G. (1990). Using student paraprofessionals in the treatment of eating disorders. *Journal of Counseling & Development, 68,* 332-335.

Lester, V., & Johnson, C. S. (1981). The learning dialogue: Mentoring. In J. Fried (Ed.), *Education for student development.* New Directions for Student Services, no. 15. San Francisco: Jossey-Bass.

Lipman-Blumen, J. (2005). *The allure of toxic leaders.* New York: Oxford University Press.

Marchese, T. J. (1990). A new conversation about undergraduate teaching: An interview with Professor J. Light, convener of the Harvard Assessment Seminars. *AAHE Bulletin, 42*(9), 3-8.

Mayhew, M. K., Rockenbach, A. N., Bowman, N. A., Seifert, T. A., Wolniak, G. C., Pascarella, E. T., & Terenzini, P. T. (2016). *How college affects students, volume 3: 21st century evidence that higher education works.* San Francisco: Jossey-Bass.

McCabe, R. H. (2000). *No one to waste: A report to public decision-makers and community college leaders.* Washington, DC: American Association of Community Colleges.

Murphy, R. O. (1989). Academic and student affairs in partnership for freshman success. In M. L. Upcraft, J. N. Gardner and Associates (Eds.), *The freshman year experience* (pp. 375-384). San Francisco: Jossey-Bass.

Northouse, P. G. (2016). *Leadership: Theory and practice* (7th ed.). Thousand Oaks, CA: SAGE.

Parks, S. D. (2008). Leadership, spirituality, and the college as a mentoring environment. *Journal of College & Character, 10*(2), 1-9.

Pascarella, E. T., Ethington, C. A., & Smart, J. C. (1988). The influence of college on humanitarian/civic involvement values. *Journal of Higher Education, 59*, 412-437.

Pascarella, E., & Terenzini, P. (1991). *How college affects students: Findings and insights from twenty years of research.* San Francisco: Jossey-Bass.

Pascarella, E. T., & Terenzini, P. T. (2005). *How college affects students, Volume 2: A third decade of research.* San Francisco: Jossey-Bass.

Peter D., Hart Research Associates. (2006). *How should college prepare students to succeed in today's global economy?* Washington, DC: American Association of Colleges & Universities.

Powell , O. B. (1959). The student who assumes counseling responsibilities. In M. D. Hardee (Ed.), *The faculty in college counseling* (pp. 225-238). New York: McGraw-Hill.

Putnam, R. D. (2000). *Bowling alone: The collapse and revival of American community.* New York: Simon & Schuster.

Rice, M. B., & Brown, R. D. (1990). Developmental factors associated with self-perceptions of mentoring competence and mentoring needs. *Journal of College Student Development, 31*, 293-299.

Rodger, S., & Tremblay, P. F. (2003). The effects of a peer mentoring program on academic success among first year university students. *The Canadian Journal of Higher Education, 33*(3), 1-18.

Salinitri, G. (2005). The effects of formal mentoring on the retention rates for first-year low achieving students. *Canadian Journal of Education, 28*(4), 853-873.

Schuh, J. H., & Laverty, M. (1983). The perceived long term effect of holding a significant student leadership position. *Journal of College Student Personnel, 24*, 28-32.

Schwitzer, A. M., & Thomas, C. (1998). Implementation, utilization, and outcomes of a minority freshman peer mentor program at a predominantly White university. *Journal of The First-Year Experience & Students in Transition, 10*(1), 31-50.

Shamir, B., & Eilam, G. (2005). "What's your story?" A life-stories approach to authentic leadership development. *Leadership Quarterly, 16*, 395-417.

Tinto, V. (1987). *Leaving college: Rethinking the causes and cures of student attrition.* Chicago: The University of Chicago Press.

Tinto, V. (1993). *Leaving college: Rethinking the causes and cures of student attrition* (2nd ed.). Chicago: The University of Chicago Press.

Tinto, V. (2012). *Completing college: Rethinking institutional action.* Chicago: The University of Chicago Press.

Vygotsky, L. S. (1978). Internalization of higher cognitive functions. In M. Cole, V. John-Steiner, S. Scribner, & E. Souberman (Eds. & Trans.), *Mind and society: The development of higher psychological processes* (pp. 52–57). Cambridge, MA: Harvard University Press.

Wagner, W. (2006). The social change model of leadership: A brief overview. *Concepts & Connections, 15*(1), p. 9.

Waldo, M. (1989). Primary prevention in university residence halls: Paraprofessional-led relationship enhancement groups for college roommates. *Journal of Counseling and Development, 67*, 465-472.

Ward, E. G., Thomas, E. E., & Disch, W. B. (2010). Goal attainment, retention and peer mentoring. *Academic Exchange Quarterly, 14*(2), 170-176.

Whitman, N. A. (1988). *Peer teaching: To teach is to learn twice.* ASHE-ERIC Higher Education Report No. 4. Washington, DC: Association for the Study of Higher Education.

Willis, J. (2006). *Research-based strategies to ignite student learning: Insights from a neurologist and classroom teacher.* Alexandria, VA: ASCD.

Winston, R. B., Jr., & Ender, S. C. (1988). Use of student paraprofessionals in divisions of college student affairs. *Journal of Counseling and Development, 66*, 466-473.

Zimmerman-Oster, K., & Burkhardt, J. C. (1999). *Leadership in the making: Impact and insights from leadership development programs in U. S. colleges and universities.* Battle Creek, MI: W. K. Kellogg Foundation.

Exercise 1.1 Quote Reflections

Review the sidebar quotes contained in this chapter and select two you think would be especially valuable to share with the students you lead or mentor.

For each quote, write a short statement explaining why you chose it.

Exercise 1.2 Journal Reflections

Journaling can stimulate leadership self-awareness and personal growth. It can also be the starting point for creating a leadership portfolio that may be presented to potential employers or included as part of your admission application to graduate and professional schools.

You can start keeping a leadership journal by recording your thoughts, either in electronic format or in a composition book, beginning with your response to the following reflection questions. (You can continue to build your learning journal and potential portfolio by responding to the journal reflection questions that appear at the end of every chapter in this book.)

1. Do you currently see yourself as a leader? Why?

2. In what specific situations have you found yourself serving as a leader?
   a. What did you learn about your leadership qualities in these situations?

   b. What did you do most effectively?

   c. What did you find most challenging?

3. In what types of leadership situations or roles do you think you have the most leadership potential?

4. Who would you like to lead/mentor and what positive changes or outcomes would you like to see?

5. What personal skills or attributes would you like to acquire or strengthen as a result of your peer leadership experience?

6. If you had the opportunity to observe or interview someone holding a leadership position on or off campus, what position would that person hold? Why would you choose to interview this particular person?

7. Think about the leadership position you're considering, preparing for, or currently occupy:
   a. Why are you pursuing or working in this particular position? (What led to your interest in it?)

   b. Would you say that your interest in leadership is motivated primarily by *intrinsic* factors— i.e., factors "inside" you, such as personal fulfillment or altruism? Or, would you say that your interests are driven more by *extrinsic* factors—i.e., factors "outside" you, such as building your resume or earning extra money?

Exercise 1.3 Gaining Self-Awareness of Your Personal Values, Talents, and Interests

No one is in a better position to know who you are—and what you want to become—than *you*. One way to gain this self-knowledge is through self-questioning. Asking yourself good questions can launch you on an inward quest toward self-discovery—the critical first step to effective leadership. You can begin the discovery process by asking yourself questions that encourage you to think deeply about your:

a) values—what you believe is *worth* doing,

b) talents—what you're *good* at doing, and

c) interests—what you *like* to do.

> The unexamined life is not worth living.
>
> —Socrates, legendary Greek philosopher

Answering the following questions should sharpen self-awareness of your interests, abilities, and values. After reading each question, jot down what comes to mind about yourself.

Personal Values

1. What matters most to you?

> In order to succeed, you must know what you are doing, like what you are doing, and believe in what you are doing.
>
> —Will Rogers, Native-American humorist and actor

2. If you were to single out one thing you really stand for or believe in, what would it be?

3. What would you say are your highest priorities in life?

4. When you're doing something that makes you feel proud, or makes you feel good about yourself, what does it usually tend to be?

5. If there were one thing in the world you could change, improve, or make a difference in, what would it be?

6. When you have extra spending money, what do you usually spend it on?

7. When you have free time, what do you usually find yourself doing?

8. For you, what would "living the good life" or "living the dream" be?

9. How would you define success? (What would it take for you to feel that you were successful?)

10. How would you define happiness? (What would it take for you to be happy?)

11. Do you have any heroes or anyone you admire, look up to, or believe has set an example worth following? (If yes, who and why?)

12. Would you rather be thought of as:

    (a) smart,

    (b) wealthy,

    (c) creative, or

    (d) caring?

    (Rank from 1 to 4, with 1 being the highest.) (Why did you rank #1 highest?)

> *Do what you value; value what you do.*
>
> —Sidney Simon, author of *Values Clarification and In Search of Values*

*From your responses to the above questions, identify a leadership role or position you think would be most compatible with your personal *values*. Explain why.

Personal Talents

1. What would you say is your greatest talent or strongest ability?

2. What are your most advanced or well-developed skills?

3. What comes naturally or easily to you that seems to come harder to others?

4. What would you say has been your greatest accomplishment or achievement in life thus far?

5. What about yourself are you most proud of, or take most pride in doing?

6. When others compliment you, what is it usually for?

7. If others come to you for help, advice, or assistance, what is it usually for and why do you think they choose you?

8. What would your best friend(s) say is your best quality, trait, or characteristic?

9. What have you accomplished or overcome that's given you a feeling that you might have a special talent for doing it?

10. If you have received awards or other forms of recognition, what have they been for?

11. On what types of learning tasks or activities have you experienced the most success?

> Never desert your line of talent. Be what nature intended you for and you will succeed.
> —Sydney Smith, 18th-century English writer and defender of the oppressed

12. In what types of courses do you tend to earn the highest grades?

*From your responses to the above questions, identify a type of leadership role or position you think would be most compatible with your personal *talents*. Explain why.

Personal Interests

1. What things are you naturally curious about or that frequently intrigue you?

2. What types of activities or experiences are you able to engage in and focus your attention on for long periods of time?

3. When time seems to "fly by" for you, what are you usually doing?

4. When your mind begins to wander, where does it usually take you?

5. What do you look forward to doing or get most excited about doing?

6. What are your favorite hobbies or pastimes?

7. When you're with friends, what do you usually talk about and spend time doing?

8. What has been your most stimulating or enjoyable learning experience?

9. If you've had previous work or volunteer experience, what jobs or tasks did you find most interesting?

10. What do you like to read?

11. When you open a newspaper or log onto the Internet, what do you tend to read first?

12. When you daydream or fantasize about your future, what do you imagine yourself doing?

*From your responses to the above questions, identify a leadership role or position that you think would be most compatible with your personal *interests*. Explain why.

Exercise 1.4 Gaining Self-Awareness of Different Forms of Intelligence

Read through the following forms of intelligence and place a checkmark next to the type that you think is your strongest form. (You can check more than one type.)

1. *Linguistic* **Intelligence:** ability to comprehend the meaning of words and communicate through language; possessing verbal skills relating to speaking, writing, listening, and learning foreign languages.

2. *Logical-Mathematical* **Intelligence:** aptitude for understanding logical patterns, making and following logical arguments; ability to work well with numbers; good at solving mathematical problems and making quantitative calculations.

3. *Spatial* **Intelligence:** aptitude for visualizing relationships among objects arranged in different spatial positions and ability to perceive or create visual images; ability to form mental images of three-dimensional objects; capable of detecting detail in objects or drawings; proficient at drawing, painting, sculpting, or graphic design; good sense of direction and ability to navigate unfamiliar places.

4. *Musical* **Intelligence:** able to appreciate or create rhythmical and melodic sounds, and play, compose, or arrange music.

5. *Interpersonal (Social)* **Intelligence:** ability to relate to people and accurately identify their needs, motivations, and emotional states; effective at expressing emotions and feelings to others; good interpersonal communication skills; ability to accurately "read" the feelings of others and meet their emotional needs.

6. *Intrapersonal (Self)* **Intelligence:** ability to introspect and understand one's own thoughts, feelings, and behaviors; capacity for engaging in personal reflection, gaining emotional self-awareness, and having clear insight into personal strengths and weaknesses.

7. *Bodily–Kinesthetic (Psychomotor)* **Intelligence:** ability to control one's own body skillfully and learn through bodily sensations or movements; skilled at tasks that involve physical coordination, working well with hands, operating machinery, building models, assembling things, or using technology.

8. *Naturalist* **Intelligence:** ability to carefully observe and appreciate features of the natural environment; keen awareness of nature and natural surroundings; ability to understand causes and consequences of events occurring in the natural world.

9. *Existential* **Intelligence:** ability to conceptualize phenomena and ponder experiences that go beyond sensory experiences and physical evidence, such as questions involving the origin, meaning, and purpose of human existence.

Source: Gardner (1993, 1999, 2006).

* Based on the checkmarks you placed next to your strongest forms of intelligence, what leadership positions, roles, or tasks do you think would best match your mental talents? Why?

Exercise 1.5 Leadership "Fit"

Using your Student Handbook or College Catalog (Bulletin), make a list of all the official peer leader positions on your campus and their primary roles or responsibilities. After compiling the list, highlight the position(s) you think best match your interests, skills (talents), and values.

Exercise 1.6 Character Strengths Assessment

Go to *www.viacharacter.org* and take the 15-minute character strengths test at this site. Review the personalized report of your results and identify:

a) your greatest character strengths, and

b) the type of leadership position(s) on campus that best reflect your character strengths.

Exercise 1.7 Leadership Information Interview

Interview someone holding a leadership position, particularly someone you consider to be an effective leader. Possible candidates for this interview include professionals working on or off campus, current peer leaders, and friends or family members. During the interview, ask some or all of the following questions. (Feel free to add or substitute questions of your own.)

1. What interested you in, or led you to, your current leadership position?

2. What advice would you give to others about how they could best prepare for the leadership position you hold?

3. During a typical day or week, what types of leadership responsibilities or activities consume most of your time?

4. What personal qualities or prior experiences have contributed most to your effectiveness as a leader?

5. What skills, perspectives, or attributes do you see as being critical for success in your particular leadership role?

6. What do you like most about your leadership role?

7. What are the most difficult or frustrating aspects of your leadership position?

8. Are there particular moral issues or ethical challenges you tend to encounter in your leadership role?

9. Do your leadership responsibilities include interacting with people of diverse ethnic/racial groups and lifestyles?

10. What impact do your leadership responsibilities have on other aspects of your life?

11. What do you do to continue learning and developing as a leader?

12. To gain additional insights into the nature of effective leadership, is there a leader you respect or admire whom you would recommend I speak with?

* Personal Reflections on the Interview:

a) What impressed you most about this leader?

b) What was the most useful leadership idea or strategy you acquired during the interview?

c) Did you learn anything during the interview that surprised or concerned you about the process of leadership?

d) As a result of conducting the interview, did your interest in or motivation for leadership increase, decrease, or remain the same? Why?

Exercise 1.8 Strategy Reflections

Review the strategies recommended for helping college students *adjust to and navigate their new social environment* on p. 12. Select two that you think students would be most receptive to learning about and putting into practice.

CHAPTER 2

The Essence of Leadership

Essential Attributes, Foundational Theories, and Powerful Practices

Reflection 2.1

If you were to name one trait or attribute that characterizes all effective leaders, what would it be?

Chapter Purpose and Preview

This chapter provides a "big picture" overview of effective leadership principles and processes, as well as a summary of the key qualities and characteristics of successful leaders. You will learn about the myths and realities of effective leadership and discover that being an effective peer leader involves more than merely showing students "the ropes" or supplying them with a laundry list of college success "tips." Outstanding leadership requires deep knowledge of research-based leadership principles and theories, such as those discussed in this chapter.

Knowledge is power.

—Francis Bacon, influential English philosopher and advocate for the scientific pursuit of knowledge

The Practice of Effective Leadership

Kouzes and Posner (2002, 2012, 2016) collected thousands of stories from leaders about their most successful leadership experiences. Employing a research method known as *content analysis*, these researchers read, reread, and picked apart the content of the leaders' stories. Their analysis revealed five universal themes or "exemplary practices" associated with effective leadership in a variety of contexts. Leaders who make extraordinarily positive changes in the individuals and groups they lead tend to engage in five key practices. These outstanding leaders:

- Inspire a Shared Vision,
- Model the Way,
- Enable Others to Act,
- Encourage The Heart, and
- Challenge the Process.

1. Inspire a Shared Vision

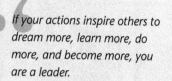

If your actions inspire others to dream more, learn more, do more, and become more, you are a leader.

—John Quincy Adams, sixth president of the United States

Great leaders share "exciting and ennobling possibilities . . . and enlist others in a common vision appealing to shared aspirations" (Kouzes & Posner, 2002, pp. 14 & 16). They are ambitious and optimistic about the possibilities of making positive change in themselves and in the individuals, groups, and organizations of which they are a part, and they get followers to share their vision and optimism. Effective leaders keep their vision front and center, and motivate others to believe in their view of the future.

2. Model the Way

Mentors don't stop with words . . . they furnish a living example.

—Tim Elmore, founder and president of Growing Leaders

Modeling the way means "demonstrating intense commitment to your beliefs with each and every action" (Kouzes & Posner, 2002, p. 63). Great leaders reflect on their values and consciously align their actions with their values. They practice what they preach; they "walk the talk"; their actions speak as loud as (or louder than) their words.

Reflection 2.2

If you don't live it, it won't come out of your horn.

—Charlie "Bird" Parker, famous jazz saxophonist, composer, and originator of Bebop

In the leadership position you hold, or may hold, what would be the most important behaviors you need to model for other students?

3. Enable Others to Act

Outstanding leaders "strengthen others by sharing power and discretion" (Kouzes & Posner, 2002, p. 301). They lead to be part of something, not the center of everything. They don't view themselves as being better than or superior to their followers; instead, they view followers as equal partners in a relationship that promotes the growth of both parties (Grayson & Speckhart, 2006; Hollander, 1992; Rost, 1991). Effective leaders enable their followers to feel capable and influential by engaging them in the execution of their leadership plan. Gradually, great leaders recede and let their followers gain more ownership of the plan, empowering them to become leaders themselves.

> Leadership isn't about you; it's about them. It's not a "me" thing; it's a "we" thing.

4. Challenge the Process

To lead, one must follow.

—Lao Tzu, ancient Chinese philosopher and founder of Taoism—a philosophy that emphasizes thought before action

Successful leaders continually "search for opportunities to change, grow and improve" (Kouzes & Posner, 2002, p. 194). They don't assume the world as it is represents the world as it should be. They seek to create and innovate. They're willing to experiment, take risks, and learn from their experiences—both setbacks and successes. Rather than settling for mediocrity, they push themselves to be the best they can be and supportively challenge their followers to do the same.

5. Encourage the Heart

Effective leaders are acutely aware of the emotional dimension of leadership. They take the time to recognize their followers' efforts, achievements, and victories. When their followers experience setbacks, they help them remain optimistic, hopeful, and resilient.

Remember that the five characteristics of outstanding leaders just discussed are not simply ideas or opinions about leadership; they are *research-based findings* of what great leaders do on a consistent basis. Throughout this book, suggestions will be made for how you can apply these five exemplary practices in different leadership contexts—such as peer tutoring, peer mentoring, and leading campus organizations.

> *Our research tells us that if we're going to make it to the summit we need someone shouting in our ear, "Come on, you can do it. I know you can do it!"*
>
> —Kouzes & Posner, *The Leadership Challenge Workbook*

Reflection 2.3

Look back at the five effective leadership practices identified by Kouzes and Posner. Which one of these practices best matches your previous ideas about what effective leaders do? Which practice did you least expect to find on the list? Why?

Myths and Misconceptions about Leaders and Leadership

Myth #1. Effective leaders are "natural" ("born") leaders. Contrary to popular belief, leadership is not an inherited personality trait or a genetic gift (Arvey et al., 2006, 2007; Bass, 1985, 1990). Leadership doesn't take place automatically and effortlessly; it's a learned skill that's developed over time through diligent practice and responsiveness to feedback (Arvey et al., 2003; Mumford et al., 2000). Studies of highly successful people in all fields, including successful leaders, show that they achieved success not solely by the grace of natural talent, but by gritty effort, dogged determination, and dedicated practice (Gladwell, 2008; Levitin, 2006).

> *The most dangerous leadership myth is that leaders are born—that people simply either have certain charismatic qualities or not. The opposite is true. Leaders are made rather than born.*
>
> —Warren G. Bennis, University professor and founding chairman of the Leadership Institute at the University of Southern California

Myth #2. Effective leaders are extroverted, bold, forceful, and aggressive. These traits may characterize some famous (or infamous) political and military leaders, but effective leaders are not typically dominant, controlling, or power-driven. Power means the ability to influence others. Successful leaders are powerful because they have the ability to influence and motivate others, not because they can dominate or overpower others (Northouse, 2016). More often than not, they display their leadership skills in subtle, socially sensitive ways (Daft & Lane, 2008). Powerful leaders don't always roar; there are many "quiet leaders" who influence and empower others with a soft voice or without doing much talking at all. Instead, they lead primarily by example—modeling positive behaviors and strategies for others to observe and emulate.

> *It's not the absence of leadership potential that inhibits the development of more leaders; it's the persistence of the myth that leadership can't be learned.*
>
> —Kouzes & Posner, *The Student Leadership Challenge*

> *At times, we have confused 'leadership' with 'dominance.'*
>
> —David Boren, president of the University of Oklahoma and longest-serving chairman of the U.S. Senate Intelligence Committee

Myth #3. Leadership is exercised by people who hold official leadership positions or have formal leadership titles. Leadership can either be *assigned* or *emergent*. Assigned leaders occupy leadership positions in an organization. People holding assigned leadership positions have the potential to be leaders but don't become leaders unless they actually use their position to exert positive influence

> *Leadership is based on inspiration, not domination.*
>
> —William Arthur Ward, American author and poet

on others. Leadership isn't automatically bestowed or guaranteed by a position or title; it's *earned* by the leader's ability to influence others positively and promote productive change (Kouzes & Posner, 2008). People who do not occupy formal leadership positions can still be leaders by positively influencing others and promoting productive change. Such people are referred to as "emergent leaders" because their positive influence develops over time and emerges from their leadership skills and attributes (Fisher, 1974; Northouse, 2016).

Leadership Theories

> *Nothing is more practical than a good theory.*
>
> — Kurt Lewin, social psychologist, and the first leading authority on group dynamics

When people hear the word "theory," they often associate it with something "impractical" that has little use in the "real world." However, theories do have practical benefits—they enable us to pull together a host of separate research findings and organize them into principles that can be used to guide and improve practice—including the practice of leadership. The leadership model developed by Kouzes and Posner presented at the beginning of this chapter is an example of a leadership theory that can guide you in the direction of becoming an effective leader. Similarly, group dynamics theory discussed in chapter 10 will help you understand how groups gradually move through different stages of development (including some early conflict) before they perform effectively as a team. Without knowledge of group dynamics theory, a group leader may lose self-confidence or give up on a group without realizing that early struggles are a normal and productive part of the process.

It's true that "there's no substitute for experience" and you will learn much about leadership through your "hands on," trial-and-error experiences as a peer leader. However, knowledge of leadership theories will help you better understand, predict, and control the outcomes of your leadership experiences. Without theories, it becomes very difficult (if not impossible) to prepare for and deal with the multiple challenges that crop up during the day-to-day practice of leadership. Said in another way, theories provide leaders with a map or compass for guiding their understanding of and response to leadership challenges. Approaching leadership with knowledge of different theoretical perspectives equips you to detect patterns across your experiences and place them into a broader conceptual framework. This will enable you to anticipate and address future leadership challenges—in college and beyond.

Another common misconception about theories is that they're merely opinions or guesses. The truth is that all legitimate theories are supported by some evidence. Don't confuse a theory, which is backed up by research, with a *hypothesis*—an informed guess or hunch that might be true but still needs to be tested to see if there's any evidence to support it.

Although theories are supported by evidence, no single theory can account for the whole truth or tell the whole story. That's why multiple theories exist in almost every field of study. Each theory in a given field may explain a portion of the total body of knowledge that exists in that field. College students often ask: "Why do we need all these theories anyway?" (Perry, 1970, 1981). If that question pops into your mind, keep in mind that explaining and improving the human experience and the world around us isn't a simple process; it's one that requires careful consideration of multiple factors and perspectives. Leadership, in particular, is a complex process that has numerous definitions (Rost, 1991) and multiple dimensions (Northouse, 2016). Thus, more than one theory of leadership is needed.

Listed below is a snapshot summary of the leading theories of leadership (Northouse, 2016), each of which is accompanied by strategies for putting it into practice.

Skills Theory

Traits refer to who leaders *are* (their personal characteristics); in contrast, *skills* refer to what leaders *do* or are *capable of doing*. Successful leaders have been found to possess a set of three key skills they develop over time (Mumford et al., 2000):

1. *Technical* skills: knowledge and expertise. Effective leaders are good at performing the tasks that their followers are expected to perform.
2. *Human* skills: ability to get along with people and work with them. Effective leaders exercise good social judgment and display outstanding interpersonal skills.
3. *Conceptual* skills: ability to generate and communicate ideas. Effective leaders clearly convey their vision to followers, solve challenging problems, and generate creative solutions.

Practical Implications and Applications of Skills Theory

To increase your effectiveness as a leader:

- Develop expertise (knowledge and skill) in the work your followers are expected to perform.
- Intentionally model your knowledge and skills for your followers to observe and emulate.
- Help your followers solve work-related problems.
- Focus on the "big picture" and communicate a big-picture vision to your followers.
- Take time to get to know your followers as individuals.
- Express interest in, and empathy toward, your followers.

Behavioral Theory

Similar to skills theory, behavioral theory focuses less on the personality traits of leaders and more on what effective leaders *do*—the actual *behaviors* they engage in while leading (Blake, 1985; Hui, 1990; Misumi, 1995; Stogdill, 1974). Researchers have discovered two core behaviors associated with effective leadership:

1. *Task* behaviors—actions that help group members successfully reach their goal.
2. *Relationship* behaviors—actions that help followers relate effectively to the leader and to each other, and to feel good about themselves.

Practical Implications and Applications of Behavioral Theory

To increase your effectiveness as a leader:

- Provide your followers with a well-designed plan for the work they are to perform.
- Ensure that your followers know exactly what they're expected to do.

- Clearly define the roles and responsibilities of each follower.
- Provide followers with criteria (performance standards) they can use to check their progress and evaluate how well they are doing.
- Focus on both the productivity and morale of your followers.
- Help your followers make a personal connection with you and with one another.
- Demonstrate concern for your followers.

Situational Theory

This leadership theory posits that effective leaders adjust and adapt their style of leadership to meet the specific leadership challenges they encounter in different contexts or situations (Blanchard, 1985; Blanchard, 1991; Blanchard, Zigarmi, & Zigarmi, 2013). To do so, the leader first assesses the situation by asking the following questions: (a) What goal are the followers being asked to achieve? (b) How complex is the task? (c) Do followers have the skills needed to accomplish the goal and the level of motivation to achieve it? (Northouse, 2016).

In short, situational theory stipulates that to determine the style of leadership needed in a particular situation, leaders must know their followers' level of competence (preparedness) and level of commitment (motivation). Once the followers' level of competence and commitment are determined, the effective leader then adapts his or her style of leadership by adjusting two key behaviors:

1. *Directive* behaviors—the amount of explicit direction or structure the followers need to understand what they have to do, how it's to be done, and who is responsible for doing it.
2. *Supportive* behaviors—the amount of social and emotional support followers need to feel comfortable with themselves, with each other, and with the task ahead of them. For instance, if the followers lack the level of skill development needed to handle the task, the leader adopts a very directive approach and explicitly teaches the skills they need to perform the task. In contrast, if followers already have the necessary skills, the leader pays less attention to task-directive behaviors and focuses more on supplying followers with social and motivational support.

Practical Implications and Applications of Situational Theory

To increase your effectiveness as a leader:

- Determine what skills your followers need to be able to successfully execute the tasks they're expected to perform.
- After determining your followers' skill level, provide them with the appropriate amount of support they need for their level of skill development. For example, provide higher levels of support (structure and direction) for followers with lower skill levels.
- Adjust your leadership style to the followers' stage of development. For example, first-year students are likely to need more direction and support than students at later stages of the college experience.
- Identify the motivational level of your followers and supply them with the appropriate amount of support for their level of motivation. For example, provide higher levels of support (inspiration and incentives) for followers with lower levels of motivation.

Path-Goal Theory

Similar to situational theory, this theory focuses on how effective leaders adjust their leadership style to different situations. However, path-goal theory places heavy emphasis on leaders meeting the *motivational* needs of their followers (House, 1996; House & Mitchell, 1974). Path-goal theory stipulates that the motivation of followers depends on whether they:

1. are aware of the personal benefits or payoffs they will experience if they achieve the goal,
2. see the work involved in reaching the goal as personally satisfying or fulfilling,
3. see a clear path to the goal, and
4. see the potential obstacles and roadblocks to reaching the goal as removable or avoidable (with the help of the leader).

In short, path-goal theory stipulates that followers will reach their goal if they think they are capable of doing the work and if doing the work will be enjoyable and rewarding. In addition, the theory states that effective leaders are those who adjust their leadership style to their followers' *motivational needs* in the following ways:

1. If followers have a strong desire for control and achievement, they need a participative style of leadership that actively involves them in the process and gives them opportunities for input and decision making.
2. If followers do not view themselves as capable or competent, they need a directive style of leadership that supplies them with clear instructions and plenty of structure.

Lastly, path-goal theory points out that the characteristics of the *work task* can affect the followers' level of motivation. For example:

1. If the task is complex or ambiguous, followers will be more motivated by a leader who gives them a substantial amount of guidance.
2. If the task is clear or simple, followers will be more motivated by a leader who gives them substantial autonomy and ample opportunity for personal control.

The bottom line of path-goal theory: Effective leaders are those who adopt a motivational leadership style that best fits the characteristics of the followers *and* the characteristics of the tasks the followers are expected to perform.

Practical Implications and Applications of Path-Goal Theory

To increase your effectiveness as a leader:

- Make sure your followers are aware of the intrinsic rewards associated with pursuing the goal (e.g., how it will be challenging, stimulating, and personal fulfilling).
- Identify the extrinsic payoffs or rewards your followers will experience if they reach the goal (e.g., how they will be recognized, gain status, or achieve personal goals).
- Make sure the steps to achieving the goal are clear and manageable.

- Anticipate potential obstacles to reaching the goal and have a plan in place for overcoming those obstacles.
- Assess the task for its level of complexity. If the task has a high level of complexity, provide followers with a high level of support (e.g., structure and direction).
- Assess your followers' level of confidence. If they have a low level of confidence, provide a high level of personal support (e.g., social and emotional).

Reflection 2.4

Review the practical implications and applications associated with the four leadership theories just discussed (Skills, Behavioral, Situational, and Path-Goal). Which of these theories do you think has the most relevance for your leadership position or leadership interests? Why?

Leader-Member Exchange Theory

The foundational principle of this theory is that the better the relationship and communication "exchange" between leaders and followers, the more likely it is that the goals of both parties will be achieved (Bauer & Berrin, 2015; Graen & Uhl-Bien, 1995). In particular, leader-member exchange theory posits that effective leadership takes place when the relationship between leader and followers is characterized by mutual trust, respect, and commitment, and is free of biases with respect to their race, ethnicity, gender, age, or religion (Northouse, 2016, p. 146).

Practical Implications and Applications of Leader–Member Exchange Theory

To increase your effectiveness as a leader:

- Seek feedback from followers about how effectively you're communicating with them.
- Seek feedback from followers about the quality of your relationship with them (e.g., check to see if they feel you understand them, trust them, and support them).
- Be sure to take an inclusive approach to leadership that incorporates members of diverse groups in the process.

Transformational Leadership Theory

This theory calls for a shift from the traditional *transactional* views of leadership that focus on give-and-take exchanges between the leader and followers (e.g., if followers do "x," the leader rewards them with "y"). In contrast, a *transformational* leader inspires followers to pursue the common good, benefitting themselves as well as the leader (Northouse, 2016), and elevating the motivation and ethical development of both parties (Burns, 1978; Wang et al., 2011). A good example of transformational leadership theory is the leadership model of Kouzes and Posner described earlier in this chapter.

According to transformational leadership theory, leadership is most powerful when: (a) the leader is a role model who exhibits the values, beliefs, and behaviors that followers should exhibit, and (b) followers are inspired by, admire, and strongly identify with the leader and what the leader stands for. Under these conditions, followers become intrinsically motivated—they do what needs to be done because they are personally committed to the cause, not because of any reward or recognition they expect to receive in return (extrinsic motivation). Because they are intrinsically motivated, followers will often do more than what's expected of them. So inspired are they by the leader's ideals and values, they transcend self-interest and go beyond the call of duty to do what's in the best interest of the group or organization to which they belong (Bass, 1985, 1990; Avolio, 1999).

> *Motivation is the art of getting people to do what you want them to do because they want to do it.*
>
> —Dwight D. Eisenhower, 34th President of the United States and five-star U.S. Army General

Practical Implications and Applications of Transformational Leadership Theory

To increase your effectiveness as a leader:

- Make sure your followers understand the mission and purpose of their work, particularly its ethical or moral value.
- Model the ethical values and moral ideals you expect your followers to display.
- Create a shared vision which identifies the ideals that you and your followers aspire to achieve.
- Communicate high expectations to your followers, inspiring them to fully commit themselves to your shared vision.
- Encourage followers to always remain mindful of whether they, and you, are enacting your shared values and ideals.

Servant Leadership Theory

The key tenet of this theory is that great leaders promote the overall growth and development of their followers, enabling them to reach their full potential (Greenleaf, 1977; Servant Leadership Institute, 2018). Servant leaders put followers first and their ultimate goal is to transfer leadership responsibilities to their followers so they, too, can become leaders (Greenleaf, 1970). Servant leaders are also concerned about the less privileged members of society and use their leadership position to reduce or remove social injustices and inequalities (Graham, 1991). The following key qualities and skills characterize servant leaders (Spears, 2002):

1. Listening—they communicate by listening first.
2. Empathy—they put themselves in the position of others and see the world from their perspective.
3. Holistic—they are concerned with the development of each follower as a whole person (intellectually, socially, emotionally, etc.)
4. Persuasive—they influence others through clear, compelling communication and personal inspiration, not through positional power, authority, or coercion.
5. Community Building—they create a sense of shared purpose, a set of common values, and collective unity among followers, inspiring them to work together in pursuit of something greater than themselves.

Practical Implications and Applications of Servant Leadership Theory

To increase your effectiveness as a leader:

- Take time to connect with your followers on a personal level by learning about their current challenges and future goals.

- Mentor your followers by serving as a trusted guide, coach, and confidante.
- Share control with your followers by allowing them to make their own decisions, to become self-leaders, and serve as leaders for others.
- Encourage followers to concern themselves with members of the wider community and society, particularly the underserved and underprivileged.

Adaptive Leadership Theory

This theory of leadership focuses on how effective leaders prepare and encourage followers to overcome resistance to change (Heifetz, 1994). An adaptive leader enables others to see the need for change, effectively engages them in the change process, and helps them deal with the stress involved in making change (Heifetz, Grashow, & Linsky, 2009). The theory posits that great leaders respond to four key challenges and sources of stress associated with the change process:

1. Closing the gap between what should be done (the ideal) and what is being done (the reality).
2. Accommodating competing and conflicting commitments; for example, helping followers balance the time they devote to their own needs and the needs of the group or organization.
3. Honestly confronting (rather than ignoring or avoiding) sensitive and controversial issues—for example, racism or sexism
4. Making difficult, but necessary, changes that require followers to overcome resistance to change by stepping outside their normal routine or familiar "comfort zone"

Practical Implications and Applications of Adaptive Leadership Theory

To increase your effectiveness as a leader:

- Be sure your followers see the need for change; at the same time, however, assure them that the change process will be manageable and not excessively stressful.
- Support followers during stressful periods of the change process, and keep their stress at a level that's moderate and productive. (e.g., if you see their stress level getting too high, reduce workload or extend deadlines.)
- Remind followers that conflict is a normal part of the change process and can be productive if it's handled respectfully and constructively.
- Listen to minority viewpoints and radical ideas; don't dismiss them simply to please the majority, minimize controversy, or maintain the status quo.
- Encourage followers to be aware of and avoid defensive behaviors that are being consciously or unconsciously used to resist change, such as: pretending there's no need for change, working on other tasks to avoid what needs to be changed, or blaming others for the change that needs to take place rather than taking personal responsibility for making change happen.

Social Change Theory of Leadership

This model of leadership was originally designed for student affairs professionals interested in promoting the leadership skills of college students (Astin & Astin, 1996). It is now being used by other leadership development professionals in a variety of settings (Skendall et al., 2017). The model posits that leadership should facilitate positive social change in institutions and communities. It rests on the following premises:

- Leadership is a process, not a position.
- Leadership is an inclusive process that develops leadership qualities among all those involved in the process, including both leaders and followers.
- Leadership is centered on seven central values, referred to as the "7 C's" of leadership development:
  1. Consciousness of Self—leaders should be aware of the beliefs, values, and attitudes that motivate them to become a leader.
  2. Congruence—the actions of leaders should be consistent with their most deeply held beliefs and convictions.
  3. Commitment—leaders should possess the energy, intensity, and passion to serve others and drive collective effort.
  4. Common Purpose—leaders should work together with followers to create a shared mission, vision, and goals.
  5. Collaboration—leaders should trust their followers, empower them, and capitalize on their diverse talents.
  6. Controversy with Civility—leaders should accept that differences in viewpoints are inevitable and allow them to be expressed openly and civilly (respectfully).
  7. Citizenship—leaders should recognize that the groups they lead should be connected to, and promote the welfare of, the local community and larger society.

Practical Implications and Applications of the Social Change Model of Leadership

To increase your effectiveness as a leader:

- Take time to reflect on the personal dimension of leadership—become aware and remain mindful of why you are a leader and what leadership roles or actions best reflect your most deeply held values and beliefs.
- Take time to focus on the interpersonal dimension of leadership—strengthen your skills for communicating, collaborating, team-building, and empowering others.
- Encourage members of the group you lead to identify aspects of social change they share in common.
- Encourage the group to go beyond itself and engage with the college community, the local community, and society at large, particularly for the purpose of promoting equity and social justice.

Reflection 2.5

Review the practical implications and applications associated with the five leadership theories just discussed (Leader-Member Exchange, Transformational, Servant, Adaptive, and Social Change). Which of these theories do you see as being most relevant to your leadership position or leadership interests? Why?

Leadership Theories: Summary and Conclusion

Don't be overwhelmed by the quantity and variety of leadership theories that have been discussed in this chapter. Although individual theories emphasize different aspects or dimensions of leadership, when viewed together they point to similar practices. Namely, to be an effective leader, you should be aware of:

1. your *purpose*–know the goal and scope of your leadership efforts, whether it be to promote positive change in individuals, groups, organizations, and/or society;
2. your *task*–know what your followers are expected to do or accomplish, including the task's level of challenge or complexity and the amount of support your followers need to successfully complete the task;
3. your *followers*–know who they are (their needs and skills) and build relationships with them (demonstrate empathy and communicate effectively);
4. your *self*–know your leadership strengths, interests, and values; be mindful of whether you are modeling the type of skills and attributes you expect your followers to exhibit; and adapt your leadership style to the specific situation– the specific characteristics of your followers and the specific demands of the task they are to perform.

As you proceed through this book, your understanding of leadership theories will become deeper as you apply them to leadership exercises and situations.

Personal Traits and Attributes of Effective Leaders

If people don't believe in the messenger, they won't believe in the message.

—James Kouzes & Barry Posner, *Student Leadership Planner: An Action Guide to Achieving Your Personal Best*

If you help others with problems of time management but you are the one who is always late to meetings, or if you give a presentation on responsible drinking yet get picked up for a DUI, much of your credibility...is quickly and decidedly undermined.

—Steven Ender & Fred Newton, *Students Helping Students*

Leadership is expressed in a variety of styles (Locke, 1999; Martindale, 2011). However, certain personal qualities tend to characterize all effective leaders. Listed below are common attributes of effective leaders that have been repeatedly identified by leadership researchers and scholars (Avolio & Luthans, 2006; Goleman, Boyatzis, & McKee, 2002; Kouzes & Posner, 2002; Northouse, 2016; Strang & Kuhnert, 2009; Wagner, 2007). As you read the following common characteristics of effective leaders, place a plus sign next to those attributes you expected to see and a negative sign next to any attribute you were surprised to see on the list.

Credible and Authentic

Effective leaders are believable and inspire others to believe in them. They're also genuine; they "keep it real," and don't pretend to be what they're not. What they profess in words, they express in deed. They just don't give "lip service" to their values by simply stating them; they embody, enact them, and live them. In short, great leaders exhibit integrity (Northouse, 2016). It's noteworthy that the word "integrity" comes from the same root as the word "integrate." This captures a key quality of true leaders: their outer self is integrated (in harmony) with their inner self–their inner character and outer behavior are in sync–what they think and feel match what they say and do.

Accountable and Dependable

Great leaders can be counted on and depended on; they follow up and follow through on their commitments (House et al., 2004). They show up when and where they're supposed to, and they do what they tell others they will do. They deliver on their promises; they don't overpromise and under-deliver (Dalla Costa, 1998).

Knowledgeable and Resourceful

Successful leaders do their homework; they learn about their followers, know the tasks they are expected to perform, and know what to do to support them. Effective leaders are also self-knowledgeable: they know who they are, including their strengths and limitations (Sanft, Jensen, & McMurray, 2008). In addition to being knowledgeable, great leaders are resourceful; they're willing to say: "I don't know, but I'll found out." They aren't too proud to seek help from others to better support their followers. Instead, they capitalize on their resources and are open to learning from others.

Dedicated and Committed

Great leaders are determined to be the best leaders they can be (Northouse, 2016). They are passionate about making a real difference in the individuals, groups, and organizations they lead, and they dedicate considerable time and energy to their work. Great leaders hustle—they go all out and give it their all; they put their whole heart and soul into it.

Things may come to those who wait, but only the things left by those who hustle.

—Author unknown

Reflection 2.6

Think about something you do with passion and commitment. What thoughts, attitudes, and behaviors do you display when you do it? In what ways might you apply this same passion and commitment to your leadership role or position?

Modest and Humble

Effective leaders are neither pompous nor pretentious. They don't let their egos become inflated by the power or prestige of the position they hold and they're not driven by the need for external recognition or status. Great leaders lead with modesty and humility (Wong & Davey, 2007); they do it for the cause not the applause.

As a peer leader, you're in a position to exert tremendous influence on less-experienced students. However, if you come across as an arrogant, overbearing know-it-all, you will lose your leadership edge. Being a strong leader means having the humility to know there are things you don't know and still need to learn.

Don't let the power go to your head.

—George Orwell, author of *Animal Farm* and Proponent of Social Justice

People don't respect know-it-alls. Hubris, excessive pride, is the killer disease in leadership. It's easy to be seduced by power and importance. Humility is the only way to resolve the conflicts and contradictions of leadership.

—Kouzes & Posner, *Student Leadership Planner: An Action Guide to Achieving Your Personal Best*

Enthusiastic and Optimistic

Effective leaders exude positive energy and enthusiasm (Goldberg, 1990) and they maintain a sense of optimism when their efforts are going slowly, nowhere,

> *Give the world the best you have, and it may never be enough; give the world the best you've got anyway.*
>
> —Mother Teresa, Catholic missionary nun and recipient of the Nobel Peace Prize

or backwards (Judge et al., 2002). Setbacks are a normal and inevitable part of the leadership challenge. Leaders cannot always control or influence the actions of others. Even when leaders are fully committed, have deep understanding of effective leadership principles, and use all the right strategies, they may not be able to make change happen quickly or consistently.

> **Creating change in individuals, groups, or organizations is an evolutionary not a revolutionary process. Great leaders remain patient, positive, and persistent during the inevitable twists and turns in the process of promoting positive change.**

Tale FROM THE Trenches

A lesson I am constantly learning is: patience, patience, patience. And you know what? Just like with everything, finding patience is challenging. But I need more patience with myself. I need more of it with other people. I need more of it as I wait for results and outcomes—instant gratification isn't always an option, and it's not always what it's cracked up to be.

—PEER LEADER

Ethical and Courageous

Great leaders are not only influential; they're ethical. They are persons of *character* who enable others to engage in higher levels of ethical conduct (Burns, 1978). According to the *Josephson Institute of Ethics*, a person of character is:

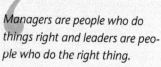

> *Managers are people who do things right and leaders are people who do the right thing.*
>
> —Warren Bennis and Burt Nanus, *Leaders: The Strategies for Taking Charge*

- Trustworthy—honest, loyal, and a person of integrity
- Respectful—courteous, accepting, non-prejudiced, and nonviolent
- Responsible—accountable, pursues excellence, and shows self-restraint
- Fair—just, equitable, reasonable, open, and unbiased
- Caring—unselfish, kind, empathetic, and compassionate (Jones & Lucas, 1994).

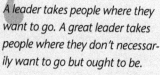

> *A leader takes people where they want to go. A great leader takes people where they don't necessarily want to go but ought to be.*
>
> —Rosalynn Carter, former United States first lady

In contrast, "toxic" or destructive leaders are arrogant, violate others' rights, and play to their followers' basest fears (Koehn, 2017; Lipman-Blumen, 2005). Great leaders don't exert power and influence at any ethical cost. They have the *courage* to do what's right—even in the face of criticism, peer pressure, or personal loss (Peterson & Seligman, 2004). Their strong set of values serves as a rudder that steers them in the right ethical direction (Avolio, Walumbwa, & Weber, 2009; Walumbwa et al. 2008). They are not moralistic—they don't impose their personal values or conventional moral standards on others—but they do raise the bar by motivating others (and themselves) to pursue ideals higher than their narrow self-interests (Bass, 1990).

Reflection 2.7

What ethical principles do you value most, and will rely on most, to guide your leadership efforts? What ethical issues or challenges do you anticipate encountering in your leadership role or position?

While strong leadership requires knowledge about leadership theories and developing effective leadership strategies, it's built on something deeper—an inner core of positive qualities (virtues) that define the leader's character and direct the leader's behavior.

The Process of Effective Leadership: Common Themes

The research findings and theoretical principles discussed in this chapter point to several recurrent themes about the *process* of effective leadership (Rost, 1991). Like playing jazz, exercising leadership is an art form. Jazz artists first learn the basic musical processes, such as scales and chords; then they apply these basic processes to play creatively in the moment. Similarly, leadership involves applying foundational processes creatively to different leadership situations and challenges. Effective leadership emanates from the following four foundational processes: (1) relational, (2) collaborative, (3) empowering, and (4) reflective.

Leadership is about a <u>process</u> that can be understood, grasped, and learned.

—Kouzes & Posner, *The Student Leadership Challenge*

1. **Leadership is a *relational* process.** "Authentic leadership" is inevitably relational—it's a process that involves leaders and followers working well together (Eagly, 2005). Leadership is grounded in effective relationship building, interpersonal communication, and harmonious interaction between the leader and followers (Murrell, 1997; Uhl-Bien, 2006).

2. **Leadership is a *collaborative* process.** Effective leadership is a process in which the leader distributes or disperses leadership responsibilities among followers, making them co-leaders (Schein, 2004). No single leader can be all things to all people. The talents of the "official" leader need to be complemented and augmented by co-leaders who bring different skills, perspectives, and approaches to the leadership process. The impact of leadership is magnified when it's not done independently by "a" leader, but done interdependently by a team of leaders. As the old saying goes, "It takes a village."

No leaders truly accomplish anything worthwhile by themselves. We achieve more when we share credit and ownership with others.

—David Boren, president of the University of Oklahoma and longest-serving chairman of the U.S. Senate Intelligence Committee

3. **Leadership is a process of *empowering* others.** Effective leaders "pass it on"; they empower their followers to become leaders and mentors (Elmore, 2008; Gould & Lomax, 1993). "The process of becoming an effective leader involves a shift of the leader's identity from thinking 'I am the leader' . . . to 'I am a leader' and 'I can engage in leadership with others'" (Komives, Lucas, & McMahon, 2007, p. 408). Leadership is a process in which followers are viewed as associates, partners, or teammates who are eventually liberated from dependence on the leader and become leaders themselves.

The fundamental task of the mentor is a liberatory task. A mentor truly believes in the autonomy, freedom, and development of those he or she mentors.

—*Mentoring the Mentor* by Paulo Freire, influential Brazilian educator and activist

Author's Experience I was a 10-year-old boy growing up in New York when I first saw the Iowa Hawkeyes football team win the Rose Bowl on national TV. I immediately became a fan of the team and eventually went to the University of Iowa for graduate school. Years later, I noticed that a surprising number of college and professional football coaches previously played at the University of Iowa. I thought it must have been a coincidence until my brother-in-law sent me an article from the *Wall Street Journal* about Iowa's legendary football coach, Hayden Fry, which documented that a remarkable number of current football coaches once played football for coach Fry.

Fry developed players into future coaches by first designating players on his team to serve as player-coaches for teammates who played the same position. His idea was to have the player-coaches develop leadership skills that would benefit the team's performance during games. As Coach Fry put it, "Those were the guys that the players would listen to, not an old coach like me" (Diamond, 2011, p. 5). The second phase of coach Fry's leadership development process was to give his player-coaches official positions on his staff as graduate assistants—after they had graduated from the university. The result: More than a dozen of his former player-coaches went on to become professional coaches.

Coach Fry's approach to developing future leaders illustrates two important points made in this book: (1) the power of peer-to-peer leadership and (2) great leaders empower others to be leaders.

—Joe Cuseo

> The leadership paradox is that leaders turn their followers into leaders.
>
> —Kouzes & Posner, *The Student Leadership Challenge*

> It's a persistent desire to do better. It's the opposite of being complacent. It's not looking backward with dissatisfaction. It's looking <u>forward</u> and wanting to grow.
>
> —Hester Lacey, journalist, commenting on a common characteristic of the highly successful people she interviewed

> SUCCESS is peace of mind which is a direct result of knowing you made the effort to become the best that you are capable of becoming.
>
> —John Wooden, college basketball coach and author of the *Pyramid of Success*

4. **Leadership is a *reflective* process that involves ongoing review, revision, and improvement.** Personal reflection and self-assessment are essential for success in any venture, including leadership. Leadership starts with a vision, followed by action, reflection, and revision. Great leaders engage in a continuous process of self-assessment and self-improvement (Bennis & Nanus, 1985; Gardner, Avolio, & Walumbwa, 2005). Yes, effective leaders begin with a thorough and thoughtful plan , but they also revise and improve that plan after putting it into action.

Like great coaches, great leaders utilize feedback to improve their own performance and the performance of those they lead. After a tough game—win or lose—a good coach replays the game film, reviews and analyzes what went well and what didn't, and uses this information as feedback to improve their coaching and their team's performance. Similarly, great leaders continuously seek ways to improve themselves and their followers. They don't fear feedback; they seek it out, learn from it, and use it to accentuate their strengths and strengthen their weaknesses. (To help you engage in this continuing process of leadership self-assessment and self-improvement, see the instrument found in Appendix B., pp. 431-440)

Don't forget that a vital source of feedback for self-improvement is YOU! Take time to pause, reflect, and self-assess, and use your self-assessment to continually improve your leadership skills and attributes.

Reflection 2.8

Which one of the following aspects of the leadership process just discussed were you least aware of?
1. Leadership is a relational process
2. Leadership is a collaborative process
3. Leadership is a process of empowering others
4. Leadership is a reflective process involving continuous review, revision, and improvement.

Now that you're more aware of this process, what's one thing you could to do put it into practice?

Internet Resources

For additional information on the process of effective leadership and the attributes of effective leaders, consult the following websites:

What is Leadership?
A New Leadership Mindset – Leadership for a New Era
http://leadershiplearning.org/system/files/New%20Leadership%20Mindset_LLC.pdf

Characteristics of Effective Leaders:
Holden Leadership Center, University of Oregon
https://holden.uoregon.edu/leadership

Psych Web
www.psywww.com/sports/leader.htm

The 21 Indispensable Qualities of a Leader
www.ansc.purdue.edu/courses/communicationskills/LeaderQualities.pdf

Principles of Transformative Leadership
http://aahea.org/articles/transformative_leadership.htm

Servant Leadership (Center for Servant Leadership):
www.greenleaf.org

References

Arvey, R. D., Rotundo, N., Johnson, W., & McGue, M. (2003, April). *The determinants of leadership: The role of genetic, personality, and cognitive factors.* Paper presented at the 18th Annual Conference of the Society of Industrial and Organizational Psychology, Orlando, FL.

Arvey, R. D., Rotundo, M., Johnson, W., Zhang, Z., & McGue, M. (2006). The determinants of leadership role occupancy: Genetic and personality factors. *Leadership Quarterly, 17,* 1-20.

Arvey, R. D., Zhang, Z., Avolio, B. J., & Kreuger, R. F. (2007). Developmental and genetic determinants of leadership role occupancy among women. *Journal of Applied Psychology, 92,* 693-706.

Astin, A. W., & Astin, H. S. (1996). *A social change model of leadership development: Guidebook, version III.* Los Angeles: Higher Education Research Institute, University of California.

Avolio, B. J. (1999). *Full leadership development: Building the vital forces in organizations.* Thousand Oaks, CA: SAGE.

Avolio, B., & Luthans, F. (2006). *The high impact leader.* New York: McGraw Hill.

Avolio, B. J., Walumbwa, F. O., & Weber, T. J. (2009). Leadership: Current theories, research, and future directions. *Annual Review of Psychology, 60,* 421-449.

Bass, B. M. (1985). *Leadership and performance: Beyond expectations.* New York: Free Press.

Bass, B. M. (1990). From transactional to transformational leadership: Learning to share the vision. *Organizational Dynamics* (Winter), 19-31.

Bauer, T., & Berrin, E. (2015). *The Oxford handbook of leader-member exchange.* New York: Oxford University Press.

Bennis, W. G., & Nanus, B. (1985). *Leaders: The strategies for taking charge.* New York: Harper & Row.

Blake, R. R. (1985). *The managerial grid III: A new look at the classic that has boosted productivity and profits for thousands of corporations worldwide.* Houston, TX: Gulf Publishing Company.

Blanchard, K. H. (1985). *SLII: A situational approach to managing people.* Escondido, CA: Blanchard Training and Development.

Blanchard, K. H. (1991). Situational view of leadership. *Executive Excellence, 8*(6), 22-23.

Blanchard, K. H., Zigarmi, P., & Zigarmi, D. (2013). *Leadership and the one minute manager: Increasing effectiveness through Situational Leadership II.* New York: William Morrow.

Burns, J. M. (1978). *Leadership.* New York: Harper & Row.

Daft, R. L., & Lane, P. G. (2008). *The leadership experience* (5th ed.). Mason, OH: South-Western Cengage Learning.

Dalla Costa, J. (1998). *The ethical imperative: Why moral leadership is good business.* Reading, MA: Addison-Wesley.

Diamond, J. (2011, December 21). Iowa: The Harvard of coaching. *The Wall Street Journal*, p. D5.

Eagly, A. H. (2005). Achieving relational authenticity in leadership: Does gender matter? *Leadership Quarterly, 16*, 459-474.

Elmore, T. (2008). *Mentoring: How to invest your life in others.* Duluth, GA: Growing Leaders Inc.

Ender, S. C., & Newton, F. B. (2000). *Students helping students: A guide for peer educators on college campuses.* San Francisco: Jossey-Bass.

Fisher, B. A. (1974). *Small group decision making: Communication and the group process.* New York: McGraw-Hill.

Freire, P., Fraser, J. W., Macedo, D., McKinnon, T. (Eds.). (1997) *Mentoring the mentor: A critical dialogue with Paulo Freire.* New York: Peter Lang Publishing.

Gardner, W. L., Avolio, B. J., & Walumbwa, F. O. (2005). Authentic leadership development: Emergent trends and future directions. In W. L. Gardner, B. J. Avolio, & F. O. Walumbwa (Eds.), *Authentic leadership theory and practice: Origins, effects, and development* (pp. 387-406). Oxford: Elsevier Science.

Gladwell, M. (2008). *Outliers: The story of success.* New York: Little, Brown.

Goldberg, L. R. (1990). An alternative "description of personality": The big-five factor structure. *Journal of Personality and Social Psychology, 59*, 1216-1229.

Goleman, D., Boyatzis, R., & McKee, A. (2002). *Primal leadership: Realizing the potential of emotional intelligence.* Boston: Harvard Business School Press.

Gould, J., & Lomax, A. (1993). The evolution of peer education: Where do we go from here? *Journal of American College Health, 45*, 235-240.

Graen, G. B., & Uhl-Bien, M. (1995). Relationship-based approach to leadership: Development of leader-member exchange (LMX) theory of leadership over 25 years: Applying a multi-level, multi-domain perspective. *Leadership Quarterly, 6*(2), 219-247.

Graham, J. W. (1991). Servant leadership in organizations: Inspirational and moral. *Leadership Quarterly, 2*, 105-109.

Grayson, D., & Speckhart, R. (2006). The leader-follower relationship: Practitioner observations. *Leadership Advance Online*, Issue 6 (Winter). Retrieved from https://www.regent.edu/acad/global/publications/lao/issue_6/pdf/grayson_speckhart.pdf

Greenleaf, R. K. (1970). *The servant as leader.* Westfield, IN: Greenleaf Center for Servant Leadership.

Greenleaf, R. K. (1977). *Servant leadership: A journey into the nature of legitimate power and greatness.* New York: Paulist Press.

Heifetz, R. A. (1994). *Leadership without easy answers.* Cambridge: MA: Belknap Press.

Heifetz, R. A., Grashow, A., & Linsky, M. (2009). *The practice of adaptive leadership: Tools and tactics for changing your organization and the world.* Boston, MA: Harvard Business School Press.

Hollander, E. P. (1992). Leadership, followership, self, and others. *Leadership Quarterly, 3*(1), 43-54.

House, R. J. (1996). Path-goal theory of leadership: Lessons, legacy, and a reformulated theory. *Leadership Quarterly, 7*(3), 323–352

House, R. J., Hanges, P. J., Javidan, M., Dorfman, P. W., & Gupta, V. (Eds.). (2004). *Culture, leadership, and organizations: The GLOBE study of 62 societies* (pp. 9-28). Thousand Oaks, CA: SAGE.

House, R. J., & Mitchell, R. R. (1974). Path-goal theory of leadership. *Journal of Contemporary Business, 3,* 81-87.

Hui, C. C. (1990). Work attitudes, leadership styles and managerial behaviors in different cultures. In R. Brislin (Ed.), *Applied cross-cultural psychology* (pp. 186-208). Newbury Park, CA: SAGE.

Jones, S. R., & Lucas, N. J. (1994). Interview with Michael Josephson. *Concepts & Connections: Rethinking Ethics & Leadership, 2*(3), 1, 3-5.

Judge, T. A., Bono, J. E., Ilies, R., & Gerhardt, M. W. (2002). *Personality and leadership: A qualitative and quantitative review. Journal of Applied Psychology, 87,* 765-780.

Koehn, N. (2017). *Forged in crisis: The power of courageous leadership in turbulent times.* New York: Scribner.

Komives, S. R., Lucas, N., & McMahon, T. R. (2007). *Exploring leadership: For college students who want to make a difference* (2nd ed.). San Francisco: Jossey-Bass.

Kouzes, J. M., & Posner, B. Z. (2002). *The leadership challenge: How to get extraordinary things done in organizations* (3rd ed.). San Francisco: Jossey-Bass

Kouzes, M. M., & Posner, B. Z. (2003). *The leadership challenge workbook.* San Francisco: Jossey-Bass.

Kouzes, M. M., & Posner, B. Z. (2006). *Student leadership planner: An action guide to achieving your personal best.* San Francisco: Jossey-Bass.

Kouzes, M. M., & Posner, B. Z. (2008). *The student leadership challenge: Five practices for exemplary leaders.* San Francisco: Jossey-Bass.

Kouzes, M. M., & Posner, B. Z. (2012). *The leadership challenge* (5th ed.). San Francisco: Jossey-Bass.

Kouzes, M. M., & Posner, B. Z. (2016). *Learning leadership: The five fundamentals of becoming an exemplary leader.* San Francisco: The Leadership Challenge—A Wiley Brand.

Levitin, D. J. (2006). *This is your brain on music: The science of a human obsession.* New York: Dutton.

Lipman-Blumen, J. (2005). *The allure of toxic leaders.* New York: Oxford University Press.

Locke, E. (1999). *The essence of leadership.* New York: Lexington Books.

Martindale, N. (2011). Leadership styles: How to handle the different personas. *Strategic Communication Management, 15*(8), 32–35.

Misumi, J. (1995). The development in Japan of the performance maintenance (PM) theory of leadership. *Journal of Social Issues, 51*(1), 213-228.

Mumford, M. D., Zaccaro, S. J., Connelly, M. S., & Marks, M. A. (2000). Leadership skills: Conclusions and future directions. *Leadership Quarterly, 11*(1), 155-170.

Murrell, K. L. (1997). Emergent theories of leadership for the next century: Towards relational concepts. *Organizational Development Journal, 15*(3), 35-42.

Northouse, P. G. (2016). *Leadership: Theory and practice* (7th ed.). Thousand Oaks, CA: SAGE.

Perry, W. (1970). *Forms of intellectual and ethical development in the college years: A scheme.* New York: Holt, Rinehart & Winston.

Perry, W. (1981). Cognitive and ethical growth. In A. Chickering & Associates, *The modern American college: Responding to the new realities of diverse students and a changing society.* San Francisco: Jossey-Bass.

Peterson, C., & Seligman, M. E. P. (2004). *Character strengths and virtues: A handbook and classification.* New York: Oxford University Press.

Rost, J. C. (1991). *Leadership for the twenty-first century.* Westport, CT: Praeger.

Sanft, M., Jensen, M., & McMurray, E. (2008). *Peer mentor companion.* Boston: Houghton Mifflin.

Schein, E. (2004). *Organizational culture and leadership* (3rd ed.). San Francisco: Jossey-Bass.

Servant Leadership Institute. (2018). *What is servant leadership?* Retrieved from https://www.servantleadershipinstitute.com/what-is-servant-leadership-1/

Skendall, K. C., Ostick, D. T., Komives, S. R., Wagner, W., & Associates. (2017). *The social change model: Facilitating leadership development.* San Francisco: Jossey-Bass.

Spears, L. C. (2002). Tracing the past, present, and future of servant-leadership. In L. C. Spears & M. Lawrence (Eds.). *Focus on leadership: Servant leadership for the 21st century* (pp. 1-16). New York: Wiley.

Stogdill, R. M. (1974). *Handbook of leadership: A survey of theory and research.* New York: Free Press.

Strang, S. E., & Kuhnert, K. W. (2009). Personality and leadership developmental levels as predictors of leader performance, *The Leadership Quarterly,* doi:10.1016/j.leaqua.2009.03.009

Uhl-Bien, M. (2006). Relational leadership theory: Exploring the social processes of leadership and organizing. *The Leadership Quarterly, 17*(6), 654-676.

Wagner, K. (2007). *Lewin's leadership styles.* Retrieved from http://psychology.about.com/od/leadership/a/leadstyles.htm

Walumbwa, F. O., Avolio, B. J., Gardner, W. L., Wernsing, T. S., & Peterson, S. J. (2008). Authentic leadership: Development and validation of a theory-based measure. *Journal of Management, 34*(1), 89-126.

Wang, G., Oh, I-S, Courtright, S. H., & Colbert, A. E. (2011). Transformational leadership and performance across criteria and levels: A meta-analytic review of 25 years of research. *Group & Organization Management, 36*(2), 223–270.

Wheatley, M. (2002). It's an interconnected world. *Shambhala Sun* (April), pp. 1-3. Retrieved from http://margaretwheatley.com/wp-content/uploads/2014/12/Its-An-Interconnected-World.pdf

Wong, T. P. T., & Davey, D. (2007). *Best practices in servant leadership.* Servant Leadership Roundtable, Regent University—School of Global Leadership and Entrepreneurship. Retrieved from http://www.gleclerc.com/2012/06/best-practices-in-servant-leadership/

Exercise 2.1 Quote Reflections

Review the sidebar quotes contained in this chapter and select two that you think would be especially valuable to share with the students you lead or mentor.

For each quote, write a short statement explaining why you chose it.

Exercise 2.2 Journal Reflections

1. Think of an example of a leader who you thought was:

   a. exceptionally effective or inspirational?

   b. particularly ineffective or deplorable?

   What specific actions or behavior(s) did each of these leaders display?

2. Reflecting back on the first interactions you had with faculty, staff, and administrators on your campus:

   a. Do you recall anyone who impressed you as being a potential mentor?

   b. What did that person say or do that most impressed you?

3. Think about other peer leaders in your program. Do you see any of them as being potential teammates with whom you could network, share resources, and exchange feedback to improve each other's leadership development? If yes, why? If not, why not?

4. Reflecting on your previous leadership experiences:
   a. What leadership strengths did you display?

   b. What positive effect(s) did your leadership strengths have on others?

   c. What could you do to further accentuate or maximize your leadership strengths?

   d. What areas or aspects of leadership do you need to improve? What could you do to improve them?

5. Think of a leadership situation in which you took a stance on a value that was important to you, or where you displayed ethical leadership behavior that could serve as a model for others to emulate.

   a. What was the situation?

   b. What did you do?

   c. How did others react?

Exercise 2.3 Self-Assessment of Exemplary Leadership Practices

Look back at the definition and description of the five "exemplary practices" of leaders identified by Kouzes and Posner (pp. 38–39).

1. Rate yourself on a scale from 1-5 (1 = lowest, 5 = highest) on the extent to which you already engage in each of these practices, or think you're capable of engaging in them.

2. Identify one of your highest-rated practices and provide a description or illustration of how you implement this practice well, or how you intend to implement it well.

3. Identify one of your lowest-rated practices and provide an action step you can take to begin implementing this practice more effectively.

Exercise 2.4 Self-Assessment of Leadership Qualities and Attributes

The box below contains a set of key *personal qualities or attributes* that are likely to promote effective leadership in a wide variety of leadership positions and situations. As you read these personal qualities, underline those you believe you already possess, and circle those you think you need to improve. (For a brief description of these five qualities, see pp. 48–49.)

Key Personal Qualities and Attributes of Effective Leaders
- **Credible and Authentic**
- **Accountable and Dependable**
- **Knowledgeable and Resourceful**
- **Dedicated and Committed**
- **Modest and Humble**
- **Enthusiastic and Optimistic**
- **Ethical and Courageous**

1. For each quality you underlined, provide a brief explanation or source of evidence that indicates you already possess this quality.

2. For each quality you circled, provide an action step you could take to begin developing this quality.

Exercise 2.5 Gap Analysis of "Real" versus "Ideal" Leadership Qualities

Look back at the four processes of effective leadership described on pp. 51–52 . Identify one in which you see the widest gap between where you'd like to be (the ideal) and where you are now (the reality).

To reduce this gap:

1. What *specific action*(s) could you take?

2. What *obstacles or roadblocks* would you have to overcome?

3. What *resources* could you draw on for help or support?

Exercise 2.6 Self-Assessment of Leadership Skills

The following box contains an alphabetized list of *skills* that leaders may need to utilize in different leadership roles and positions. As you read these skills, underline those you believe you already possess and circle those you need to improve.

Personal Skills Relevant to Successful Leadership Performance

advising	delegating	partnering
coaching	designing	persuading
collaborating	evaluating	planning
communicating	explaining	problem solving
coordinating	initiating	producing
creating	motivating	referring
	negotiating	resolving
	networking	summarizing
		supervising
		synthesizing

1. For each skill you underlined, provide a brief explanation or source of evidence that indicates you already possess this quality.

2. For each skill you circled, provide an action step you could take to begin developing this quality.

CHAPTER 3

The College Experience

Applying Student Development Research and Theory to the Practice of Peer Leadership

Reflection 3.1

What would you say are three key differences between high school and college? Which one of these differences do you think poses the greatest challenge for the students you lead or mentor?

Chapter Purpose and Preview

During the 1960s, record numbers of baby-boom children attended college. It was at this time that research on the college student experience began to explode. Studies continued over the next four decades, leaving us now with more than 50 years of research on how students learn and develop in college. The purpose of this chapter is to synthesize the major findings of this research and help you apply them to promote the success of the students you lead and mentor.

The First-Year Experience: Transitioning from High School to Higher Education

The first year of college is generally considered to be the most critical stage of the college experience. It's the year when students undergo the greatest amount of learning and personal growth; it's also the time when they experience the most stress, the most academic difficulties, and are most likely to withdraw from college (Cuseo et al., 2016).

Students transitioning to college encounter different adjustments at different times during their first year on campus. They're most likely to be receptive to information and advice for handling these adjustments at times when they're currently experiencing them. Simply stated, students are more willing and "ready" to acquire timely knowledge they can apply to their immediate circumstances. By remaining aware of issues that new students are likely to encounter at different points during their first term in college, you can anticipate their needs and respond to them in a timely fashion.

Keep in mind that new students often experience multiple adjustment issues at the same time. For instance, new students may be initially dealing with social issues about leaving home and fitting in, while at the same time, they're confronted with such academic tasks as figuring out how to take effective notes during professors' lectures and how to keep up with college reading assignments. You may be able to provide "just-in-time" support to new students at times when they most need it by thinking of the first college year as unfolding in three major stages: early, middle, and late.

The *Early* Stage (First Six Weeks)

According to psychologist Abraham Maslow's classic "need hierarchy" theory of human motivation, social acceptance and self-esteem are basic human needs that must be met before personal growth and self-actualization can take place (Maslow, 1954). (See Figure 3.1)

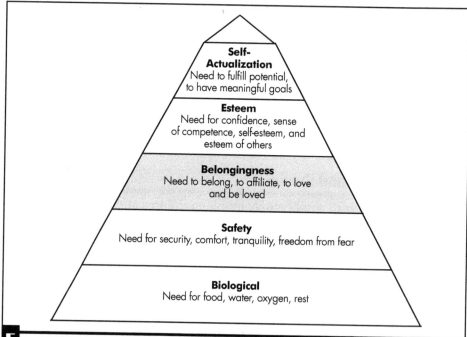

Figure 3.1   Maslow's Hierarchy of Needs suggests that social belongingness is a basic need that must be met before humans can reach their full potential.

Consistent with Maslow's theory, research on college students indicates that they have a strong need to "fit in" socially at the very start of their college experience (Brower, 1997; Shanley & Johnson, 2008; Tinto, 1988). Social needs, such as finding friends, overcoming shyness, and dealing with homesickness, are often high-priority needs for students during their first few weeks of college. As a peer leader, you can help them meet these needs by creating early opportunities for new students to connect with peers, faculty, and student-support agents on campus. (Specific strategies for doing so are provided on pp. 81-86.)

Author's Experience It's ironic that I am co-authoring this book because I was a "college drop-out" (or at least a stop-out) the first time around. I attended a rather large university about a five-hour drive from home. Unfortunately, campus housing was limited so I wasn't able to live on campus. A few weeks before school started, I fell in love (or at least infatuation) with a girl who was living back home. My heart and mind were not focused on school. By December, I was home again.

I eventually returned to college and graduated, so my story had a happy ending. However, during my first turn at college I would have benefitted immensely from a peer leader or mentor—someone who I could have turned to, someone who could have helped me think through my decisions, or someone who could have connected me with a campus professional to receive the support and direction I needed at that stage of my life.

— *Greg Metz*

As a peer leader I have seen students struggle with homesickness, pregnancy, forceful coaches, hostile roommates, death, and more. Freshmen have to deal with all of these issues while trying to adjust to an entirely new way of life.

—Peer leader

The *Middle* Stage (Just Before and After Midterm Exams)

The middle stage of students' first-year experience in college may be defined as the time around midterm—the midpoint of the term when students are likely to encounter their first wave of college exams, assignment deadlines, and course grades. Research indicates that student satisfaction with college varies at different times during the term and an appreciable "dip" in satisfaction tends to takes place around midterm (Pennington, Zvonkovic, & Wilson, 1989). Midterm also marks the end of the "honeymoon period" for new students—when the novelty or rush of simply being in college (and attending lots of social gatherings and meeting lots of new people) is replaced by the pressure of meeting the academic demands and expectations of college. The terms "midterm slump" and "midterm crunch" have been coined to capture the stresses associated with this stage of the semester (Duffy & Jones, 1995).

Reflection 3.2

Think about your first term in college:

1. During your first two weeks on campus, what were you most concerned or worried about?

2. At midterm, were your concerns and worries the same, or had they shifted to different issues?

3. Do you think that most new students experience concerns and worries similar to yours?

4. To help new students better deal with the issues they will experience, what could peer leaders and mentors do?

Since students often receive their first wave of academic evaluation and feedback around midterm, this is a time when they're most likely to be receptive to your recommendations and referrals to academic-support services. (See pp. 87-88 for tips on making effective referrals.) Another way you can provide support at this stage of the term is by helping new students reflect on their midterm grades. If their initial grades are low, remind them that it's a normal part of the process of adjusting to the higher demands of higher education. Also, remind them that their midterm grades are not their final grades and are not counted in their grade-point average. Encourage them to view their midterm results as feedback that can be used to improve their performance during the second half of the term and pull up their final course grades. Here are some questions you can use to get this process going:

- Were these the grades you expected to receive?
- Are you pleased or disappointed by them?
- Do you see any pattern in your performance that points to things you're doing well and things you need to improve?
- What strategies and resources could you use to improve your performance in areas that need the most improvement?

(See chapter 7, pp. 215-216 for more detailed strategies on how to help students use their midterm exam results as feedback to improve their subsequent performance.)

Many campuses have adopted "early alert" or "early warning" systems that notify students much earlier than midterm (after the first 2-3 weeks of class) if they're at risk for a poor or failing grade by exhibiting behaviors such as:

1. Frequent class absences
2. Chronic class tardiness or leaving class early
3. Not acquiring textbook or other course materials
4. Not bringing required course materials to class (e.g., notebook, lab materials)
5. Being disengaged or disruptive in class (e.g., not taking notes, talking, texting, or unwillingness to participate in class discussions)
6. Failure to complete reading assignments
7. Missing or poor performance on early quizzes
8. Missing, late, or weak effort on early assignments.

If you see students exhibiting any of these behaviors, or if they have received an early-alert notice about these behaviors, strongly encourage them to meet with their course instructor or academic advisor to discuss how to modify their behavior before it results in a poor course grade or course withdrawal.

The *Late* Stage (Between Midterm and Final Exams)

Students are likely to encounter different issues and challenges toward the end of the term as they try to cope with the pressures of final projects, final exams, and returning home for the holidays (Thanksgiving and Christmas). This may be the time when you need to be sensitive and responsive to the wellness needs of students. End-of-term projects and upcoming final exams are often accompanied by sleep loss (pulling all-nighters), disruption of normal eating and exercise routines, and elevated levels of stress associated with test anxiety or fear of failure. (See chapter 7 for specific wellness strategies you can share with your students.)

The Second Semester

Once students have completed their first term in college and received their first full set of college grades, they tend to focus less on making a successful transition *to* college and more on making a successful transition *through* college—thinking about what's ahead of them (Brower, 1997). At this time, students may be most receptive to questions that ask them to reflect on their first term in college and identify what they did well, what setbacks or mistakes they made, and what they learned from those mistakes that could be used to improve their future performance. The second semester may also be the time when undecided students are trying to reach a decision on a major, or when decided students start thinking about changing their major based on their first-term course experiences and grades (Cuseo, 2005). Check in with your students about their academic plans, and if they seem confused or unclear about their future goals, encourage them to meet with an academic advisor.

One way to remain sensitive and responsive to the different adjustments that new students encounter at different times during their first-year experience is to remember that college adjustments typically fall into three key categories:

1. *Social* adjustments (Do I belong here?)—forming and sustaining new relationships while undergoing changes in the prior relationships they had with family members and high school friends.
2. *Academic* adjustments (Will I make it?)—dealing with the heavier academic workload in college and the reality that their initial college grades are likely to be lower than the grades they earned in high school.
3. *Motivational* adjustments (Is it worth it?)—thinking about whether the benefits of college outweigh its costs—in terms of money, time and effort.

Remain aware of, and responsive to, students' needs by checking in with them about how things are going in each of these three key areas of their college experience (academic, social, and motivational) and offer them support in any areas where they may be struggling. Specific strategies for providing student support in each of these areas is provided in chapter 4 (social support), chapter 5 (motivational support), and chapter 7 (academic support).

For students who may be struggling with motivational questions about whether college is really worth it, share with them the information contained in Box 3.1.

Box 3.1

Why College Is Worth It: The Economic and Personal Benefits of a College Education

Despite the belief that earning a college degree is as common as earning a high school diploma, only 31% of Americans hold a 4-year college degree (Lumina Foundation, 2016). When college graduates are compared with others from similar social and economic backgrounds who did not continue their education beyond high school, research shows that a college degree is well worth the time and effort it takes to achieve it. Summarized below are positive outcomes associated with a college education and a college degree (Cuseo, et al., 2016). As you can see, a college education has multiple benefits on multiple aspects of the student's future life.

1. Economic and Career Benefits

- Job Security and Stability—college graduates have higher rates of employment and are less likely to be laid off work.

- Higher Income—the gap between the earnings of high school and college graduates is large and *growing*. Individuals holding a bachelor's degree earn an average weekly salary that's approximately $17,500 higher than high school graduates. When these differences are calculated over a lifetime, the income of families headed by someone with a bachelor's degree is over a million dollars more than families headed by people with a high school diploma. (See Figure 3.2)

> *It's an irrefutable fact that college gives you a significant and persistent advantage decade after decade.*
>
> —Mary C. Daly, Vice President of the Federal Reserve Bank of San Francisco

- Better Retirement and Pension Benefits
- Career Versatility and Mobility—greater ability to move from one position to another. (College graduates have more job options.)
- Career Advancement—greater opportunity to move up to higher-level positions. (College graduates have more opportunities for job promotions.)
- Career Satisfaction—college graduates are more likely to find themselves in careers that interest them and in positions they find stimulating, challenging, and personally fulfilling.

- Career Autonomy—college graduates have more opportunities to work independently (without supervision) and make their own on-the-job decisions.

- Career Prestige—college graduates are more likely to hold higher-status positions (jobs considered to be highly desirable and highly regarded by society).

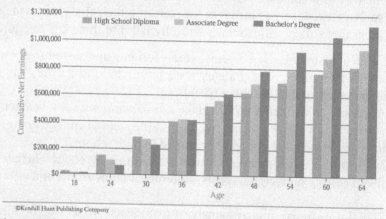

©Kendall Hunt Publishing Company

Figure 3.2

2. Advanced Intellectual Skills

- Are more knowledgeable
- Have more effective problem-solving skills—better ability to deal with complex and ambiguous problems
- Are more open to new ideas
- Have more advanced levels of moral reasoning
- Make more effective consumer choices and decisions
- Make wiser long-term investments
- Have a clearer sense of self-identity, including self-awareness and knowledge of personal talents, interests, values, and needs
- Are more likely to continue learning throughout life

3. Physical Health Benefits

- Have better health insurance—college graduates are more likely to be insured and have more comprehensive coverage
- Have better dietary habits
- Exercise more regularly
- Have lower rates of smoking and obesity
- Live longer and healthier lives

4. Social Benefits

- Greater social self-confidence
- Stronger interpersonal and human relations skills
- More effective leadership skills
- Greater popularity
- Higher levels of marital satisfaction

5. Emotional Benefits

- Lower levels of anxiety
- Higher levels of self-esteem
- Greater sense of self-efficacy—more likely to believe they can influence or control the outcomes of their life
- Higher levels of psychological well-being
- Higher levels of life satisfaction and personal happiness

6. Effective Citizenship

- Greater interest in national issues—both social and political
- Greater knowledge of current events
- Higher voting participation rates
- Higher rates of participation in civic affairs and community (volunteer) service
- Less likely to be incarcerated

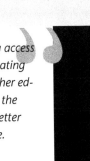

For the individual, having access to and successfully graduating from an institution of higher education has proved to be the path to a better job, to better health and to a better life.

—The College Board

7. Higher Quality of Life for Their Children

- Less likely to smoke during pregnancy
- Provide better health care for their children
- Spend more time with their children
- More likely to involve their children in stimulating educational activities that advance their cognitive (mental) development
- More likely to save money for their children to go to college
- Have children who are more likely to graduate from college
- Have children who are more likely to work in higher-status, higher-salary careers

Reflection 3.3

Which of the eight benefits of a college education listed in Box 3.1 were you least aware of? Which of the eight benefits do you think would be most important to share with your students?

Remind students that the short-term sacrifices they make now to complete college will bring lifelong benefits. Attaining a college degree is still a major accomplishment and it's an accomplishment that will enrich the quality of their life for the rest of their life.

Theories of College Student Development

By becoming familiar with student development theory, you acquire a framework for anticipating common patterns of college student behavior that will enable you to become a more effective peer leader and mentor. Three theories in particular can provide you with an essential overview of the key factors that affect student development and success in college:

- Student Involvement Theory (Alexander Astin),
- Interactionalist Theory of Student Retention (Vincent Tinto), and
- Student Identity Development Theory (Arthur Chickering).

Astin's Student Involvement Theory

Alexander Astin, a prominent researcher and scholar, developed an influential theory on the relationship between the degree of student involvement in the college experience and college success. Simply stated, Astin's involvement theory posits that success in college depends directly on the amount of time and energy students invest in the learning process—both *inside* and *outside* the classroom (Astin, 1984, 1993).

How Peer Leaders and Mentors Can Apply Astin's Student Involvement Theory

Peer leaders can apply this theory to their work by making an intentional effort to get students involved in the college experience. Here are some specific strategies for doing so.

Encourage students to *act* (engage in some action) on what they're learning. Students can be sure they're actively involved in the learning process if they engage in one or more of the following *actions*:

- *Writing*—when they write about what they're trying to learn (e.g., take notes on what they're reading, rather than passively highlight sentences).
- *Speaking*—when they state aloud what they're trying to learn (e.g., explain course concepts to a study partner, rather than just looking over the material silently).
- *Organizing*—when they connect or integrate the ideas they're learning into an outline, diagram, or concept map.

Urge students to attend all their classes in all their courses. Not surprisingly, the more time students devote to the task of learning, the more they learn and the more deeply they learn. This relationship leads to a straightforward recommenda-

It is not so much what the individual thinks or feels, but what the individual does, how he or she behaves, that defines and identifies involvement.

—Alexander Astin, Professor Emeritus, UCLA

tion you can make to students: Get to all classes in all courses. New students are often tempted to skip or cut classes because, unlike the teachers they had in high school, college professors are less likely to monitor class attendance or take roll. Remind students not to let this newfound freedom fool them into thinking that missing classes will not affect their course grades. Over the past 75 years, numerous studies have shown a direct relationship between class attendance and course grades—as one goes up or down, so does the other (Credé, Roch, & Kieszczynka, 2010; Launius, 1997; Shimoff & Catania, 2001; Tagliacollo, Volpato, & Pereira, 2010). Figure 3.3 depicts the results of one major study that clearly show the relationship between students' class attendance during the first 5 weeks of the term and their final course grades.

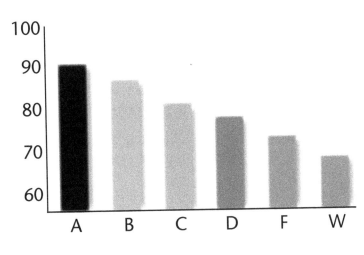

Figure 3.3 Relationship between Class Attendance Rate and Final Course Grades

Point out to new students that a full load of college courses (15 units) only requires that they be in class about 13 hours per week. If they think of college as a full-time job that only requires them to show up somewhere for 13 hours a week, that's a pretty sweet deal which leaves them with much more educational freedom than they had in high school. To miss class when they're being asked to spend such a limited time in class is a terrible abuse of this freedom. It's also an abuse of the money that they, their family, and taxpaying citizens are paying for their college education.

> **Emphasize to new students that if they want to withdraw from a class, they should see an academic advisor. Make sure they understand that if they just stop attending class, even if they stop attending during the first few weeks of the term, it doesn't mean they're automatically dropped from the course.**

Encourage students to stay actively involved in class. During college lectures, the best way students can apply the principle of active involvement is to engage in the action of taking notes. Writing down what someone is saying essentially "forces" the listener to pay closer attention to what's being said and reinforces retention of what's been heard. Remind students that their role in the college classroom is not to be an absorbent sponge or passive spectator who simply sits back and soaks up information. Instead, their role should be that of a detective or investigative reporter who's on a search-and-record mission. They should actively search for knowledge, pick the instructor's brain, pick out the instructor's key points, and record their "pickings" in their notebook (or on their laptop).

All genuine learning is active, not passive. It is a process in which the student is the main agent, not the teacher.

—Mortimer Adler, American professor of philosophy and educational theorist

Remind students that since they're spending much less time sitting in class than they did in high school, they're expected to spend much more time engaged in schoolwork outside of class. Since they're spending much less time in class than they did in high school, new students are often pleasantly surprised by how much "free time" they have in college. However, college students have much more "homework" and much of that work doesn't involve simply turning in assignments on a

> *In high school we were given a homework assignment every day. Now we have a large task assigned to be done at a certain time. No one tells [us] when to start or what to do each day.*
>
> —First-year college student

daily or weekly basis. Out-of-class work assigned in college may not even be collected and graded. Instead, it's expected that students do it for their own benefit to help them prepare for exams and assignments (e.g., acquiring knowledge from assigned readings that will appear on course exams). Rather than formally collecting homework, college professors expect students to do assigned work on their own, without supervision or enforced accountability.

Consistent with student involvement theory, studies repeatedly show that the more time students spend on academic work outside of class, the higher their grades (National Survey of Student Engagement, 2009). College faculty expect that for each hour students spend on coursework in class, they should spend at least two hours outside of class (Kuh, 2005). For example, in a three-credit course that meets three hours per week, students should devote at least six hours of out-of-class work per week. Unfortunately, less than 10% of beginning college students report putting in at least two hours of work out of class for every hour they spend in class (Kuh, 2005). This has to change if college students are to earn good grades. Just as successful athletes need to put in a significant amount of practice time to improve their athletic performance, successful students need to do the same to improve their academic performance.

Encourage new students to approach college like it's a full-time job. If they're taking a full load of courses, they're in class about 13 hours per week, which means they should spend about 26 hours a week working on those courses outside of class time. This adds up to a 40-hour work week—similar to a full-time job. In one study of more than 25,000 college students it was found that the percentage of students who spent 40 or more hours per week on academic work that received "A" grades was almost three times higher than it was for students who spent between 20 and 40 hours per week on academic work. For students who spent 20 or fewer hours per week on academic work outside of class, twice as many of them received a grade of "C" or below than did students who spent 40 or more hours on out-of-class work (Pace, 1990, 1995). (For tips you can share with students on course-related work they could and should do outside of class, see chapter 6, pp. 177-179.)

If students need further convincing about the importance of putting in time outside of class to earn good grades, remind them that earning higher grades translates into greater career benefits. Research on college graduates indicates that the higher their grades were in college, the higher: (a) their starting salary, (b) the status (prestige) of their first job, and (c) their career mobility—ability to change jobs or move into different positions (Cuseo et al., 2016). This relationship between higher college grades and career benefits exists for students at all types of colleges and universities, regardless of the reputation or prestige of the institution attended (Pascarella & Terenzini, 1991, 2005). In other words, students' level of academic achievement in college matters more to their career success than what college they attended.

> *Do not be a PCP (Parking Lot-Classroom-Parking Lot) student. The time you spend on campus will be a sound investment in your academic and professional success.*
>
> —Drew Appleby, Professor Emeritus of Psychology and Director of Undergraduate Studies, IUPUI

Encourage students to get actively involved in campus life, such as participating in student clubs and organizations, recreational programs, leadership activities, and volunteer experiences. Research consistently shows that learning experiences outside the classroom contribute as much to students' personal and career development as their coursework (Gallup-Purdue Index Report, 2014; Kuh, 1995; Kuh, Douglas, Lund, & Ramin-Gyurnek, 1994). This is one reason why most campuses no longer use the term "*extra*curricular" activities. Instead, they are referred to as "*co*-curricular" experiences to convey the message that both in-class and out-of-class learning experiences combine to educate the student as a whole person.

Research shows that students who become actively involved in campus life are more likely to:

- Enjoy their college experience;
- Graduate from college; and
- Develop leadership skills that enhance their career performance after college (Astin, 1993).

> **Remind students that co-curricular experiences are resumé-building experiences and that the campus professionals with whom they interact while engaging in these experiences (e.g., Director of Student Life or Dean of Students) can serve as personal references and resources for letters of recommendation.**

Be sure your students know that devoting a reasonable amount of time to co-curricular experiences should not interfere with their academic performance and lower their college grades. Since college students spend considerably less time inside the classroom than they did in high school, it leaves them with more time to engage in learning experiences outside the classroom. Research indicates that students' academic performance and progress to degree completion are not impaired if they spend 20 or fewer hours outside of class on co-curricular experiences and part-time work (Advisory Committee on Student Financial Assistance, 2008). In fact, students who get involved in co-curricular experiences tend to earn higher grades than students who do not get involved at all (Pascarella, 2001; Pascarella & Terenzini, 2005).

Encourage students to take advantage of student success workshops offered on campus (e.g., workshops on time management and study strategies) and to get involved with student clubs or organizations whose activities relate to their educational, personal, or career plans. If there are none that appeal to them, suggest they start one of their own. However, advise them not to get involved in more than two or three major campus organizations at a time. Restricting their total number of out-of-class activities will not only enable them to keep up with their studies, it will also be a more impressive resumé-builder. A long list of involvement in numerous activities can send the message that students are padding their resumé with activities they participated in temporarily or superficially (or not at all).

> *Just a [long] list of club memberships is meaningless; it's a fake front. Remember that quality, not quantity, is what counts.*
>
> —Lauren Pope, former director of the National Bureau for College Placement

Reflection 3.4

For the students you lead and mentor, what campus clubs or student organizations do you think would be most relevant to their educational, personal, or career plans?

▌into's Interactionalist Theory of Student Retention

Over the course of the past forty years, the opportunity to attend college has expanded dramatically in the United States. Since 1990, the proportion of high school graduates going to college has increased sharply (NASH & Education Trust, 2009; Snyder & Dillow, 2011), including students from low-income minority groups (Engle et al., 2012). More than 75% of high school graduates now enter college immediately after graduation (Hurley & Coles, 2015). Unfortunately, these gains in college *access* are not being matched by gains in college *success* (Hunt & Carruthers, 2004; Radford et al., 2010). The United States has one of the highest college-going rates in the world, yet its college graduation rates (both 2-year and 4-year) rank near the bottom half of all industrialized nations (Organisation for Economic Cooperation and Development, 2016). Only 40% of students who enroll in four-year colleges and universities earn a bachelor's degree in four years and only 60% graduate within six years. For students enrolling in two-year colleges, approximately 28% of them complete a certificate or degree within three years (National Center for Education Statistics, 2015).

One reason why campuses have developed peer leadership programs is to improve these disappointing graduation rates by improving student retention—students' ability to persist in college until they graduate. Vincent Tinto, an educational sociologist, has developed a highly regarded theory of student retention. His work has strongly influenced how campus leaders and student development professionals think about retention and what actions colleges should take to improve it (Tinto, 1987, 1993, 2012). According to Tinto, promoting student retention involves understanding the experiences that students have *before* college and the interactions they have *during* college.

Before–College Factors

Students enter college with different sets of what Tinto calls "pre-entry attributes," such as whether they will be the first member of their family to graduate from college and their level of academic preparedness or readiness for college. Some students enter college with less well-developed reading and writing skills and receive less guidance from family members who have already graduated from college. Such before-college experiences influence the amount and nature of support students will need to succeed in college.

Students' level of commitment to college at the time they enter college also affects the likelihood they will persist to graduation. Students who are less committed to college in general, or to the particular college they're attending, are less likely to graduate and will need more support and motivation to hang in there and graduate.

During–College Factors

Although students' experiences prior to college influence their retention and college-completion rates, Tinto asserts that students' experiences *during* college have the greatest effect on student persistence to graduation. These experiences include interactions with faculty, student support professionals, and peer leaders. His theory stipulates that two key factors impact college success: academic integration and social integration. As the college experience unfolds, students be-

Call it a clan, call it a network, call it a tribe (or) call it a family. Whatever you call it, whoever you are, you need one.

—Elizabeth Jane Howard, award-winning British novelist

come connected to ("integrated" into) the campus to various degrees. The greater their academic and social integration, the more likely they will persist to graduation. Simply stated, when students see themselves as integral members of the college community, they are more likely to remain in college and graduate from college (Tinto, 1987, 1993, 2012).

How Peer Leaders and Mentors can Apply Tinto's Interactionalist Theory of Student Retention

As a peer leader, you can increase students' commitment to college by articulating the benefits of a college education and a college degree (see pp. 74-75). You can also increase students' commitment to *your* college by: (1) reminding them of its exceptional and distinctive features, (2) encouraging them to take advantage of exciting opportunities and programs it offers, and (3) connecting them with its successful alumni.

The powerful role that peer leaders can play in socially integrating new students into the campus community is suggested by research indicating that college students who receive peer mentoring during their first term on campus report feeling significantly more connected to the college community than non-mentored students (Sanchez, Bauer, & Paronto, 2006; Yomov et al., 2017). Further evidence for the positive influence of peer leaders is highlighted by a national study of 41,000 first-year college students on 72 different campuses. The study revealed that new students who interacted with peer leaders and mentors reported stronger connections with their peers and their faculty, were more involved in campus life outside the classroom, and felt a greater sense of "belonging" (Barefoot, 2003).

As a peer leader and mentor, you are well positioned to help students make these key connections. By doing so, you will be effectively applying Tinto's Interactionalist Theory to enhance students' academic and social integration, and ultimately, their likelihood of persisting to college graduation.

Connecting Students with Their Peers

As you already know, students are more likely to listen to (and be influenced by) other students than by faculty, staff, or administrators. One of the most powerful things you can do as a peer leader is to facilitate the development of mutually supportive social networks among students.

These networks can supply students with valuable social capital—the sociological network that enables them to bond together and stay together until they graduate. When students make meaningful interpersonal connections with other students, it strengthens their sense of membership in the campus community and improves the overall quality of their college experience.

Capitalize on the power of peer networking by connecting students with each other early and often. You can be a connection catalyst by:

- Bringing students together to share meals,
- Encouraging students to attend cultural or athletic events on campus and being there with them,
- Playing sports or working out together, and
- Facilitating learning teams. (For specific strategies, see chapter 7, p. 212.)

Connecting Students with Key Members of the Campus Community

In addition to connecting with classmates and peer mentors, students can connect with a variety of other people on campus who can promote their college success. Listed below are other important interpersonal connections that students could and should make in college. Encourage students to begin making these connections during their first year so they can begin building a social-support network they can rely on throughout their college experience.

Help students to:

- Connect with a student development professional they may have met during orientation.
- Join a college club, student organization, campus committee, intramural team, or a community service (volunteer) group whose members share the same personal or career interests as they do. If they don't see a club or organization they were hoping to join, encourage them to start one of their own, especially one that relates to their educational or career goals. For example, if they are English majors, suggest they start a Writing Club or a Book Club. If they plan to become lawyers, they could start a pre-law club.
- Connect with an academic advisor to discuss and develop an educational plan.
- Connect with academic support professionals in the Learning Resource Center or Academic Success Center for tutoring related to any course in which they'd like to improve their performance and achieve academic excellence.
- Connect with a college librarian to get early assistance and a head start on any research projects they've been assigned.
- Connect with a personal counselor to discuss issues related to college adjustment or personal growth.
- Connect with peers who live near them or who commute to campus from the same area in which they live. If their schedules are similar, encourage them to carpool together. (See Box 3.2 for additional strategies for promoting connections among commuter students and to other members of the campus community.)

Connecting Students with Faculty

Research repeatedly shows that the more contact students have with faculty members during their time in college, the more likely they are to complete college and earn their degree (Astin, 1993). Studies also show that students who have more contact with faculty outside of class are more likely to exhibit stronger academic performance, stronger critical thinking skills, higher levels of college satisfaction, and greater motivation to continue their education after college (Cuseo, 2018; Pascarella & Terenzini, 2005).

First-year students often have fears and preconceptions about approaching college faculty because they may think that "they're not interested in spending time with students" or that "I wouldn't know what to say to them." New students may need your help to develop the self-confidence to approach faculty, pose questions to them, and create relationships with them. Remind them that faculty are more likely to remember students whom they've interacted with outside the

Box 3.2

Promoting the Social Integration of Commuter Students

- Design a special, commuter-student module or strand within new-student orientation during which commuters are given the opportunity to meet and interact with each other.
- Construct a commuter-student directory (including phone numbers and e-mail addresses) to facilitate carpooling, networking, and a sense of group identity.
- Create a special Facebook page for commuter students containing information especially for them (e.g., information on off-campus opportunities for housing and social gatherings).
- Organize a "commuter awareness" event on campus (e.g., a commuter appreciation day at which commuters are given tickets for free lunch in the student café).
- Encourage and support the development of a commuter-student club or council.
- Encourage commuter students to become representatives in student government and on campus committees or task forces.
- Help form commuter teams who participate in intramural sports and other forms of on-campus competition (e.g., competition between teams of students living in different campus residences and teams of commuters living in different geographical areas off campus).
- Help organize college services or events in off-campus geographical areas populated with high concentrations of commuter students (e.g., dinners at a local restaurant, movie night at a local theatre, or study sessions at a local library).

classroom and that faculty are more likely to write letters of recommendation for students with whom they've had personal interaction.

New students may also need to be reminded that college faculty hold office hours for the express purpose of interacting with students beyond the classroom. Unlike high school, college students don't see instructors outside of class only if they're "in trouble" (e.g., doing poorly or need to be disciplined).

As a peer leader, you can help students connect with faculty by:

- Suggesting they converse briefly with them after class and communicate with them via e-mail.
- Encouraging them to use faculty office hours. Urge students to seek out their instructors for help with understanding course concepts and course assignments, and for information about majoring in a faculty member's field of study. Share with students the ways in which you approach faculty outside of class and what you talk about when you visit with faculty.
- Recommending particular faculty whom you know are very approachable and helpful, and who may share similar educational or recreational interests as the student.
- Advising students to participate in activities with faculty, such as field trips and undergraduate research, particularly in a field they're majoring in, or considering as a major.
- Inviting faculty to meetings that you are holding with your students.

Author's Experience I tell first-year students to see their course instructors during their office hours at least three times during the term. In fact, I've made this a requirement for students in my college success course. At the end of the term, my students complete a course evaluation. Almost always, the number-one positive statement students make about the course was how helpful the faculty office visits were. They tell me that those visits not only helped them learn the course material, but also enabled them to view and interact with their instructors in a different, more personal way.

— *Aaron Thompson*

Reflection 3.5

Given the importance of student-faculty contact outside the classroom, what recommendations would you have for faculty and administrators to increase out-of-class contact between faculty and students on your campus?

Connecting Students with Academic Advisors

Regardless of your particular leadership role on campus, make a point of stressing to your students the importance of connecting with an academic advisor. Too often, students view academic advisors as people they only go for class scheduling or to see if their graduation requirements have been completed. Yes, advisors do those things, but they also do much more. Advisors:

- Help students choose or change majors.
- Advise students about whether or not to drop a class.
- Alert students to educational and career opportunities relating to their chosen major.
- Refer students to campus resources and off-campus opportunities that are appropriate at different stages of their college experience.
- Help students construct an educational plan that will enable them to graduate in a timely manner.
- Assist students with finding educational and career opportunities after graduation.

In short, academic advisors are much more than course schedulers; they can be mentors, support agents, and partners with whom students can collaborate to promote their success in college and beyond.

Serving as an Effective Referral Agent

A leader need not be a superhero or a superstar. You cannot do everything for everybody. There will be times when you're able to help students solve problems, but there will be other occasions when you will need to connect them with campus resources for professional assistance. You can play this important connecting role by: (a) asking students about their needs, concerns, and interests; (b) acquiring knowledge about campus support services and student opportunities on your campus; and (c) referring students to student-support professionals who are most qualified to address particular student needs or concerns. If you do not know who to refer your students to, find somebody who does know. Someone on campus almost always has an answer or can direct you to someone else who has an answer.

> **You provide the first line of defense for your students. By providing accurate and timely referrals, you can short-circuit student problems and issues before they turn into full-blown crises.**

I have helped students close the gap between their potential and performance by listening to their concerns and giving them information about things that can help them, whether it is the counseling center on campus, the tutoring services, or the student groups they can get involved in.

—Peer leader

Get to know the student-support professionals on your campus. Visit the people associated with the resources available to students. Have their contact information handy, cultivate relationships with them, and connect students to them. Introduce your students to these other support agents so they can build networks of interpersonal support and increase their stock of social capital.

Successful people have lots of mentors. It's been said that "it takes a village" and your college community is that village; it contains the collective knowledge and wisdom of multiple villagers with whom you can partner to help students succeed. Some of your key campus partners include:

- Faculty,
- Academic Advisors,
- Career Counselors and Specialists,
- Student Life Professionals,
- Residence Advisors and Assistants
- Personal Counselors,
- Campus Ministers,
- Financial Aid Counselors,
- Community Service Specialists,
- Graduate Teaching and Research Assistants, and
- Working Professionals in the Local Community.

Obtain a copy of their brochures and program descriptions, ask them about what they do, the challenges they face, their most essential advice for students, and how you can most effectively partner with them.

Also network with other student leaders and use them as a resource. You never know who may be able to exert the most influence on whom, or what particular relationship will prove to be life-changing for a student.

Reflection 3.6

Which campus partners mentioned in the above list do you think your students would: (a) most benefit from interacting with, and (b) be least likely to interact with unless you strongly encouraged them to do so?

Connect students to campus resources. According to Tinto's Interactionalist Theory, students are more likely to remain in college and complete their degree when they interact with both the social and academic systems of their college or university. Studies show that students who interact with campus resources designed to support their academic development report higher levels of satisfaction with their college experience and are more likely to complete their college education (Chaney, 2010; Pascarella & Terenzini, 1991, 2005).

It's probably safe to say that, after college, students will never again be part of another organization or community with so many resources and services at their fingertips that are intentionally designed to promote their personal development and future success. By helping students take advantage of all the resources available to them, you're helping them capitalize on a once-in-a-lifetime opportunity. As a peer leader, you can play a key role in helping students connect with and capitalize on campus resources by:

- Increasing student awareness of their purpose and the value of using them.
- Sharing positive experiences you have had with these resources or the positive experiences of other students who you know have benefitted from them.
- Actively referring students to them. (See pp. 87-88 for specific ways to make effective student referrals.)

> Remind students that their use of campus resources comes free of charge—the cost of these services is already covered by their tuition. By investing time and energy in campus resources, students are not only increasing their prospects for college success, they're also maximizing the return on their financial investment in college. In other words, they're getting a bigger bang for their buck!

Take time to learn about the campus resources available to your students. An essential step in the process of referring students to campus resources is being fully aware of what they are designed to do and what they have to offer. Familiarize yourself with your college catalogue (whether in print or online), especially the parts that are most relevant to the needs of the students you're working with. Also, peruse websites (and Facebook pages) for campus- and community-based resources that may benefit your students. If you know where to refer students, they are less likely to get the "runaround" and are more likely to get around to using the resources available to them. (Appendix A, pp. 427-430 contains a list of key campus resources designed to support student success, their primary purposes, and key reasons for using them that you can share with students to motivate them to take advantage of these resources.)

> Helping students capitalize on campus resources helps them develop *resourcefulness*—a habit or disposition that promotes success in college and life.

Making Referrals Sensitively and Strategically

Effective referral agents know *what* resources are available and know *how* to motivate students to use them. There's an art and a science to making successful referrals that goes well beyond simply telling students what resources are available to them. An effective referral agent inspires students to capitalize on available resources by supplying them with a compelling rationale for doing so, instilling confidence in the referred person or resource, and helping them take action on the referral. Described below are key strategies for making effective referrals.

- First and foremost: take time to *listen* closely to the student's problem before making a referral. If you refer too quickly, it can send the message that you're disinterested, dismissive, or giving the student the "brush off." Explain why you're referring rather than trying to help the student yourself. Make it clear that you cannot provide advice because the issue or problem is beyond your area of expertise and qualifications. Be sure students know you're making a referral to ensure that they receive the best advice and support, not because you're disinterested in their problem or issue.

- **Respect and maintain student confidentiality.** Make it explicitly clear up front that you intend to keep your conversation private and confidential.

- **Provide a clear description of the referred resource and its purpose.** Explain why the resource exists, how it relates to the student's current issue or concern, and what good things are likely to take place if the student uses it. Students can have reservations, doubts, and sometimes be downright skeptical about using particular resources (e.g., "tutoring is just for dummies") or about approaching certain people (e.g., "counselors are for people with mental health problems"). By providing a clear rationale for the referral and painting a positive picture of what the referred person can do for the student, you increase the likelihood that the student will actually follow through on your referral.

- **Personalize the referral: Refer the student to a *person*, not than an office or position.** Referring a student to a human being, not an anonymous entity, serves to humanize the referral process and increases the student's sense of personal connection to the referred resource.

- **Use your best judgment about what particular support professional on campus provides the best match or "fit" for the student's particular personality and needs.** If you're unsure who that person might be, seek input from your program director.

- **Reassure students that the person you're referring them to is caring, concerned, and qualified.** Vouch for the credibility and character of the referred person. A calculus tutor knows calculus and knows how to explain it to students. An academic advisor understands academic requirements and options, and knows how to help students make informed educational decisions about their coursework. Personal counselors understand how to help students cope with minor college adjustments and more serious personal issues.

  If you know other students who have benefitted from the support-service professional, mention it. For instance, "I know the person I'm referring you to; she's qualified, she cares, and she knows her stuff—I know because I have referred other students to her with problems similar to yours and they really benefitted from her advice."

- **Help students prepare for the first visit.** Assist them in clarifying their purpose for going, and discuss how to approach the resource person. Such prepping will reduce any trepidation they may have about going and will increase the likelihood that they'll follow through with the appointment.

- **Help students take the steps needed to make an appointment.** Since it's best to "strike while the iron is hot," try to persuade students to make an appointment with the person you're referring them to at the time they've come to see you. If they're unwilling to make the appointment right away, let them know that you're ready and willing to help them set up an appointment whenever they're ready.

- **If possible, walk the student to the referred person's office.** This will ensure that the student knows where to go and how to get there. It may also provide the student with the social support needed to actually get there.
- **Follow up with the referred student.** Encourage the student to get back to you about how the referral went in general. You don't want to probe for specific details because the student may not feel comfortable divulging them to you, or you may not have the right to know them. However, it's okay to ask if they saw the referred person, if it helped, and if there's anything else you can do to provide further assistance. Even if students don't act on your initial recommendation or don't get back to you, following up with them serves to remind them about the referral and show them that you're still thinking about them.
- **Compliment students for seeking support and striving for self-improvement.** Praising students for using a resource raises their awareness that help-seeking is not a sign of weakness, but a sign of personal strength and resourcefulness.

> **Always respect the boundaries of your position. As you know, you're not a professional counselor, therapist, or academic-support specialist. You're a peer mentor—a trusted guide, one role of which is to direct and connect students to the right campus resources and to campus professionals who are best prepared to deal with their particular challenges, problems, or issues.**

Reflection 3.7

What student issues do you think you'll encounter in your leadership role that will fall beyond the professional boundaries of your position and require referral to a professional on campus?

Helping Your Campus Identify Sources of Student Dissatisfaction and Causes of Student Withdrawal

In addition to connecting students to campus resources and student-support professionals, you can promote student retention at your college or university by keeping an eye and ear out for underlying causes of student dissatisfaction that can lead to their withdrawal. Peers are often more aware of student intentions to leave college—and their reasons for doing so—long before these intentions become apparent to faculty, staff, and administrators. Students are also more likely to feel comfortable sharing their true feelings with a trusted peer than with an older authority figure employed by the college.

As a peer mentor, you can promote student retention by engaging in any of the following practices.

- Help gather information on students' campus experiences, including their sources of satisfaction and dissatisfaction (e.g., conducting personal interviews or focus groups).
- Identify and support students who show signs of intended withdrawal (e.g., students who have not pre-registered for next term's classes or haven't reapplied for financial aid).

- Serve as a student representative on your college's retention committee.
- Conduct "exit interviews" with students who are in the process of withdrawing. (A peer is likely to receive more honest responses from a departing student than an older professional employed by the college.)
- Survey students who have withdrawn from your college to assess: (a) their reasons for leaving, (b) whether there was anything the college could have done to help them stay, and (c) if they may be interested in coming back.

Chickering's Theory of Student Identity Development

Arthur Chickering, student development researcher and scholar, formulated a highly acclaimed theory of college students' identity development. Chickering's theory identifies seven key "vectors" of personal identity that are developed during the college experience (Chickering, 1969; Chickering & Reiser, 1993). Listed below are short descriptions of these seven vectors of student development.

1. *Achieving Competence:* gaining a stronger sense of self-efficacy and self-confidence about one's intellectual and interpersonal capabilities.
2. *Managing Emotions:* learning to recognize and control emotions—such as anxiety, anger, and frustration.
3. *Moving through Autonomy to Interdependence:* growing more independent, while at the same time coming to appreciate the value of interdependence and collaboration.
4. *Developing Mature Interpersonal Relationships:* becoming open to developing new relationships, more intimate relationships, and relationships with people from different cultural backgrounds.
5. *Establishing Identity:* becoming comfortable with oneself (e.g., one's sexuality, ethnicity, and beliefs) and developing a personal identity that's self-determined—as opposed to being defined or determined by someone else.
6. *Developing Purpose:* finding one's calling or purpose in life and making intentional plans about the future.
7. *Developing Integrity:* developing a coherent system of personal values and ethical principles, and acting in ways that are consistent with those values and principles.

The challenges and opportunities associated with Chickering's seven areas of development do not end at college graduation; they are experienced throughout life. However, it's during the college years that these challenges come at a fast and furious pace. Chickering stresses that college students do not move through these vectors in a strictly sequential or linear fashion. Instead, students typically "spiral" through them—going forward, backward, then forward again—depending on their personal circumstances and particular college experiences. Thus, it's best not to view these seven vectors as sequential stages of development, but as general target areas for your peer leadership efforts, keeping in mind that student development in these areas will not always progress smoothly across time. In fact, they may actually regress from time to time. So, be patient and persistent; your efforts to promote student development may occasionally hit a wall or bounce backward, but that's just part of the maturational process of moving forward.

Reflection 3.8

Which one of Chickering' seven developmental challenges do you think will pose the greatest challenge for the students you're working with? As a peer leader or mentor, what kind of support could you provide to help students meet this challenge?

How Peer Leaders and Mentors Can Apply Chickering's Theory of Student Identity Development Theory

As a peer leader, you can support students in their quest to meet the challenges associated with each of these vectors of development. Students' growth is maximized when they experience moderate challenges to their current level of development that's accompanied by effective support (Sanford, 1967; Upcraft, Gardner, & Barefoot, 2005). You can both challenge and support students' personal growth along Chickering's seven vectors by applying the knowledge you acquire from chapters in this book that correspond to each of these vectors :

1. *Achieving Competence:* chapters 5 and 6
2. *Managing Emotions:* chapters 4 and 7
3. *Moving through Autonomy toward Interdependence:* chapters 5 and 8
4. *Developing Mature Interpersonal Relationships:* chapters 4 and 9
5. *Establishing Identity:* chapters 5 and 7
6. *Developing Purpose:* chapter 5
7. *Developing Integrity:* chapters 1 and 7.

You, too, will continue to advance along these seven vectors of development as you proceed through your college experience. Your advancing level of development will increase your ability to identify and empathize with the students you mentor (and they with you). To jumpstart this identification and empathy-building process, complete Exercise 3.6 at the end of this chapter.

Internet Resources

For additional information on concepts contained in this chapter, consult the following websites.

Differences between High School and College
smu.edu/alec/transition.asp

Different Stages of Student Challenges/Adjustments during the First Year of College
www.sandiego.edu/parents/documents/TheWCurveRevised.pdf

Benefits of the College Experience and College Degree
https://trends.collegeboard.org/education-pays

Theories of College Student Development
https://ir.library.illinoisstate.edu/cgi/viewcontent.cgi?referer=https://www.bing.com/&httpsredir=1&article=1029&context=fpml

References

Advisory Committee on Student Financial Assistance. (2008, September). *Apply to succeed: Ensuring community college students benefit from need-based financial aid.* Washington, DC: Author. Retrieved from https://www2.ed.gov/about/bdscomm/list/acsfa/applytosucceed.pdf

Astin, A. W. (1984). Student involvement: A developmental theory. *Journal of College Student Personnel, 25,* 297-308.

Astin, A. W. (1993). *What matters in college?* San Francisco: Jossey-Bass.

Barefoot, B. O. (2003). *Findings from the second national survey of first-year academic practices, 2002.* Brevard, NC: Policy Center for the First Year of College.

Brower, A. M. (1997). Prototype matching for future selves: Information management strategies in the transition to college. *Journal of The Freshman Year Experience & Students in Transition, 9*(1), 7-42.

Bureau of Labor Statistics. (2015). December 8). *Earning and unemployment rates by educational attainment.* Retrieved from http://www.bls.gov/emp/ep_chart_1001.htm

Chaney, C. H. (2010). *National evaluation of Student Support Services: Examination of student outcomes after six years.* Washington, DC: U.S. Department of Education.

Chickering, A. W. (1969). *Education and identity.* San Francisco: Jossey-Bass.

Chickering, A. W., & Reiser, L. (1993). *Education and identity* (2nd ed.). San Francisco: Jossey-Bass.

Credé, M., Roch, S. G., & Kieszczynka, U. M. (2010). Class attendance in college: A meta-analytic review of the relationship of class attendance with grades and student characteristics. *Review of Educational Research, 80*(2), 272-295.

Cuseo, J. (2005). "Decided," "undecided," and "in transition": Implications for academic advisement, career counseling, and student retention. In R. S. Feldman (Ed.), *Improving the first year of college: Research and practice* (pp. 27-50). New York: Erlbaum.

Cuseo, J. (2018). Student-faculty engagement. In J. Groccia, & W. Buskist (Eds.), *Student engagement: A multidimensional perspective* (pp. 87-98). New Directions for Teaching and Learning, No. 154. San Francisco: Jossey-Bass.

Cuseo, J., Thompson, A., Campagna, M., & Fecas, V. (2016). *Thriving in college & beyond: Research-based strategies for academic success and personal development* (4th ed.). Dubuque, IA: Kendall Hunt.

Duffy, D. K., & Jones, J. W. (1995). *Teaching within the rhythms of the semester.* San Francisco: Jossey-Bass.

Engle, J., Yeado, J., Brusi, R., & Cruz, J. (2012). *Replenishing opportunity in America: The 2012 midterm report of public higher education systems in the access to success initiative.* Washington, DC: The Education Trust.

Gallup-Purdue Index Report. (2014). *Great jobs, great lives: A study of more than 30,000 college graduates across the U.S.* Retrieved from https://www.luminafoundation.org/files/resources/galluppurdueindex-report-2014.pdf

Gordon, V. N., & Steele, G. E. (2003). Undecided first-year students: A 25-year longitudinal study. *Journal of the First-Year Experience and Students in Transition, 15*(1), 19-38.

Hunt, J., Jr., & Carruthers, G. (2004). Foreword. *Measuring up 2004: The national report card on higher education.* San Jose, CA : National Center for Public Policy in Higher Education.

Hurley, S., & Coles, A. (2015). College counseling for Latino and underrepresented students. National Association for College Admission Counseling & Excelencia in Education. Retrieved from http://www.edexcelencia.org/research/college-counseling-latino-and-underrepresented-students

Kuh, G. D. (1995). The other curriculum: Out-of-class experiences associated with student learning and personal development. *Journal of Higher Education, 66*(2), 123–153.

Kuh, G. D., (2005). Student engagement in the first year of college. In M. L. Upcraft, J. N. Gardner, B. O. Barefoot, & Associates, *Challenging and supporting the first-year student: A handbook for improving the first year of college* (pp. 86-107). San Francisco: Jossey-Bass.

Kuh, G. D., Douglas, K. B., Lund, J. P., & Ramin-Gyurnek, J. (1994). *Student learning outside the classroom: Transcending artificial boundaries.* ASHE-ERIC Higher Education Report No. 8. Washington, DC: George Washington University, School of Education and Human Development.

Launius, M. H. (1997). College student attendance: Attitudes and academic performance. *College Student Journal, 31*(1), 86-93.

Lotkowski, V. A., Robbins, S. B., & Noeth, R. J. (2004). *The role of academic and non-academic factors in improving student retention.* ACT Policy Report. Retrieved from https://www.act.org/research/policymakers/pdf/college_retention.pdf

Lumina Foundation. (2016). *A stronger nation through higher education.* Indianapolis, IN: Author. Retrieved from https://www.luminafounation.org/files/publications/stronger_nation/2016/A_Stronger_Nation

Maslow, A. H. (1954). *Motivation and personality.* New York: Harper & Row.

NASH (National Association of System Heads) & Education Trust. (2009). *Charting a necessary path: The baseline report of public higher education systems in the access to success initiative.* Washington, DC: Authors.

National Center for Education Statistics. (2015). *Digest of education statistics, 2015: Selected cohort entry years, 1996 through 2008.* Washington, DC: U.S. Department of Education. Retrieved from https://nces.edgov/programs/digest/d15/tables/dt15_326.10asp

National Survey of Student Engagement. (2009). *NSSE Annual Results 2009. Assessment for improvement: Tracking student engagement over time.* Bloomington, IN: Author.

Organization for Economic Cooperation and Development. (2016). *Education at a glance, 2016; OECED indicators.* Paris: Author.

Pace, C. (1990). *The undergraduates: A report of their activities.* Los Angeles: University of California, Center for the Study of Evaluation.

Pace, C. (1995, May). *From good processes to good products: Relating good practices in undergraduate education to student achievement.* Paper presented at the meeting of the Association for Institutional Research, Boston.

Pascarella, E. T. (2001, November/December). Cognitive growth in college: Surprising and reassuring findings from the National Study of Student Learning. *Change,* pp. 21–27.

Pascarella, E. T., & Terenzini, P. T. (1991). *How college affects students: Findings and insights from twenty years of research.* San Francisco: Jossey-Bass.

Pascarella, E. T., & Terenzini, P. T. (2005). *How college affects students, Volume 2: A third decade of research.* San Francisco: Jossey-Bass.

Pennington, D. C., Zvonkovic, R. M., & Wilson, S. L. (1989). Changes in college satisfaction across an academic term. *Journal of College Student Development, 30*(6), 528-535.

Radford, A., Berkner, L., Wheeles, S., & Shepherd, B. (2010). *Persistence and attainment of 2003-2004 beginning postsecondary students: After 6 years.* NCES 2011-151. U.S. Department of Education, Office of Educational Research and Improvement.

Sanchez, R. J., Bauer, T. N., & Paronto, M. E. (2006). Peer-mentoring freshmen: Implications for satisfaction, commitment, and retention to graduation. *Academy of Management Learning and Education, 5*(1), 25-37.

Sanford, N. (1967). *Where colleges fail.* San Francisco: Jossey-Bass.

Shanley, M. K., & Johnson, J. (2008). 8 things first-year student fear about college. *Journal of College Admission* (Fall), 1-6.

Shimoff, E., & Catania, C. A. (2001). Effects of recording attendance on grades in Introductory Psychology. *Teaching of Psychology, 23*(3), 192-195.

Snyder, T. D., & Dillow, S. A. (2011). Digest of educational statistics, 2010. (NCES 2011-0105). Washington, DC: National Center for Education Statistics, Institute of Education Sciences, U.S. Department of Education. Retrieved from https://nces.ed.gov/pubs2011/2011015.pdf

Tagliacollo, V. A., Volpato, G. L., & Pereira, A., Jr. (2010). Association of student position in classroom and school performance. *Educational Research, 1*(6), 198-201.

Tinto, V. (1987). *Leaving college: Rethinking the causes and cures of student attrition.* Chicago: The University of Chicago Press.

Tinto, V. (1988). Stages of student departure: Reflections on the longitudinal character of student leaving. *The Journal of Higher Education, 59*(4), 438-455.

Tinto, V. (1993). *Leaving college: Rethinking the causes and cures of student attrition* (2nd ed.). Chicago: The University of Chicago Press.

Tinto, V. (2012). *Completing college: Rethinking institutional action.* Chicago: The College of Chicago Press.

Upcraft, M. L., Gardner, J. N., & Barefoot, B. O. (2005). The first year of college revisited. In M. L. Upcraft, J. N. Gardner, B. O. Barefoot, & Associates, *Challenging & supporting the first-year student: A handbook for improving the first year of college* (pp. 1-12). San Francisco: Jossey-Bass.

Yomov, D., Plunkett, S. W., Efrat, R., & Marin, A. G. (2017). Can peer mentors improve first-year experiences of university students. *Journal of College Student Retention: Research, Theory & Practice, 19*(1), 25-44.

Exercise 3.1 Quote Reflections

Review the sidebar quotes contained in this chapter and select two that you think would be especially valuable to share with the students you lead or mentor.

For each quote, write a short statement explaining why you chose it.

Exercise 3.2 Journal Reflections

1. If you were to make a short presentation to high school seniors about the most important *difference* between high school and college, what would you focus on?

2. If you were asked to share your top-three tips for college success with new students during orientation, what would they be?

3. Based on your first-year experience in college, what do you think will be the most difficult or significant challenge your students will face?

4. a) What practices or policies on your campus do you think are working to *increase* student satisfaction and retention? Why?

   b) What practices or policies on your campus do you think are *decreasing* student satisfaction and retention? How could these practices or policies be improved? As a peer leader, do you see any way you could help make these improvements happen?

Exercise 3.3 Identifying College Stressors

Read the list of college stressors in the box below and rate them in terms of how stressful each one is likely to be for the students you are leading or mentoring.

(1 = low, 5 = high)

College Stressor	Stress Rating				
Tests and exams	1	2	3	4	5
Writing assignments	1	2	3	4	5
Class workload	1	2	3	4	5
Pace of courses	1	2	3	4	5
Performing up to expectations	1	2	3	4	5
Speaking up in class or in front of groups	1	2	3	4	5
Handling personal freedom	1	2	3	4	5
Time pressure (e.g., meeting deadlines)	1	2	3	4	5
Financial pressure (e.g., managing money)	1	2	3	4	5
Organizational pressure (e.g., organizing time and tasks)	1	2	3	4	5
Living independently	1	2	3	4	5
Deciding on a major or career	1	2	3	4	5
Worrying about the future	1	2	3	4	5
Finding meaning and purpose in life	1	2	3	4	5
Moral and ethical decisions	1	2	3	4	5
Emotional issues	1	2	3	4	5
Physical health	1	2	3	4	5
Intimate relationships	1	2	3	4	5
Sexuality	1	2	3	4	5
Family responsibilities	1	2	3	4	5
Family conflicts	1	2	3	4	5
Peer pressure	1	2	3	4	5
Loneliness or isolation	1	2	3	4	5
Roommate conflicts	1	2	3	4	5
Conflict with professors	1	2	3	4	5
Campus policies or procedures	1	2	3	4	5
Transportation	1	2	3	4	5
Technology	1	2	3	4	5
Safety	1	2	3	4	5

Other stressors you would add to this list:

_____	1 2 3 4 5
_____	1 2 3 4 5
_____	1 2 3 4 5

Review your ratings and identify three items you rated highest:

a) What *time or stage* during the college experience are students most likely to experience this source of stress, or experience it most intensely?

b) What *coping strategy* would you suggest to students to help them deal with each source of stress?

c) What *campus resource* would you recommend to students to help them deal with each source of stress?

Exercise 3.4 Facilitating Students' Social Integration

Construct a short "sales pitch" or "elevator speech" you could share with students to persuade them to make a personal connection with:

(a) a faculty member

(b) an academic advisor.

Deliver your pitch to a fellow student leader or friend and ask for feedback on its persuasiveness.

Exercise 3.5 Creating a Master List of Student-Support Resources

1. Construct a comprehensive list of all student-support resources available on your campus. Your final product should be a list that includes the following information:

Campus Resource   Types of Support Provided   Campus Location   Contact Person

_____   _____   _____   _____

(After you finish constructing this master list, save it for future use when making referrals.)

2. List what you think are the most common problems or issues that students experience on your campus, and, next to each one, list the campus resource or support professional that's best qualified to deal with that particular problem or issue.

Name _____ Date _____

Exercise 3.6 Applying Chickering's "7 Vectors" of Development

Think of a situation or scenario that students are likely to experience with respect to each of Chickering's seven vectors of development (described on p. 89).

Write a short description of this scenario that includes information relating to the following questions:

1. How does the scenario capture or relate to that particular vector of Chickering's theory?

2. What could a peer leader or mentor do to help students develop along the vector depicted in the scenario ?

Name _____ Date _____

Exercise 3.7 Strategy Reflections

Review the strategies for how peer leaders and mentors can apply *Astin's Student Involvement Theory* recommended on pp. 76-79. Select three strategies that you think students would be most receptive to learning about and putting into practice.

CHAPTER 4

Social and Emotional Intelligence

The Foundation of Effective Leadership

Reflection 4.1

When you hear the word "intelligence," what characteristics come to mind?

Chapter Purpose and Preview

Relating well to others, and communicating effectively with them, is a key leadership skill and an essential element of "social intelligence." Similarly, "emotional intelligence"–the ability to identify and manage our emotions and be aware of how our behavior influences the emotions of others–is critical for effective leadership. This chapter identifies specific ways in which you can exhibit social and emotional intelligence. It also supplies you with interpersonal communication and human relations strategies for developing positive relationships with students, which, in turn, will enhance your effectiveness as a peer leader.

The Importance of Social and Emotional Intelligence

Human intelligence was once considered to be a general intellectual trait that could be measured by an intelligence test (IQ). Scholars have since discovered that the singular word "intelligence" is inaccurate and should be replaced with the plural "intelligences" to reflect the fact that humans can and do display intelligence (mental ability) in multiple forms that cannot be captured in a single test score. One of these multiple forms of intelligence is *social intelligence* (a.k.a. "interpersonal intelligence")–the ability to communicate and relate effectively to others (Gardner, 1993, 1999; Goleman, 2006). It's long been known that social intelligence is essential for effective leadership (Avolio, Walumbwa, & Weber, 2009; Zaccaro et al., 1991) and more recent research indicates that it's a better predictor of personal and professional success than intellectual ability (Carneiro, Crawford, & Goodman, 2006; Goleman, 2006).

Another recently recognized form of intelligence is *emotional intelligence*—the ability to recognize and manage one's own emotions, the emotions of others, and to behave in ways that have a positive impact on the emotions of others (Matthews, Zeidner, & Roberts, 2007; Mayer, Salovey, & Caruso, 2000). As

Relationships are the key to leadership effectiveness . . . Leadership is inherently relational.

—Komives, Lucas, & McMahon, *Exploring Leadership: For College Students Who Want to Make a Difference*

> *Knowing and managing your emotional response while helping another is crucial to your own well-being and to your ability to help.*
>
> —Ender & Newton, *Students Helping Students*

discussed in chapter 2, *empathy*—the ability to stand in another's emotional shoes—is a key tenet of servant leadership theory (Spears, 2002).

Similar to research findings on social intelligence, emotional intelligence has also been found to be a better predictor of personal and occupational success than performance on intellectual tests (Goleman, 1995, 2000). Research also shows that emotional self-awareness is a key characteristic of effective leaders (Avolio & Luthans, 2006; Goleman, Boyatzis, & McKee, 2013).

Key Elements of Social and Emotional Intelligence

Interpersonal communication and human relations skills provide the foundation for effective leadership (Clarke, 2018; Hogan, Curphy, & Hogan, 1994; Johnson & Bechler, 1998). Leaders in all contexts and roles need to be skilled at initiating and maintaining good working relationships with the people they lead. When peer leaders develop these relationship skills, the students they lead gain more trust in them and become more receptive to their efforts to support them.

Developing relationships doesn't happen by chance, but through an intentional process that involves: (1) initiating interpersonal contact, (2) getting to know others as individuals, and (c) showing genuine interest in others.

Initiating and Developing Interpersonal Relationships

Creating and sustaining open, meaningful relationships with students is a key component of effective peer leadership and mentoring. Here are some specific strategies for doing so.

- If you're working as peer leader in the classroom, arrive early to strike up conversations with students and stick around afterward to interact with them individually.
- Periodically invite your students to informal get-togethers and hold them in a comfortable environment that's conducive to conversation. For your first get-together, make it a short meeting (e.g., not longer than an hour) so that it doesn't seem like you're asking for a major commitment. You can always go overtime if the conversation is going well.
- On the day before the get-together, remind your students about the time, place, and purpose of your meeting. Reminders not only stimulate students' memory of the event, they also increase students' commitment to participating in the event.
- At your first meeting, learn about your students' backgrounds, interests, experiences, and goals.

Keep track of what you learn in this initial meeting and build on it to guide your conversations in future meetings. (See chapter 1, Exercise 1.3, for a wide range of questions you could ask students to get to know them as individuals.)

Reflection 4.2

Would you say you're good at initiating relationships? If yes, why? If no, why not? Which of the just-discussed strategies for initiating relationships would you feel most comfortable using in your particular peer leadership role?

Tale FROM THE Trenches

I met with all my students for a minimum of a half-hour, usually to grab lunch, and discuss what they have going on outside of classes, how they feel about the upcoming year, and if they've thought about what they'll do with their education/degree. Initially I was just a little bit nervous to meet individually with some of my students, but it went well and I did just fine facilitating conversation.

—PEER LEADER

Effective and Professional Communication Strategies

In any leadership role, effective communication is vital. Communication skills keep your followers in the loop, strengthen your credibility with them, and enable you to share your experiences with campus partners in an effective manner. Listed below are some key suggestions and strategies for doing so.

You must earn the right and privilege of helping another. This will occur during the early phase of the helping relationship if you are demonstrating the skills of effective communication.

—Ender & Newton, *Students Helping Students*

- Ask students for their contact information and how they prefer to be contacted (e.g., e-mail, cell phone, Facebook, Twitter). Be willing to utilize different communication media to maximize the probability that your message reaches all those you'd like it to reach and reaches them through a medium that they're most comfortable using.
- Establish mutual agreements (norms) about what your students can expect from you regarding your communications and what you expect of them.
- Communicate regularly with your students (e.g., at least weekly) to:
  1. Keep them informed about upcoming events, activities, and meetings. (Consider developing a website for your program that includes planned activities, key resources, and helpful links.)
  2. Help them stay on track with respect to their tasks and goals.
  3. Seek feedback about their needs and areas of concern.
  4. Acknowledge their academic achievements, accomplishments, birthdays, and educational milestones (e.g., completing their first midterms, first term or first year in college).
- Personalize your communications—make them sound less like formal correspondences and more like personal letters coming from one human being to another (e.g., type the name of the person[s] at the start of the message and your name at the end of the message).
- Unless the communication needs to be kept confidential, keep your partners and supervisors in the loop by copying messages to them about what your program or organization is doing. This serves to heighten others' interest in and sense of involvement with your program, and it gives them the opportunity to provide you with advice and resources.

Students may prefer to communicate via informal texting or Facebook, but communication with professional partners and supervisors should take place through standard campus media (e.g., campus e-mail or Blackboard).

- When communicating with others online, do it with the same care and social sensitivity as you would when communicating with them face-to-face. The terms "e-mail etiquette" and "netiquette" have made their way into popular language because people often forget to apply everyday principles of social warmth and etiquette when communicating electronically. In fact, it's particularly important to use effective interpersonal skills when communicating online, because unlike communicating in person, we cannot reinforce and clarify our message with body language. (Hence, the creation and proliferation of emojis.)

- At all times and in all communication media, keep it professional. Others will judge you on the quality and professionalism of your communications. Don't forget that your e-mails and Facebook posts can be instantaneously transmitted to almost anybody anywhere. So be sure not to make negative remarks about any student or member of the campus community and always use appropriate language. Slangs, slurs, or profanity not only run counter to expectations that peer leaders be role models, such unprofessional or insensitive language may also violate campus codes of conduct.

Reflection 4.3

What mode(s) of communication do you think are most effective for communicating with students on your campus?

The Power of Listening

> Listening well is as important to critical thinking as is contributing brilliantly.
>
> —Stephen Brookfield, *Developing Critical Thinkers*

Interpersonal communications and human relations experts report that most people should spend less time talking and more time listening and listening well (Nichols, 1995; Nichols & Stevens, 1957; Wolvin, 2009). When people are surveyed and asked to identify what they like most about their best friend, "good listener" ranks among the top characteristics cited (Berndt, 1992). Effective listening is also a key characteristic of effective problem solvers (Steil & Bommelje, 2007) and ranks among the top skills sought by employers when hiring and promoting employees (Gabric & McFadden, 2001; Wolvin, 2010b).

> We have been given two ears and a single mouth in order that we may hear more and talk less.
>
> —Zeno of Citium, ancient Greek philosopher

Influential and powerful leaders are often thought of as being eloquent and dynamic speakers. Although spectacular oratory skills may be important for certain leadership roles, effective listening skills are equally, if not more, important. In fact, listening has been identified as one of the top-ranking characteristics of effective leaders (Johnson & Bechler, 1998; Wolvin, 2010a). Students will not hear you if you don't hear them. They may initially be interested in your wisdom and advice, but in the long run, they're likely to be more interested in being heard. If they feel listened to, they're more likely to listen to you (and to each other).

Active Listening Strategies

Humans can listen to and understand words spoken to them at an average rate that is four times faster than the average rate at which words can be spoken (Barker & Watson, 2000). Consequently, when listening to others speak, there's plenty of time for us to slip into *passive listening*—hearing the words through our ears, but not thinking about those words in our mind (because our mind is somewhere else). *Active listening* is a communication skill that involves: (a) focusing our *full attention* on the speaker's message (as opposed to just waiting for our turn to talk or thinking about what we're going to say next); (b) being an *empathic* listener who not only attends to the spoken message but also to the speaker's feelings and nonverbal signals; and (c) being an *engaged* listener who checks for understanding, expresses interest, and encourages elaboration.

> **When we listen actively and empathically to others, and give their thoughts and feelings our undivided attention, we send them the undeniable message that we respect them.**

Active listening doesn't happen automatically. It's a skill developed through sustained effort and practice which eventually becomes a natural habit. According to servant leadership theory, effective leaders realize that effective communication starts with active listening and is a learned habit that requires discipline (Spears, 2002). The following practices may be used to develop the disciplined habit of active listening.

- When listening, monitor your understanding of what's being said. Good listeners take personal responsibility for following the speaker's message. In contrast, poor listeners put all the responsibility on the speaker to make the message clear and interesting. To check if you're following a spoken message, particularly if it's a complex or emotional message, occasionally paraphrase what you hear the speaker saying in your own words (e.g., "Let me make sure I understand . . ." or "What I hear you saying is . . ."). Such check-in statements ensure that you're following what's being said; they also send a message to the speaker that you're listening closely to what's being said and taking the message seriously.

- In addition to checking occasionally to see if you're following the speaker's message, check to be sure you're understanding what the speaker is *feeling* (e.g., you could say: "I get the sense you're feeling . . ."). Pay particularly close attention to the speaker's nonverbal messages—such as tone of voice and body language—which often provide clues to the emotions behind the words. For instance, speaking at a fast rate and at high volume may indicate frustration or anger and speaking at a slow rate and at low volume may indicate dejection or depression.

- Avoid the urge to interrupt the speaker when you think you have something important to say. Wait until the speaker has paused or completed her train of thought.

- If the speaker pauses and you start to say something at the same time the speaker starts speaking again, let her continue before expressing your thought.

> The most important thing in communication is to hear what isn't being said.
>
> —Peter F. Drucker, Austrian author and founder of the study of "management"

- If your questions are followed by periods of silence, don't become uncomfortable and rush in to ask something else. Silence may simply mean that the speaker is reflecting and taking time to formulate a thoughtful response.
- Be sure your "body language" while listening sends a message to the speaker that you're interested and non-judgmental. It's estimated that more than two-thirds of all human communication is nonverbal and it often sends a stronger message than verbal communication (Driver, 2010; Navarro, 2008). When a speaker perceives inconsistency between a listener's verbal and nonverbal signals (e.g., one shows interest, the other disinterest), the nonverbal message is more likely to be perceived as the true message (Ekman, 2009). Consequently, body language may be the most powerful way a listener can communicate genuine interest in the speaker's message and convey respect for the speaker. (See **Box 4.1** for positive, nonverbal communication messages to send while listening.)

Box 4.1

Nonverbal Signals Associated with Active Listening

Good listeners listen nonverbally; they use their whole body to communicate that they are paying full attention to, and are fully interested in, the speaker. The acronym "SOFTEN" has been created by communication experts to summarize and help us remember the key body-language signals we should send while listening.

S = **Smile.** Smiling sends signals of acceptance and interest. However, it should be done periodically, not continuously. (A continuous, non-stop smile can come across as inauthentic or artificial.)

Sit Still. Fidgeting or squirming sends the message that you're bored or growing inpatient (and can't wait to move onto something else).

O = **Open Posture.** Avoid closed-posture positions, such as crossing your arms or folding your hands—such nonverbal signals can send a message that you're not open to what the speaker is saying or passing judgment on what's being said.

F = **Forward Lean.** Leaning *forward* sends the message that you're looking forward to what the speaker is going to say next. In contrast, leaning back can send a signal that you're backing off from (losing interest in) what's being said, or that you're evaluating (psychoanalyzing) the speaker.

Face the Speaker Directly. Try to line up your shoulders directly or squarely with the speaker's shoulders—as opposed to turning one shoulder toward the speaker and one away from the speaker—which may send the message that you want to get away or are giving the speaker the "cold shoulder."

T = **Touch.** A light touch on the arm or hand once in a while, particularly to reassure a person who's speaking about something they're worried about or uncomfortable with, can be a good way to communicate warmth. However, touch sparingly and make it more like a pat, not sustained touching, stroking, or rubbing—which could be interpreted as inappropriate intimacy (or sexual harassment).

E = **Eye Contact.** Lack of eye contact with the speaker can send the message that you're looking elsewhere to something more interesting or stimulating than what's being said. On the other hand, eye contact shouldn't be continuous or relentless because it could be interpreted as staring or glaring. Instead, strike a happy medium by making *periodic* eye contact—occasionally look away and then return your eye contact to the speaker.

N = **Nod Your Head.** Nodding slowly and periodically while listening sends the signal that you're following what's being said and affirming the person saying it. However, avoid rapid and repeated head nodding; this can send the message that you want the speaker to hurry up so you can start talking, or want the speaker to finish up so you can get out of there!

Sources: Barker and Watson (2000), Nichols (2009), Purdy and Borisoff (1996)

To gain greater awareness of your nonverbal communication habits, ask a few people who know you well (and whose judgment you trust) to imitate your body language. This exercise can often be revealing and illuminating, as well as entertaining.

Reflection 4.4

Were there any effective nonverbal-listening messages cited in **Box 4.1** you weren't already aware of, or you need to work on? If yes, which one(s)?

Speaking Skills

In addition to effective listening skills, relationship building also requires effective *speaking* skills—the ability to communicate orally.

Described below are top tips for strengthening oral communication skills. Some of these recommendations may appear to be very obvious or fundamental, but they're also very powerful. Don't be fooled by their seeming simplicity, and don't underestimate their importance for effective leadership and mentoring.

Communicate your ideas precisely and concisely. When speaking, your objective should be to get to the point, make your point, get off stage, and give someone else a chance to speak. Nobody appreciates a "stage hog" who dominates the conversation and gobbles up more than his or her fair share of talk time, even if that person happens to be a peer leader.

Your spoken messages become less time-consuming, less boring, and more to the point when you avoid tangents, unnecessary details, and empty fillers—such as: "like," "kinda like," "I mean," "I'm all," and "you know." Such fillers simply "fill up" time while adding nothing substantive or meaningful to the conversation. Excessive use of fillers can also result in the listener losing patience, interest, and respect for the speaker (Daniels & Horowitz, 1997; Ward, 2018).

Be sincere; be brief; be seated.
—Top tip for public speakers offered by Franklin D. Roosevelt, 32nd president of the United States and noted orator

It does not require many words to speak the truth.
—Chief Joseph, Leader of the Nez Percé, Native-American Indian tribe

Take time to gather your thoughts mentally before expressing them orally. It's better to figure out what you're going to say *before* saying it than to do so *while* saying it. Instead of making others listen to their thoughts while they think through them, effective conversationalists (and leaders) give forethought to what they're going to say before beginning to speak, which enables them to speak more economically, minimize fillers, and open up more time for others to speak and be heard.

To talk without thinking is to shoot without aiming.
—An old English proverb

Be comfortable with silent spells during conversations. Silence can sometimes cause discomfort (like riding in an elevator with a stranger). To relieve the discomfort of silence, it's tempting to rush in and say anything to get the conversation going again, particularly if you're the leader. Although this urge to break the silence may be well intended, it can result in speaking before or without forethought. More often than not, it's better to hold back our words and think them through before blurting them out and risk saying something thoughtless or meaningless.

Silence is better than unmeaning words.
—Pythagoras, Greek philosopher and mathematician

Silent spots in a conversation shouldn't be automatically viewed as a "communication breakdown." Instead, they may indicate that the people involved in the conversation are pausing to think deeply about what they're saying to each other and are comfortable enough with one another to allow these reflective pauses to take place.

Reflection 4.5

Would you say you're a good conversationalist?

If yes, what makes you so?

If no, what prevents you from being one?

Interpersonal Relationship Skills (a.k.a. Human Relations Skills)

In addition to communicating effectively with others, interpersonal relationship or human relations skills is another key component of social intelligence (Goleman, 2006) and effective leadership (Northouse, 2016). These skills involve relating well to others and building positive relationships with them.

How can you help students view you as approachable and interested in forming relationships with them? The first step is getting to know them and showing interest in them. As important as knowing how to lead is knowing *who* you are leading. Students are likely to be interested in what you know, but they're more likely to be interested in knowing that you're interested in them. Listed below are specific strategies for getting to know your students.

Learn and remember *names.* When you know students by name and refer to them by name, you affirm their individuality and uniqueness. You've probably heard people say they have a good memory for faces, but not names, which implies that they will never be good at remembering names. The truth is that the ability to remember names is not some kind of natural-born talent or inherited ability. Instead, it's a skill that's developed through intentional effort and effective use of memory-improvement strategies, such as those described below.

- When you meet someone, pay close attention to that person's name when you first hear it. The crucial initial step to remembering someone's name is to get the name into your brain in the first place. As obvious as this may seem, when we first meet someone, instead of listening actively and carefully for that person's name, we're often more concerned about the first impression we're making on them after being introduced, or what we're going to say to them once we've just met them. Consequently, we *forgot* the name because we never *got* the name into our brain in the first place (because our mind was focused on something else).

- Strengthen your memory for a person's name by saying the name soon after you first hear it. For instance, if your friend Gertrude has just introduced you to Geraldine, you might say: "Geraldine, how long have you known Gertrude?" When you state a person's name shortly after you first hear it, you

> *In all helping situations, the interaction between two people— the quality of the relationships— is probably the most important factor in the success and helpfulness that occurs.*
>
> —Ender & Newton, *Students Helping Students*

> *We should be aware of the magic contained in a name. The name sets that individual apart; it makes him or her unique among all others. Remember that a person's name is to that person the sweetest and most important sound in any language.*
>
> —Dale Carnegie, author of the bestselling book, *How to Win Friends and Influence People* and founder of The Dale Carnegie Course—a worldwide leadership training program for business professionals

prevent memory loss at the time when forgetting is most likely to take place–during the first minutes after the brain takes in new information (Averell & Heathcote, 2011). There's also another benefit of saying the person's name right after you've heard it: It makes the person feel welcomed and accepted.

- Associate the person's name with other information you've learned or know about the person. For instance, you can associate the person's name with (a) some physical characteristic of the person, (b) the place where you met, or (c) your first topic of conversation. By making a mental connection between the person's name and something else, you capitalize on the brain's natural tendency to store (retain) information in the form of interconnected networks rather than as isolated bits of information (Zull, 2011).

- Keep a name journal that includes the names of new people you meet and information about them (e.g., what they do and what their interests are). We write down things we want to remember to do or to buy, so why not write down the names of people whose names we want to remember? Whenever you meet someone new, make note of that person's name by recording it in a name journal and accompany it with a short note about that person (e.g., where you met and what you talked about).

> *When I joined the bank, I started keeping a record of the people I met and put them on little cards, and I would indicate on the cards when I met them, and under what circumstances, and sometimes [make] a little notation which would help me remember a conversation.*
>
> —David Rockefeller, prominent American banker, philanthropist, and former CEO of the Chase Manhattan Bank

> **Remembering names is not only a good way to make friends and improve your social life, it's also a skill for improving your effectiveness as a leader and a professional in any career you may choose to pursue.**

Refer to people by name when you greet them and interact with them. Once you've learned students' names, refer to them by name whenever you see them. Saying, "Hi, Waldo" will mean a lot more to Waldo than simply saying "Hi" or "Hi, there"–which sounds like you've just encountered an unidentifiable object "out there" in public space (like addressing a letter, "to whom it may concern.") By continuing to use people's names after you've first learned them, you strengthen your memory for their names and show them that you remember who they are (and that they're important to you).

Remember information that people share with you and mention it when you interact with them. Listen closely to what others share with you during conversations, especially to things that seem important to them and they really care about (for one person that may be politics, for another it may be sports, and for another it may be relationships). Remember these topics and bring them up in your future conversations.

When you see people from time to time, mention something you discussed with them the last time you were together. Get beyond the stock, generic questions that people routinely ask when they see each other (e.g., "What's up? What's going on?"). Instead, ask about something you talked about last time (e.g., "How did you make out on that math test last week?"). Our memories often reflect our priorities–we remember what's important to us. By remembering what others share with us, we show them that they're important to us.

There's another advantage of showing interest in others: You're likely to begin hearing them say what a great listener and conversationalist you are! In addition, you're likely to see them becoming more interested in you and hearing what you have to say.

> *You can make more friends in 2 months by becoming interested in other people than you can in 2 years by trying to get other people interested in you.*
>
> —Dale Carnegie, *How to Win Friends and Influence People*

Studies show that college students' success is enhanced when they experience *personal validation*—when they're recognized as *individuals,* and feel that they *matter* to others and that others *care* about their success (Rendón-Linares & Muñoz, 2011; Schlossberg, Lynch, & Chickering, 1989). As a peer leader and mentor, you can provide students with personal validation by knowing them by name, referring to them by name, and showing interest in them.

The Art of Questioning

Asking questions of others is an effective way to demonstrate interest in and build rapport with them. If you give forethought to the type of questions you ask and the sequence in which you ask them, you can increase the likelihood that the conversation will flow smoothly and you begin building relationships conducive to effective peer leadership and mentoring. Described below are four key types or categories of questions that you can ask students to get to know them and support them.

1. "Check-in" Questions
A check-in is a type of question that can get conversations going in one-on-one and group situations. It involves asking students to share their responses to a prompt, such as:

- What's your favorite bumper sticker and why?
- What's your favorite movie?
- What would you do tomorrow if you won the lottery?

Check-ins are effective conversation starters because they're not too personal or too threatening. If you do a Google search with the phrase "conversation starters," you'll find hundreds of check-in prompts; the possibilities are endless.

> Talking first about topics that may appear trivial or superficial is often a necessary prerequisite for talking later about topics that are more personal and meaningful.

2. "How's it Going Questions"
A simple way to show interest in others and generate conversations with them is by posing "how's it going" questions about their:

- Social life (e.g., roommates, friends, and family)
- Academic life (e.g., classes, tests, and assignments)
- Emotional life (e.g., stress level)
- Physical well-being (e.g., general health)
- College life (e.g., "Was it what you expected it to be?" "Are you happy you came here?")

3. "Open-ended" Questions
Once your students become comfortable speaking with you, you may then begin to kick off conversations by asking a wide-open question such as: "What would like to talk about today?" This is called an *open-ended question* because it opens the door to a variety of answers and leaves the respondent with plenty of room to

elaborate. In contrast, "close-ended" questions are those that can be answered in a single word. Compare the following two types of questions:

a. "What grade did you get on your last chemistry test?" (close-ended question)
b. "What could you have done differently to improve your grade on your last chemistry test? (open-ended question)

The first question calls for a one-word response and the second question opens up opportunities for elaboration and exploration. The second question also allows you to learn more about the student's strategies and acquire information that can be used to help the student improve.

Reflection 4.6

What three open-ended questions do you think would be useful to ask the students you're working with?

_____

4. "Probing" Questions
Probing is a conversational process that invites and encourages others to share more details about their experiences, needs, concerns, attitudes, or feelings. When you learn more details or specifics about students' experiences, it gives you more information to assist them. Probes often come up spontaneously during the course of a conversation and cannot always be scripted. However, you can plan ahead to use effective probes like the following:

a. "That's interesting. Can you tell me more about ____?"
b. "It seems like there's a lot going on with ____. Can you give me some details?"

The process of probing may feel awkward initially because it can sound like you're digging into their personal affairs. Certainly, you don't want to force students to elaborate on topics that they seem reluctant to discuss. However, by using probes selectively and sensitively, you can encourage students to open up to you. Like a spider's web, artful probing can weave simple conversations into more elaborate and meaningful patterns.

Tale FROM THE Trenches

So far, the biggest thing I have noticed is how the conversation has evolved beyond just the questions I had prepared and how willing the students are to talk. All of them feel open talking to me about whatever problems they are facing. It has been cool to see them open up. I can now ask them more focused questions and interact with them on a deeper level.

—PEER LEADER

Asking Deeper, More Meaningful Questions

Initially, your goal is just to have students feel comfortable talking with you about anything. After you've built rapport and solidified your relationship with them, you may then ask more significant questions. As a peer leader and mentor, here are some deeper questions you could pose to students:

- What have you done well in college thus far? What could or should you be doing differently?
- Who have you connected with on campus? Do you think you're developing the type of relationships that will contribute to your success? What could you do to expand your connections to other people and campus resources?
- How are things going academically? What learning strategies are working well for you and what do you seem to be struggling with? What would you say are the major sources of stress in your life right now? Have you been able to keep these sources of stress at a manageable level?
- Do you feel you're changing (or have changed) since coming to college? In what way(s)?

Keep track of the type of questions that generate the most passionate and enthusiastic responses from your students. When students give very detailed and strongly expressed responses, this can serve as a clue to what's most important to them. These may also be the areas in which students are most likely to be receptive to your support, guidance, or leadership.

Reflection 4.7

List three "deep" questions that might be useful to ask the students you're leading or mentoring. Briefly explain why you chose each of these questions.

Emotional Intelligence

The leaders who have the most influence on people are those who are the closest to them.

—Kouzes & Posner, *The Student Leadership Challenge*

I've learned that people will forget what you said, people will forget what you did, but people will never forget how you made them feel.

—Maya Angelou, African-American poet, educator, and best-selling author

In addition to social skills—such as listening, speaking, and questioning—effective leadership requires relating to people with emotional sensitivity and emotional intelligence. Listed below are suggestions for doing so. These practices will help students feel more emotionally "close" to you and increase their willingness to confide in you.

Express genuine interest in and concern for others' feelings. Instead of asking the routine questions like, "How are you?" or "How's it goin'?" ask the question, "How are you feeling?" Showing genuine concern for others' feelings increases the likelihood that they will share their feelings with you, and when they have, their feelings validated by you, they feel better about themselves (Laurenceau, Barrett, & Pietromonaco, 1998; Reis & Shaver, 1988).

Share information about yourself.
How often have you witnessed this rapid, ritualistic interchange between two people?

Person A: "Hi, how's it goin'?"
Person B: "Fine, how ya' doin'?"
Person A: "Good. Thanks."

In this exchange, no meaningful information is shared by either person and chances are that neither person expects nor wants to hear about how the other person is truly feeling. Such social rituals are understandable and acceptable when people first interact with each other. However, if their relationship is to move to a closer, more meaningful level, they'll need to move beyond social rituals toward mutual sharing of personal experiences (Goffman, 1967).

Building close, authentic relationships is a give-and-take process in which two people begin to share progressively more personal information with one another—an interpersonal process that human relations specialists call the *intimacy spiral* (Cusinato & L'Abate, 1994). You can start this reciprocal sharing process by noticing the kinds of personal information students share with you and respond, in turn, by sharing something similar about yourself that's a little more personal or intimate. Relating a similar experience of your own demonstrates *empathy*— your ability to understand the feelings of others.

Naturally, this sharing should be done in small doses; you don't want to suddenly blow others away with hot blasts of intimacy and private details about your personal life. Instead, gradually and sensitively share more about yourself. As you continue to have more contact and conversations with your students, engage in more self-disclosure—share or disclose a little more of yourself. If someone asks you, "How's it going?" or "How are you?" take these questions seriously and respond by sharing something meaningful about yourself. That includes sharing your aspirations, fears, success stories and stumbling blocks. By so doing, you model the type of sincerity and authenticity that you'd like for them to display toward you. When you share yourself with others, it shows that you trust them, and in turn, they're likely to trust you (Adler & Towne, 2014).

> *People are more willing to follow someone they like and trust. To be trustworthy, you must trust and be open both with and to others. That means . . . telling people the same things you'd like to know about them.*
>
> —Kouzes & Posner, *The Student Leadership Challenge*

Look for opportunities to provide others with genuine compliments. Look for positive behaviors and praise them when you see them. Providing students with sincere compliments elevates their self-esteem and increases the probability that they'll continue to do whatever you complimented them for doing. Simply stated, people like to be around others who make them feel good about themselves and who provide them with feedback on what they're doing well.

Remember that you can compliment others for many things besides their physical appearance. Complimenting others about their actions or inner character is more powerful than complimenting them on their external features because you're recognizing them for *who* they genuinely are and *what* they actually do.

If you notice students improving and succeeding, you can acknowledge them with kind words, a quick e-mail, a Facebook message, or a modest celebration. Even the smallest victories can be noted, such as students finishing a major assignment or completing their first term in college. Small, simple compliments for little accomplishments can often have large, long-term impact on reinforcing positive behaviors and sustaining positive relationships.

> *Kind words can be short and easy to speak, but their echoes are truly endless.*
>
> —Mother Teresa of Calcutta, Albanian Catholic nun and winner of the Nobel Peace Prize

Leaders can demonstrate good human relations skills by complimenting members of the community who may not rank high in the "organizational pecking order" but who perform critical jobs and provide essential services for those in leadership positions, such as support staff and administrative assistants.

Stay positive and enthusiastic. Not surprisingly, people prefer to be around others who are upbeat and enthusiastic. Studies show that when people see others in a good mood, they respond more positively to them (Branscombe & Baron, 2016;

Byrne, 1997). As the old adage goes, "Enthusiasm is contagious"—others can "catch" our good mood and, when they do, their own mood improves. In contrast, when we're pessimistic, angry, or "down," we bring others down with us, and we drive down our chances of connecting with them and influencing them. A major study of effective student leaders revealed that one of their distinguishing features was extraordinary enthusiasm and ability to spread that enthusiasm to the students they led (Kouzes & Posner, 2008).

Reflection 4.8

In the leadership role you play, what do you think will be the biggest threat or challenge to your remaining optimistic and enthusiastic? What could you do, or what resources could you use, to help you handle this threat or challenge?

Helping Students with Personal Issues and Problems

Good mentors are ready, willing, and able to help others in need. Given your leadership position on campus, it's likely that students will come to you for advice about personal issues, particularly if you've taken the time to establish a close relationship with them. Listed below are strategies for helping others with personal issues and problems.

> " A friend is a person with whom I may be sincere. Before him, I may think aloud.
>
> —Ralph Waldo Emerson, American author, philosopher, and orator

> " A problem well-defined is half solved.
>
> —John Dewey, influential philosopher, psychologist and educational reformer

- First and foremost: Be a good listener and lend an empathetic ear. By just providing a sounding board and letting others bounce their thoughts and feelings off you, a solution may bounce right back to them. Sometimes, the best help you can provide is just by being available, asking questions, listening (and listening some more), and reaffirming your support. Simply giving others a chance to get their personal feelings out in the open and allowing them the opportunity to think out loud can lead them to discover effective solutions on their own. Their problem may be solved with your doing little more than listening in a concerned and compassionate way.
- After listening actively and empathically, ask questions to help students clarify the problem or issue. You can do this by using phrases such as: "It seems like . . ." "Could it be that . . . ?" "I get the impression that . . ." An effective helper assists others to get a deeper understanding of their problem. Often, help is best provided by asking the right question, not by giving the right answer. Good questions empower others to help themselves, leading them to see their problem more clearly, which, in turn, can lead them to a clear solution.
- Share with the student any experiences you may have had with a similar problem, or if you have had other students come to you with a similar issue. It's always good for people to know that that they're not the only ones who are facing challenges and struggling with certain issues. Don't be afraid to let your students know that others have encountered similar obstacles and difficulties. This will help them realize their problem is not "abnormal," strengthen their self-esteem, and increase their self-confidence that the problem is solvable.

However, avoid using the common expression, "I know how you feel." This statement may be well intended, but it's presumptuous to say you *know* how someone else feels because there's no way you can get into the person's head and know what that person is actually feeling. Also, avoid saying things like, "Oh, don't worry about it, everything will be alright" or, "You'll get over it." Comments like these may send a message to help-seeking students that their feelings are exaggerated and unjustified, or that they're overreacting and "making a mountain out of a molehill."

> *When I ask you to listen to me and you begin to tell me why I shouldn't feel that way, you are trampling my feelings.*
> —Author unknown

- Try to avoid directly instructing or dictating what should be done to solve the student's problem. An effective helper is someone who helps others see their options clearly and allows them to make their own choice rather than making the choice for them. When students reach their own decision, they "own" that decision, are more likely to take action on it, and experience an increased sense of self-control and self-esteem. They also learn not to depend on you to solve problems for them. Instead, you help them develop the self-confidence needed to become independent, self-reliant problem solvers.

> *The point of being a mentor is not to create dependency but to promote self-responsibility, not to decide for someone, but to encourage self-direction.*
> —Ender & Newton, *Students Helping Students*

> **Peer mentors are not experts who make decisions for students; they are facilitators who empower students to make their own decisions.**

- If supportive listening and questioning are not enough to lead the student to discover a solution to the problem, move to "Plan B": work with the student to generate possible solutions. An effective method for doing so is a process called *brainstorming*. See **Box 4.2** for a summary of its key steps.

Box 4.2

The Process of Brainstorming

Key Steps:
1. Working together with the student, generate as many solutions to the problem as possible. At this stage of the process, the goal is to think creatively and imaginatively without worrying about whether the ideas generated may be ineffective or impractical. Studies show that initial concerns about whether ideas will work often block the ability to generate ideas that have the potential to work (Basadur, Runco, & Vega, 2000).
2. Use the list of ideas and strategies generated as a springboard to trigger additional ideas.
3. After all possible ideas are listed, critically evaluate them and eliminate those that the student thinks would be least effective or realistic.
4. From the remaining list of ideas, encourage the student to choose the best option (or combination of options) for solving the problem.

The point of brainstorming is to create as many good options as possible and allow students to choose the one they're most comfortable with, believe in, and is most consistent with their values (not your values). Helping students identify options and make their own choices serves to respect their individuality and promotes their sense of control or ownership of the choices they make.

Students can use the process of brainstorming to solve any problem they may encounter. Thus, by exposing students to the process, you not only help them solve their current problem, you empower them with a strategy they can use to solve future problems on their own.

- After helping students lay out all their options, if they still cannot make a decision and seek your advice about what choice to make, start by sharing ideas that have worked for you in the past or that have worked for other students. Be sure to offer your advice as a concerned friend, not as an expert authority. For instance, before giving advice, introduce it by saying, "This is just a suggestion . . ." or, "I wonder if this might . . . ." Offer your recommendations as reasonable possibilities, not as sure-fire solutions. The last thing you want to do is to come off as an arrogant know-it-all by saying things like: "What your problem is . . ." or, "What you need to do is . . . ."

- Before ending your discussion, review and summarize the next steps that need to be taken to solve the problem or resolve the issue (e.g., what specific actions will be taken and when those actions will take place).

- If the problem appears too serious or beyond your ability to deal with, encourage the student to seek professional help (e.g., from an advisor or counselor on campus). Know your limitations; don't be afraid to say, "I don't know, but I can refer you to someone who does know." Another option would be to consult with a campus professional who has more experience or expertise dealing with the particular type of problem the student has come to you with, and then come back to the student with different options suggested by the professional. (If you decide to do this, as a courtesy, let the student know your intention to do so.)

- Last and most important, if someone comes to you for help or assistance with a personal problem, any information that person shares with you must remain confidential. This is not only the legally correct thing to do; it's also the ethically responsible thing to do. It respects the person's privacy and reinforces the person's trust in you. The only exception to this rule is when students share information with you that strongly suggests they're in immediate danger of harming themselves or someone else.

The *Family Education Rights and Privacy Act* (a.k.a. *FERPA* or the "Buckley Amendment") legally prohibits communicating student information to others. If you have any doubt about whether you can share information about a student, before sharing it, check with your program supervisor.

Reflection 4.9

Do you often find people coming to you for advice or help?

If yes, on what issues do they typically seek your advice or help?

Does this tell you anything about where your leadership strengths or talents may lie?

Handling Serious Student Issues and Crises

As students come to know and trust you, it's likely that emotionally intense and sensitive matters will be brought to your attention—for example, issues involving relationships and sexuality, alcohol and drug abuse, anxiety, depression, or suicidal thoughts. Although it's unlikely you'll be dealing with crises on a regular basis, you need to be prepared for the possibility. Helping students in crisis can be extremely challenging but also very rewarding because it can promote tremendous personal growth—in the person who overcomes the crisis and in the person who lends a helping hand.

Specific procedures for dealing with serious student problems and crises are likely to be provided in a peer leadership handbook or handout you received during leadership training. In addition to information contained in these resources, the following may be used as general guidelines.

- Let the student know you are very concerned and want them to hear about all the details relating to their problem or issue.
- Strongly encourage the student to make an appointment immediately with a personal counselor or advisor. If possible, escort the student to the appropriate office, and remain with the student until an appropriate professional becomes available.
- If the student elects not to act on your urgent recommendation to seek help and you fear the student is in danger or putting others in danger, immediately and discretely inform your program supervisor. If your supervisor person cannot be reached, inform the campus police.
- Keep a record of the steps you took during the crisis and the parties you contacted.

> In a crisis situation, a student's right to privacy or confidentiality is outweighed by the need to ensure the student's safety or the safety of others.

> *When written in Chinese, the word 'crisis' is composed of two characters. One represents danger and the other represents opportunity.*
>
> —John F. Kennedy, 35th president of the United States

Internet Resources

For additional information on leadership relating to social and emotional intelligence, consult the following websites.

Social Intelligence
http://www.socialintelligenceinstitute.org/

Interpersonal Communication Skills
www.skillsyouneed.co.uk/IPS/What_is_Communication.html

Active Listening and Leadership
https://hbr.org/2014/01/three-ways-leaders-can-listen-with-more-empathy

Crisis Referral Strategies
www.blinn.edu/counseling/Faculty_Referral_Resources.pdf

References

Adler, R. B., & Towne, M. (2014). *Looking out, looking in.* Boston: Cengage.

Averell, L., & Heathcote, A. (2011). The form of the forgetting curve and the fate of memories. *Journal of Mathematical Psychology, 55*(1), 25-35.

Avolio, B., & Luthans, F. (2006). *The high impact leader.* New York: McGraw Hill.

Avolio, B. J., Walumbwa, F. O., &. Weber, T. J. (2009). Leadership: Current theories, research, and future directions. *Annual Review of Psychology, 60,* 421-449.

Barker, L., & Watson, K. W. (2000). *Listen up: How to improve relationships, reduce stress, and be more productive by using the power of listening.* New York: St. Martin's Press.

Basadur, M., Runco, M. A., & Vega, L. A. (2000). Understanding how creative thinking skills, attitudes, and behaviors work together. *Journal of Creative Behavior, 34*(2), 77-1000.

Berndt, T. J. (1992). Friendship and friends' influence in adolescence. *Current Directions in Psychological Science, 1*(5), 156–159.

Branscombe, N. R., & Baron, R. A. (2016). *Social psychology* (14th ed.). Essex, England: Pearson.

Brookfield, S. (1987). *Developing critical thinkers.* San Francisco: Jossey-Bass.

Byrne, D. (1997). An overview (and underview) of research and theory within the attraction paradigm. *Journal of Personality and Social Psychology, 14*(3), 417-431.

Carnegie, D. (1936). *How to win friends & influence people.* New York: Simon & Schuster.

Carneiro, P., Crawford, C., & Goodman, A. (2006). *Which skills matter?* Centre for the Economics of Education, London School of Economics, Discussion Paper 59. Retrieved from http://cee.lse.ac.uk/ceedps/ceedp59.pdf

Clarke, N. (2018). *Relational leadership: Theory, practice and development.* London: Routledge.

Cusinato, M., & L'Abate, L. (1994). A spiral model of intimacy. In S. M. Johnson & L. S. Greenberg (Eds.), *The heart of the matter: Emotion in marital therapy.* New York: Brunner/Mazel.

Daniels, D., & Horowitz, L. J. (1997). *Being and caring: A psychology for living.* Prospect Heights, IL: Waveland Press.

Driver, J. (2010). *You say more than you think: A 7-day plan for using the new body language to get what you want.* New York: Crown Publishers.

Ekman, P. (2009). *Telling lies: Clues to deceit in the marketplace, politics, and marriage* (revised ed.). New York: W. W. Norton.

Ender, S. C., & Newton, F. B. (2000). *Students helping students: A guide for peer educators on college campuses.* San Francisco: Jossey-Bass.

Gabric, D., & McFadden, K. L. (2001). Student and employer perceptions of desirable entry-level operations management skills. *American Business Law Journal, 16*(1), 50-59.

Gardner, H. (1993). *Frames of mind: The theory of multiple intelligences* (2nd ed.). New York: Basic Books.

Gardner, H. (1999). *Intelligence reframed: Multiple intelligences for the 21st century.* New York: Basic Books.

Goffman, E. (Ed.). (1967). *Interaction ritual: Essays in face-to-face behavior.* Chicago: Adine.

Goleman, D. (1995). *Emotional intelligence: Why it can matter more than IQ.* New York: Random House.

Goleman, D. (2000). *Working with emotional intelligence.* New York: Bantam Dell.

Goleman, D. (2006). *Social intelligence: The new science of human relationships.* New York: Dell.

Goleman, D., Boyatzis, R., & McKee, A. (2013). *Primal leadership: Realizing the potential of emotional intelligence.* Boston: Harvard Business School Press.

Hogan, R., Curphy, G. J., & Hogan, J. (1994). What we know about leadership: Effectiveness and personality. *American Psychologists, 49,* 493-504.

Johnson, M. (2012). Integrating technology into peer leader responsibilities. In J. R. Keup (Ed.), *Peer leadership in higher education* (pp. 59-71). San Francisco: Jossey-Bass.

Johnson, S., & Bechler, C. (1998). Examining the relationships between listening effectiveness and leadership emergence: Perceptions, behaviors, and recall. *Small Group Research, 29*(4), 452-471.

Komives, S. R., Lucas, N., & McMahon, T. R. (2007). *Exploring leadership: For college students who want to make a difference* (2nd ed.). San Francisco: Jossey-Bass.

Kouzes, M. M., & Posner, B. Z. (2008). *The student leadership challenge: Five practices for exemplary leaders.* San Francisco: Jossey-Bass.

Laurenceau, J.-P., Barrett, L. F., & Pietromonaco, P. R. (1998). Intimacy as an interpersonal process: The importance of self-disclosure, partner disclosure, and perceived partner responsiveness in interpersonal exchanges. *Journal of Personality and Social Psychology, 74,* 1238–1251.

Matthews, G., Zeidner, M., & Roberts, R. D. (2007). *The science of emotional intelligence: Knowns and unknowns.* New York: Oxford University Press.

Mayer, J. D., Salovey, P., & Caruso, D. R. (2000). Models of emotional intelligence. In R. J. Sternberg (Ed.), *Handbook of intelligence* (pp. 396-420). Cambridge, UK: Cambridge University Press.

Navarro, J. (2008). *What every BODY is saying.* New York: Harper Collins.

Nichols, M. P. (1995). *The lost art of listening.* New York: Guilford Press.

Nichols, M. P. (2009). *The lost art of listening.* New York: Guilford Press.

Nichols, M. P., & Stevens, L. A. (1957). *Are you listening?* New York: McGraw-Hill.

Northouse, P. G. (2016). *Leadership: Theory and practice* (7th ed.). Thousand Oaks, CA: SAGE.

Purdy, M., & Borisoff, D. (Eds.). (1996). *Listening in everyday life: A personal and professional approach.* Lanham, MD: University Press of America.

Reis, H. T., & Shaver, P. (1988). Intimacy as an interpersonal process. In S. W. Durck (Ed.), *Handbook of personal relationships* (pp. 367-389). New York: Wiley.

Rendón-Linares, L. I., & Muñoz, S. M. (2011). Revisiting validation theory: Theoretical foundations, applications, and extensions. *Enrollment Management Journal, 5*(2), 12-33.

Schlossberg, N. K., Lynch, A. Q., & Chickering, A. W. (1989). *Improving higher education environments for adults: Responsive programs and services from entry to departure.* San Francisco: Jossey-Bass.

Spears, L. C. (2002). Tracing the past, present, and future of servant-leadership. In L. C. Spears & M. Lawrence (Eds.), *Focus on leadership: Servant-leadership for the 21st century* (pp. 1-16). New York: Wiley.

Steil, L. L., & Bommelje, R. (2007). *Listening leaders: The ten golden rules to listen: Lead and succeed.* Edina, MN: Beaver Pond Press.

Ward, S. (2018). *How to stop saying 'um' and 'you know': How to stop using annoying filler words when you speak.* Retrieved from https://www.thebalancesmb.com/speak-for-success-speech-problem-of-fillers-2948544

Wolvin, A. D. (2009). Listening, understanding and misunderstanding. In W. F. Eadie (Ed.), *21st century communication* (pp. 137-146). Thousand Oaks, CA: SAGE.

Wolvin, A. D. (2010a). Listening. In R. A. Couto (Ed.), *Political and civic leadership: A reference handbook* (pp. 922-927). Thousand Oaks, CA: SAGE.

Wolvin, A. D. (2010b). *Listening and communication in the 21st century.* Malden, MA: Blackwell.

Zaccaro, S. J., Gilbert, J., Thor, K. K., & Mumford, M. D. (1991). Leadership and social intelligence: Linking social perceptiveness and behavioral flexibility to leader effectiveness. *Leadership Quarterly, 2,* 317-331.

Zull, J. E. (2011). *From brain to mind: Using neuroscience to guide change in education.* Sterling, VA: Stylus.

Exercise 4.1 Quote Reflections

Review the sidebar quotes contained in this chapter and select two that you think would be especially valuable to share with the students you lead or mentor.

For each quote, write a short statement explaining why you chose it.

Exercise 4.2 Journal Reflections

1. Should peer leaders give out their cell-phone number? Why?

2. What would be a reasonable timeframe for peer leaders to respond to student phone calls or text messages?

3. What ways of using social networking sites would be inappropriate or unethical for peer leaders?

4. Should peer leaders be friends with their students on Facebook?

5. Should student leaders limit access to certain parts of their social-network profile? (If yes, what privacy setting should be used?)

6. Should peer leaders filter their comments, group members' comments, and photograph albums? If yes, in what way(s)?

Source: Johnson (2012).

Exercise 4.3 Relationship Self-Assessment

On a scale of 1-5 (1 = low, 5 = high), rate yourself on each of the following characteristics.

___ I effectively initiate relationships.

___ I am accessible.

___ I am approachable.

___ I am a good listener.

Provide a reason or explanation for each of your ratings that describes: (1) what you're doing well, (2) what you'd like to improve, and (3) what you could do to improve (or what resource you could use to help you improve).

Exercise 4.4 Probing Question Role-Play

1. Pair up with a fellow student (ideally another peer mentor), and practice the process of questioning, listening actively, and probing (described on pp. 116–117). One partner takes the role of peer mentor and the other takes the role of student.

2. Switch roles.

3. Share your thoughts about how it went—from the perspective of your role as student and as peer mentor. Give each other feedback on what worked well and what seemed awkward or needed improvement.

Exercise 4.5 Crisis-Referral Role Play

Partner with a fellow student leader. Think of an incident or scenario that would call for a crisis referral. Make the referral using the steps outlined on p. 123. Ask your partner for feedback on how effectively you implemented the referral process.

Exercise 4.6 Strategy Reflections

Review the strategies suggested for *interacting with others in emotionally sensitive and intelligent ways* on pp. 118-120. Select two that you would be most confident about (or comfortable with) putting into practice.

CHAPTER 5
Setting Goals and Maintaining Motivation

Reflection 5.1

What does being "successful" mean to you?

Chapter Purpose and Preview

One of the goals of peer leadership is to help students be successful, and since success is often defined as achieving one's goals, one role of peer leaders is to help students identify their goals and the means (succession of steps) needed to reach their goals. Studies show that people are more likely to be successful when they set specific goals for themselves rather than simply telling themselves they're going to "try hard" or "do their best." This chapter supplies you with practical leadership strategies for helping students set specific, realistic goals and maintain their motivation until their goals are reached.

Introduction

Deep within them, students often have the passion to succeed, but need help discovering that passion and converting it into action. As a peer mentor and leader, you're in a position to inspire students to aim high and keep climbing by encouraging them to set ambitious, yet realistic, goals. Studies show that peer mentors can have positive influence on student attitudes toward setting and pursuing academic, social, and career goals (Sanchez, Bauer, & Paronto, 2006; Ward, Thomas, & Disch, 2010). Dare your students to dream, but also challenge them to transform their dreams into specific goals, create plans for achieving their goals, and take action on the plans they create.

> Student leaders breathe life into the hopes and dreams of others and enable them to see the exciting possibilities that the future holds.
>
> —Kouzes & Posner, *The Student Leadership Challenge*

The Relationship between Goal Setting and Success

The word "success" derives from the Latin root "*successus*"—meaning "to follow or come after"—as in the word "successive." Thus, by definition, success involves a succession or sequence of actions that leads to a desired outcome. The process starts with identifying an end (goal) followed by identifying the means (sequence of steps) for reaching that goal. Research shows that successful people set goals on a regular basis (Locke & Latham, 1990) and devise specific plans for reaching their goals (Halvorson, 2010). As Duckworth (2016) puts it: "They not only had determination, they had *direction*" (p. 8).

> The tragedy of life doesn't lie in not reaching your goal. The tragedy of life lies in having no goal to reach.
>
> —Benjamin Mays, minister, scholar, activist, and former president of Morehouse College

> *Dreams can be fulfilled only when they've been <u>defined</u>.*
>
> —Ernest Boyer, former United States Commissioner of Education

Characteristics of a Well-Designed Goal

Studies show that people who set specific, well-constructed goals are more likely to achieve them than are people who simply tell themselves they're going to try hard and do their best (Halvorson, 2010; Latham & Locke, 2007). The acronym "SMART" is a well-known mnemonic device (memory strategy) for recalling all the key components of a well-designed goal (Doran, 1981; Meyer, 2003). Box 5.1 describes the different components of a SMART goal. Share this goal-setting strategy with your students to help them define and design goals that are both meaningful and achievable.

Box 5.1

The SMART Method of Goal Setting

A **SMART** goal is one that's:

- **S**pecific—defines precisely what the goal is, targets exactly what needs to be done to achieve it, and provides a clear picture of what successfully reaching the goal looks like.

  Example: By spending 25 hours per week on my coursework outside of class and by using effective learning strategies (such as those recommended in chapter 7 of this book), I will achieve at least a 3.0 grade-point average this term. (Note how much more specific goal this goal is than saying, "I'm really going to work hard this term.")

- **M**eaningful (and **M**easurable)—the goal being pursued is personally important to me (meaningful) and I can clearly measure my progress toward achieving it.

  Example: Achieving at least a 3.0 grade-point average this term is important to me because it will enable me to get into the field I'd like to major in; I'll measure my progress toward this goal by calculating the grade I'm earning in each of my courses at regular intervals throughout the term. (Note: At www.futureme.org, students can set up a program to send themselves e-mails reminding them to check on the progress they're making toward the goals they have set for themselves.)

- **A**ctionable (i.e., Action-Oriented)—the actions or behaviors to be taken to reach my goal are concrete and specific.

  Example: I will achieve at least a 3.0 grade-point average this term by (a) attending all classes in all courses, (b) taking detailed notes in my classes, (c) completing reading assignments by their due dates, and (d) studying in advance (rather than cramming) for my exams..

- **R**ealistic—the time, effort, and skills needed to reach my goal are reasonable and manageable, so I have a good chance of achieving it.

  Example: Achieving a 3.0 grade-point average this term is a realistic goal because (a) I have a reasonable course load, (b) I will work no more than 15 hours per week at my part-time job, and (c) I will be able to get help from campus support services if I run into academic difficulty.

- **T**ime-framed—the goal has a definite deadline and a clear timetable with a short-range (daily), mid-range (weekly), and long-range (monthly) timeline.

  Example: To achieve at least a 3.0 grade-point average this term, first I'll be sure to acquire all the information I need to learn by taking complete notes in my classes and completing all my reading assignments (short-range step). Second, I'll learn the information I've acquired from my notes and readings by breaking it into parts and studying the parts in separate sessions in advance of major exams (mid-range step). Third, the day before the exam I'll review all information I previously studied in parts, get a good night's sleep, and be well rested on the day of the exam (long-range step).

Note: This SMART goal-setting process can be used to set goals in any area of one's life and for any aspect of self-development (see chapter 8, p. 236), such as:

- self-management (e.g., setting goals for managing time and money)
- physical development (e.g., setting health and fitness goals)
- social development (e.g., setting relationship goals)
- emotional development (e.g., setting goals for managing stress or frustration)
- intellectual development (e.g., setting goals for learning and academic achievement)
- career development (e.g., setting goals for career exploration, preparation, or development).

Author's Experience Once I set a goal to lose 35 pounds in 7 months, going from 210 to about 175. My goal was:

Specific—I had a clear target to shoot for (175 lbs.)

Meaningful—I wanted to improve my health (lower my cholesterol) and be a quicker basketball player, and **M**easurable—I could measure my progress in terms of pounds lost

Actionable—The actions I would engage to lose weight were to exercise regularly and consume fewer calories

Realistic—175 lbs. is a reasonable weight for someone of my height and body type, and

Time-framed—I set out to lose 1-2 pounds per week.

It worked!

— *Greg Metz*

> **Goal setting is a strategic and systematic process that could (and should) be applied to achieve any personal goal set at any stage of life.**

Reflection 5.2

If you were to set a goal for your leadership development right now, what would you choose and why would you choose it?

In addition to specific goal-setting methods, such as the SMART, research reveals that the following practices and attributes characterize people who successfully set and achieve goals. Encourage students to be mindful of these qualities and practices when they set and pursue their own goals.

Successful goal setters set *self-improvement (get-better) goals* that focus on personal progress and growth rather than perfection (be-good) goals. Studies show that when people set get-better goals, they pursue them with greater interest, intensity, and joy (Halvorson, 2010). This is probably due to the fact that get-better goals give us a sense of progress by focusing on how far we've come. In contrast, perfection (be-good) goals focus on how far we still have to go.

Successful goal setters focus on outcomes they can *influence or control.* For an aspiring actress, a controllable goal would be to increase her acting skills and professional acting opportunities, not to become a famous movie star—a desirable outcome but not something that's totally within her control.

Successful goal setters set goals that are *challenging and effortful.* Goals worth achieving force us to stretch ourselves and break a sweat; they call for endurance, persistence, and resiliency. Studies of successful people in all occupations indicate that when they set goals that are attainable but also *challenging,* they pursue those goals more strategically, with more intensity, and with greater commitment (Latham & Locke, 2007; Locke & Latham, 2002). There's another advantage of setting a challenging goal: When it's achieved, the person achieving it experiences a strong sense of personal accomplishment, satisfaction, and self-esteem.

Accomplishing something hard to do.

—First-year student's response to the question: "What does being successful mean to you?"

Nothing ever comes that is worth having, except as a result of hard work.

—Booker T. Washington, born-in-slavery Black educator, author, and advisor to Republican presidents

Successive goal setters anticipate *obstacles* that may be encountered along the path to their goals and have a plan for dealing with these potential obstacles. One characteristic of successful people is that they imagine what their life would be like if they didn't reach their goals. Imagining this scenario drives them to prepare for events or circumstances that might interfere with their plans and aspirations (Gilbert, 2006; Harris, Griffin, & Murray, 2008). They remain optimistic about succeeding, but they're not blind optimists; they realize the road may be tough so they have a realistic plan in place in case they encounter roadblocks or rough spots along the way (Oettingen, 2014; Oettingen & Stephens, 2009). Thus, effective goal-setters have both a plan for reaching their goal and a plan for surmounting potential impediments.

Encourage students to identify potential obstacles along the path to completing college as well as campus resources they can use to help them overcome these obstacles. Research indicates that success in college involves a combination of what students do for themselves (personal responsibility) and how well they capitalize on available resources designed to promote their success (Pascarella & Terenzini, 1991, 2005).

> Successful people are *resourceful*—they're aware of, and take advantage of, resources they can use to help them reach their goals.

> *Develop an inner circle of close associations in which the mutual attraction is not sharing problems or needs. The mutual attraction should be values and goals.*
>
> —Denis Waitley, former mental trainer for U.S. Olympic athletes and author of *Seeds of Greatness*

Remind students that their peers represent another resource for goal achievement. The power of social support groups is well documented by research in multiple fields (Brissette, Cohen, & Seeman, 2000; Duckworth, 2016; Ewell, 1997). Students can harness the power of social support by surrounding themselves with peers who are committed to achieving their educational goals and distancing themselves from "toxic" people who can poison their plans or dampen their dreams.

Urge your students to find motivated peers and make mutual-support "pacts" to help each other reach their goals. These peer-support pacts may be viewed as "social contracts" signed by "co-witnesses" who hold one another accountable to fulfilling their goal commitments. Studies show that when an individual commits to a goal in the presence of others, the commitment is strengthened because it becomes both a personal and an interpersonal commitment (Hollenbeck, Williams, & Klein, 1989; Locke, 2000).

Tale FROM THE Trenches

I gave the students a worksheet to write down their individual goals. They created academic, professional, and social goals that could have been short term or long term. I then had them put their goals into an envelope and hand them to me. I chose this process because I would be able to have their goals with me and be able to keep up with them during meetings. We are going to have an evaluation of their goals during the middle of the term and near the end. I will be sending out e-mails to them to see how they are doing and will check in on them to see if they are working towards their goals.

—PEER LEADER

Helping Students Maintain Motivation and Make Progress Toward Their Goals

The word "motivation" derives from the Latin root "movere," meaning "to move." As its root meaning implies, motivation involves overcoming inertia. Motivated people get off their butts and get moving, and once they get moving, they maintain momentum and keep moving until their goals are reached. Studies show that goal setting is just one step in the motivational process; it must be accompanied by a strong commitment to achieve the goal that's been set (Locke, 2000; Locke & Latham, 1990). Goal setting establishes the intention to act, but motivation transforms intention into action.

Reaching challenging goals requires maintaining motivation and sustaining effort over an extended period of time. Listed below are strategies you can share with students to help them stay motivated and continue to pursue their goals.

Ask students to put their goals in writing and keep them visible. A written goal can operate like a written contract—a formal statement that holds us accountable for following through on our commitment. Placing a written goal in a place where we can't help but see it on a daily basis (e.g., on our laptop, refrigerator, or bathroom mirror) ensures that we don't "lose sight" of it and are continually reminded to pursue it. Said in another way: what we keep in sight, we keep in mind.

> **The next best thing to actually doing something is to write down our intention to do it and keep that written intention visible (and memorable).**

Encourage students to visualize reaching their long-range goals. To maintain motivation over time, we need to keep the "big picture" in mind and continue to keep our "eye on the prize." One way to do so is by creating vivid mental images or pictures of reaching our goal and experiencing its positive consequences. For beginning college students, if their long-rage goal is a college degree, they could visualize a crowd of cheering family, friends, and faculty at their graduation. (They could even add musical accompaniment to their visualization by playing a motivational song in their head—e.g., "We are the Champions" by Queen).

Ask students to visualize completing all the key steps leading to their goal. For visualization to be an effective motivator, it's important not only to visualize the success itself (the end goal), but also the successive steps to be taken along the way. "Just picturing yourself crossing the finish line doesn't actually help you get there—but visualizing how you run the race (the strategies you will use, the choices you will make, the obstacles you will face) not only will give you greater confidence, but also leave you better prepared for the task ahead" (Halvorson, 2010, p. 208).

Yes, reaching a long-term goal requires focusing on the prize—the dream and why the dream is important. Such "big picture" thinking serves to inspire us. However, we also need to focus on the little things that need to be done to get us there—the to-do lists, the day-to-day tasks, the due dates, etc. (See chapter 6 for specific strategies you can share with students.) This nitty-gritty stuff represents the effortful perspiration that converts inspiration into action, enabling us to plug away and persist until our goals (and dreams) and are reached.

It could be said that successfully achieving a long-term goal requires two lenses with different focus points. We need a wide-angle lens to give us a big-picture view of the future far ahead of us (our ultimate goal) and a narrow-angle lens that zooms our focus in on the here and now—the steps that lie immediately ahead of us. For college students, alternating between these two perspectives

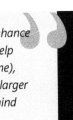

You can lead a horse to water, but you can't make him drink.
—Author unknown

To get motivated and enhance your self-control (or to help someone else do the same), think why. Consider the larger meaning or purpose behind what you are doing."
—Heidi Grant Halvorson, social psychologist, and author of *Succeed: How We Can Reach Your Goals*

You've got to think about 'big things' while you're doing small things, so that all the small things go in the right direction.

—Alvin Toffler, American futurologist and author who predicted the future effects of technology on our society

allows them to view their smaller, short-term chores and challenges (e.g., completing an assignment that's due next week) in light of the larger, long-range picture (e.g., college graduation and a successful future).

Author's Experience

I once coached a youth soccer team (5 to 6-year-old boys) and noticed that many of the less successful players tended to make either of two mistakes when trying to advance the ball down the field. Some of the less successful players spent too much time looking down, focusing on the ball at their feet, trying to be sure that they didn't lose control of it. By not occasionally lifting his head and looking ahead, this player often missed open territory, open teammates, or an open goal. Other unsuccessful players made the opposite mistake: They spent too much time with their heads up, trying to see where they were headed. By not periodically glancing down to see the ball right in front of them, this player often lost control of it, moved ahead without it, or sometimes stumbled over it and fell flat on his face. In contrast, the more successful players had developed the habit of shifting their focus between looking down to maintain control of the ball in front of them and lifting their eyes to see where they were headed.

The more I thought about how the successful soccer players alternated between these two perspectives, it struck me that this was a metaphor for success in life. Successful people alternate between long-range and short-range perspectives; they remain mindful of both the long-term goal far ahead of them and the short-term tasks right in front of them.

— *Joe Cuseo*

> **We need to keep our future dreams and current tasks in dual focus. Integrating these two perspectives provides us with both the inspiration to set goals and the determination to reach them.**

Advise students to keep a record of their personal progress. Highly effective people reflect regularly on their daily progress to ensure they're on track and making progress toward their goals (Covey, 1990). Research indicates that even the simple act of monitoring and recording progress toward our goals can increase our motivation to continue pursuing them (Locke & Latham, 2005; Matsui, Okada, & Inoshita, 1983). Keeping a regular record of our personal progress increases motivation because it provides us with frequent *feedback* about whether we're on track and positive *reinforcement* for staying on track (Bandura & Cervone, 1983; Schunk, 1995).

Ask your students to record their short- and mid-range goal achievements in red on a calendar, or in a journal. These recordings can serve as benchmarks that provide them with visible markers (and reminders) of their progress. Students could also mark their progress on a chart or graph, or list their achievements in a resumé or portfolio. By placing these markers of progress where they can be seen on a daily basis, students are supplied with a visible source of motivation that can help them to continue striving toward their ultimate long-term goal (Halvorson, 2010).

Encourage students to reward themselves for completing the stepping-stones along the road to their long-range goal. Not only should students document their progress, they should celebrate their success. Reaching a long-range goal is clearly cause for celebration because it marks the end of the trip and the thrill of reaching our desired destination. Reaching short- and mid-range goals, however, are not as obviously rewarding because they're merely stops along the way. We're more likely to complete these intermediate steps along the path to our long-range goal if we reward ourselves for completing them. The process of setting short-range and mid-range goals and rewarding ourselves for reaching them is a simple yet powerful self-motivational strategy. It helps us maintain momentum over an extended period of time, which is exactly what's needed to reach a long-range goal.

Reflection 5.3

To reach your ultimate goal of becoming an outstanding peer leader, what would are the stepping-stones or sub-goals you'll need to complete along the way? How would you reward yourself for completing them?

Supply students with motivational feedback. Encouraging feedback can keep students striving for and progressing toward the goals they've set for themselves. You can provide students with motivational feedback that has the six key features listed in Box 5.2

Box 5.2 — Six Attributes of Motivational Feedback

1. **Proactive:** it's delivered in the *early stages* of the process while there's still time to make adjustments and improvements before students veer too far off track or fall too far behind.
2. **Prompt:** it's delivered *soon after* the students engage in goal-related actions or behaviors.
3. **Precise:** it focuses *specifically* on what students need to do to stay on track and make progress toward their goal.
4. **Practical:** it provides suggestions for improvement that are *manageable* and *do-able* by targeting behaviors that students can *realistically* change.
5. **Persuasive:** it provides students with reasons *why* improvement should be made, thereby *motivating* them to take action on the feedback provided.
6. **Positive:** it begins and ends on an *optimistic* note and delivered in a way that preserves the student's *self-esteem*, recognizes personal *strengths*, and reinforces personal *progress*.

How can you deliver feedback that's positive yet challenging? How can you remain optimistic and enthusiastic, while at the same time being honest and realistic with students about things they need to change? One way to do so is by using the following "warm-cool-warm" feedback sequence:

1. *Warm* (compliment)
2. *Cool* (challenge)
3. *Warm* (compliment)

For example:

(1) Start with a positive statement about the student's effort and prior achievement.
(2) Follow with a challenging yet supportive suggestion about what the student could do better.
(3) End with a positive statement that reminds the student about what is going well and expresses confidence that the student can use your suggestion to do even better.

By starting with positive feedback, you create a positive "first impression" that decreases defensiveness and increases receptivity to the constructive criticism that follows. Concluding the interchange on an optimistic note creates a positive "last impression" that inspires the student to act on the feedback you've provided.

Naturally, it's hard to stay upbeat, enthusiastic, and deliver positive feedback to students who are continually messing up. That will happen, but don't give up on students when they stumble, and don't give up on yourself as a leader when things don't go according to your hopes and plans. Keep in mind that each student's pace of development is affected by his or her unique circumstances and degree of readiness for the college experience—academically, socially, and emotionally. Continue to challenge your students to commit to their goals and to engage in behaviors that are consistent with their aspirations; and continue to support them by providing positive, empathetic, and effective feedback.

> Your leadership experiences will test your confidence and resilience; it's all about how you deal with it. Continue to believe in your students' potential to improve and continue to believe in your ability to make a difference.

Reflection 5.4

In your position as a peer leader, what challenges do you think will provide the strongest test of your leadership confidence and resiliency?

Helping Students Explore and Set Career Goals

Goals may be classified into three general categories: top-level, mid-level, and low-level, depending on the order or sequence in which they are to be achieved (Duckworth, 2016). Short-level goals must be reached before a mid-level goal can be achieved, and a mid-level goal must be reached before a long-range goal can be achieved. This process of goal setting is called *means-end analysis*. It starts with identifying a top-level goal (the end) and working backward to identify the mid-level and short-level goals (the means) needed to reach the ultimate goal (Brooks, 2009; Newell & Simon, 1959). For instance: "Getting out the door by eight a.m. is a low-level goal. It only matters because of a mid-level goal: arriving at work on time. Why do you care about that? Because you want to be punctual. Why do you care about that? Because being punctual shows respect for the people with whom you work. Why is that important? Because you strive to be a good leader" (Duckworth, 2016. p. 63).

For first-year students, a career goal would be a high-level goal. Most professional careers require a college degree, so completing all coursework for a degree would be a mid-level goal. To reach that mid-level goal, students need to start completing the courses they're taking right now (low-level goal).

In a national survey of first-year college students, almost 60% of them strongly agreed that it's important to be thinking about their career, but only 25% said they had a clear idea about how to achieve their career goals (HERI, 2014). Remind students that designing a career plan doesn't mean that the plan cannot be adjusted or modified. Goals can change as students develop and change, acquire new knowledge and skills, and discover new interests and talents. Making a tentative career plan doesn't mean that students are limiting their options, forfeiting flexibility, or locking themselves into premature plans about what they're going to do for the rest of the lives. Instead, when students engage in career planning, they're simply sketching out a roadmap that: (a) enables them to begin anticipating the type of future they'd like to create for themselves, (b) provides them with a sense of direction for getting there, and (c) gets them moving in the right direction. More specifically, career goal setting and planning involves three key steps:

You've got to be careful if you don't know where you're going because you might not get there.

—Yogi Berra, Hall of Fame baseball player

1. **Awareness of self**—gaining insight into your interests, abilities and talents, and values.
2. **Awareness of goal options**—knowing what goal (career) options are available to you.
3. **Awareness of what goal options provide the best self-match or "fit"**—knowing what goal (career) options align most closely with your abilities, interests, values, and needs.

Here are specific strategies you can share with students to help them take each of these steps in the process of setting a career goal.

Step 1. Self-Awareness

Success begins when you develop a clear understanding of who you are, where you want to go, and how to get there. The career goal you set for yourself says a lot about who you are and what you want from life. Thus, self-awareness is a critical first step in the process of career goal setting. You need to know yourself in order to know what career is best for you. While this may seem obvious, self-awareness and self-discovery are often overlooked aspects of the career goal-setting process. By helping students deepen their self-awareness, you put them in a better position to choose a career goal and pursue a career path that's true to who they are and who they want to become.

Know thyself.

—Plato, ancient Greek philosopher

To thine own self be true.

—William Shakespeare in *Hamlet*

> **Meaningful personal goals and wise life choices are built on a deep understanding of self.**

As a peer leader, you can help sharpen students' self-awareness by asking them questions that encourage introspection. Introspective questions can launch students on an inner quest that leads to greater self-insight and self-discovery.

The unexamined life is not worth living.

—Socrates, ancient Greek philosopher and a founding father of Western philosophy

> *In order to succeed, you must know what you are doing, like what you are doing, and believe in what you are doing.*
>
> —Will Rogers, Native American humorist and actor

You can initiate this introspective process by asking students questions relating to their personal:

- **Interests:** what they *like* to do;
- **Talents:** what they're *good* at doing;
- **Values:** what they believe is *important* to do or really *worth* doing.

Reflection 5.5

Would you say that the purposes and responsibilities associated with your particular leadership role "fit" or "match" your talents, interests, and values? If yes, why? If no, why not?

For a career goal to be attainable, the person pursuing it needs to have the personal interest, ability, and passion to attain it. You can use the questions listed in Exercise 5.3 (p. 161) to get students thinking about their personal interests, talents, and values. After students respond to the questions, ask them to reflect on their answers by posing this follow-up challenge: "Based on your responses to these questions, identify a career goal that would be most compatible or consistent with who you are."

Another way students can gain greater self-knowledge is by taking career self-assessment tests or inventories. These tests enable students to see how their personal characteristics (e.g., interests and values) compare with satisfied and successful professionals working in different careers. If the student's responses tend to be similar to the responses of satisfied and successful professionals in a particular career, this suggests the career might be a good fit for the student. Although career interest inventories don't tell the whole story, they are useful tools for students to have in their toolbox when setting career goals. Encourage students to see the Career Development Office on your campus to take a career interest inventory and other types of career self-assessments.

Step 2. Awareness of Career Options

The second step in the career goal-setting process involves students becoming aware of different career options available to them and what work is really like in these different careers (as opposed to how it's e depicted or glorified in popular media). To help students gain this knowledge, encourage them to consult the *Occupational Outlook Handbook* (www.bls.gov/ooh) and connect with a career development specialist on campus.

Step 3. Awareness of Career Options that Provide the Best Personal "Match" or "Fit"

In addition to (and more important than) starting salary, students need to be aware of how well the career they're considering matches or aligns with their personal talents, interests, and values. Since a career choice is a long-range decision that will affect their life beyond college, students need to think about how that choice will affect their long-term happiness. The ideal career choice should lead students to the following future-life scenario: They wake up on a workday morning and hop out of bed enthused and excited about going to work. When they're working, time seems to fly by, and before they know it, the day's over. After work, they feel good about the work they did and how well they did it. Remind students that for this ideal scenario to become (or even approach) reality, they should make every attempt to identify a career goal that's "in sync" with their *talents*—what they do well, their *interests*—what they like to do, and their *values*—what they're proud to do.

Characteristics of Successful People

Achieving success involves use of effective use of goal-setting and motivational strategies, but it takes something more. Ultimately, success emerges from the inside out—it flows from personal qualities and attributes found within a person. Studies of successful people who achieve goals reveal they possess the personal characteristics discussed below. Share these characteristics with your students, model them for your students, and encourage your students to exhibit them.

Self-Efficacy

Self-efficacy is the belief that you can positively influence the *outcomes* of your life (Bandura, 1994, 2001). People with self-efficacy have what psychologists call an "internal locus of control"—they believe that the locus (location or source) of control for events in their life is primarily *internal*—"inside" them and within their control, rather than *external*—outside them and beyond their control. They believe that success is influenced more by attitude, effort, and commitment than by luck, chance, or fate (Carlson et al., 2009; Jernigan, 2004; Rotter, 1966). In contrast, people with low self-efficacy tend to feel helpless and powerless; they think (and allow) things to happen to them rather than taking charge and making things happen for them.

College students with a strong sense of self-efficacy believe they're in control of their educational success and can shape their future—regardless of what their past experience or current circumstances may be. Research on students with a strong sense of *academic self-efficacy* shows that they:

1. Put considerable effort into their studies;
2. Use active-learning strategies;
3. Capitalize on campus resources; and
4. Persist in the face of obstacles (Multon, Brown, & Lent, 1991; Zimmeman, 1995, 2000).

Students with a strong sense of self-efficacy also possess a strong sense of personal responsibility. As the breakdown of the word "responsible" implies, they believe they're "response" "able"—able to respond effectively to personal and educational challenges.

Set yourself earnestly to discover what you are made to do, and then give yourself passionately to the doing of it.

—Martin Luther King, Jr., American clergyman, prominent leader in the African-American Civil Rights Movement, and winner of the Nobel Peace Prize

If you do not find it within yourself, where will you go to get it?

—Zen saying (Zen is a branch of Buddhism that emphasizes seeing deeply into the nature of things and ongoing self-awareness.)

I'm a great believer in luck, and I find the harder I work the more I have of it.

—Thomas Jefferson, third president of the United States

Reflection 5.6

In what area of your life do you think you have the strongest sense of self-efficacy? Is there anything you can take from the strong self-efficacy you have in this area and apply it to your work as a peer leader?

Growth Mindset

A *mindset* is a powerful belief. People with a *"growth mindset"* believe that intelligence and other positive qualities can be grown or developed. In contrast, people with a "fixed mindset" believe that intelligence and other abilities are fixed, inborn traits that cannot be modified or acquired (Dweck, 2006, 2015). Supporting the concept of growth mindset are studies indicating that IQ scores are not fixed, but can change significantly over time (Ramsden, 2011). Research also shows that the human brain isn't fixed; it changes with experience and parts of the brain responsible for learning a particular skill (e.g., math) grow and develop when those skills are practiced (Brown University, 2000).

Listed below are opposing pairs of traits—one representing a fixed mindset (FM) and the other a growth mindset (GM). As you read through these pairings, honestly assess yourself in terms of whether you lean more toward a fixed or growth mindset by circling either the FM (Fixed Mindset) or GM (Growth Mindset) option.

I try to get better at what I do. (GM)
I try to show others (including themselves) how good I am. (FM)

I try to validate myself by proving how smart or talented I am. (FM)
I validate myself by stretching trying to become smarter and more talented than I am now. (GM)

If I cannot learn something easily or quickly, I think that means I'm not smart or good at it. (FM)
I believe I can get good at something even if it doesn't come easily to me at first. (GM)

I evaluate my performance by comparing it to my past performances. (GM)
I evaluate my performance by comparing it to the performance of others. (FM)

I believe the amount of intelligence people start with doesn't predict the amount they'll end up with. (GM)
I believe people are born with a certain amount of intelligence and not much can be done to change it. (FM)

I think success is a matter of having ability. (FM)
I think success is a matter of getting ability. (GM)

I focus on demonstrating my skills to others. (FM)
I focus on developing my skills for myself. (GM)

I like to improve myself (by getting better). (GM)
I like to prove myself (as being good or smart). (FM)

I feel smart when I complete tasks quickly and without mistakes. (FM)
I feel smart when I struggle with tasks at first, but then succeed at them. (GM)

I seek out feedback from others to improve myself. (GM)
I avoid seeking feedback from others for fear it will expose my weaknesses. (FM)

> *If you believe you can develop yourself, then you're open to accurate information about your current abilities, even if it's unflattering.*
>
> —Carol Dweck, *Mindset: The New Psychology of Success*

I feel threatened by the success of others. (FM)
I feel I can be inspired by and learn from the success of others. (GM)

I tend to show progressive improvement in my performance over time. (GM)
I tend to peak early and don't progress to higher levels of performance. (FM)

I think success should be effortless. (FM)
I think success should be effortful. (GM)

I view challenges as opportunities to develop new skills. (GM)
I view challenges as threatening because they may prove I'm not smart. (FM)

I believe effort creates talent. (GM)
I believe effort is for those who can't make it on talent. (FM)

I focus on self-improvement—about becoming the best I can be. (GM)
I focus on self-validation—about proving I'm already good. (FM)

I look at grades as labels that judge or measure my intelligence. (FM)
I look at grades as a source of feedback for improving my performance. (GM)

> *No matter what your ability is, effort is what ignites that ability and turns it into accomplishment.*
>
> —Carol Dweck, Stanford psychologist and author of *Mindset: The New Psychology of Success*

Reflection 5.7

Look back at the previous pairs of statements and compare the total number of fixed mindset (FM) and growth mindset (GM) statements you circled.

a) Do your totals suggest that, in general, you lean more toward a growth or fixed mindset?

b) Do you see any patterns in your responses that suggest you're more likely to have a growth mindset for certain characteristics or situations and a fixed mindset for others?

c) How do you think your responses would compare to those of the students you lead or mentor?

Numerous studies show that growth mindset is strongly associated with goal achievement and personal success (Dweck, 2006). For example, when growth-mindset students do poorly on a test, they improve on the next one. In contrast, the performance of fixed-mindset students shows no pattern of improvement (or shows decline) over time, particularly if their first exam score is low (Halvorson, 2010). It's also been found that students can have different mindsets for different subjects and situations. Some students may have a fixed mindset for math, but a growth mindset for other subjects.

The most important thing to remember and convey to the students you mentor about mindset is that although it plays a powerful role in motivation and success, it's just a belief and it can be changed from "fixed" to "growth" for any subject or situation (Dweck, 2006). Ask students to take a look at their beliefs about what makes someone intelligent or talented. If their beliefs suggest they have a fixed mindset, they may need to change that mindset to reach the goals they've set for themselves and realize their full potential.

You can promote students' growth mindset by the language you use when providing them with feedback about their successes and setbacks. When students are given positive feedback on the effort they expend and the strategies they use, that feedback focuses on behavior they can readily change and continually improve; in contrast, praising talent and intelligence focuses on traits which students may view as fixed and unalterable. There's also another danger of praising students for their talent or intelligence: "It give them a boost, a special flow—but for the moment. The minute they hit a snag, their confidence goes out the window and their motivation hits rocks bottom. If success means they're smart, then failure means they're dumb" (Dweck, 2006, p. 175).

Listed below are examples of how language that commonly reinforces a fixed mindset (FM) after a successful or unsuccessful performance can be changed into language that reinforces a growth mindset (GM) (Duckworth, 2016).

1. After successful performance:

   "You're so talented!" (FM) → "You learn so well!" (GM)

   "Great job! (FM) → "Great job! If you were to do it over again, is there any thing you could have done even better?" (GM)

2. After unsuccessful performance:

   "Well, at least you tried." (FM) → "I know that wasn't the outcome you were hoping for. What do you think went wrong and how might it be corrected?" (GM)

   "That was hard. Don't feel bad about not being able to do it." (FM) → "That was hard. Don't feel bad about not being able to do it *yet*." (GM)

> *Our words have a far greater motivational impact than most of us realize, and that's a responsibility that should be taken seriously.*
>
> —Heidi Grant Halvorson, social psychologist, and author of *Succeed: How We Can Reach Your Goals*

Grit

When a person sustains significant effort, energy, and perseverance over an extended period of time to achieve a goal, that person is demonstrating *grit* (Duckworth et al., 2007; Stoltz, 2014). People with grit have been found to possess the following qualities (Duckworth, 2016).

> *Grit is perseverance and passion for long-term goals. Sticking with your future day in, day out, not just for the week, not just for the month, but for years and working really hard to make that future a reality.*
>
> —Angela Duckworth, psychologist, University of Pennsylvania

Passion. Many people associate passion with infatuation or obsession. However, interviews with high achievers about what it takes to be successful reveal that, for them, passion is about *consistency over time*. It's more about stamina than intensity. "Grit is about working on something you care about so much that you're willing to stay loyal to it. It's doing what you love, but not just falling in love—staying in love" (Duckworth, 2016, p. 54).

Perseverance. Gritty people pursue goals with relentless determination. If they encounter something along the way that's hard to do, they work harder to do it. Studies of highly successful people—whether they be scientists, musicians, writers, chess masters, or basketball stars—consistently show that achieving performance excellence requires repeated effort and dedicated practice (Charness &

Schultetus, 1999; Levitin, 2006). This is even true for very famous people who the public views as being naturally talented, brilliant, or gifted. For example, before they burst into musical stardom, the Beatles performed live an estimated 1,200 times over a four-year period; many of these performances lasted five hours or more per night. They performed (practiced) for more hours during their first four years together than most bands perform during their entire career. Similarly, before Bill Gates became a computer software giant and creator of Microsoft, he logged almost 1,600 hours of computer time during one seven-month period alone, averaging 8 hours a day, 7 days a week (Gladwell, 2008).

These extraordinary success stories point strongly to the conclusion that reaching goals and achieving success takes dedication, determination, and perseverance. Share these stories with your students and remind them that for these famous people, their success was not just a gift; it took grit.

Reflection 5.8

Think about something you succeeded at in your life that involved considerable dedication, determination, and perseverance. Do you see ways in which you could apply the same qualities to achieve success as a peer leader?

How smart you are will influence the extent to which you experience something as difficult (for example, how hard a math problem is), but it says nothing about how you will deal with difficulty when it happens. It says nothing about whether you will be persistent and determined or feel overwhelmed and helpless.

—Heidi Grant Halvorson, social psychologist, and author of *Succeed: How We Can Reach Your Goals*

Resilience. Grit involves hanging in there, sustaining effort until the goal is reached, and displaying the fortitude to push forward in the face of frustration or adversity. A gritty person bounces back from setbacks turns them into comebacks.

Remind students that it takes courage not to get discouraged. How they initially react to a setback affects what action they take in response to it. For instance, if they react to a poor test grade by knocking themselves down with self-putdowns ("I'm a loser" or "I screw up everything"), they're likely to become discouraged and give up. Notice that these reactions have two resilience-destroying characteristics: they're *permanent* (a "loser" is always a loser) and *pervasive* (screwing up "everything" means not screwing up one thing, but all things). A permanent and pervasive explanation for a setback turns a molehill into a mountain (Seligman, 2006). If you catch students engaging in such negative self-talk, make them aware of it. Challenge them to replace it with positive self-talk that reacts to the setback as *temporary* (not permanent) and *specific* (not pervasive). For instance, encourage them to respond to a setback by saying: "I'm going to let this one failure define who I am; I'll learn from it and use it as motivation to get it right next time."

What happens is not as important as how you react to what happens.

—Thaddeus Golas, *Lazy Man's Guide to Enlightenment*

Interestingly, the root of the word *failure* is "fallere"–to "trip" or "fall." Thus, failing doesn't mean we've been defeated; it just means we've stumbled and taken a temporary spill. Similarly, the word "problem" derives from the Greek root "proballein"–"to throw forward"–suggesting that a problem is an opportunity to move ahead. You can help students take this approach to a problem or setback by advising them to react to it by rewording or rephrasing it as a positive goal statement. (e.g., "I'm flunking math" can be reframed as: "My goal is to get a grade of C or better on the next exam to pull my overall course grade into passing territory.") Also remind them to think about previous setbacks they've experienced and recovered from. Ask them what they did to bounce back from those setbacks and if they could use similar strategies or resources to overcome their current setback.

> *The harder you fall, the higher you bounce.*
>
> —Chinese proverb

It's intriguing that the root of the word *success* is "*successus*"—meaning "to follow or come after." This suggests that success can still be achieved after a fall if we don't give up, but get up and continue taking steps toward our goal. Encourage students to view poor academic performances and other setbacks (particularly those occurring early in their college experience) not as failures but as opportunities for learning and growth. Also, be sure to recognize and reinforce students' resilient behavior when you witness it by delivering *affirmations*, such as: "You demonstrated a lot of grit when you overcame . . ." "You showed a lot of perseverance by sticking with . . ." (Sobell & Sobell, 2013).

In the movies, a clipboard is used to signal the next "take" (shooting) if the previous take was unsuccessful. You can use this as a metaphor to remind students that if they make early mistakes in college, it's their "first take"; they can learn from it, improve their performance on the next take, and achieve success on their final take.

Reflection 5.9

What is the most significant setback or obstacle you've encountered in college thus far?

How did you overcome it? (What actions did you take to get past it or prevent it from holding you back?)

What did you learn from this experience that you might use as a peer leader to help other students succeed?

People can grow grit "from the inside out"—by developing it themselves, and they can grow grit "from the outside in"—with the help of coaches and mentors (Duckworth, 2016). One potentially powerful role you can play as a peer leader and mentor is to help students develop the grit they need to reach their long-term goals.

Internet Resources

For additional information to share with students on goal setting and motivation, consult the following websites:

Goal Setting
www.siue.edu/SPIN/activity.html

Self-Motivational Strategies
www.selfmotivationstrategies.com

Self-Efficacy
https://www.psychologytoday.com/us/blog/flourish/201002/
if-you-think-you-can-t-think-again-the-sway-self-efficacy

Grit and Resilience
https://learningconnection.stanford.edu/resilience-project
Growth Mindset
https://www.ted.com/talks/carol_dweck_the_power_of_believing_
that_you_can_improve

References

Bandura, A. (1994). Self-efficacy. In V. S. Ramachaudran (Ed.), *Encyclopedia of human behavior* (Vol. 4, pp. 71–81). New York: Academic Press.

Bandura, A. (2001). Social cognitive theory: An agentic perspective. *Annual Review of Psychology, 52*(1), 1–26,

Bandura, A., & Cervone, D. (1983). Self-evaluative and self-efficacy mechanisms governing the motivational effects of goal systems. *Journal of Personality and Social Psychology, 45*(5), 1017–1028.

Brissette, I., Cohen, S., & Seeman, T. E. (2000). Measuring social integration and social networks. In S. Cohen, L. G. Underwood, & B. H. Gottlieb (Eds.), *Social support measurement and intervention* (pp. 53–85). New York: Oxford University Press.

Brooks, K. (2009). *You majored in what? Mapping your path from chaos to career.* NY: Penguin.

Brown University. (2000, October 20). *Study describes brain changes during learning. ScienceDaily.* Retrieved from www.sciencedaily.com/releases/2000/10/001020092659.htm

Carlson, N. R., Miller, H., Heth, C. D., Donahoe, J. W., & Martin, G. N. (2009). *Psychology: The science of behaviour* (7th ed.). Toronto, ON: Pearson Education Canada.

Charness, N., & Schultetus, R. S. (1999). Knowledge and expertise. In F. T. Durso, R. S., Nickerson, R. W. Schvaneveldt, S. T. Dumais, D. S. Lindsay, & M. T. H. Chi (Eds.), *Handbook of applied cognition* (pp. 57-81). Chichester, United Kingdom: John Wiley & Sons.

Covey, S. R. (1990). *Seven habits of highly effective people* (2nd ed.). New York: Fireside.

Doran, G. T. (1981). There's a S.M.A.R.T. way to write management's goals and objectives. *Management Review, 70*(11), 35-36.

Duckworth, A. (2016). *Grit: The power of passion and perseverance.* London: Vermillion.

Duckworth, A. L., Peterson, C., Matthews, M. D., & Kelly, D. R. (2007). Grit: Perseverance and passion for long-term goals. *Journal of Personality and Social Psychology, 92*(6), p. 1087-1101.

Dweck, C. S. (2006). *Mindset: The new psychology of success.* New York: Random House.

Dweck, C. (2015). "Carol Dweck revisits the 'growth mindset.'" *Education Week, 35*(5), pp. 20, 24. Retrieved from https://www.edweek.org/ew/articles/2015/09/23/carol-dweck-revisits-the-growth-mindset.html

Ewell, P. T. (1997). Organizing for learning. *AAHE Bulletin, 50*(4), 3–6.

Gilbert, P. T. (2006). *Stumbling on happiness.* New York: Alfred A. Knopf.

Gladwell, M. (2008). *Outliers: The story of success.* New York: Little, Brown.

Halvorson, H. G. (2010). *Succeed: How we can reach our goals.* New York: Plume.

Harris, P., Griffin, D., & Murray, S. (2008). Testing the limits of optimistic bias: Event and person moderators in a multilevel framework. *Journal of Personality and Social Psychology, 95,* 1225-1137.

HERI (Higher Education Research Institute). (2014). *Your first college year survey 2014.* Los Angeles: Cooperative Institutional Research Program, University of California-Los Angeles

Hollenbeck, J. R., Williams, C. R., & Klein, H. J. (1989). An empirical examination of the antecedents of commitment to difficult goals. *Journal of Applied Psychology, 74*(1), 18–23.

Jernigan, C. G. (2004). What do students expect to learn? The role of learner expectancies, beliefs, and attributions for success and failure in student motivation. *Current Issues in Education* [Online], *7*(4). Retrieved January 16, 2012 from http://cie.ed.asu.edu/volume7/number4/

Kouzes, M. M., & Posner, B. Z. (2008). *The student leadership challenge: Five practices for exemplary leaders.* San Francisco: Jossey-Bass.

Latham, G., & Locke, E. (2007). New developments in and directions for goal-setting research. *European Psychologists, 12,* 290-300.

Levitin, D. J. (2006). *This is your brain on music: The science of a human obsession.* New York: Dutton.

Locke, E. A. (2000). Motivation, cognition, and action: An analysis of studies of task goals and knowledge. *Applied Psychology: An International Review, 49,* 408-429.

Locke, E. A., & Latham, G. P. (1990). *A theory of goal setting and task performance.* Englewood Cliffs, NJ: Prentice Hall.

Locke, E. A., & Latham, G. P. (2002). Building a practically useful theory of goal setting and task motivation. *American Psychologist, 57,* 705-717.

Locke, E. A., & Latham, G. P. (2005). Goal setting theory: Theory building by induction. In K. G. Smith & M. A. Mitt (Eds.), *Great minds in management: The process of theory development.* New York: Oxford.

Matsui, T., Okada, A., & Inoshita, O. (1983). Mechanism of feedback affecting task performance. *Organizational Behavior and Human Performance, 31,* 114–122.

Meyer, P. L. (2003). *Attitude is everything: If you want to succeed above and beyond.* Waco, Texas: Meyer Resource Group, Incorporated.

Multon, K. D., Brown, S. D., & Lent, R. W. (1991). Relation of self-efficacy beliefs to academic outcomes: A meta-analytic investigation. *Journal of Counseling Psychology, 38*(1), 30–38.

Newell, A., & Simon, H. A. (1959). *The simulation of human thought.* Santa Monica, CA: Rand Corporation.

Oettingen, G. (2014). *Rethinking positive thinking: Inside the new science of motivation.* New York: Penguin.

Oettingen, G., & Stephens, E. (2009). Mental contrasting future and reality: A motivationally intelligent self-regulatory strategy. In G. Moskowitz & H. Grant (eds.), *The psychology of goals.* New York: Guilford.

Pascarella, E., & Terenzini, P. (1991). *How college affects students: Findings and insights from twenty years of research.* San Francisco: Jossey-Bass.

Pascarella, E., & Terenzini, P. (2005). *How college affects students: A third decade of research* (Vol. 2). San Francisco: Jossey-Bass.

Ramsden, S., Richardson, F. M., Josse, G., Thomas, M. S. C., Ellis, C., Shakeshaft, C., Seghier, M. L., & Price, C. J. (2011). Verbal and non-verbal intelligence changes in the teenage brain. *Nature, 479,* 113-116.

Rotter, J. (1966). Generalized expectancies for internal versus external controls of reinforcement. *Psychological Monographs: General and Applied, 80*(609), 1–28.

Sanchez, R. J., Bauer, T. N., & Paronto, M. E. (2006). Peer-mentoring freshmen: Implications for satisfaction, commitment, and retention to graduation. *Academy of Management Learning and Education, 5*(1), 25-37.

Schunk, D. H. (1995). Self-efficacy and education and instruction. In J. E. Maddux (Ed.), *Self-efficacy, adaptation, and adjustment: Theory, research, and application* (pp. 281-303). New York: Plenum Press.

Seligman, M. E. P. (2006). *Learned optimism: How to change your mind and your life.* New York: Vintage Books.

Sobell. L. C., & Sobell, M. B. (2013). *Motivational techniques and skills for health/mental health coaching and counseling.* Retrieved from http://www.nova.edu/gsc/forms/mi-techniques-skills.pdf

Stoltz, P. G. (2014). *Grit: The new science of what it takes to persevere, flourish, succeed.* San Luis Obispo: Climb Strong Press.

Ward, E. G., Thomas, E. E., & Disch, W. B. (2010). Goal attainment, retention and peer mentoring. *Academic Exchange Quarterly, 14*(2), 170-176.

Zimmerman, B. J. (1995). Self-efficacy and educational development. In A. Bandura (Ed.), *Self-efficacy in changing societies.* New York: Cambridge University Press.

Zimmerman, B. J. (2000). Self-Efficacy: An essential motive to learn. *Contemporary Educational Psychology, 25,* 82–91.

Exercise 5.1 Quote Reflections

Review the sidebar quotes contained in this chapter and select two that you think would be especially valuable to share with the students you lead or mentor.

For each quote, write a short statement explaining why you chose it.

Exercise 5.2 Clarifying Leadership Goals

Take a moment to answer the following questions honestly.

- What are my highest priorities?
- What competing needs and priorities do I need to keep in check?
- How will I maintain balance across different aspects of my life?
- What am I willing or able to give up in order to achieve success as a peer leader?
- How will I maintain motivation for my leadership role on a day-to-day basis?
- Who will I collaborate with to reach my leadership goals and how will that collaboration take place?

Exercise 5.3 Setting a SMART Goal to Reduce the Real-vs.-Ideal Gap

Think of an aspect of your leadership where there's a significant gap between what you'd like it to be (the ideal) and where you are (the reality).

Use the following form to identify a goal you could pursue to reduce this gap.

Goal: _____

What specific *actions* will be taken?

When will these actions be taken?

What *obstacles* or *roadblocks* do you anticipate?

What *resources* could you use to overcome these anticipated obstacles or roadblocks?

How will you *measure your progress*?

How will you know when you *reached or achieved* your goal?

Exercise 5.4 Designing a SMART Leadership Goal

Think about a leadership goal that you'd like to reach this year. Apply the SMART method of goal setting (described on p. 140) to create a plan for achieving it.

Exercise 5.5 Converting Setbacks into Comebacks: Transforming Pessimism into Optimism through Positive Self-Talk

In *Hamlet*, Shakespeare wrote: "There is nothing good or bad, but thinking makes it so." His point was that experiences have the potential to be positive or negative, depending on how people interpret them and react to them. Listed below is a list of negative reaction statements students may make in response to a personal setback. For each of these self-defeating statements, reword or rephrase it to make a more positive, self-motivating statement for students. (For examples, see the section on resilience, p. 153.)

a) "I'm just not good at this."

b) "There's nothing I can do about it."

c) "Nothing is going to change."

d) "This always happens to me."

e) "Everybody is going to think I'm a loser."

Exercise 5.6 Strategy Reflections

Review the strategies for helping students *maintain motivation and progress toward their goals* on pp. 142–144. Select three strategies that you think students would be most receptive to learning about and putting into practice.

CHAPTER 6

Managing Time and Tasks

Reflection 6.1

Complete the following sentence with the first thought that comes to mind:
For me, time is ...

Chapter Purpose and Preview

Setting goals may be the first step in the process of achieving success, but managing time and completing the tasks needed to reach those goals is the critical second step. This chapter supplies you with a comprehensive set of mentoring strategies to help students establish personal priorities, manage time, combat procrastination, and complete tasks.

The Relationship between Goal Setting, Managing Time, and Managing Tasks

Time is a powerful personal resource; when we gain greater control of it, we gain greater control of our life and our ability to reach our goals. If students are to have a realistic chance of achieving their goals, they need a plan for spending their time in ways that aligns with their goals and enables them to progress toward their goals. Thus, setting goals, reaching goals and managing time are essential, interrelated skills. They involve asking and answering the following questions: How can I break down big goals into smaller, more manageable steps? What specific tasks do I need to complete in order to reach each step? How much time will it likely take to complete each step?

Goal attainment is achieved through step-by-step accomplishments that take place on a day-by-day basis. Each and every day, whether they plan to or not, students make decisions about what they will do that day. To reach their goals, they need to remain mindful of whether their daily actions are moving them in the direction of their goals. This practice of ongoing (daily) assessment of how time is being spent is a simple yet important form of self-reflection. Research on highly effective people reveals that they are planners who reflect regularly on their daily progress to check if they're on track and making steady progress toward their goals (Covey, 2004). This includes highly creative people in the arts and sciences; in a study of the typical day in the life more than 150 innovative artists and scientists, what they all had in common was daily rituals—they developed day-by-day work routines and habits (Currey, 2013).

> Ultimately, a student (and all of us) should craft a 'dream' but the dream must be broken down into bite-size pieces.
>
> —Brad Johnson & Charles Ridley, *The Elements of Mentoring*

The Importance of Time Management for College Students

National surveys indicate that almost 50% of first-year college students report difficulty managing their time effectively (HERI, 2014). Time management is particularly challenging for students transitioning directly from the lockstep schedule of high school to the less tightly controlled schedules of college—where there is less in-class "seat time" per week, leaving students with much more "free time" to manage outside of class.

Simply stated, students who have difficulty managing their time in college have difficulty managing their college experience. When college sophomores were interviewed in a national study about their first-year experience, one key difference was found between students who had an outstanding first year (both academically and personally) and those who struggled during their first year: The successful students frequently brought up the topic of time management during the interviews. They said they had to think carefully about how to spend time and intentionally budget their time. In contrast, sophomores who had experienced difficulty during their first year of college hardly talked about the topic of time at all during their interviews, even when they were specifically asked about it (Light, 2001).

Research indicates that it's not only college students who have time-management challenges. People of all ages report that managing time is a critical aspect of their life and setting priorities and balancing multiple responsibilities (e.g., work and family) is often a stressful juggling act for them (Harriott & Ferrari, 1996). These findings suggest that time management is more than just a college success skill; it's also a life-management and life-success skill (Gupta, Hershey, & Gaur, 2012). When people improve their ability to manage time, other aspects of their life also improve, including lowering their level of stress (Janata, 2008). In fact, studies show that people who have good time-management skills also have higher levels of life satisfaction and personal happiness (Myers, 1993, 2000).

Reflection 6.2

What do you think will be the biggest time-management challenge you'll face in your peer-leadership role or position?

As a peer leader and mentor, you can help students succeed in college by helping them remain mindful of the importance of time management and by equipping them with strategies for managing their time and tasks. Here are some strategies you can share with (and model for) them. The following ideas may look very simple, but that may be the reason why they're often simply overlooked.

Strategies for Managing Time and Tasks

Effective time- and task-management involves three key steps:

1. Analysis—breaking down time to see how we're spending it;
2. Itemization—listing *what* tasks need to be done and *when* they need to be done;
3. Prioritization—ordering our tasks in terms of their importance and tackling them in that order.

The following strategies can be shared with students to help them execute these three steps.

Analysis: breaking down time into smaller units to gain greater awareness of how it's being spent. How often have you heard someone say, "Where did all the time go?" or "I just can't seem to find the time!" One way to find out where our time goes and find more time for getting things done is by doing a *time analysis*—a detailed examination of how much total time we have and what we're spending it on, including patches of wasted time when little gets done or nothing gets accomplished. A time analysis only needs to be done for a week or two to give us a pretty good idea of where our time is going and help us find ways to use our time more productively (Morgenstern, 2004).

Doesn't thou love life? Then do not squander time, for that is the stuff life is made of.

—Benjamin Franklin, 18th-century inventor, newspaper writer, and cosigner of the Declaration of Independence

> What we spend our time on is often a true test of who we are and what we value. Taking some time to see how we're spending time is more than a clerical activity. When done well, it's an exercise in self-awareness that gives us deeper insight into our personal priorities and values.

Itemization: listing *what* tasks are to be done and *when* they are to be done. Just as we make lists to remember items to buy at a grocery store or people to invite to a party, we can make to-do lists of things we need to do and when they are due. One characteristic of highly successful people is that they are list makers; they create lists for things they want to accomplish each day (Covey, 2004).

Reflection 6.3

Do you think most students make daily to-do lists of things they need to get done? If not, why not?

To help students itemize their time and tasks, encourage them to take advantage of the following time-planning and task-management tools.

- *Small, portable planner.* Students can use this planner to list all their course assignments and exams, along with their due dates. (It can also be used in sync with the same calendar programs available on their desktop or laptop.) Pulling together all work tasks required in each course and getting them in the same place makes it much easier for students to keep track of what they have to do and when they have to do it.

- *Large, stable calendar.* In the calendar's date boxes, students can record their major assignments for the term. The calendar should be posted in a place where they can't help but see it every day (e.g., bedroom or refrigerator door). By repeatedly seeing the things they have to do, students are less likely to overlook them, forget them, or subconsciously repress them because they rather not do them.

- *Smartphone.* Students can use this device for purposes other than checking social networking sites and sending or receiving text messages. It can be used as a calendar tool to record due dates and set up alert functions to remind students of deadlines. Many smartphones also allow the user to set up task or "to-do" lists and set priorities for each item entered. A variety of apps are now available for planning tasks and tracking the amount of time we spend on them (e.g., see: http://www.rememberthemilk.com).

Students should take advantage of these cutting-edge tools, but at the same time, remind them that planners don't plan time, people do. Ultimately, any effective time-management strategy depends on committing fully to one's goals and establishing personal priorities.

> Time management is rooted in goal commitment. When the roots of goal commitment are strong, effective time-management can grow and develop into lifelong habits.

Using a calendar is an effective way for students to itemize their academic commitments.

©Noyna/Shutterstock.com

Reflection 6.4

a) Do you have a paper calendar you carry with you or do you use an electronic calendar tool on your cell phone?

b) If you don't use either of these tools, why not?

c) How do you think most students would answer the above two questions?

Prioritization: ordering tasks in terms of their importance and tackling them in that order. After itemizing tasks that need to be done, the next step is *prioritizing* them—determining the *order or sequence* in which they will get done. Prioritizing is basically a process of ranking tasks in order of their priority and completing high-priority tasks first. Here are two key criteria (standards of judgment) you can suggest to students for determining high-priority tasks:

- **Urgency.** Tasks that are closest to their deadline or due date should receive high priority. Starting an assignment that's due next week takes precedence over starting an assignment that's due next month (even if the latter assignment is more appealing or stimulating).
- **Gravity.** Tasks that carry greater weight (count more) should receive higher priority. If an assignment that's worth 100 points and an assignment worth 10 points are due at the same time, the 100-point task should receive higher priority. Students should be sure to spend their work time on tasks that matter most. Similar to investing money, time should be invested on tasks that yield the greatest dividends.

A simple but effective strategy for prioritizing tasks is to divide them into "A," "B," and "C" lists (Lakein, 1973; Morgenstern, 2004). List "A" is reserved for *essential* (non-negotiable) tasks—those that *must* be done now. List "B" is for *important* tasks—those that *should* be done soon. List "C" is for *optional* tasks—those that *could* or *might* be done if there's time remaining after the more important tasks on lists A and B have been completed.

Organizing tasks and time in these three lists can help students make rational decisions about how to divide their labor and tackle their tasks. They shouldn't be wasting time on less important things to deceive themselves into thinking they're "getting stuff done"—when, in reality, all they're doing is "keeping busy" and distracting themselves (and subtracting time) from the more important things they should be doing.

Developing a Time-Management Plan

Like successful chess players, successful time managers plan ahead and anticipate their next moves. Warn students not to buy into the myth that if they spend time planning their time, they're taking time away from getting things done.

You've probably heard of the old proverb: "A stitch in time saves nine." Planning time is a "stitch" (one unit of time) that saves "nine" (additional units of time). Actually, time-management experts estimate that the amount of time it takes to plan our work reduces our total work time by a factor of three; in other words, for every one unit of time we spend planning, we save three units of time working (Goldsmith, 2010; Lakein, 1973). Thus, 5 minutes of planning time typically saves us 15 minutes of total work time, and 10 minutes of planning time saves us 30 minutes of work time.

Taking time to plan our work saves us work time in the long run because it gives us a map of where we're going, thus reducing our risk of veering off track or getting sidetracked. Developing a plan of attack also reduces the likelihood of "false starts"—starting our work, then discovering later we didn't start off on the right track, which forces us to backtrack and start all over again.

Things that matter most must never be at the mercy of things that matter least.

—Johann Wolfgang von Goethe, German poet, dramatist, and author of the epic *Faust*

When I have lots of homework to do, I suddenly go through this urge to clean up and organize the house. I'm thinking, 'I'm not wasting my time. I'm cleaning up the house and that's something I have to do.' But all I'm really doing is avoiding schoolwork.

—College sophomore

If you fail to plan, you plan to fail.

—Benjamin Franklin

Key Elements of an Effective Time-Management Plan

Once students have accepted the idea that taking time to plan isn't a waste of time and will actually save time in the long run, you can help them to design a plan for managing their time. Listed below are components of an effective time-management plan that you can share with students.

An effective time-management plan includes short-, mid- and long-range tasks, such as the following:

1) *Long-range* tasks (e.g., tasks to be completed before final exams, and reports or papers due the end of the term);
2) *Mid-range* tasks (e.g., tasks to be completed by midterm); and
3) *Short-range* tasks (e.g., tasks to be completed by the next class session).

An effective time-management plan transforms intention into action. Step one is to plan the work; step two is to work the plan. Students can transform a plan on paper (or on screen) into a plan of action by: (a) previewing what they intend to do, (b) reviewing whether they actually did what they intended to do, and (c) closing any gaps between their intentions and actions. This process involves creating a *daily to-do list* at the start of the day and reviewing the list at the end of the day to determine what got done and what didn't get done. The tasks that didn't get done become high-priority tasks for the next day's to-do list.

If students frequently find lots of unchecked items on their to-do list at the end of the day, this probably means they're spreading themselves too thin and are trying to accomplish too much too soon. They may need to be more realistic about how much they can get done in a single day and reduce the number of items they include on their daily to-do list. Difficulty completing all tasks on daily to-do lists may also mean that students need to adjust their time-management plan by substituting work time for time they're spending on other activities (e.g., time spent on Facebook and responding to text messages or phone calls). If your students are consistently failing to complete daily tasks, they may have to ask themselves if they're truly committed to investing the amount of time and effort that's needed to reach their goals.

Murphy's Laws:

1. Nothing is as simple as it looks.

2. Everything takes longer than it should.

3. If anything can go wrong, it will.

—Murphy's Laws (named after Captain Edward Murphy, a naval engineer)

An effective time-management plan reserves time for the unexpected. We should plan for the best, but also prepare for the worst. A good plan includes a buffer zone or safety net of extra (unscheduled) time to accommodate unforeseen developments and unexpected emergencies. Just as we should have extra funds in our savings account to accommodate unexpected expenses (e.g., car repairs or medical treatments), we should reserve extra time in our schedule to accommodate tasks that end up taking more time than we budgeted for, as well as for tasks that may unexpectedly crop up (e.g., handling a family emergency).

An effective time-management plan should schedule time for both work and play. A time-management plan shouldn't consist only of a dry and daunting list of work tasks that have be done; it should also include things that are fun to do. The plan shouldn't turn us into robotic workaholics, but contain a balanced blend of work tasks and activities that allow us to relax, recreate, refuel, and recharge.

This balance may be created by suggesting to students that they follow a daily "8-8-8 rule": 8 hours for sleep, 8 hours for school and 8 hours for other activities. They are more likely to faithfully execute a time-management plan that includes play time along with work time, and if they use their play activities as rewards for completing their work tasks.

> If a time-management plan includes things we *like* to do, we're more likely to do the things we *have* to do.

From my perspective, time management is about efficiently accomplishing the necessary things in the time you've got so that the free time you've allotted is stress free.

—Peer leader

Reflection 6.5

What relaxing and recreational activities do you engage in to maintain work-play balance in your life? Do you develop an intentional plan for engaging in these activities on a regular basis? (If not, why not?)

An effective time-management plan should have some flexibility. The plan shouldn't be rigid and unalterable, but should have the flexibility to be modified if necessary. Just as work commitments and family responsibilities can crop up unexpectedly, so, too, can fun activities. A good time-management plan should allow us the freedom to take advantage of enjoyable opportunities that may emerge spontaneously. However, *bending* the plan doesn't mean *breaking* the plan. If play time is substituted for work time, the work time needs to be rescheduled for another time. In other words, we can borrow time, but not steal it.

Helping Students Make Productive Use of "Free Time" Outside the Classroom

Compared to high school, college students are expected to put in a lot more independent work outside of class. Thus, using out-of-class time strategically and productively is critical to college success. Listed below are strategies you can share with students to help them work independently and in advance of exams and assignments. Building time for each of these activities into their time-management plan will enable them to make more productive use of their out-of-class time and strengthen their overall academic performance

- Review **lecture notes** from the last class before the next class. After taking class notes, students often don't look at them again until it's close to test time. Don't let your students fall into this habit; instead, urge them to review their notes regularly between class sessions, rewrite any notes that may have been sloppily written the first time, and reorganize their notes so that different bits of information relating to the same point are put in the same place. Lastly, if they find any information gaps or confusing points in their notes, encourage them to seek out the course instructor or a trusted classmate to clear them up before the next class session.

If students take some time to review and refine their course notes between class sessions, they can build mental bridges between classes, helping them connect information they will learn in the upcoming class with information they learned in the previous class.

- **Complete reading assignments pertaining to an upcoming lecture topic *before* that topic is discussed in class.** This will make lectures easier to understand and enable students to participate more effectively in class (e.g., ask meaningful questions and make informed contributions to class discussions).

- **Review and take notes on information highlighted in assigned readings.** Students often do not review material they've highlighted in their reading until they're about to be tested on that material. Encourage students to reflect on their reading highlights and take short notes on them in advance of exams; this will reduce the need for last-minute cramming and give them time to clear up confusing information found in the reading with a fellow classmate or with the course instructor.

- **Integrate class notes and reading notes relating to the same point or concept.** Advise students to connect information in their lecture notes with information in their reading notes that pertain to the same idea and get them in the same place (e.g., on the same index card).

- **Use a "part-to-whole" study method.** Encourage students to study in advance of exams by breaking the material into small parts (pieces) and studying those parts in short, separate study sessions. This strategy will enable them to avoid last-minute cramming and enable them to use their last study session right before the exam to review the "whole"—all the parts they previously studied. (For more details about the part-to-whole study method, see chapter 7, p. 208.)

- **Work on large, long-term assignments due at the end of the term by breaking them into smaller short-term tasks, and complete them in successive stages throughout the term.** For instance, if students have a large term paper due toward the end of the term, advise them to divide it into the following smaller tasks and complete each of them in separate installments.
  1. Search for and decide on a topic.
  2. Locate sources of information on the topic.
  3. Organize information obtained from the sources into categories.
  4. Develop an outline of the paper's major points, including the order or sequence in which they'll be covered.
  5. Construct a first draft of the paper.
  6. Review and refine the first draft (and, if necessary, write additional drafts).
  7. Complete a final draft.
  8. Proofread the final draft for spelling and grammatical errors before turning it in.

Reflection 6.6

Do you think most students make productive use of their time between classes? If not, what could or should they be doing instead of what they're currently doing?

Encourage students to carry *portable* schoolwork with them during the day—work they can bring with them and get done in anyplace at anytime. This will enable them to take "dead time" (time spent doing nothing), such as waiting for appointments or transportation, and resurrect it into "live" (productive) time.

Helping Students Combat Procrastination

A major enemy of effective time management is procrastination. Research indicates that 80-95% of college students procrastinate (Steel, 2007) and almost 50% report that they procrastinate consistently (Onwuegbuzie, 2000). Procrastination is such a serious issue that some college campuses have opened "procrastination centers" especially for students experiencing this problem (Burka & Yuen, 2008).

> *Many people take no care of their money 'til they come nearly to the end of it, and others do just the same with their time.*
> —Johann Wolfgang von Goethe, German poet, dramatist, and author of the epic *Faust*

Instead of abiding by the proverb, "Why put off till tomorrow what can be done today?" the procrastinator's philosophy is just the opposite: "Why do today what can be put off till tomorrow?" Adopting this philosophy leads to a perpetual pattern of postponing what needs to be done until the last possible moment, forcing the procrastinator to rush frantically to finish work just before the deadline and turn in work that is inferior or incomplete (or turn in nothing at all).

Myths That Promote Procrastination

To have any hope of putting a stop to procrastination, students need to let go of two popular myths (misconceptions) about time and performance. If your students believe in either of the following myths, challenge them to think otherwise.

Myth 1. "I work better under pressure" (on the day or night before something is due). Procrastinators often confuse desperation with motivation. Their rationale for thinking that they work *better* under pressure is really not a rationale at all; instead, it's a rationalization used to justify the fact they *only* work under pressure—when they're forced to because they've run out of time and are under the gun of a looming deadline.

It's certainly true that when we're under the pressure of a deadline, we're more likely to *start* working and work *faster*, but that doesn't mean we're working *smarter*, more *effectively,* or producing work of better *quality*. Because procrastinators repeatedly play "beat the clock," they focus more on beating the buzzer than delivering their best shot. The typical result is a work product of poorer quality than they could have produced if they began working sooner.

> *Haste makes waste.*
> —Benjamin Franklin

Myth 2. "Studying in advance is a waste of time because you'll forget it all by test time." Procrastinators use this belief to justify putting off all studying until the night before an exam. As will be discussed in chapter 7, studying that's distributed (spread out) over time is more effective than massed (crammed) studying. Furthermore, last-minute studying can lead to pulling "late-nighters" or "all-nighters." This fly-by-night practice deprives the brain of dream sleep (a.k.a. REM sleep), which retains information and reduces stress (Hobson, 1988; Voelker, 2004).

Working under time pressure also increases performance pressure because it leaves procrastinators with little time to seek help on their work and no time to accommodate last-minute emergencies or random catastrophes.

Strategies for Preventing and Overcoming Procrastination

Listed below are strategies you can share with students to help them reduce procrastination and prevent it from happening in the first place.

Consistently use effective time-management strategies. It's been found that procrastinators are less likely to procrastinate when they convert their intentions or vows ("I swear I'm going to start tomorrow") into concrete action plans (Gollwitzer, 1999; Gollwitzer & Sheeran, 2006). Studies show that if people consistently use effective time-management plans and practices (such as those cited in this chapter) and apply them to tasks that they procrastinate on, their procrastination habit begins to fade and is replaced by more productive work habits (Ainslie, 1975; Baumeister, Heatherton, & Tice, 1994).

Organization matters. Research indicates that disorganization contributes to procrastination (Steel, 2007). If students' workspaces and work materials are well organized and ready to go, they're more likely to get going and start working. Having the right materials in the right place at the right time not only makes it easier to begin work, it also helps to maintain momentum by reducing the need to stop, find stuff that's needed to continue working, and then restart the work process all over again. For procrastinators, anything that delays the start of their work, or interrupts their work once it's begun, can supply them with just enough time (and the right excuse) to postpone working.

> The less time and effort it takes to start working and continue working, the more likely it is that work will be started, continued, and completed.

A simple, yet effective, way for students to organize their college work materials is to develop a personal file system. Encourage them to start filing (storing) materials from separate courses in separate notebooks or folders (paper or electronic). This enables them to keep all materials related to the same course in the same place and gives them immediate access to these materials when they need them. A file system not only helps get students organized, it reduces the risk of procrastination by reducing the time (and effort) it takes for students to get started. It also reduces stress that can be triggered by the unsettling feeling of having things "all over the place." Instead, everything is "in place" and set to go.

Location matters. Effective time and task management includes effective management of one's work environment. *Where* work takes place can influence *whether* the work is begun and gets done. Working in an environment that minimizes distractions and maximizes concentration reduces the risk of procrastination (Steel, 2007). Encourage students to arrange their work environment to minimize social distractions (e.g., friends nearby who are not working) and social media distractions (e.g., texting or tweeting). Better yet, suggest they remove everything from their work site that's not related to the work they're doing. A student's risk for procrastination can also be reduced by working in an environment that includes positive social-support networks—e.g., working with a group of motivated students who make work more attractive, less distractive, and more productive.

Make the start of work as inviting or appealing as possible. For many procrastinators, initiating work—getting off the starting blocks—is their stumbling block. They experience what's known as "start-up stress"—when they're about to start a task, they start having negative feelings about it—expecting it to be difficult, stressful, or boring (Burka & Yuen, 2008).

The secret to getting ahead is getting started.

—Mark Twain (Samuel Clemens), acclaimed American humorist and author

If your students have trouble starting their work, encourage them to sequence their work tasks in a way that allows them to work first on tasks they're likely to find more interesting or are more likely to do successfully. Beginning with these tasks can give students a "jump-start," enabling them to overcome inertia and create momentum. Once this initial momentum is generated, they can ride it and use it as motivational energy to attack less appealing work they encounter later in the work sequence, which often ends up being less onerous or anxiety-provoking than they thought it would be. Many times, the anticipation of a daunting task is worse than the task itself. In one major study of college students who didn't start a project until just before its due date, it was found that that they experienced anxiety and guilt while they were procrastinating, but once they began working, these negative emotions subsided and were replaced by more positive feelings of progress and accomplishment (McCance & Pychyl, 2003).

Did you ever dread doing something, and then it turned out to take only about 20 minutes to do?

—Conversation between two college students overheard in a coffee shop

If you know students who have trouble beginning their work due to start-up stress, you might also advise them to start their work at a place they find pleasant and relaxing while doing something they find pleasant and relaxing (e.g., working in their favorite coffee shop while sipping their favorite beverage).

If your students do not have trouble starting their work, but lose motivation before completing their work, suggest they schedule easier and more interesting work tasks *in the middle or toward the end* of their planned work time. Some procrastinators have difficulty starting work; others have trouble continuing and finishing the work they've started (Pierro et al., 2011). As previously mentioned, if students have trouble beginning their work, it might be best for them to start with tasks they find easier or more interesting. On the other hand, if their procrastination involves stopping before completing the work they've started, it might be better for them to attack easier and more interesting tasks at a later point in their work sequence—at a time when their interest and energy normally tends to fade. Knowing that there are more stimulating and manageable tasks ahead of them can also provide these students with an incentive for completing the less enjoyable and more difficult tasks first.

I'm very good at starting things but often have trouble keeping a sustained effort.

—First-year college student

If students are close to completing a task, encourage them to "go for the kill"—finish it then and there—rather than stopping and going back to it later. As the old saying goes, "There's no time like the present." Continuing to work on a task that's already been started capitalizes on the momentum that's already been generated. In contrast, postponing work on a task that's near completion and going back to it again later means that the student has to overcome start-up inertia and regenerate momentum all over again.

There's another advantage of finishing a task that's already been started: it creates a sense of *closure*—the feeling of personal accomplishment and self-satisfaction that comes with knowing we've "closed the deal." Seeing a task checked off as completed serves as a visible sign of achievement that can motivate us to keep going and complete the next task.

Divide large work tasks into smaller, bite-sized pieces. Work becomes less overwhelming and less stressful when it's handled in small chunks or segments. Procrastination relating to large work tasks can be reduced by using a "divide and conquer" strategy—divide the large task into smaller, more manageable subtasks and tackle the small tasks one at a time. By dividing a large task into smaller pieces, students can take quick jabs at the tall task, poke holes in it, and whittle down its size with each successive punch. This step-by-step approach reduces the pressure of having to deliver one, big knockout punch right before the final bell (deadline or due date). Remind students not to underestimate the power of short work sessions. These sessions can be more productive than marathon sessions because it's easier to maintain concentration and energy for a more limited period of time.

> *To eat an elephant, first cut it into small pieces.*
> —Author unknown

Author's Experience

The two biggest projects I've had to complete in my life were writing my doctoral thesis and writing this textbook. The strategy that enabled me to compete both of these large tasks was to set short-term deadlines for myself (e.g., complete 5-10 pages each week). I psyched myself into thinking that these little, self-imposed due dates were really drop-dead deadlines that I had to meet. This strategy allowed me to divide one monstrous chore into a series of smaller, more manageable mini-tasks. It was like taking a huge, hard-to-digest meal and breaking it into small, bite-sized pieces that I could easily ingest and gradually digest over time.

— *Joe Cuseo*

Reflection 6.7

a) Would you say you're a procrastinator?

b) If yes, do you think you procrastinate to such a degree that it reduces the quality of your work or adds to your level of stress?

c) How do you think most students would answer the above two questions?

P sychological Causes of Procrastination

In some cases, procrastination doesn't simply result from poor time-management habits but has deeper psychological roots. People can and do use procrastination as a psychological strategy for protecting their self-image or self-esteem. One of these strategies is called *self-handicapping*, which some procrastinators use (often unconsciously) to "handicap" themselves by giving themselves a limited amount of time to prepare for and complete work tasks. This way, if their work performance turns out to be less than spectacular, they can always conclude (rationalize) it was because they were performing under a handicap—lack of time (Chu & Cho, 2005; Rhodewalt &Vohs, 2005). For example, if a student receives a low grade on a test or paper, he can "save face" (self-esteem) by saying that he had the ability or intelligence to earn a high grade, but just didn't put much time into it. Better yet, if he happens to get a good grade—despite his last-minute, last-ditch effort—it proves just how smart he is because he was able to earn a high grade without putting in much time at all! Thus, self-handicapping creates a fail-safe or win-win scenario that always protects the procrastinator's self-image.

In addition to self-handicapping, listed below are other psychological factors that have been found to contribute to procrastination.

Procrastinators would rather be seen as lacking in effort than lacking in ability.

—Joseph Ferrari, professor of psychology and procrastination researcher

- **Perfectionism.** The procrastinator has unrealistically high personal standards or expectations, which leads to the belief that it's better to postpone work, or not do the work at all, than to risk doing it less than perfectly (Kachgal, Hansel, & Nuter, 2001).
- **Fear of failure.** The procrastinator feels that turning in work and getting negative feedback on it is worse than turning in nothing at all (Burka & Yuen, 2008; Solomon & Rothblum, 1984).
- **Fear of success.** The procrastinator fears that doing well will show others that she's capable of performing at a high level, which will create expectations that she continue to maintain this high level of performance (Beck, Koons, & Milgram, 2000; Ellis & Knaus, 2002).
- **Indecisiveness.** The procrastinator has difficulty making decisions in general, including decisions about what to do first, when to do it, or whether to do it (Anderson, 2003; Steel, 2007).
- **Thrill seeking.** The procrastinator loves the adrenaline rush associated with rushing to get things done just before a deadline (Szalavitz, 2003).

Striving for excellence motivates you; striving for perfection is demoralizing.

—Harriet Braiker, psychologist and best-selling author

When you're given a positive label, you're afraid of losing it, and when you're hit with a negative label, you're afraid of deserving it.

—Carol Dweck, professor of Psychology, Stanford University

If any of these psychological issues is the root of procrastination, it needs to be uprooted and dealt with before the problem can be solved. This may require that you refer the student to a counseling psychologist (either on or off campus) who is professionally trained to deal with emotional issues. (For effective referral strategies, see chapter 3, pp. 86-88.)

Whether the cause is lack of time-management skills or deeper psychological issues, procrastination continues to be a problem for many students and one that can have significant impact on their success in college. Be on the lookout for it and be ready to help students combat it.

■nternet Resources

For additional information to share with students on managing time and preventing procrastination, consult the following websites:

Time-Management Strategies for Students
www.studygs.net/timman.htm
https://pennstatelearning.psu.edu/time-management

Beating Procrastination
www.mindtools.com/pages/article/newHTE_96.htm
https://success.oregonstate.edu/learning/stop-procrastinating

References

Ainslie, G. (1975). Specious reward: A behavioral theory of impulsiveness and impulse control. *Psychological Bulletin, 82,* 463–496.

Anderson, C. J. (2003). The psychology of doing nothing: Forms of decision avoidance result from reason and emotion. *Psychological Bulletin, 129,* 139–167.

Baumeister, R. F., Heatherton, T. F., & Tice, D. M. (1994). *Losing control: How and why people fail at self-regulation.* San Diego, CA: Academic Press.

Beck, B. L., Koons, S. R., & Milgram, D. L. (2000). Correlates and consequences of behavioral procrastination: the effects of academic procrastination, self-consciousness, self-esteem, and self-handicapping. *Journal of Social Behavior and Personality, 15,* 3-13.

Burka, J. B., & Yuen, L. M. (2008). *Procrastination: Why you do it, what to do about it now.* Cambridge, MA: De Capo Press.

Chu, A. H. C., & Cho, J. N. (2005). Rethinking procrastination: Positive effects of "active" procrastination behavior on attitudes and performance. *The Journal of Social Psychology, 145*(3), 245-264.

Covey, S. R. (2004). *Seven habits of highly effective people* (3rd ed.). New York: Fireside.

Currey, M. (2013). *Daily rituals: How artists work.* New York: Knopf.

Ellis, A. & Knaus, W. J. (2002) *Overcoming procrastination* (Rev. ed.). New York, NY: New American Library.

Erickson, B. L., & Strommer, D. W. (2005). Inside the first-year classroom: Challenges and constraints. In J. L. Upcraft, J. N. Gardner, & B. O. Barefoot (Eds.), *Challenging and supporting the first-year student* (pp. 241–256). San Francisco: Jossey-Bass.

Goldsmith, E. B. (2010). *Resource management for individuals and families* (4th ed.). Upper Saddle River, NJ: Prentice Hall.

Gollwitzer, P. M. (1999). Implementation intentions: Strong effects of simple plans. *American Psychologist, 54*(7), 493-503.

Gollwitzer, P. M., & Sheeran, P. (2006). Implementation intentions and goal achievement: A meta-analysis of effects and processes. *Advances in Experimental Social Psychology, 38,* 69-119.

Gupta, R., Hershey, D. A., & Gaur, J. (2012). Time perspective and procrastination in the workplace: An empirical investigation. *Current Psychology, 31*(2), 195-211.

Harriott, J., & Ferrari, J. R. (1996). Prevalence of chronic procrastination among samples of adults. *Psychological Reports, 73,* 873-877.

HERI (Higher Education Research Institute). (2014). *Your first college year survey 2014.* Los Angeles: Cooperative Institutional Research Program, University of California-Los Angeles.

Hobson, J. A. (1988). *The dreaming brain.* New York: Basic Books.

Janata, J. (2008). *How does time management reduce stress, and what are some tips for managing time better?* Retrieved from https://abcnews.go.com/Health/StressCoping/story?id=4672836

Johnson, W. B., & Ridley, C. R. (2008).*The elements of mentoring: The 65 key elements of mentoring.* New York: St. Martin's Press

Kachgal, M. M., Hansen, L. S., & Nutter, K. T. (2001). Academic procrastination prevention/intervention: Strategies and recommendations. *Journal of Developmental Education, 25*(1), 2-12.

Lakein, A. (1973). *How to get control of your time and your life.* New York: New American Library.

Light, R. J. (2001). *Making the most of college: Students speak their minds.* Cambridge, MA: Harvard University Press.

McCance, N., & Pychyl, T. A. (2003, August). *From task avoidance to action: An experience sampling study of undergraduate students' thoughts, feelings and coping strategies in relation to academic procrastination.* Paper presented at the Third Annual Conference for Counseling Procrastinators in the Academic Context, University of Ohio, Columbus, Ohio.

Morgenstern, J. (2004). *Time management from the inside out: The foolproof system for taking control of your schedule—and your life* (2nd ed.). New York: Henry Holt & Co.

Myers, D. G. (1993). *The pursuit of happiness: Who is happy—and why?* New York: Morrow.

Myers, D. G. (2000). *The American paradox: Spiritual hunger in an age of plenty.* New Haven, CT: Yale University Press.

Onwuegbuzie, A. J. (2000). Academic procrastinators and perfectionistic tendencies among graduate students. *Journal of Social Behavior and Personality, 15,* 103–109.

Pierro, A., Giacomantonio, M., Pica, G., Kruglanski, A. W., & Higgins, E. T. (2011). On the psychology of time in action: regulatory mode orientations and procrastination. *Journal of Personality and Social Psychology, 101*(6), 1317-1331.

Rhodewalt, F., & Vohs, K. D. (2005). Defensive strategies, motivation, and the self. In A. Elliot & C. Dweck (Eds.). *Handbook of competence and motivation* (pp. 548-565). New York: Guilford Press.

Solomon, L. J., & Rothblum, E. D. (1984). Academic procrastination: Frequency and cognitive-behavioral correlates. *Journal of Counseling Psychology, 31*(4), 503-509.

Steel, P. (2007). The nature of procrastination: A meta-analytic and theoretical review of quintessential self-regulatory failure. *Psychological Bulletin, 133*(1), 65-94.

Szalavitz, M. (2003). Tapping potential: Stand and deliver. *Psychology Today* (July/ August), 50-54.

Voelker, R. (2004). Stress, sleep loss, and substance abuse create potent recipe for college depression. *Journal of the American Medical Association, 291,* 2177–2179.

Exercise 6.1 Quote Reflections

Review the sidebar quotes contained in this chapter and select two that you think would be especially valuable to share with the students you lead or mentor.

For each quote, write a short statement explaining why you chose it.

Exercise 6.2 Time Analysis Inventory

1. Go to the following website: pennstatelearning.psu.edu/resources/study-tips/time-mgt
   Click on the link titled "time-management exercise."

2. Complete the time management exercise at this site. The exercise asks you to estimate the amount of time per day or week that you engage in various activities (e.g., sleeping, employment, and commuting). When you enter the amount of time devoted to these activities, the website will automatically compute the total number of remaining hours you have available in the week for academic work and co-curricular experiences (e.g., leadership and mentoring).

3. After completing your entries, answer the following questions (or provide your best estimate).

   a) How many hours per week will you devote to academic work?

   b) How many hours per week will you devote to peer leadership activities and other co-curricular experiences?

4. Ask the students you lead or mentor to complete this exercise as well.

Exercise 6.3 Procrastination Self-Assessment

1. Go to https://www.psychologytoday.com/tests/career/procrastination-test-abridged. Take the self-assessment questionnaire at this site.

2. What do the results suggest about your overall tendency to procrastinate?

3. In the areas where your answers indicated tendencies toward procrastination, what could you start doing now to reduce those tendencies?

4. In the areas where your answers indicate that you do *not* procrastinate, what behaviors do you engage in or strategies do you use to prevent procrastination? Do you think any of these strategies could be shared with the students you mentor to help them combat procrastination?

Exercise 6.4 Case Study

Procrastination: The Vicious Cycle

Delayla has a major paper due at the end of the term. It's now past midterm and she still hasn't begun working on it. She keeps telling herself, "I should have started sooner" but continues to postpone her work and is now beginning to feel anxious and guilty. To relieve her anxiety and guilt, Delayla starts doing other tasks instead, such as cleaning her room and organizing files on her computer. These tasks keep her busy, take her mind off the term paper, and give her the feeling that she's getting something accomplished. Time continues to pass and the deadline for the paper grows dangerously close. Delayla now finds herself in the position of having lots of work to do and little time left to do it.

Adapted from *Procrastination: Why You Do It, and What to Do About It* (Burka &Yuen, 2008)

Reflection and Discussion Questions:

1. What do you expect Delayla will do at this point? Why?

2. What grade do you think she'll end up receiving on her paper?

3. Can you relate to this student's experience, or know students who have similar experiences?

4. Other than simply starting sooner, what else could Delayla (and other procrastinators like her) have done to break this procrastination cycle?

Exercise 6.5 Strategy Reflections

Review the strategies recommended for *preventing and overcoming procrastination* on pp. 180–182. Select three strategies that you think students would be most receptive to learning about and putting into practice.

CHAPTER 7

Academic Coaching

Helping Students Learn Deeply and Think Critically

Reflection 7.1

What would you say is the key difference between learning and memorizing?

Chapter Purpose and Preview

This chapter prepares you to be a "learning coach"—a peer educator who helps students learn deeply, think at a higher level, and achieve peak levels of academic performance. The chapter provides specific, research-based strategies you can share with and model for students that relate to the key academic tasks they're expected to perform in college, such as: taking lecture notes, completing reading assignments, studying and test-taking. Equipping students with these strategies will help them acquire learning and thinking habits they can apply across the curriculum and throughout life.

What Is Deep Learning and Why Is It Important?

Learning is the fundamental mission of all colleges and universities, and it's something that doesn't stop after graduation. It's a lifelong process that is essential for personal and professional success in the 21st century. The continued growth in information technology, coupled with increasing global interdependence, is creating a high demand for college graduates who have "learned how to learn" and who can apply their learning skills throughout life in different occupational and cultural contexts (Niles & Harris-Bowlsbey, 2012; SECFHE, 2006).

When students learn deeply, they dive below the surface of shallow memorization and build mental bridges between what they are learning and what they already know (David, 2015; Piaget, 1978; Vygotsky, 1978). Deep learning doesn't take place by the passive absorption of information into the brain—as if it were a sponge. Instead, it involves actively building new ideas onto ideas that are already stored in the brain. When this happens, memorizing isolated facts and bits of information is transformed into a deeper learning process that involves acquisition of *conceptual knowledge*—networks of connected ideas that are stored in the brain in the form of actual physical (neurological) networks of brain cells (LeDoux, 2002). (See **Figure 7.1**.)

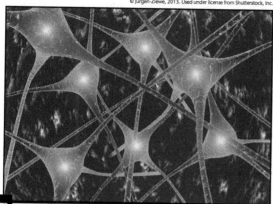

Figure 7.1   Deep learning involves making connections between what we're trying to learn and what we already know. When we learn something deeply, it's stored in the brains as part of an interconnected network of brain cells.

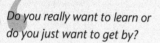

Do you really want to learn or do you just want to get by?

—Question posed by a student to another student in a coffee shop

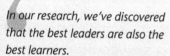

In our research, we've discovered that the best leaders are also the best learners.

—Kouzes & Posner, *Student Leadership Planner*

Studies suggest that most college students are not in the habit of engaging in deep learning (Arum & Roksa, 2011; Kuh, 2005; Nathan, 2005). They show up for class most of the time, copy down some notes, highlight information in their textbooks, memorize what they think they'll be tested on and regurgitate what they've memorized on exams. Students may get by with these practices, but they are not learning deeply, not retaining what they learn beyond test time, and not applying what they learn to their lives.

Change is needed to create a culture of deep learning on college campuses. As a peer leader, you can be a key catalyst in this change process by serving as a *learning coach* who motivates, models, and empowers students to develop the attributes of a deep, lifelong learner. All student leaders, regardless of their specific leadership role on campus, can embrace the role of learning coach by: (a) sharing their knowledge of effective leaning strategies with students, (b) modeling effective learning practices for students to emulate, (c) supplying students with feedback on whether their learning habits are effective, and (d) inspiring students to value learning and continue learning throughout life.

> The word "educate" derives from the Latin root "educere" meaning to "bring out" or "lead forth." Thus, leading and educating are closely related processes; both involve promoting positive change in others.

Reflection 7.2

Do you think most students on your campus engage in deep learning? What would you say is the major change that students must make in their approach to learning in order for them to become deep learners?

Sharing and Modeling Effective Learning Strategies

Academically successful students invest significant time and energy at each of the following stages of the learning process: (1) acquiring information they need to know (e.g., by listening actively and taking quality notes in class and completing assigned readings outside of class), (2) converting the information they acquire into knowledge by learning it deeply (e.g., using effective study strategies), and (3) reflecting on the knowledge they acquire and thinking critically about it (e.g., evaluating it and applying it). You can serve as a learning coach at each of these stages in the deep-learning process by sharing and modeling the following strategies.

Coaching for Note-Taking

Starting in the very first week of the term, college students are expected to listen actively to lectures and take quality notes in class. Studies show that most test questions (and test answers) on college exams come from professors' lecture notes (Cuseo et al., 2016). As a learning coach, you can remind students to take note-taking seriously and supply them with specific strategies for taking notes effectively.

You may encounter students who think that if they write down notes in class it will interfere with their ability to pay attention to what their instructor is saying. If you hear students saying this, point out to them that research consistently shows that college students who record and review their own notes taken in class earn higher scores on tests of their ability to retain that information than do students who do not take notes or review notes provided for them (Jairam & Kiewra, 2009; Kiewra, 2005). You can also point out research showing that when students are tested for their comprehension and retention of key concepts presented in lectures, those students who take notes in longhand outperform students who type notes on a keyboard (Mueller & Oppenheimer, 2014). This is likely due to the fact that the physical movements made when writing by hand leave a stronger motor (muscle) memory trace in the brain, which deepens learning and strengthens retention of the information being written down (Herbert, 2014).

See Box 7.1 for specific strategies you can share with students to boost the quality of their note-taking. In addition to sharing these effective note-taking strategies, you can offer to review the notes that students take in class and provide them with feedback. Or, better yet, you could offer to attend a class session with them, take notes yourself, and compare their notes with yours. (Naturally, seek the professor's permission first.)

Box 7.1

Top Tips to Share with Students on Lecture Listening and Note-Taking

1. **Get organized.** Bring the right equipment to class. Get a separate notebook for each class, write your name on it, date each class session, and store all class handouts in it.
2. **Get to class on time.** During the first few minutes of class, instructors often share valuable information—such as reviews, previews, and important reminders.
3. **Get in the right frame of mind.** Come to class with the attitude that you're there to pick your instructor's brain, pick up answers to test questions, and pick up points to build up your course grade.
4. **Get in the right position.**
   - The ideal place to sit: "front and center" (of the room)—where you're in the best position to hear and see what's going on.
   - The ideal posture to adopt: upright and leaning forward. The body influences the mind, so if the body is in an alert and ready position, the mind is likely to follow suit.
   - The ideal social position to occupy: a seat near classmates who will not distract you, but motivate you to listen actively and take notes aggressively.
5. **Get it down—in writing.** Actively look, listen, and record important points from start to finish of class. Remember that college professors do not record all important lecture information on the board or include it on their PowerPoint slides. They expect students to listen carefully for important ideas and make note of them on their own.

If you're not sure if information being delivered during a lecture is important and should be written down, use the following rule: When in doubt, write it out; it's better to have it and not need it than to need it and not have it.

Studies show that writing improves students' attention to, and retention of, information presented during lectures. In addition, writing leaves a visible (written) record of information that can be reviewed and studied later. (You can't study information you have no record of.)

6. **Finish strong.** During the last few minutes of class, instructors often share valuable information, such as timely reminders, reviews, and previews.

7. **Stick around.** When class ends, resist the temptation to immediately bolt out of the room. If possible, hang out for a while and quickly review your notes (alone or with a classmate). This quick end-of-class review helps the brain lock-in and retain information it's just received. During your end-of-class review, if there are gaps or confusing points in your notes, try to catch the instructor after class to clear them up.

Using the above strategies is particularly important in larger classes where students are likely to feel more anonymous, less accountable, and less engaged.

Finish class with a rush of attention, not a rush out the door!

The Cornell Note-Taking System

This method of note-taking was first developed by a college professor at Cornell University (Pauk, 1962). Frustrated by his students' poor test scores, he designed a system that students could use to take better notes in class and later use the notes they took to better prepare for exams. Since he taught at Cornell University, his method came to be called the Cornell Note-Taking System; it has become one of the most well known and frequently recommended college note-taking methods. Listed below are its key steps.

Steps:

• On a single 8½ x 11 page of notepaper, draw a vertical line about 2½ inches from the left edge of the page and a horizontal line about 2 inches from the bottom edge of the page (as depicted in the scaled-down illustration below). This creates three separate spaces—labeled below as areas A, B, and C.

```
              ← 8½" →

  ← 2½" →  │          ← 6" →

           │
           │
           │
           │
           │
           │
           │
           │
           │
           │              ↑
           │              9"        Area A
  Area C   │
           │              ↓
           │
           │
           │
           │
  - - - - -│- - - - - - - - - - - - - -
   ↑       │
   2"      │                Area B
   ↓       │
```

- Use area A (right side of the vertical line) to record notes during lectures.
- Use area B (bottom of page) to summarize the main points—which should be done as soon as possible after class.
- Use area C (left side of the page) to formulate questions about the material after class. Use the lecture notes taken in areas A and B to answer the questions in area C.

After students have formulated their questions, they can then quiz themselves, team up with a classmate to quiz one another, or go to their professor to ask if the questions they created are relevant and represent the type of higher-level thinking the instructor expects them to engage in on exams and assignments (see pp. 218-219 for a list of higher-level thinking questions that students could apply to information contained in their class notes).

The Cornell method of note taking promotes deep learning by prompting students to reflect on their notes and by challenging them to restate the material in their own words—which ensures they're not simply memorizing it, but truly understanding it. The Cornell method is an effective note-taking strategy; however, it's not the only one. Another effective strategy for summarizing notes is in the form of concept maps or "mind maps" that make diagrammatic connections among key concepts. (For an example, see **Figure 7.2.**)

Whatever particular note-taking method students choose to use, the most important thing is that they fully commit to an approach that actively involves them in the process of taking notes, followed by a reflective review of the notes they have taken. As a learning coach, you can help students develop this commitment.

6

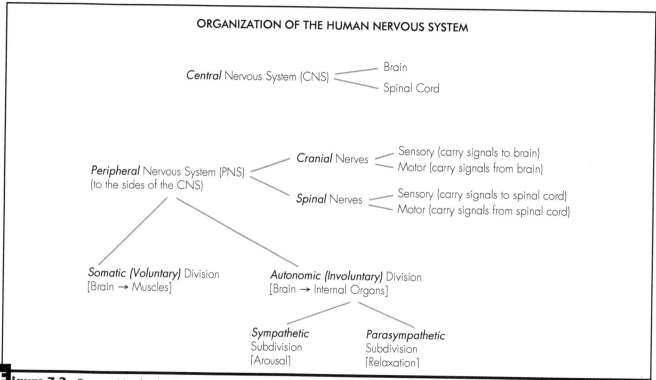

Figure 7.2   Concept Map for the Human Nervous System

Author's Experience When I was in college, I didn't give much thought about learning strategies, such as note-taking methods. However, I always attended classes and took thorough notes. Not only did taking notes help me review the lecture material later, it kept me attentive while in class. Later, when I became a graduate student, I began teaching a course on college-success strategies and learned more about the learning process and effective methods for taking lecture notes (for instance, the Cornell note-taking system). I began to employ this method as a learner in my graduate classes while teaching them to my students in my college-success course. That's when I truly realized: Wow, this stuff really works!

— *Greg Metz*

Reflection 7.3

Do you think the majority of new college students know the importance of:

(a) attending class consistently?

(b) taking notes consistently in class?

(c) reviewing notes from their last class prior to their next class?

Do you see yourself being able to influence students' attitudes or habits with respect to the above three behaviors? If yes, how?

Coaching for Reading

Reading assignments in college are likely to be lengthier and more challenging than those given in high school and college students are expected to do the assigned reading entirely on their own. Not surprisingly, college reading research shows that students who complete their assigned readings earn higher course grades (Sappington, Kinsey, & Munsayac, 2002).

Information contained in assigned readings ranks right behind information from lectures as a source of test questions on college exams (Brown, 1988; Cuseo et al., 2016). College students are likely to find questions on exams about information contained in reading assignments that their professors didn't talk extensively about in class, or didn't even mention in class. College professors may also expect students to relate or connect lecture material contained in lectures with material found in assigned reading. Furthermore, professors often deliver their lectures with the expectation that students have completed the assigned reading on the topic they're lecturing about. Consequently, if students haven't completed the reading before class, they're likely to have a harder time following lectures in class.

It's important to stress to students that assigned reading is not optional reading; it's required reading and they should do it according to the schedule their instructor has established. By completing assigned reading in a timely manner, students will: (a) be better positioned to understand class lectures, (b) improve the quality of their participation in class, and (c) obtain information that will appear on exams that's not covered in class.

As a learning coach, you can share and model the effective textbook reading strategies contained in Box 7.2

Box 7.2

Top Tips to Share with Students for Reading College Textbooks

1. **Get the textbooks required for your courses as soon as possible and get your reading assignments done on time.** If you're short on funds and cannot purchase the textbook right away, you can: (a) check to see if your instructor has placed a copy at the reserve desk in the library, (b) ask your instructor if there's an extra copy of the book available that you can use temporarily, or (c) speak with someone in the Business or Financial Office about whether you can get an emergency book scholarship.

2. **Read with the right equipment.**
   - Bring a writing tool (pen, pencil, or keyboard) to record important information about what you're reading and create a storage space (notebook or computer) where you can save and later retrieve that information to prepare for exams and assignments.
   - Have a dictionary (electronic or paper) nearby to look up the meaning of unfamiliar words. This practice not only helps you understand what you're reading, it also builds your vocabulary. Strengthening your vocabulary will improve your reading comprehension in all courses, as well as your performance on standardized tests—such as those required for admission to graduate and professional schools.

I recommend that you read the first chapters right away because college professors get started promptly with assigning certain readings. Classes in college move very fast because, unlike high school, you do not attend class five times a week but two or three times a week.

—Advice to new college students from a first-year student

- Check the back of your textbook for a glossary or list of key terms used in the book. Each college field of study (academic discipline) uses its own special language, and decoding that language is a stepping-stone to understanding its key ideas. The glossary that appears at the end of the textbook is more than an ancillary appendage; it's a valuable tool for helping you comprehend course concepts. In fact, it's a good idea to make a photocopy of the textbook's glossary and have it in hand while reading—as you would a dictionary. This will save you the time and trouble of holding your place on the page that you were reading, going to the back of the book to find the glossary, and then returning to the page you were reading.

3. **Get in the right position.** To maximize attention, sit upright. If you need light, have it come from behind you and over the side of your body that's opposite the hand you use to highlight and take notes. Arranging your source of light in this position will reduce glare and shadows on the pages you're reading, which can be distracting and fatiguing.

4. **Get a sneak preview.** Before jumping right in and starting to read a new chapter, take a little time to look at its boldface headings and any chapter outline, summary, and end-of-chapter questions that may accompany it. This preview will supply you with a map of the chapter, give you an aerial ("big picture") overview of its major ideas, and help you keep these key ideas in sight once you start reading the particular details. As the old saying goes, "Don't lose the forest for the trees."

5. **Finish your reading sessions with a short review of what you've read.** Rather than using the last few minutes to cover a few more pages, end it with a review of the information that you highlighted and noted as important. Most memory loss for information received takes place immediately after the brain processes (takes in) that information and starts doing something else. Thus, it's best to use the last minutes of a reading session to "lock in" the key information you've just read.

The goal of strategic reading is not simply to "cover" the assigned pages, but to *discover* the key ideas contained on those pages and retain those ideas.

Reflection 7.4

Based on your experience, do most college students consistently complete their reading assignments? As a peer leader and mentor, do you see yourself being able to have a positive influence on students' reading habits? If yes, how? If no, why not?

Strategic Studying: Coaching Students to Learn Deeply

Studying isn't a short sprint that takes place just before test time; it's more like a long-distance run that takes place over an extended period of time. Studying that takes place the night before an exam should be students' last step in a sequence of test-preparation steps that begins well before test time. These steps include: (a) taking accurate and complete notes in class, (b) doing the assigned reading, and (c) seeking help from professors or peers about any concepts contained in lectures or readings that are unclear or confusing. Once these steps have been taken, students are then positioned to study the information they've acquired and learn it deeply.

Described below is a series of study strategies you can share with students to promote deep and durable learning.

Give studying your undivided attention. The human attention span has limited capacity. We can devote all of it or part of it to whatever task we're engaging in at the moment. As the phrase "paying attention" suggests, we can pay in full or pay in part. If students engage in multiple tasks simultaneously, such as studying while also watching for texts or watching videos, each task consumes a part of their total attention span. Thus, studying receives their "divided" not "undivided" (full) attention.

Studies show that doing challenging academic work while multitasking divides up attention and drives down comprehension and retention.

Studies show that when humans multitask, they are not really able to pay equal and full attention to all tasks at the same time; instead, they divide up their attention by shifting it back and forth from one task to another (Howard, 2014). When this happens, performance on the task that's most complex or mentally demanding is the one that suffers the most (Crawford & Strapp, 1994). The brain cannot handle a challenging mental task while accommodating other tasks at the same time. For deep learning to take place, it needs uninterrupted processing and reflection time to create connections between neurons (brain cells) (Jensen, 2008).

Urge students to give study time their undivided attention. Suggest they unplug all electronic accessories. They can even use apps to help them do so (e.g., a cell-phone silencer). If they cannot commit to this recommendation, suggest they set aside a short block of time to check electronic messages after they've engaged in a certain amount of study time. This will allow social media to serve as a reward *after* studying, not as a distraction *while* studying.

Make meaningful associations. Deep learning doesn't take place through osmosis—passively soaking up information in exactly the same form as it appears in a textbook or lecture. Instead, it occurs when learners actively translate the infor-

> *You can do several things at once, but only if they are easy and undemanding. You are probably safe carrying on a conversation with a passenger while driving on an empty highway [but] you could not compute the product of 17 x 24 while making a left turn into dense traffic, and you certainly should not try.*
>
> —Daniel Kahneman, professor Emeritus of Psychology, and author of *Thinking Fast and Slow*

mation they receive into a form that's meaningful to them (Biggs & Tang, 2007; Mayer, 2002).

> **Deep learning does not take place through the simple *transmission* of information from teacher or textbook *to* learner; it involves effortful *transformation* of information into knowledge *by* the learner.**

The human brain is naturally wired to convert unfamiliar information into a form that's familiar and meaningful. You can demonstrate this to students by having them read the following passage:

> *Aoccdrnig to rscheearch at Cmabridge Uinverstisy, it deos't mattaer in what order the ltteers in a word are, the only iprmoetnt thing is that the frist and lsat ltteer be at the rghit pclae. The rset can be a total mses and you can still raed it wouthit a porbelm. This is bcusae the human mind deos not raed ervey lteter by istlef, but the word as a wlohe. Amzanig huh?*

Notice how natural it was for you to transform these meaningless, misspelled words into familiar, meaningful words that were already stored in your brain. This exercise can be used to show students that whenever they are learning something new, they should capitalize on the brain's natural meaning-making tendencies to find meaning in unfamiliar information by relating it to what they already know. For instance, if they're learning an unfamiliar academic term, before trying to beat the term into their brain through repetition and memorization, they should first attempt to find some meaning in the term that makes sense to them. One way to do so is by looking up the etymology or "root" of unfamiliar academic terms. For instance, suppose students are taking a biology course and studying the autonomic nervous system—the part of the nervous system that operates without our conscious awareness or voluntary control (e.g., heart and lungs). The meaning of this biological term is found in its prefix "auto," meaning self-controlling or "automatic"—as in automatic transmission. Once students find meaning in abstract terms, they can learn them faster and retain them longer than by trying to memorize them through sheer repetition.

If looking up the etymological root of an academic term still doesn't make it meaningful, students can make the term meaningful in other ways. For example, looking up the root of "artery" will reveal nothing about its meaning or purpose. However, by taking its first letter, "a," and having it stand for "*away*," it gives the term meaning (an *a*rtery carries blood *a*way from the heart). Thus, an unfamiliar term that would require repeated rehearsal to be remembered is transformed into a term that's immediately meaningful and forever memorable.

Another way students can make learning meaningful is by *comparing* or *contrasting* what they're learning with something they already know. Students can do this by getting in the habit of asking themselves the following questions:

(a) How is this idea similar to something I previously learned or already know? (Compare)

(b) How is this idea different from what I previously learned or already know? (Contrast)

Research indicates that asking these simple questions is a powerful learning strategy (Marzano, Pickering, & Pollock, 2001). It works because the new idea being learned becomes more meaningful when it's connected to something the learner already knows.

> **Deep learners dive below the shallow surface of memorization by connecting what they're currently learning to what they've previously learned.**

Organize related pieces of information into conceptual categories. Encourage students to integrate bits of information relating to the same topic or idea into separate categories. When ideas pertaining to the same point or concept are spread all over the place externally, they're likely to take the form internally (in our minds)—they're spread all over the place in the brain, are mentally disconnected, and are not deeply learned. Suggest to students that they get related ideas in the same place by getting them on the same index card under the same category heading. Index cards can work like a portable file cabinet. Each card functions as a separate file folder or hub in the wheel—connected to which are related pieces information—the spokes of the wheel.

> **Deep learners ask questions like: How can this specific piece of information be categorized or classified into a larger concept? How does this particular idea relate to or "fit into" a bigger picture?**

Distribute study time across separate study sessions. Deep learning depends not only on *how* we learn (our method), but also on *when* we learn (our timing). How students distribute or spread out their study time out across time is as important as how much total time they spend studying. For students of all abilities and ages, research consistently shows that distributing study time over several shorter sessions results in deeper learning and longer retention than loading all study time into one long session (Brown, Roediger, & McDaniel, 2014; Carey, 2014; Dunlosky et al., 2013).

Although cramming before exams is better than not studying at all, it's far less effective than spacing out studying across time. Advise students not to frantically cram all of their study time into a massive, one-shot session ("massed practice"), but to use *distributed practice*—"distribute" or spread out study time over several shorter sessions. Distributed practice improves learning and memory in two major ways:

- It minimizes loss of attention due to fatigue or boredom.
- It reduces mental interference by giving the brain some downtime to cool down and lock in information it has just processed (taken in) without having to process additional incoming information (Malmberg & Murnane, 2002; Murname & Shiffrin, 1991). Memory works like a muscle: After it's been exercised, if given some "cool down" time before it's exerted again, it builds greater strength (memory) for information it has been processing (Carey, 2014). On the other hand, if the brain's downtime is interfered with by the arrival of a new wave of information, it gets overloaded and is less able to retain information it's taking in. That's exactly what cram-

Hurriedly jam-packing a brain is akin to speed-packing a cheap suitcase—it holds its new load for a while, then most everything falls out.

—Benedict Carey, author, *How We Learn: Throw Out the Rule Book and Unlock Your Brain's Potential*

ming does—it overloads the brain with lots of information in a limited period of time. In contrast, distributed study does just the opposite—it uses shorter sessions with downtime in between sessions—giving the brain time to slow down and retain the information it previously processed (studied) and giving it the opportunity to move that information from short-term to long-term memory (Willis, 2006).

In addition, distributed study has emotional advantages: it's more motivating and less stressful than cramming. Students' motivation to study is likely to be stronger if they know they're going to be doing it for a short, manageable period of time rather than a long, exhausting stretch of time.

Reflection 7.5

Do you study in advance of exams or cram just before exams? How do you think most college students would answer this question?

Use the "part-to-whole" study method. This method of learning is a natural extension of the distributed practice strategy. It involves breaking up the material to be learned into smaller parts, studying those parts in separate sessions in advance of the exam, and using the very last study session just before the exam to review (restudy) "the whole"—all the parts that were previously studied in separate sessions. Thus, the final session isn't a cram session or even a study session; it's a review session.

Research shows that students of all ability levels learn material in college courses more effectively when they study the material in small units and move on to the next unit only after material from the previous has been learned and understood (Pascarella & Terenzini, 1991, 2005). Another major advantage of breaking up material into smaller parts and studying those parts in advance of an exam is that it gives students a chance to check their understanding of each part before moving on to learn the next part. This is a particularly important advantage in courses where students' ability to learn the next unit builds on and depends on their understanding of the previous unit (e.g., math and science courses).

Make sure that students don't buy into the myth that studying in advance is a waste of time because what was previously studied will all be forgotten by test time. (As discussed in chapter 6, procrastinators often use this argument to rationalize their habit of putting off studying until the very last moment.) Memory research demonstrates that if we temporarily forget information studied previously, once we start reviewing it, we're able to relearn and retain it much faster than we did the first time. Even if we cannot recall the information right away, it doesn't mean it's completely forgotten and that previous study time was a waste of time because there still is a memory trace of it in the brain. All it takes is a quick review to strengthen that memory trace and enable us to recall the previously studied information (Kintsch, 1994).

Capitalize on the power of visual learning. The human brain consists of two hemispheres (half spheres)—the left hemisphere and the right hemisphere (see **Figure 7.3**). Each of these hemispheres specializes in a different type of learning. Typically, the left hemisphere specializes in verbal learning; it primarily processes words, both spoken and written. In contrast, the right hemisphere typically specializes in visual–spatial learning; it deals primarily with perceiving images, patterns, and objects that occupy physical space. If students engage both hemispheres while studying, two different memory traces are recorded—one in each major hemisphere (half) of the brain. This process of laying down dual (verbal and visual) memory traces is referred to as *dual coding* (Paivio, 1990). Since two memory traces are better than one, dual coding results in deeper learning and longer retention of what was learned.

To capitalize on the advantage of dual coding, encourage students to use all the visual aids available to them, including those used by the instructor in class and those found in the textbook. Students can also create their own visual aids by representing what they are learning in the form of pictures, symbols, or concept maps—such as flowcharts, timelines, spider webs, and wheels (with hubs and spokes), or branching tree diagrams. As mentioned above, representing verbal information in visual form doubles the number of memory traces recorded in your brain. (Or, as the old saying goes, "A picture is worth a thousand words.")

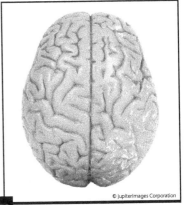

© JupiterImages Corporation

Figure 7.3 The human brain includes two half spheres (hemispheres): the left specializes in verbal learning and the right specializes in visual learning.

Learn with and through multiple sensory channels. All our senses channel information into the brain. Seeing something may start with our eyes, but we don't experience "seeing" it until that sensory input reaches the visual center of the brain. Similarly, input from other senses, such as hearing and touch, reach areas of the brain that are specialized for processing information received through those particular senses. **Figure 7.4** contains a map of the outer surface of the human brain. It shows how different parts of the brain are specialized to receive input from different sensory modalities. When students use multiple sensory modalities while learning, multiple memory traces of what's being studied are recorded in separate areas of the brain, resulting in deeper learning and stronger memory for what has been studied.

I have to <u>hear</u> it, <u>see</u> it, <u>write</u> it, and <u>talk</u> about it.

—First-year college student responding to the question: "How do you learn best?"

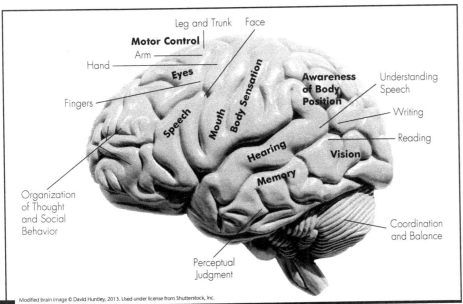

Modified brain image © David Huntley, 2013. Used under license from Shutterstock, Inc.

Figure 7.4   A Map of the Functions Performed by the Outer Surface of the Human Brain

Information that reaches the brain through multiple sensory modalities is learned more deeply and retained longer because it: (a) forms interconnections across multiple areas of our brain, and (b) supplies more routes or avenues through which information can be retrieved (recalled) (Shams & Seitz, 2011; Willis, 2006; Zull, 2002).

> When I have to remember something, it's better for me to do something with my hands so I could physically see it happening.
>
> —First-year college student

Remind students that movement is also a sensory channel. When we move, our brain receives kinesthetic stimulation—sensations generated by our muscles. Memory traces for movement are stored in an area of the brain that plays a major role for all types of learning (Middleton & Strick, 1994; Jensen, 2005). Thus, incorporating movement into the learning process improves our ability to retain what's being learned by adding a motor (muscle) memory trace of it to our brain. Students can use movement to help them learn and retain academic information by using their body to act out what they're studying or by symbolizing it with their hands (Kagan & Kagan, 1998). For instance, if they're trying to remember five points relating to a topic or concept, they can strengthen their learning and memory of those points by counting them out on their fingers while studying them.

Author's Experience

I was talking about memory in class one day and told my students that when I have trouble remembering how to spell a word, its correct spelling often comes back to me as soon as I start writing out the word. One of my students raised her hand and said the same thing happens to her when she forgets a phone number—it comes back to her when she starts punching it in. Both of these experiences point to the power of movement for improving learning and memory.

— Joe Cuseo

Also, remember that talking involves movement—of our lips and tongue. Thus, speaking aloud when studying, either to a friend or to oneself, not only improves memory by supplying auditory (sound) input to the brain, it also supplies kinesthetic (motor) input.

Learn with emotion. There are networks of neurons (brain cells) running between the emotional and memory centers of the brain (Zull, 2011); thus, the emotions we experience while learning can affect how we learn. Research indicates that positive emotions, such as excitement and enthusiasm, can strengthen memory of academic information just as it does for memory of life events and personal experiences. When we're excited or enthused about what we're learning, adrenaline is released into our bloodstream and carried to the brain. Once adrenaline reaches the brain, it increases blood flow and glucose production, stimulating learning and strengthening memory (LeDoux, 1998; Rosenfield, 1988). Thus, if students approach what they're learning with passion and positivity, they're more likely to learn it deeply and remember it longer (Howard, 2014; Minninger, 1984).

One way students can generate these feelings while learning is by being aware of the relevance or significance of what they're learning. For instance, if they are learning about the process of photosynthesis, they should be aware that they're not just memorizing steps of a boring chemical reaction, but learning about the underlying force that sustains the life of all forms of plant life on planet Earth. If students don't know why the concept they're studying is significant, encourage them to find out by doing a quick computer search, talking it over with their instructor, or asking an advanced student majoring in the field.

> **Remind students that they will learn more deeply and retain what they learn much longer when it's a "total body experience"—when they to put their whole self into it—their mind (thinking), their body (movement), and their heart (emotion).**

Learn collaboratively. In a national study that involved in-depth interviews with more than 1,600 college students, it was discovered that almost all students who struggled academically had one particular learning habit in common: They always studied alone (Light, 2001). In contrast, research from kindergarten through college shows that when students learn collaboratively in teams, they experience significant gains in both academic performance and development of interpersonal skills (Cross, Barkley, & Major, 2005; Gilles & Adrian, 2003; Johnson, Johnson, & Smith, 1998).

If you want to go quickly, go by yourself—if you want to go farther, go in a group.

—African proverb

Learning is strengthened when it takes place in a social context characterized by interpersonal interaction. As learning scholars put it, knowledge is "socially constructed"—it's built up through interpersonal dialogue and interchange of ideas. These external (social) conversations get converted into internal (mental) ideas that shape our thoughts (Bruffee, 1993). Thus, when students have frequent, thought-provoking conversations about what they're learning with other students, they broaden their knowledge base, deepen their learning, and elevate their level of thinking.

When seniors at Harvard University were interviewed, nearly every one of them who had participated in learning teams considered the experience to be crucial to their academic progress and success (Light, 1990, 1992, 2001). The power of teamwork is magnified further when students make wise choices about teammates who will enrich the quality and productivity of their learning teams. To help students make wise choices about their learning teammates and study partners, share with them the following two guidelines:

TEAM = Together Everyone Achieves More

—Author unknown

1. Keep a keen eye out for classmates who may be good learning teammates. Look for motivated students who attend class consistently, come to class prepared, and participate actively in class. These are the students who are likely to make significant contributions to your learning team (not freeloaders or hitchhikers looking for a free ride).
2. Include members on your learning team whose personal characteristics, backgrounds, and experiences differ from your own. Homogenized teams composed of students with similar characteristics and experiences , or who are very familiar with each other, often end up being the least productive teams. Their similarity and familiarity can turn them from a work group into a social group or gabfest that gets them off task and onto topics that have nothing to do with the learning task (e.g., what they did last weekend or what they're planning to do next weekend). Instead, include at least some teammates who are not friends or close acquaintances and who differ from you in terms of age, gender, race or ethnicity, and cultural or geographical background. Such variety brings different life experiences, thinking strategies, and learning approaches to the team, which, increases the team's social diversity and learning capacity.

For additional strategies on leading and facilitating effective learning teams, see Box 7.3.

Reflection 7.6

In your peer leadership role, will you be in a position to help students form learning teams or study groups? If yes, do you think they would respond positively to your efforts to bring them together for such academic purposes? Why or why not?

Box 7.3

Strategies for Leading and Facilitating Effective Learning Teams

1. **Before jumping right into group work, give team members a little time to interact informally and get to know one another.** If teammates are allowed some social "warm up" time before getting right to work, they're more likely to develop a stronger sense of team identity and feel more comfortable about expressing their ideas openly. Taking time to establish this sense of group trust at the outset is particularly important when teammates are unfamiliar with one another and come from different personal or cultural backgrounds.

2. **Have teammates work together to complete a unified work product.** When a team is asked to create a single, unified product (e.g., a jointly completed sheet of answers to questions, or a comprehensive list of ideas), its members are more likely to unify their efforts and work as a true team, rather than as a group of separate individuals. Completing a common final product keeps teammates thinking in terms of "we" (not "me"), keeps the team moving in the same direction toward the same goal, and, when they reach that goal, leaves them with a sense of collective achievement that they did it *together*.

3. **Have each teammate make an equal and identifiable contribution to the team's final product.** Each teammate should be responsible for making an indispensable contribution to the team's end product. Said in another way, each group member should be responsible for contributing an essential piece that's needed to complete the whole puzzle. For example, each member could contribute: (a) a different piece of *knowledge* (e.g., a specific chapter of the textbook or a particular topic the instructor covered in class), (b) a different *perspective* (e.g., national, international, or global), or (c) a different form of *thinking* (e.g., analysis, synthesis, or application).

In addition to making different contributions to the group's final work *product*, teammates should be expected to make different contributions to the work *process*. Similar to how members of a sports team have different roles to play during a game, members of a learning team should have specific roles to play during the learning process, such as:

- manager—assures that the team stays on track and keeps moving toward its goal;
- moderator—ensures that all teammates have equal opportunity to contribute;
- summarizer—monitors the team's progress and identifies what's been accomplished and what still needs to be done;
- recorder—keeps a written record of the team's ideas.

Research shows that when team learning takes place under the above-three conditions, significant gains are made in student learning and social development (Johnson, Johnson, & Smith, 1995, 1998; Slavin, 1995).

Remind students that learning teams are more than just study groups formed the night before an exam. Students can team-up with classmates earlier and more frequently to work on a variety of other academic tasks, such as those listed below.

Note-Taking Teams. Immediately after class, students can take a couple of minutes to team-up with one another to compare and share notes. Since listening is a demanding task, it's likely that one student will pick up a key point that the other missed and vice-versa. Students could engage in a two-step procedure called "cooperative note-taking pairs," in which one member of the pair summarizes his notes for the other—who adds any information to her notes that she missed; the partners then reverse roles—the summarizer becomes the listener and adds information to his notes that he missed. During the process, teammates could ask each other questions such as: "What main ideas did you take away? "What did you feel was most important"? "What did you find most challenging or confusing"? "What test questions could be asked of us that are based on these notes?" (Johnson, Johnson, & Smith, 1991, 1995).

Author's Experience During my first term in college, I was having difficulty taking complete notes in my biology course because the instructor spoke very rapidly and with a foreign accent. I noticed another student (Alex) sitting in the front row who was having similar difficulties. Following one particularly fast and complex lecture, we looked at each other and noticed that we were both shaking our heads in frustration. We started talking about how exasperated we were and decided to join forces immediately after every class to compare notes and identify points we missed or found confusing. First, we helped each other by comparing and sharing our notes to see if one of us got something the other missed. Next, we looked to see if there were gaps in both of our notes; if there were, we went to the front of the classroom together to consult with the instructor before he left the room. Alex and I ended up with the highest grades in the course.

— *Joe Cuseo*

Reading Teams. After completing reading assignments, classmates team up to compare their highlighting and margin notes, and identify information they think should be studied for upcoming exams.

Writing Teams. Students provide each other with feedback to revise and improve their own writing. Studies show that when peers assess each other's writing, the quality of their individual writing improves and they develop more positive attitudes about writing (Topping, 1998). Students can form peer-writing teams to help each other at any or all of the following stages in the writing process:

1. **Topic selection and refinement**—to help each other come up with a list of possible topics and subtopics to write about;
2. **Pre-writing**—to clarify their writing purpose, thesis statement, and audience;
3. **First draft**—to improve the organization, style, or tone of their writing; and
4. **Final draft**—to proofread their writing, detecting and correcting clerical errors before turning it in.

Library Research Teams. First-year students are often unfamiliar with the process of using a college or university library to conduct academic research. Some students actually experience "library anxiety" and will do their very best to avoid even stepping foot in the library, particularly if it's a large and intimidating place (Malvasi, Rudowsky, & Valencia, 2009). By forming a library research team, students can develop a social support group and make library research less intimidating, transforming it from a solitary experience done alone to a collaborative venture done together. Such collaboration not only reduces library anxiety, it also generates collective energy that can result in a better work product than working individually.

Study Teams. Research on study groups indicates that they are most effective when each member has done all the required course work prior to the group meetings—for example, each teammate has attended class, taken notes, and completed all the required readings (Light, 2001). The power of study teams is also magnified when its members: (a) study *individually* before meeting as a group, (b) come to group meetings prepared with answers or ideas to share with teammates, and (c) come armed with specific questions to ask. This ensures that all team members are both individually accountable for their own learning and collectively responsible for contributing to the learning of their teammates.

Test-Review Teams. After receiving their results on course examinations and assignments, students can collaborate to review their performance in teams. By comparing their work, all teammates get a better idea about why they lost and earned points. Having the opportunity to view the work of teammates who received the maximum number of points on certain test questions can provide students with models of work they can emulate and use to improve their future performance. It's especially effective for students to team-up after tests and assignments *early in the term*, which would enable them to get early feedback that can be used to diagnose their initial mistakes, improve their subsequent performance, and raise their overall course grade—while there's still plenty of time left in the term to do so.

Reflection 7.7

Think about the students you are coaching or mentoring this term. Do they have classmates they could connect with to form test-review teams after exams? Would you be able to facilitate the formation of these teams?

Helping Students Self-Monitor and Self-Assess Their Learning

Deep learners are *reflective* learners—they reflect on *how* they go about learning (their learning habits and strategies) and *if* they are learning deeply. They self-monitor and self-assess to check their comprehension by asking questions such as: "Am I actually understanding this?" and "Do I really know it?"

How can students know if they really know it? In general, the best answer to this question is when a student can say: "I find *meaning* in it—I can relate to it personally or put it in terms that make sense to me" (Ramsden, 2003). Listed below are self-assessment questions you can share with students to help them check to see if they have moved beyond memorization to deeper, more meaningful learning. Their answers to these specific questions will help them answer the bigger question: "How do I know if I really know it?"

- **Can you paraphrase (restate or translate) what you're learning in your own words?** One way to check if you really know something is to see if you can state it differently than how your instructor or textbook stated it. If you can, it's a good sign that you've moved beyond surface memorization (mental regurgitation) to a deeper level of comprehension. If you can take what you're learning and complete the following sentence: "In other words . . .," it shows you've transformed it into a form that's meaningful to you.
- **Can you explain what you're learning to someone who is unfamiliar with it?** Another way to gain awareness of how well you know or don't know something is by trying to explain it to someone who doesn't know it (just ask any teacher). Studies confirm that students gain a deeper level of understanding of what they're learning when they're asked to explain it to someone else (Chi et al., 1994; Mayhew et al., 2016). If you can translate the concept into language that's understandable to a peer who hasn't learned it, this is a good sign that you've learned it deeply.

> *When you know a thing, to recognize that you know it; and when you do not, to know that you do not know; that is knowledge.*
>
> —Confucius, influential Chinese thinker and educator

> *You do not really understand something unless you can explain it to your grandmother.*
>
> —Albert Einstein, considered the "Father of Modern Physics"

> *I learn best through teaching. When I learn something and teach it to someone else, I find that it really sticks with me a lot better.*
>
> —College sophomore

- **Can you think of an example of what you've learned?** If you can come up with a specific instance or illustration of the concept that differs from any provided by your instructor or supplied in your textbook, this suggests you really know it. It shows you're able to take an abstract concept and represent it in the form of a concrete experience (Bligh, 2000).
- **Can you think of an analogy between the concept you're learning and something you already know or have previously learned?** (e.g., "This concept is like ____ or is similar to ____.")
- **Can you apply what you're learning to a new situation or problem that you haven't seen before?** The ability to apply what you've learned in a different situation or context is a good indicator of deep learning (Erickson & Strommer, 2005). Learning specialists refer to this mental process as *decontextualization*–taking what's been learned in one context and transferring it to another context (Bransford, Brown, & Cocking, 2000). For instance, you know you've learned a mathematical concept deeply when you can take that concept and use it to solve math problems different than those solved by your instructor or the author of your textbook. This is why math instructors rarely include the same problems on exams that they solved in class or were solved in the textbook. They're not trying to "trick" students at test time; they're trying to see whether their students have learned the concept deeply.

> *Most things used to be external to me—out of a lecture or textbook. It makes learning a lot more interesting and memorable when you can bring your experiences into it. It makes you want to learn.*
> —Returning adult student

Encouraging Students to Use Test Results as Feedback for Improving Their Future Performance

Often, when students get a quiz or test back, they just check to see what grade they got, then stuff it in a binder or toss it into the nearest wastebasket. You can help students break this unproductive habit by strongly encouraging them to reflect on their academic performances with an eye toward: (a) determining where they lost and gained points, and (b) developing a strategic plan for improving their next test performance. Suggest to students that they STOP and ask themselves questions like the following:

- Were these the results I expected?
- What do the results suggest about the effectiveness of my approach to learning the material?
- How can I use my results as constructive feedback to improve my next test grade?

Mistakes should neither be ignored nor neglected; they should be detected and corrected (and prevented from happening again).

> *When you make a mistake, there are only three things you should do about it: admit it; learn from it; and don't repeat it.*
> —Paul "Bear" Bryant, legendary college football coach

Summarized in Box 7.4 are strategies you can suggest to students for identifying sources of lost points on exams. They can use these strategies to pinpoint the particular step in the learning process where the breakdown occurred and focus on that step when preparing for the next exam.

Box 7.4

Strategies for Helping Students Pinpoint Sources of Lost Points on Exams

1. On test items where students lost points, you can help them identify the stage in the learning process that may have accounted for the lost points by asking them the following questions.

- **Did you have the information you needed to answer the question correctly?** If you didn't, where should the information have been acquired in the first place? Was it information presented in class that didn't get into your notes? If yes, consider adopting strategies for improving your lecture listening and note-taking. (Suggest the strategies cited on pp. 199-200.) If the missing information was contained in your assigned reading, check to see if you're using effective reading strategies (such as those listed on pp. 203-204).

- **Did you have the information, but didn't remember it?** Failing to remember information on a test can usually be traced back to the following factors:

   (a) You may have tried to cram in too much study time just before the exam and didn't give your brain enough time to "digest" (consolidate) the information and store it in long-term memory. The solution could be distributing your study time more evenly in advance of the next exam and using the "part-to-whole" study method. (Suggest they try the strategies provided on p. 208.)

   (b) You didn't cram, but you didn't learn the material deeply enough to be able to recall it at test time. You may need to study smarter or more strategically. (Recommend to them the strategies cited on pp. 205-212.)

   (c) Test anxiety may have interfered with your concentration and memory. (If students report to you that they experience test anxiety, connect them with a professional in the Academic Support Center or Counseling Center.)

- **Did you study the material but didn't really understand it?** This suggests you may need to self-monitor your comprehension more closely while studying to determine whether you're truly understanding it or just memorizing it. (Share with students the self-monitoring and self-assessment strategies on pp. 214-215.)

- **Did you know the material but lost points due to careless test-taking mistakes?** If this happened, the solution may simply be a matter of taking more time to review your test after completing it and checking for absentminded errors before turning it in.

2. **Get feedback from your instructor.** Start by carefully reading any written comments that your instructor made on your exam. Keep these comments in mind when you prepare for the next test. You can seek additional feedback by making an appointment to confer with your instructor during office hours. (If you do make an office visit, your purpose should not be to challenge the validity of the test or complain about your last test grade, but to get feedback you can use to improve your next test grade.

3. **Seek feedback from professionals in your Learning Center or Academic Support Center.** Tutors and other learning support professionals on campus can supply you with constructive feedback on how to improve your test-preparation and test-taking strategies. Ask these professionals to take a look at your previous test results and seek their advice about how to improve your subsequent test results .

4. **Seek feedback from classmates.** Peers can also be a valuable source of information on how to improve your academic performance and course grades. Consider reviewing your tests with a trusted classmate, particularly someone who did well. Their test answers can provide you with models of what type of work your instructor expects on exams. Ask successful students what they did to be successful, such as how they prepared for the test and what strategies they used during the test.

Reflection 7.8

When you get a test back, do you carefully review the results to see where you gained and lost points? Do you use this information as feedback to improve your next test performance? How do you think most students would answer the above-two questions?

elping Students to Think Critically

The term "critical thinking" often means different things to different people, but almost everyone would agree that it's a higher form of thinking that goes beyond just acquiring factual knowledge and memorizing information. It involves reflecting thoughtfully on acquired information and knowledge and engaging in a more advanced or rigorous form of mental action on it—such as evaluating its validity, integrating it with other information, or applying it to solve a problem or resolve an issue.

Studies show that students' memory for factual information learned in college has a short shelf life—it fades quickly over time. In contrast, critical thinking skills developed in college have longevity (Pascarella & Terenzini, 1991, 2005); critical thinking is a "habit of mind" that can last a lifetime.

National surveys of college professors teaching freshman-level through senior-level courses in variety of academic fields show that more than 95% of them believe that the most important goal of a college education is developing students' ability to think critically (Gardiner, 2005; Milton, 1982). Similarly, college professors teaching introductory first- and second-year courses report that the primary educational purpose of their classes is to develop students' critical thinking skills (Higher Education Institute, 2009; Stark et al., 1990). Simply stated, college instructors are more concerned about teaching students *how* to think than they are about teaching students what to think or what facts to remember.

This isn't to say that acquiring knowledge is unnecessary or unimportant. When students acquire a broad and deep body of knowledge, they acquire mental material to which they can apply critical thinking skills (Willingham, 2008). It could be said that knowledge supplies students with the raw material to work with and the stepping-stones to build on and climb to higher-level thinking—as illustrated in **Figure 7.5.**

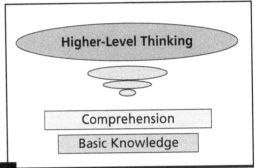

Figure 7.5   "Higher-level thinking" builds on basic knowledge and comprehension to move to more advanced levels of thought.

ajor Forms of Critical Thinking

When college professors ask students to "think critically," they're usually asking them to engage in the higher forms of thinking listed in Box 7.5. A simple yet powerful way to help students develop these higher-level thinking skills is by encouraging them to reflect on their own thinking through self-questioning. Thinking often involves talking silently to ourselves, so if students can get in the habit of asking themselves questions that call for higher-level thinking, they can begin training their minds to think at a higher level. Once students develop the habit of asking themselves higher-level thinking questions, they can apply these questions to the material they're learning, demonstrate higher levels of thinking on their exams and assignments, and earn higher college grades.

If you do not ask the right questions, you do not get the right answers.

—Edward Hodnett, British poet

Box 7.5

Questions Students Can Ask Themselves to Develop Higher-Level Thinking Skills

1. **ANALYSIS (ANALYTICAL THINKING)**—breaking down information into its essential elements or parts.
   * What are the main ideas contained in _____?
   * What are the key issues raised by _____?
   * What hidden assumptions or values are embedded in _____?
   * What are the reasons behind _____?
   * What are the underlying causes of ____?
   * How are the ideas contained in _____ similar to or different than ____?
   * How might this ____ be broken down into its component parts and tackled in a systematic, step-by-step fashion?
   * What additional information do I need to understand or complete this ____?

2. **SYNTHESIS**—integrating separate pieces of information into a more complete, coherent product or pattern.
   * In what way(s) is this idea related to ____?
   * How could these different _____ be grouped together into a more general class or category?
   * How can this idea be joined or connected with _____ to create a more comprehensive answer or solution?
   * How might these separate _____ be reorganized or rearranged to get a better understanding of the "big picture"?

3. **APPLICATION (APPLIED THINKING)**—using knowledge for practical purposes to solve problems and re-solve issues.
   * What purpose or function could ____ serve?
   * What are the practical implications or consequences of _____?
   * How can ____ be used to improve or strengthen_____?
   * How might this theory or principle be applied to _____?
   * How could _____serve to prevent or eliminate _____?

4. **BALANCED THINKING**—carefully considering reasons for and against a particular position or viewpoint.
   * What are the strengths (advantages) and weaknesses (disadvantages) of _____?
   * What evidence supports and contradicts _____?
   * What are arguments for and against _____?
   * What are the major costs and benefits of _____?
   * What are the potential risks and rewards of _____?

5. **MULTIDIMENSIONAL THINKING**—thinking about ourselves and the world around us from multiple an-gles or perspectives.
   * What viewpoints need to be considered in order to get a complete understanding of ____?
   * What factors or variables may combine to influence ____?
   * What aspects of personal development should be considered when ____?
   * How would people from different cultural backgrounds interpret or react to _____?
   * What dimensions of the self (personal development) would be affected by ____?
   * What dimensions of the world (global development) would be affected by ____?

6. **EVALUATION**—critically judging the soundness of arguments and evidence used to draw conclusions.
   * What examples support the argument that _____?
   * What research evidence is there for _____?
   * What statistical data document or back up this ____?
   * What assumptions are being made to reach the conclusion that ____?

- If ____ is true, would it follow that ____ is also true?
- If people believe in _____, what actions or practices would be consistent with this belief?
- What criteria (standards) are being used to judge the validity of ____?
- What criteria are being used to judge the ethicality or morality of ____?
- What criteria are being used to judge the aesthetic value (beauty) of ____?

7. **CREATIVE THINKING**—generating ideas that are unique, original, or innovative.
- What would happen if _____?
- What could be invented to _____?
- What might be a different method for _____?
- What changes could be made to improve _____?
- What would be a novel approach to _____?
- What strategies have not yet been tried for solving the problem of ___?
- What are alternative ways of looking at _____?

In your role as learning coach or peer educator, you can pose questions like these to your students to elevate their level of thinking. You can also encourage them to ask these questions of themselves when they prepare for exams, write papers or reports, and participate in class discussions or study-group sessions. To further encourage thinking self-awareness—a process known as *metacognition*—ask students to keep a "thinking log" or "thinking journal" in which they note the type of thinking they're using in their courses (analysis, synthesis, application, etc.). This strategy will not only help students develop higher-level thinking skills, it will also help them reference these skills during job interviews and in letters of application for career positions or graduate schools.

Reflection 7.9

Review the seven higher-level thinking questions listed in Box 7.5. Identify one way in which you could use each of these skills in your peer leadership role or position.

Internet Resources

For additional information on deep learning and critical thinking, consult the following websites:

Learning Strategies and Study Skills
https://dus.psu.edu/academicsuccess/studyskills.html

Brain-Based Learning
http://www.brainrules.net/the-rules

Critical and Creative Thinking
http://www.criticalthinking.org/pages/for-students/610
http://www.umich.edu/~elements/probsolv/strategy/crit-n-creat.htm

References

Arum, R., & Roska, J. (2011). *Academically adrift: Limited learning on college campuses.* Chicago: The University of Chicago Press.

Biggs, J., & Tang, C. (2007) *Teaching for quality learning at university* (3rd ed.). Buckingham: SRHE and Open University Press.

Bligh, D. A. (2000). *What's the use of lectures?* San Francisco: Jossey Bass.

Bransford, J. D., Brown, A. L., & Cocking, R. R. (2000). *How people learn: Brain, mind, experience and school.* Washington, DC: National Academies Press.

Brown, R. D. (1988). Self-quiz on testing and grading issues. *Teaching at UNL (University of Nebraska–Lincoln), 10*(2), 1-3.

Brown, P. C., Roediger III, H. L., & McDaniel, M. A. (2014). *Make it stick: The science of successful learning.* Cambridge, MA: The Belknap Press of Harvard University Press.

Bruffee, K. A. (1993). *Collaborative learning: Higher education, interdependence, and the authority of knowledge.* Baltimore: Johns Hopkins University Press.

Carey, B. (2014). *How we learn.* London: Random House.

Chi, M., de Leeuw, N., Chiu, M. H., & LaVancher, C. (1994). Eliciting self-explanations improves under-standing. *Cognitive Science, 18,* 439-477.

Cook, S. W. (1984). Cooperative interaction in multiethnic contexts. In N. Miller & M. B. Brewer (Eds.), *Groups in contact: The psychology of desegregation.* New York: Academic Press.

Crawford, H. J., & Strapp, C. M. (1994). Effects of vocal and instrumental music on visuospatial and verbal performance as moderated by studying preference and personality. *Personality and Individual Differences, 16*(2), 237-245.

Cross, K. P., Barkley, E. F., & Major, C. H. (2005). *Collaborative learning techniques: A handbook for college faculty.* San Francisco: Jossey-Bass.

Cuseo, J. B., & Thompson, A., Campagna, M., & Fecas, V. S. (2016). *Thriving in college & beyond: Research-based strategies for academic success and personal development* (4th ed.). Dubuque, IA: Kendall Hunt.

David, L. (2015, June 20). *"Constructivism," in learning theories.* Retrieved from https://www.learning-theories.com/constructivism.html

Dunlosky, J., Rawson, K. A., Marsh, E. J., Nathan, M. J., & Willingham, D. T. (2013). Improving students' learning with effective learning techniques: Promising directions from cognitive and educational psychology. *Psychological Science in the Public Interest, 14*(1), 4-58.

Erickson, B. L., & Strommer, D. W. (2005). Inside the first-year classroom: Challenges and constraints. In J. L. Upcraft, J. N. Gardner, & B. O. Barefoot (Eds.), *Challenging and supporting the first-year student* (pp. 241-256). San Francisco: Jossey-Bass.

Gardiner, L. F. (2005). Transforming the environment for learning: A crisis of quality. *To Improve the Academy, 23,* 3-23.

Gilles, R. M., & Adrian, F. (2003). *Cooperative learning: The social and intellectual outcomes of learning in groups.* London: Farmer Press.

Herbert, W. (2014). *Ink on paper: Some notes on note taking.* Association for Psychological Sciences (APS). Retrieved from http://www.psychologicalscience.org/index.php/news/were-only-human/ink-on-paper-some-notes-on-note-taking.html

Higher Education Research Institute (HERI). (2009). *The American college teacher: National norms for 2007-2008.* Los Angeles: HERI, University of California, Los Angeles.

Howard, P. J. (2014). *The owner's manual for the brain: Everyday applications of mind-brain research* (4th ed.). New York: HarperCollins.

Jairam, D., & Kiewra, K. A. (2009). An investigation of the SOAR study method. *Journal of Advanced Academics* (August), 602-629.

Jensen, E. (2005). *Teaching with the brain in mind* (2nd ed.). Alexandria, VA: ASCD.

Jensen, E. (2008). *Brain-based learning.* Thousand Oaks, CA: Corwin Press.

Johnson, D., Johnson, R., & Smith, K. (1998). Cooperative learning returns to college: What evidence is there that it works? *Change, 30,* 26-35.

Johnson, D. W., Johnson, R. T., & Smith, K. A. (1991). *Cooperative learning: Increasing college faculty instructional productivity.* ASHE-ERIC Higher Education Report No. 4. Washington, D. C.: Association for the Study of Higher Education.

Johnson, D. W., Johnson, R. T., & Smith, K. A. (1995). Cooperative note-taking pairs. *Cooperative Learning and College Teaching, 5*(3), 10-11.

Kagan, S., & Kagan, M. (1998). *Multiple intelligences: The complete MI book.* San Clemente, CA: Kagan Cooperative Learning.

Kahneman, D. (2011). *Thinking, fast and slow.* New York: Farrar, Strauss & Giroux.

Kiewra, K. A. (2005). *Learn how to study and SOAR to success.* Upper Saddle River, NJ: Pearson Prentice Hall.

Kintsch, W. (1994). Text comprehension, memory, and learning. *American Psychologist, 49*, 294–303.

Kouzes, M. M., & Posner, B. Z. (2006). *Student leadership planner: An action guide to achieving your personal best.* San Francisco: Jossey-Bass.

Kuh, G. D. (2005). Student engagement in the first year of college. In M. L. Upcraft, J. N. Gardner, B. O. Barefoot, & Associates, *Challenging and supporting the first-year student: A handbook for improving the first year of college* (pp. 86-107). San Francisco: Jossey-Bass.

LeDoux, J. (1998). *The emotional brain: The mysterious underpinnings of emotional life.* New York: Simon & Schuster.

LeDoux, J. (2002). *Synaptic self: How our brains become who we are.* New York: Penguin Books.

Light, R. J. (2001). *Making the most of college: Students speak their minds.* Cambridge, MA: Harvard University Press.

Light, R. L. (1990). *The Harvard assessment seminars.* Cambridge, MA: Harvard University Press.

Light, R. L. (1992). *The Harvard assessment seminars, second report.* Cambridge, MA: Harvard University Press.

Malmberg, K. J., & Murnane, K. (2002). List composition and the word-frequency effect for recognition memory. *Journal of Experimental Psychology: Learning, Memory, and Cognition, 28*, 616-630.

Malvasi, M., Rudowsky, C., & Valencia, J. M. (2009). *Library Rx: Measuring and treating library anxiety, a research study.* Chicago: Association of College and Research Libraries.

Marzano, R. J., Pickering, D. J., & Pollock, J. (2001). *Classroom instruction that works: Research-based strategies for increasing student achievement.* Alexandria, VA: Association for Supervision and Curriculum Development.

Mayer, R. E. (2002). Rote versus meaningful learning. *Theory into Practice, 41*(4), 226-232.

Mayhew, M. K., Rockenbach, A. N., Bowman, N. A., Seifert, T. A., Wolniak, G. C., Pascarella, E. T., & Terenzini, P. T. (2016). *How college affects students, volume 3: 21st century evidence that higher education works.* San Francisco: Jossey-Bass.

Middleton, F., & Strick, P. (1994). Anatomical evidence for cerebellar and basal ganglia involvement in higher brain function. *Science, 226*(5184), 458–461.

Milton, O. (1982). *Will that be on the final?* Springfield, IL: Charles C. Thomas.

Minninger, J. (1984). *Total recall: How to boost your memory power.* Emmaus, PA: Rodale.

Mueller, P. A., & Oppenheimer, D. M. (2014). The pen is mightier than the keyboard: Advantages of longhand over laptop note taking. *Psychological Science, 25*(6), 1159-1168.

Murname, K., & Shiffrin, R. M. (1991). Interference and the representation of events in memory. *Journal of Experimental Psychology: Learning, Memory, & Cognition, 17*, 855-874.

Nathan, R. (2005). *My freshman year: What a professor learned by becoming a student.* Ithaca, NY: Cornell University Press.

Niles, S. G., & Harris-Bowlsbey, J. (2012). *Career development interventions in the twenty-first century.* Upper Saddle River, NJ: Pearson Education.

Paivio, A. (1990). *Mental representations: A dual coding approach.* New York: Oxford University Press.

Pascarella, E., & Terenzini, P. (1991). *How college affects students: Findings and insights from twenty years of research.* San Francisco: Jossey-Bass.

Pascarella, E., & Terenzini, P. (2005). *How college affects students: A third decade of research* (Vol. 2). San Francisco: Jossey-Bass.

Pauk, W. (1962). *How to study in college.* Boston: Houghton Mifflin.

Piaget, J. (1978). *Success and understanding.* Cambridge, MA: Harvard University Press.

Ramsden, P. (2003). *Learning to teach in higher education* (2nd ed.). London: RoutledgeFalmer.

Rosenfield, I. (1988). *The invention of memory: A new view of the brain.* New York: Basic Books.

Sappington, J., Kinsey, K., & Munsayac, K. (2002). Two studies of reading compliance among college students. *Teaching of Psychology, 29*(4), 272-274.

SECFHE. (2006). *A national dialogue: The Secretary of Education's Commission on the future of higher education.* (U.S. Department of Education Boards and Commissions: A Draft Panel Report). Retrieved from http://www.ed.gov/about/bdscomm/list/hiedfuture/reports/0809-draft.pdf

Shams, W., & Seitz, K. (2011). Influences of multisensory experience on subsequent unisensory processing. *Frontiers in Perception Science, 2*(264), 1-9.

Slavin, R. E. (1995). *Cooperative learning* (2nd ed.). Boston: Allyn & Bacon.

Stark, J. S., Lowther, R. J., Bentley, M. P., Ryan, G. G., Martens, M. L., Genthon, P. A., et al. (1990). *Planning introductory college courses: Influences on faculty.* Ann Arbor: National Center for Research to Improve Postsecondary Teaching and Learning, University of Michigan. (ERIC Document Reproduction Services No. 330 277 370).

Topping, K. (1998). Peer assessment between students in colleges and universities. *Review of Educational Research, 68*(3), 249-276.

Vygotsky, L. S. (1978). Internalization of higher cognitive functions. In M. Cole, V. John-Steiner, S. Scribner, & E. Souberman (Eds. & Trans.), *Mind in society: The development of higher psychological processes* (pp. 52–57). Cambridge, MA: Harvard University Press.

Willingham, D. T. (2008). Critical thinking: Why is it so hard to teach? *Arts Education Policy Review, 109*(4), 21-29.

Willis, J. (2006). *Research-based strategies to ignite student learning: Insights from a neurologist and classroom teacher.* Alexandria, VA: ASCD.

Zull, J. E. (2002). *The art of changing the brain: Enriching the practice of teaching by exploring the biology of learning.* Sterling, VA: Stylus.

Zull, J. E. (2011). *From brain to mind: Using neuroscience to guide change in education.* Sterling, VA: Stylus.

Name _____   Date _____

Exercise 7.1 Quote Reflections

Review the sidebar quotes contained in this chapter and select two that you think would be especially valuable to share with the students you lead or mentor.

For each quote, write a short statement explaining why you chose it.

Name _____ Date _____

Exercise 7.2 Assessment of Effective Note-Taking Strategies

Answer the following items as you think the students you mentor would answer them.

4 = always, 3 = sometimes, 2 = rarely, 1 = never

1.	I take notes aggressively in class.	4	3	2	1
2.	I sit near the front of class.	4	3	2	1
3.	I adopt an alert, active-listening posture when seated in class by sitting upright and leaning forward.	4	3	2	1
4.	I take notes on what my instructors say, not just what they write on the board.	4	3	2	1
5.	I pay special attention to information presented at the start and end of class.	4	3	2	1
6.	I have an effective system or strategy for taking notes in class.	4	3	2	1
7.	I review my notes immediately after class to check if they're complete and accurate.	4	3	2	1

Which one of the above note-taking strategies do you think is most important for students to use, but you see them not using (or not using consistently)?

Would you be able to persuade students to use this strategy? (If yes, how? If no, why not?)

Exercise 7.3 Assessment of Effective Study Strategies

Answer the following items as you think the students you mentor would answer them.

4 = always, 3 = sometimes, 2 = rarely, 1 = never

1.	I avoid multitasking while studying.	4	3	2	1
2.	I try to make connections between what I'm currently studying and what I've previously learned.	4	3	2	1
3.	I pull together information from my class notes and readings that relate to the same concept and get it in the same place.	4	3	2	1
4.	I use as many senses as possible while studying (e.g., say it aloud, map it out, act it out).	4	3	2	1
5.	I self-monitor (check myself) while studying to be sure I'm learning deeply and not just memorizing.	4	3	2	1
6.	I distribute (spread out) my study time over several short sessions in advance of exams and use my last study session before exams to review the information I previously studied.	4	3	2	1
7.	I participate in learning teams or study groups with classmates.	4	3	2	1

Which one of the above study strategies do you think is most important for students to use, but you see them not using (or not using consistently)?

Would you be able to persuade students to use this strategy? (If yes, how? If no, why not?)

Exercise 7.4 Critical Thinking Scenario

Trick or Treat: "Confusing" Test or "Challenging" Test?

Students just had their first exam returned to them in Professor Plato's philosophy course and they're going over the test together in class. Some students are angry because they feel the professor deliberately included "trick questions" to confuse them. Professor Plato responds by saying that his test questions were not designed to trick or confuse them but to "challenge them to think."

Reflection and Discussion Questions

1. What do you think led some students to conclude that Professor Plato was trying to trick or confuse them?

2. What type of test questions do you think the professor created to "challenge students to think"?

3. On future tests, what might the students do to reduce the likelihood they'll be tricked or fooled again?

4. As a learning coach, what could you do to help students avoid or handle this scenario?

Exercise 7.5 Midterm Self-Evaluation

About halfway through the term, students are likely to experience the "midterm crunch"—a wave of major exams and assignments. This is a good time to check in with them about their academic progress. Using the form below, ask students to list the courses they're taking this term and the grades they're receiving in these courses. If they don't know what their grade is in a particular course, ask them to check the syllabus for the instructor's grading scale and estimate their own grade based on the scores they've received on completed tests and assignments. This should give them at least a rough idea of where they stand in the course. If they're still having difficulty determining their course grade, even after checking the course syllabus and the results of their returned tests and assignments, suggest they seek out the instructor to see where they stand in the class.

Course No.	Course Title	Grade
1.		
2.		
3.		
4.		
5.		

Pose the following questions to students about their midterm grades:

1. Were these the grades you *expected*? Were they better or worse than you anticipated?

2. Were these the grades you were *hoping* for? Are you pleased or disappointed?

3. Do you see any patterns in your performance that point to things you're doing well and things you need to improve?

4. If you had to pinpoint one action you could take right now to improve your lowest course grade, what would it be?

Exercise 7.6 Strategy Reflections

Review the strategies recommended on pp. 205–212 for *coaching students to study strategically and learn deeply*. Select three strategies that you think students would be most receptive to hearing about and putting into practice.

CHAPTER 8

Holistic Leadership

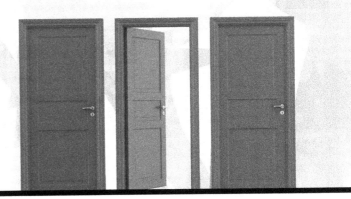

Mentoring and Developing the Whole Person

Reflection 8.1

What does it mean to you to be a "well-rounded" person and lead a "well-balanced" life?

Chapter Purpose and Preview

Learning and development in college is maximized when students maintain physical wellness, are mindful of what they put into their body (healthy food), what they keep out of it (unhealthy substances), and how well they restore it (quality of sleep). Students' academic performance in college and their ability to persist to college completion also depend on how well they maintain their mental health and cope with emotional stressors, particularly anxiety and depression. This chapter supplies you with leadership and mentoring strategies for helping students deal with the stress of college life, attain optimal physical and mental wellness, and develop holistically—as full ("whole") human beings.

The Importance of Holistic ("Whole Person") Development for College Success

Effective peer leaders and mentors go beyond helping students succeed academically. They are also concerned about their students' overall well-being and contribute to their development as a "whole" human being (a.k.a. holistic development) (Bordes & Arredondo, 2005; Gould & Lomax, 1993; Harmon, 2006; Sanft, Jensen, & McMurray, 2008). Success in college is affected by many factors that aren't strictly academic in nature. Research shows that the vast majority of students who withdraw from college are in good academic standing at the time of their withdrawal. Most students do not depart because they've "flunked out" or have been "forced out" (academically dismissed); they leave for a variety of personal reasons (Cuseo et al., 2016; Gardiner, 1994; Tinto, 1993, 2012). Even when students are experiencing academic difficulty at the time of their withdrawal, their poor grades are often a result or symptom of personal issues that are interfering with their academic performance.

Key Dimensions of the Holistic Development

National surveys reveal that the number-one reason why students go to college is to get a good job (Pryor et al., 2012). While finding employment and earning a decent living are certainly important outcomes of a college education, vocational development is just one piece of the larger pie of holistic development. A college education should not only enrich students economically; it should enrich them personally, enabling them to become well-rounded, fully developed human beings.

Figure 8.1   Key Elements of Holistic (Whole-Person) Development

As illustrated in **Figure 8.1,** the self is a multidimensional entity composed of multiple components, all of which are interrelated and interdependent. We are not just thinking (intellectual) beings or working (vocational) beings; we're also social, emotional, physical, ethical, and spiritual beings.

Holistic development is a comprehensive process that includes growth of the following dimensions of self:

1. **Intellectual:** acquiring a broad base of knowledge; learning how to learn and how to think critically.
2. **Emotional:** understanding, managing, and expressing emotions.
3. **Social:** improving the quality and depth of interpersonal relationships.
4. **Ethical:** building moral character—making sound ethical judgments, developing a clear value system to guide personal decision-making, and demonstrating consistency between one's convictions (beliefs) and commitments (actions).
5. **Physical:** acquiring knowledge about the human body and applying that knowledge to prevent disease, promote wellness, and achieve peak performance.
6. **Spiritual:** pondering the "big questions," such as the meaning and purpose of life, the inevitability of death, and the origins of human life and the natural world.
7. **Vocational:** exploring career options and pursuing a career path that is consistent with one's true talents, interests, and values.
8. **Personal:** developing a sense of personal identity, a coherent self-concept, and the ability to manage personal affairs and resources effectively.

(For a more detailed description of these eight elements of self-development, see Exercise 8.2, pp. 267-270.)

> Everyone is a house with four rooms: a physical, a mental, an emotional, and a spiritual. Most of us tend to live in one room most of the time but unless we go into every room every day, even if only to keep it aired, we are not complete.
>
> —Native American proverb

Reflection 8.2

Which of the eight dimensions of self-listed above do you have the most interest in helping students develop? Why?

As can be seen in **Figure 8.1**, the different dimensions of self are interrelated. They do not act independently but interdependently—they interact with one another to influence our overall development and total well-being (Gallup-Purdue Index, 2014; Kegan, 1994; Love & Love, 1995). Our intellectual performance is influenced by our emotional state (whether we're enthusiastic or anxious), our emotional state is influenced by our social relationships (whether we're socially supported or isolated), and our social relationships are influenced by our physical self-concept (whether we have a positive or negative body image). If one link in the chain is strengthened or weakened, other dimensions of the self are likely to be strengthened or weakened simultaneously. For example, research shows that when college students make gains in intellectual development, they also make gains in social self-confidence and self-esteem (Pascarella & Terenzini, 1991, 2005).

The Relationship between Holistic Development and Wellness

Wellness can be defined as a state of optimal health in which our risk of illness is minimized and our physical and mental performance is maximized. Research indicates that when people attend to and develop multiple dimensions of the self and live a well-rounded, well-balanced life, they're more likely to be healthy (physically and mentally) and successful (personally and professionally) (Covey, 2004; Goleman, 1995; Heath, 1977). As a peer mentor, you can play an important role in helping students achieve this balance by sharing and modeling the wellness strategies discussed in the following sections of this chapter.

> *Wellness is a multidimensional state of being describing the existence of positive health in an individual as exemplified by quality of life and a sense of well-being.*
>
> —Charles Corbin and Robert Pangrazi, president's Council on Physical Fitness and Sports

Author's Experience On my bedroom door, I've posted a list of key components of wellness to remind me to keep my life balanced. Every Sunday night I reflect on the previous week and ask myself if I've ignored any component of the holistic wheel. If I have, I try to make an earnest attempt to pay more attention to that aspect of my life during the upcoming week. For instance, if my previous week's activities reveal that I've neglected to spend enough time on my social self, I plan to spend more time the following week with family and friends. If I've neglected to attend to my physical self, I plan to exercise more consistently and eat more healthily the next week. Having the holistic wheel in full view provides me with a constant visual reminder to strive for "wholeness" and "balance" in my life.

— *Joe Cuseo*

Physical Wellness

It could be said that physical wellness is a precondition or prerequisite that enables other elements of personal wellness to be experienced. It's hard to grow intellectually and emotionally if we're not well physically, and it's hard to become wealthy and wise without first being healthy. A healthy physical lifestyle includes the following key elements:

1. Supplying our body with effective fuel (nutrition) to generate energy;
2. Resting our body (sleep) so it can recover and replenish the energy it has expended; and
3. Avoiding risky behaviors that can threaten our bodily health and safety.

Reflection 8.3

Have you seen students change their eating habits after they've been in college for awhile? If yes, in what way(s)?

Nutrition Management Strategies

> *Tell me what you eat and I'll tell you what you are.*
>
> —Anthelme Brillat-Savarin, French gastronomist

> *If we are what we eat, then I'm cheap, fast, and easy.*
>
> —Steven Wright, award-winning comedian

In addition to eating for pleasure or out of convenience, we should "eat to win" by intentionally consuming foods that sustain our health and enable us to attain peak levels of physical and mental performance. Unfortunately, national surveys reveal that less than 40% of college students report having a healthy diet (Sax et al., 2004); additional studies confirm these students' self-reports by showing that their diets include too much fat and too little fruits and vegetables (Li et al., 2012). To maintain wellness and maximize performance, college students need to eat in a more thoughtful, nutritionally conscious way. You can help them do so by sharing and modeling the following nutrition-management strategies.

Follow a dietary plan that supplies nutritional variety and balance. Doing some advanced planning about what foods we're going to consume will help us from falling into the impulsive habit of just grabbing what's available, quick, and convenient—such as "fast food" and pre-packaged or processed food—which are the least healthy options.

Because different foods contain different types of nutrients (carbohydrates, protein, and fat) in different amounts, no single food group can supply all the nutrients our body needs. Thus, consuming a balanced blend of different food groups is needed for us to function at maximum capacity. **Figure 8.2** depicts the American Dietetic Association's *MyPlate* chart, an updated version of what was formerly called the "Food Guide Pyramid." To find the daily amount of food that should be consumed from each of the major food groups for one's age and gender, see the following websites: *www.ChooseMyPlate* or *www.cnpp.usda. gov/dietaryguidelines.*

Students can use the guidelines at these sites to develop and follow a personal nutritional plan which ensures that each of these key food groups is consumed on a consistent basis.

Another nutrition-management strategy you can share with students is "eating the rainbow"—consuming a variety of colorful fruits and vegetables. This is a simple but surefire way to get an ample amount of vitamins, minerals, and disease-fighting nutrients. The external color of fruits and vegetables can reveal the specific nutrients found within them. Fruits and vegetables that are:

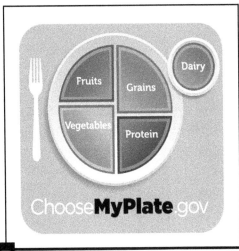

- Orange and Yellow (e.g., carrots, squash, melons) contain high amounts of vitamins A and C as well as nutrients that prevent cataracts and other types of eye disease
- Green (e.g., spinach, broccoli, avocado) contain high levels of vitamins B, E, and K as well as anti-cancer agents
- Red (e.g., tomatoes, strawberries, cherries) contain an antioxidant that reduces the risk of cancer and heart disease
- Purple and Blue (e.g., grapes, eggplant, red cabbage) contain abundant amounts of vitamins C and K as well as antioxidants that reduce the risk of cancer and cardiovascular disease

Figure 8.2   MyPlate. Source: USDA.

- Brown and White (e.g., cauliflower, mushrooms, bananas) contain chemicals that attack viruses and bacteria, reducing the risk of infectious diseases (Nutrition Australia, 2015).

Reflection 8.4

Do you regularly eat fruits and vegetables that fall into each of the above-five color categories? What are your weakest categories? To strengthen your weakest color category, what could you eat that you'd be willing to eat?

Examine the contents of packaged food products. Effective nutrition management requires awareness of the ingredients contained in packaged food products—before putting them into your shopping cart and into your body. This analysis can be done by simply taking a little time to read the labels on packaged food products to determine what healthy nutrients (vitamins and minerals) and unhealthy ingredients (fats, sugar, and sodium) they contain. To help students critically read and evaluate the nutrient labels on packaged food products, steer them to the following website: https://www.fda.gov/food/guidanceregulation/guidancedocumentsregulatoryinformation/labelingnutrition/ucm2006828.htm

> **Don't forget to hydrate. Even mild dehydration (shortage of fluid) can drain physical energy and create feelings of fatigue. Men should drink about 15.5 cups of fluids per day and women about 11.5 cups (Mayo Clinic Staff, 2017).**

Eating Disorders

While some students experience the "freshman 15"—a 15-pound weight gain during the first year of college (Levitsky et al., 2006), others may experience eating disorders associated with weight loss and loss of control of their eating habits.

These disorders are more common among females (National Institute of Mental Health, 2014), largely because Western cultures place more emphasis (and pressure) on females to maintain lighter body weight and size. Studies show that approximately one of every three college females report worrying about their weight, body image, or eating habits (Leavy, Gnong, & Ross, 2009).

Box 8.1 provides a short summary of the major eating disorders experienced by college students. These disorders are often accompanied by emotional issues (e.g., depression and anxiety) that are serious enough to require psychotherapy (National Institute of Mental Health, 2014). The earlier these disorders are identified and treated, the better the prognosis—the speed and probability of recovery. If you see students exhibiting symptoms (signs) of the following eating disorders, advise them to seek professional help immediately. (Use the referral strategies described in chapter 3, pp. 86-88.)

Box 8.1

Major Eating Disorders

Anorexia Nervosa

Students experiencing this disorder are dangerously thin, but see themselves as overweight and have an intense fear of gaining weight. They are obsessed with losing weight, eat infrequently, and, when they do eat, consume extremely small portions. They may also use different methods to lose weight, such as exercising compulsively and taking diet pills, laxatives, diuretics, or enemas. Anorexics are typically in denial about their condition. Even if their weight drops to the point where they may look like walking skeletons, they still fail to see themselves as being dangerously underweight.

I had a friend who took pride in her ability to lose 30 lbs. in one summer by not eating and working out excessively. I know girls that find pleasure in getting ill so that they throw up, can't eat, and lose weight.

—Comments written in a first-year student's journal

Bulimia Nervosa

This disorder is characterized by repeated episodes of "binge eating"—consuming an exorbitant amount of food (bingeing) within a short period of time. They lose self-control during the binge, and after the binge, they attempt to purge themselves of the calories they consumed (and their guilt about consuming them) by such methods as: self-induced vomiting, consuming excessive amounts of laxatives or diuretics, using enemas, or fasting. If this binge-purge pattern takes place at least twice a week and continues for three or more months, the person would be diagnosed as suffering from bulimia.

Like anorexics, bulimics aren't happy with how their bodies look, fear gaining weight, and are driven by an intense desire to lose weight. However, unlike anorexics, it's harder to identify bulimics because their binges and purges typically take place secretly and their body weight looks about normal for their age and height.

Binge-Eating Disorder

Similar to bulimics, binge eaters engage in repeated, out-of-control eating episodes during which they consume large amounts of food. However, unlike bulimics, binge eaters don't purge after their binging episodes. To be diagnosed with binge-eating disorder, the person must exhibit at least three of the following symptoms, two or more times per week, for several months:

1. Eating at an extremely rapid rate.
2. Eating until becoming uncomfortably full.
3. Eating large amounts of food when not physically hungry.
4. Eating alone because of embarrassment about others seeing how much they eat.
5. Feeling guilty, disgusted, or depressed after overeating.

Sources: American Psychiatric Association (2013); National Institute of Mental Health (2014).

R est and Sleep

In addition to eating well, sleeping well is another key component of wellness. The quantity and quality of our sleep we get plays a key role in preserving our health and optimizing our performance. The most obvious purpose of sleep is to rest and reenergize the body. However, sleep has other important benefits, including:

- Preserving and restoring the power of the immune system (National Institutes of Health, 2012),
- Coping with stress (Dement & Vaughan, 2000), and
- Enabling the brain to form and store memories (Ellenbogen, Payne, & Stickgold, 2006).

Sleep researchers agree that in today's information-loaded, multi-tasking world, humans are not getting the quantity and quality of sleep needed to perform at peak levels (Centers for Disease Control and Prevention, 2015a). College students, in particular, tend to have poorer sleep habits and experience more sleep problems than the general population. Because college students are dealing with heavier academic workloads than they had in high school, have more opportunities for late-night socializing, and are more likely to cram for tests by engaging in late-night (or all-night) study sessions, they often get into irregular sleep schedules and experience sleep deprivation. It's estimated that 60% of college students get an insufficient amount of sleep—a rate twice that of the general population (Kingkade, 2014).

> *Sleep deprivation is a major epidemic in our society. Americans spend so much time and energy chasing the American dream that they don't have much time left for actual dreaming.*
>
> —William Dement, pioneering sleep researcher and founder of the American Sleep Disorders Association

Reflection 8.5

How many hours of sleep per night do you need to perform at a peak level, both mentally and physically? Do you typically get this amount of sleep each night? If not, why not? How do you think most students would answer the above two questions?

> *First of all, you should probably know that your body will not function without sleep. I learned that the hard way.*
>
> —Words written by a first-year student in a letter of advice to incoming college students

Strategies to Share with Students for Improving the Quality of Their Sleep

Since sleep has powerful benefits for both the body and the mind, if we can improve the quality of our sleep, we can improve our physical and mental well-being. Listed below are specific strategies you could share with students for improving their sleep quality, which, in turn, should improve their overall health and performance.

Gain greater awareness of your sleep habits by keeping a sleep log or sleep journal. Tracking your sleep experiences in a journal may enable you to discover patterns in the things you do, or don't do, just before to going to bed on nights when you sleep well compared to nights when you sleep poorly. If you discover a pattern, you can use this information to help you develop a pre-bedtime routine that gets you a good night's sleep on a more consistent basis.

Try to get into a regular sleep schedule by going to bed and getting up at about the same time each day. The human body functions best when it runs on a rhythm of set cycles. If you can get your body on a regular sleep cycle, you can get into a biological rhythm that makes it easier for you to fall asleep, stay asleep, and wake up naturally according to the your body's "internal alarm clock."

Getting on a regular sleep schedule that's conducive to high-quality sleep is particularly important for students at times when they need to perform at peak levels, such as midterms and finals. Sleep research shows that to be at their physical and mental best for upcoming exams, students should get on a regular sleep schedule of getting to sleep and getting up at about the same time at least one week before major exams are to be taken (Dement & Vaughan, 1999). Unfortunately, for many college students, the opposite happens. Midterms and finals are the times during the term when their regular sleep cycles are likely to be disrupted by the need to stay up later to cram for exams, get up earlier to squeeze in extra study time, or pull all-nighters and not sleep at all. To help students avoid this cramming pattern and get into a regular sleep schedule near midterms and finals, advise them to use the "distributed" practice and "part-to-whole" study method described in chapter 7 (pp. 207-208).

Attempt to get into a relaxing pre-bedtime ritual each night. Taking a hot bath or shower, consuming a hot (non-caffeinated) beverage, or listening to relaxing music are bedtime rituals that can get us into a worry-free state before sleep and help us fall asleep sooner (Epstein & Mardon, 2007). Also, making a list of things we intend to do the next day before going to bed may help us relax and fall asleep because we know we're organized and ready to handle the following day's tasks.

Because sleep helps us retain what we experienced before falling asleep, a light review of class notes or reading highlights just before bedtime might be another good pre-bedtime practice. Many years of research indicates that the best thing humans can do to retain information they've just learned or studied is to "sleep on it." This is probably due to the fact that sleep gives the brain time to process and store the information without having to deal with external stimulation or outside distractions (Kuriyama et al., 2008; National Institutes of Health, 2013).

Reflection 8.6

Just before going to bed at night, what do you typically do? Do you think this helps or hinders the quality of your sleep?

Keep the temperature in the room where you sleep no higher than 70 degrees Fahrenheit. Warm temperatures often make us feel sleepy, but they usually don't help us stay asleep or sleep deeply. This is why people have more trouble sleeping on hot summer evenings. High-quality, uninterrupted sleep is more likely to take place at cooler room temperatures that don't exceed 70 degrees (Lack et al., 2008).

Avoid intense mental activity just before going to bed. Light mental work may serve as a relaxing pre-sleep ritual, but intense reading, writing, or studying before bedtime induces a heightened state of mental arousal that can interfere with your ability to wind down and fall asleep (National Institutes of Health, 2012).

Avoid intense physical exercise before bedtime. Vigorous physical activity elevates muscle tension and increases oxygen flow to the brain, both of which hinder our ability to fall asleep. If you know students who like to exercise in the evening, advise them to do it at least three hours before bedtime (Epstein & Mardon, 2007).

Avoid consumption of sleep-interfering foods, beverages, or drugs in the late afternoon or evening. In particular, avoid the following sleep-disruptive substances near bedtime:

- **Caffeine.** It's a stimulant drug; for most people, it stimulates the nervous system and keeps them awake.
- **Nicotine.** Another stimulant drug that's likely to reduce the depth and quality of sleep. (Note: Smoking hookah through a water pipe delivers the same amount of nicotine as a cigarette.)
- **Alcohol.** It's a depressant (sedative) substance that makes us feel sleepy in larger doses; however, in smaller doses, it can have a stimulating effect. Furthermore, alcohol disrupts sleep quality by reducing the amount of time spent in dream-stage sleep. (Marijuana does the same.)
- **High-fat foods.** Eating just before bedtime (or during the night) increases digestive activity in the stomach. This "internal noise" can interfere with the depth and quality of sleep. In particular, high-fat foods such as peanuts, beans, fruits, raw vegetables, and high-fat snacks should be avoided before bedtime because these foods require more digestive effort and activity.

> Alcohol and marijuana are substances that make us feel sleepy but that doesn't mean they enhance sleep quality. In fact, these two substances typically reduce the quality of sleep by interfering with dream-stage sleep.

A lcohol Use among College Students

Research indicates that first-year college students drink more than they did in high school (Johnston et al., 2006) and have higher rates of alcohol abuse than do high school students and students at more advanced stages of the college experience (Bergen-Cico, 2000; White, Jamieson-Drake, & Swartzwelder, 2002). Because they think so many other college students drink, the number-one reason why first-year students drink is to "fit in" and feel socially accepted (Meilman & Presley, 2005). However, research shows college students overestimate how many of their peers drink and how much they drink. This overestimation can lead students to believe they need to conform to the norm, and if they don't, they won't be "normal" (Cail & LaBrie, 2010).

Whatever the legal age for drinking may be, the reality is that first-year college students will be confronted with the following choices:

1. To drink or not to drink.
2. To drink responsibly or irresponsibly.

If they choose to drink, remind them that it should be *their* choice, not a choice imposed on them by social pressure or peer conformity. For students who drink, listed below are some quick tips you can share with them for drinking safely and responsibly. To minimize the risk that students will respond defensively to your advice, share these tips as recommended strategies, not as pious platitudes or preachy warnings.

- **Don't feel pressured to drink to an excessive degree.** Remind them of the research showing that college students overestimate how many of their peers drink and how much they drink. They shouldn't feel "uncool," unusual, or abnormal if they prefer to drink only occasionally and in moderation, rather than consistently and excessively.
- **Don't drink with the intention of getting intoxicated; set a limit about how much you will drink.** Use alcohol as a beverage, not as a mind-altering drug.
- **Eat well before drinking and snack while drinking.** This helps lower the peak level of alcohol in the bloodstream.
- **Drink slowly.** Sip, don't gulp; avoid "shot-gunning" or "chug-a-lugging" drinks.
- **Spread out drinking over time so that drinks are consumed intermittently, not consecutively.** If you're having more than one drink during the course of an evening, space out the drinks over time. This gives the body time to metabolize the alcohol consumed and keeps the percentage of alcohol in the bloodstream at lower, more manageable levels.
- **Monitor your physical and mental state while drinking.** Don't continue to drink after you've reached a state of moderate relaxation or a mild loss of inhibition. Drinking to the point where you're drunk or bordering on intoxication will not improve your physical health or social life. Slurring your speech, nodding out, or vomiting in the restroom isn't likely to make you the life of the party.

> **Remind students that alcohol can be costly, in terms of both dollars and calories. So, by monitoring the amount of alcohol they consume, they're not only managing their health and safety, they're also managing their weight and money.**

Alcohol Abuse

Alcohol is a legal substance (at least for people who've reached a certain age) and it's ingested as a beverage, not injected, smoked, or snorted. That being said, alcohol is still a *drug*, particularly when consumed in large quantities (doses). In moderate amounts, alcohol could be described as a relaxing beverage; however, in larger doses, it's a mind-altering substance that contains a mind-altering ingredient: ethyl alcohol (see **Figure 8.3**). Thus, like other mind-altering substances, alcohol has the potential to be addictive; approximately 7-8% of people who drink experience alcohol dependency (alcoholism) (Julien, Advokat, & Comaty, 2011). Alcohol dependency has genetic roots, so if you know students with a history of alcohol abuse in their family, gently remind them to be cautious about their drinking habits.

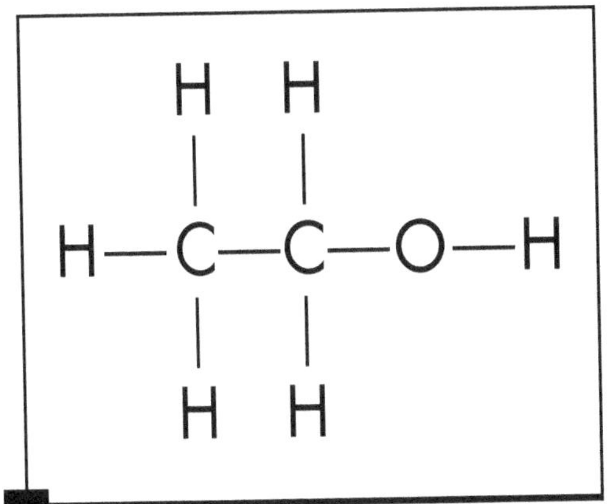

Students' expectations that drinking (or drinking to excess) is an expected and normal part of the college experience is probably why the number-one "drug" problem on college campuses is *binge drinking*—episodes during which large amounts of alcohol (4-5 or more drinks) are consumed in short period of time, resulting in an acute state of intoxication—more commonly referred to as a "drunken state" (Marczinski, Estee, & Grant, 2009).

Although binge drinking isn't necessarily a form of alcohol dependency, it's still a form of alcohol *abuse* because it has direct, negative effects on the physical or mental well-being of the drinker. Research indicates that every time a person drinks to the point of drunkenness, it reduces the size and effectiveness of the part of the brain involved with memory formation (Brown et al., 2000). This finding has led researchers to a simple but disturbing conclusion: Each time a person gets drunk, the dumber that person gets (Weschsler & Wuethrich, 2002).

Figure 8.3 Ethyl Alcohol

Binge drinking also reduces a person's inhibitions about engaging in risk-taking behavior, which, in turn, increases their risk of personal accidents, injuries, and illnesses. It's noteworthy that the legal age for consuming alcohol was once lowered to 18 years, but it was raised back to 21 because the number of drunk-driving accidents and deaths among teenage drinkers increased dramatically after the legal age was lowered (Mothers Against Drunk Driving, 2015; NHTSA/FARS & US Census Bureau, 2012). Traffic accidents still account for more deaths of Americans between the ages of 15 and 24 than any other cause (Centers for Disease Control & Prevention, 2015b).

When people consume alcohol in substantial amounts, they become substantially less cautious about doing things they normally would be hesitant or reluctant to do. This chemically induced sense of self-confidence—colloquially referred to as "liquid courage"—can override the process of logical thinking and rational decision making, increasing the likelihood that the drinker will engage in irrational, risk-taking behavior—such as fighting others or destroying property. Binge drinkers are also more likely to engage in reckless driving—increasing their risk of injury or death, and are more willing to risk unprotected sex—increasing their risk of pregnancy and contracting sexually transmitted infections (STIs).

Arguably, no other drug reduces a person's inhibitions as dramatically as alcohol. It's been said that binge drinking disinhibits and deludes drinkers into thinking they're "invincible, immortal, and infertile." The loss of inhibition that takes place during binge-drinking episodes stems from the fact that alcohol is a depressant drug: It depresses (slows down) signals normally sent from the upper, front part of the brain (the "human brain")—which is in charge of rational thinking and controls or inhibits the lower, middle part of the brain (the "animal brain")—which is responsible for basic animal drives, such as sex and aggression (see **Figure 8.4**). When the upper (rational) brain is slowed down by alcohol, the animal brain is freed from the signals that normally restrain or inhibit it, thus allowing basic drives to be released and expressed. This is the underlying biological reason why binge drinking increases the drinker's risk of engaging in aggressive behavior, such as sexual harassment, sexual abuse, and relationship violence (Abbey, 2002; Bushman & Cooper, 1990).

If you drink, don't park. Accidents cause people.

—Steven Wright, American comedian

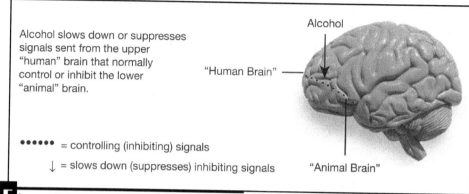

Alcohol slows down or suppresses signals sent from the upper "human" brain that normally control or inhibit the lower "animal" brain.

Alcohol

"Human Brain"

•••••• = controlling (inhibiting) signals

↓ = slows down (suppresses) inhibiting signals

"Animal Brain"

Figure 8.4   How Alcohol Works in the Brain to Reduce Personal Inhibitions

As a peer mentor, your objective shouldn't be to scare students away from even thinking about drinking or to lay a heavy "guilt trip" on students who do drink. Instead, it should be to educate students about the pros and cons of drinking, and to assure students who prefer not to drink that they shouldn't feel pressured to drink. For students who prefer to drink, advise them is to use alcohol moderately and safely, not excessively and dangerously.

Reflection 8.7

Do you drink alcohol? If yes, why? If no, why not? How do you think most students on your campus would answer these questions?

Use and Abuse of Illegal Drugs

In the United States, alcohol is a substance that citizens can use legally once they reach a certain age. Other substances cannot be used legally at any age. While the college years are often a time for exploring and experimenting with different ideas, feelings, and experiences, experimenting with illegal drugs can be risky business. Unlike legal drugs, which have to pass through rigorous testing by the Federal Drug Administration before being approved for public consumption, similar safeguards are not in place for the production and packaging of illegal drugs. We don't know if or what illegal drugs have been "cut" (mixed) during the production process. Thus, consuming an illegal substance is not only a criminal risk, it's also a health risk because it involves consumption of an *unregulated* substance. For these reasons, the best bottom-line advice you can give students about using illegal drug is: When in doubt, keep it out. Don't put anything into your body that's totally unregulated, possibly adulterated, and potentially unpredictable.

Listed below are the major types of illegal drugs, accompanied by a short description of their primary physical and psychological effects.

- **Cocaine (coke, crack).** A stimulant that's typically snorted or smoked and produces a strong "rush" (an intense feeling of euphoria)
- **Amphetamines (speed, meth).** A strong stimulant that increases energy and general arousal; it's usually taken in pill form but may also be smoked or injected

- Ecstasy (X). A stimulant typically taken in pill form that speeds up the nervous system and reduces social inhibitions
- Hallucinogens (psychedelics). Drugs that alter or distort perception—for example, LSD ("acid") and hallucinogenic mushrooms ("shrooms")
- Narcotics (e.g., heroin and prescription pain pills). Sedative drugs that slow down the nervous system and produce feelings of relaxation. (Heroin is a particularly powerful narcotic that's typically injected or smoked and produces an intense "rush" of euphoria.)
- Marijuana (weed, pot). A legal drug in some states, but still illegal in most states; it works primarily as a depressant or sedative, slowing down the nervous system and producing feelings of relaxation
- Date Rape Drugs. Depressant (sedative) drugs that induce sleepiness, memory loss and possible loss of consciousness, thus rendering the drinker vulnerable to rape or other forms of sexual assault. These drugs are typically colorless, tasteless and odorless; thus, they can be easily mixed into a drink without the drinker noticing it. Common date-rape drugs include Rohypnol ("roofies") and GHB ("liquid E").

Reflection 8.8

What illegal drugs (if any) have you seen students use? Have you seen students use an illegal drug that does not appear on the above list? Do you think that drug use at your campus is widespread or serious enough to be considered a "problem" that needs attention?

Motives (Reasons) for Drug Use

People use drugs for a variety of reasons, the most common of which are listed below. Increasing students' awareness of the motives behind drug use can help reduce their tendency to do drugs for unconscious or subconscious reasons.

- Social Pressure. To "fit in" or feel socially accepted (e.g., drinking alcohol because everyone else seems to be doing it)
- Recreational (Party) Use. For fun, stimulation, or pleasure (e.g., smoking marijuana at parties to relax, loosen inhibitions, and have a "good time")
- Experimental Use. Doing drugs out of curiosity—to test out their effects (e.g., experimenting with LSD to see what it's like to have a psychedelic or hallucinogenic experience)
- Therapeutic Use. Using prescription or over-the-counter drugs for medical purposes (e.g., taking Prozac for depression or Adderall to treat attention deficit disorder)
- Performance Enhancement. To improve physical, mental, or social performance (e.g., taking steroids to improve athletic performance or stimulants to stay awake and cram for exams)
- Escapism. To escape a personal problem or an unpleasant emotional state (e.g., taking ecstasy to escape depression or boredom)
- Addiction. Physical or psychological dependence (e.g., habitually using cocaine or prescription drugs because stopping use of them triggers uncomfortable withdrawal symptoms)

"For fun." "To party." "To fit in."
"To become more talkative, outgoing, and flirtatious."
"To try anything once."
"To become numb." "To forget problems." "Being bored."

—Responses of freshmen and sophomores to the question, "Why do college students take drugs?"

Reflection 8.9

What motives for drug use listed above would you say are the most common reasons for drug use on your campus? Do you think students' common motivations (reasons) for using drugs could be satisfied by substituting drug-free experiences? If yes, what would those experiences be?

Any drug has the potential to be addictive, especially if it's injected intravenously (directly into a vein) or smoked (inhaled through the lungs). These routes of intake are particularly dangerous because they deliver the drug to the brain faster and heighten the drug's peak effect (its highest level of impact). When a drug has a fast and high-peak effect ("rush"), it's soon followed by a sharp and sudden drop in its effect ("crash") (see **Figure 8.5**). This peak-to-valley, roller-coaster-like experience can create a stronger need or craving to use the drug again after its intense impact suddenly bottoms out, which, in turn, increases the user's tendency to use it again and use it repeatedly, thus increasing the risk of dependency (addiction).

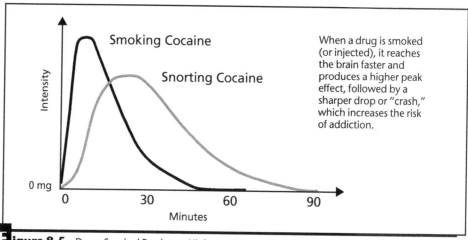

Figure 8.5   Drugs Smoked Produce a Higher and More Rapid Peak Effect

Listed below are the most common signs that a person's drug use (including alcohol) is moving in the direction of *dependency (addiction)*:
- Steadily increasing the amount (dose) of the drug and/or using it more consistently
- Difficulty cutting back (e.g., unable to reduce the frequency of drug use or use the drug in smaller amounts)
- Difficulty controlling or limiting the amount taken after starting
- Keeping a steady supply of the drug on hand
- Spending more money on the drug than can be afforded
- Using the drug alone
- Hiding or hoarding the drug
- Lying about drug use to family and friends
- Reacting angrily or defensively when questioned about using the drug
- Rationalizing drug abuse (e.g., "I'm just partying. It's a normal part of the college experience.")

- Being "in denial" about abusing the drug (e.g., "I don't have a problem")
- When continuing use of the drug matters more to the user than the continuing personal and interpersonal problems its use is causing.

Helping someone deal with drug dependency or other psychological problems (e.g., eating disorders and abusive relationships) can be challenging because the person is often in *denial*—that is, doesn't "see" the problem because it has been pushed out of conscious awareness. Denial is not simply lying; it's a defense mechanism used unconsciously to protect one's self-image or self-esteem. Thus, the first step involved in helping students overcome drug abuse or a psychological disorder often involves helping them overcome denial. Guidelines for doing so are provided in **Box 8.2**

Box 8.2

Top Tips for Helping Students Overcome Denial

1. First, ask permission to talk about the issue. People are more likely to talk about their behavior and change their behavior when they have some sense of decision-making control over the process, rather than having the process imposed on them.
2. Make sure the student knows that you're there not to criticize or condemn, but because you care and want to provide support.
3. Avoid heavy "guilt trips." Don't attack the student's character; instead, simply share your perceptions by using "I messages" (e.g., "What I'm seeing is . . . .").
4. Assure the student that what he or she is experiencing is not unusual. (For example, "normalize" the student's experience by saying: "A lot of people have struggled with . . .").
5. Don't focus on the student's character or personal traits. Instead, focus on: (a) the student's behavior, (b) the negative consequences that the behavior is having on the student and others, and (c) the positive consequences that will take place once the student's behavior is changed.
6. Mention that other people view the student's behavior the same way as you do. This will help assure the student that it's not just your perception (or misperception). However, don't share the names of other people without their permission.
7. When you approach the student, try to bring the student's closest friends or family members with you. This will assure the student that it's not just your personal "crusade" or "rescue mission."
8. If possible, introduce the student to someone who had experienced denial and overcame it. This will help assure the student that the challenge isn't insurmountable and positive change can be made.
9. If the student is unwilling or unable to take action, summarize what was discussed during your meeting and ask if it would be okay to check back sometime later.
10. If your first attempt to help fails, don't give up. Be patient and persistent because people in denial can be persistently resistant. It may take more than one attempt to make a breakthrough.

Sources: Ogden and Biebers (2010), Sobell and Sobell (2013).

Reflection 8.10

In your leadership or mentoring role, do you expect to encounter situations in which you may need to help students overcome denial?

Are you familiar with the concept of *intervention*—a planned attempt by a group of people (usually family and friends) to intervene with someone in denial and persuade that person to seek professional help? If yes, what was the problem and how well did the intervention work?

U nhealthy Relationships

An unhealthy relationship is one that threatens a person's physical or psychological well-being. (See **Box 8.3** for a summary of the major types of unhealthy relationships.) If you know of students who are involved in a relationship in which they are repeatedly disrespected, excessively controlled, or concerned about their safety, strongly encourage them to acknowledge it and do something about it. If they don't take action early, they run the risk that the abusive relationship may escalate and become violent. Whether the abuse is emotional, psychological, physical, or sexual—it's a threat to personal wellness that should never be tolerated. Behaviors that qualify as abusive include, but are not limited to, degrading language, dominating or dictating a partner's actions, and physical or sexual assault (Murray & Kardatzke, 2007).

Unfortunately, the prevalence of relationship abuse among college students is high. A survey conducted by the National Institutes of Health revealed that 44.7% of college students experienced partner or non-partner violence, 72.8% of whom were women and 27.2% were men (Forke et al., 2008). Relationship abuse occurs among college students of all races, ethnicities, and socioeconomic groups (Malik, Sorenson, & Aneshensel, 1997), including students who are gay and bisexual (Freedner et al., 2002).

Victims and offenders of relationship abuse are often unwilling to admit, or are in complete denial about, the abuse that's taking place. Even if victims of relationship abuse are aware of the situation, they often don't seek help because they're embarrassed or fear retaliation from their abusive partner. If you know or suspect that a student is involved in an abusive relationship, it's imperative that you encourage that student to seek immediate help. Connect the student with your college's Counseling Office. This office may be staffed with a professional who has special expertise working with victims and perpetrators of relationship abuse. If not, your campus counselors should be able to refer the students to an off-campus professional who specializes in relationship abuse.

Reflection 8.11

Have you known anyone who was involved in an abusive relationship? In what way(s) was the relationship abusive? How did the abused partner handle it?

Box 8.3

Unhealthy Relationships

Listed below are various forms of unhealthy relationships. Note that the examples cited are not just physical or sexual in nature; they include emotional and psychological abuse—which can be just as harmful.

Abusive Relationships

An abusive relationship may be defined as one in which one partner is abused physically, verbally, or emotionally. Abusers are often dependent on their partners for their sense of self-worth and fear their partner will abandon them, so they attempt to prevent this from happening by over-controlling their partner. Abusers may also feel powerless or weak in other areas of their life and attempt to bolster their self-esteem or self-efficacy by exerting power over their partner.

Potential Signs of Abuse:

- The abuser is possessive and tries to dominate or control all aspects of the partner's life (e.g., discourages the partner from having contact with friends or family members).
- The abuser frequently yells, shouts, intimidates, or physically threatens the partner.
- The abuser constantly puts down the partner and attempts to damage the partner's self-esteem.
- The abuser displays intense and irrational jealousy (e.g., accusing the partner of infidelity without evidence).
- The abuser demands affection or sex, even when the partner is uninterested or unwilling.
- The abuser often appears charming to others in public settings, but is abusive toward the partner in private.
- The abused partner behaves differently (typically more reserved or inhibited) in the partner's presence.
- The abused partner fears the abuser.

Strategies to Share with Students for Avoiding or Escaping Abusive Relationships:

- Minimize relationship isolation by continuing to maintain social ties with friends outside of the relationship.
- Don't rationalize or make excuses for the abuser's behavior (e.g., he was drinking or she was under stress).
- Get an objective, "third party" perspective by asking close friends for their views on your relationship. (Love can be "blind," so it's possible to be in denial about an abusive relationship and not "see" what's really going on.)
- Speak with a professional counselor on campus to help you view your relationships more objectively.

Sexual Assault, a.k.a. Sexual Violence

Sexual assault refers to nonconsensual (unwanted or unwilling) sexual contact forced on another person without that person's consent. *Rape* is a form of sexual assault or sexual violence that's defined legally as forced sexual penetration (intercourse) imposed through physical force, by threat of bodily harm, or when the victim is incapable of giving consent due to alcohol or drug intoxication. Rape typically falls into two major categories:

(1) Stranger Rape—when a total stranger forces sexual intercourse on the victim.
(2) Acquaintance Rape or Date Rape—when the victim knows, or is dating, the person who forces unwanted sexual intercourse.

It's estimated that 85-90% of reported rapes on college campuses are committed by someone the victim is acquainted with, and 50% take place during a date. Alcohol is frequently associated with acquaintance rapes because it lowers the rapist's inhibitions and reduces the victim's ability to determine if it's a potentially dangerous situation. Since the partners are familiar with each other, the victim may feel that what happened was not really rape. However, acquaintance rape *is* rape and it's still a crime because it involves nonconsensual sex.

Recommendations to Share with Female Students for Avoiding Sexual Assault:

- Avoid drinking to the point of intoxication or associating with those who do.
- If you drink, or go to places where others drink, remain aware of the possibility of date-rape drugs being dropped into your drink. To guard against this risk, don't let others give you drinks and hold onto your drink at all times (e.g., don't leave it, go to the restroom, and come back to drink it again).

- When you attend parties, go with at least one other friend so you can keep an eye out for each other.
- Clearly and assertively communicate what your sexual limits are. Use "I messages" to firmly resist unwanted sexual advances by focusing specifically on the person's actions or behavior (e.g., "I'm not comfortable with you touching me like that").
- Carry mace or pepper spray and be prepared to use it if necessary.
- Take a self-defense class. Research shows that taking a course on avoiding or resisting sexual assault reduces the course taker's risk of rape by almost 50% (Senn et al., 2015).

Recommendations to Share with Male Students for Reducing Their Risk of Committing Sexual Assault:
- Don't assume a woman wants to have sex just because she's:
  (a) very friendly or flirtatious,
  (b) dressed in a particular way, or
  (c) drinking alcohol.
- If a woman says "no," take it as a firm no. Don't interpret it to mean that she's really saying "yes."
- Don't think that just because you're "the man," you have to be the sexual initiator or aggressor.
- Don't interpret a woman's rejection of your sexual advances as a personal insult or a blow to your masculinity; it simply meaning that she's not ready or willing to have sex.

Sexual Harassment

In college settings, sexual harassment includes any unwanted or unwelcome sexual behavior initiated by another student or an employee of the college that interferes with a student's education. Sexual harassment can take the following forms:
(1) **Physical**—initiating contact by touching, grabbing, pinching, or brushing up against a person's body.
(2) **Verbal**—making sexual comments about someone's body or clothes; sexual jokes; teasing—including spreading sexual rumors about a person's sexual activity or orientation; or requesting sexual favors in exchange for a better grade, job, or promotion.
(3) **Nonverbal**—staring or glaring at another person's body; making erotic or obscene gestures toward the person; sending obscene messages or unsolicited pornographic material to the person.

Recommendations to Share with Students for Dealing with Sexual Harassment:
- Make your objections clear and firm. Tell the harasser directly that you're offended by the unwanted behavior and that you know it constitutes sexual harassment.
- Keep a written record of any harassment. Record the date, place, and specific details about the harassing behavior.
- Become aware of the sexual harassment policy on campus. (The school's policy is likely to be found in the *Student Handbook* or may be obtained from the Office of Human Resources.)
- If you are unsure about whether you're experiencing sexual harassment, or what to do about it, contact the Counseling Center or Office of Human Resources.

Note: Sexual harassment is a form of *peer harassment*—a broader category of harassment that includes taunting, bullying (in person or online), and harassing others based on their race or sexual orientation. All these behaviors violate a federal law that guarantees the right of all students to experience a learning environment conducive to learning. If you know of students who are experiencing any of these forms of harassment, be sure they don't tolerate them silently, but report them immediately to school authorities.

Sources: Karjane, Fisher, and Cullen (2005); National Center for Victims of Crime (2012); National Institute of Justice (2008); Ottens and Hotelling (2001); Penfold (2006)

Mental Health and Emotional Wellness

Physical health and mental health represent the "twin towers" of personal wellness; the latter involves attaining and maintaining emotional well-being. One role of an effective peer mentor is to help students stay in tune with their emotional self and seek professional help if they're experiencing mental health issues. You may need to assure students that they shouldn't feel guilty or embarrassed if they are experiencing mental health problems. These are common occurrences and they often have biochemical roots that have nothing to do with personal weakness or lack of will power (Meynen, 2010; Rüsch, Angermeyer, & Corrigan, 2005)

Anxiety and depression are two of the most common emotions that adversely affect the mental health of people in general (Anxiety and Depression Association of America, 2017) and college students in particular (Center for Collegiate Mental Health, 2017). Discussed below are the key signs (symptoms) of anxiety and depression, along with strategies you can share with students to help them manage these emotions.

Stress and Anxiety

Students report experiencing higher levels of stress in college than they did in high school (Bartlett, 2002; Sax, 2003). But what exactly is *stress*? Stress is rooted in the "fight-or-flight" response—an automatic physical reaction wired into the human body that enabled our ancient ancestors to survive by fighting or fleeing from life-threatening predators. The word "stress" itself derives from Latin, meaning "to draw tight." As its root meaning suggests, stress isn't necessarily bad; in the right amount, it can actually be productive. For instance, a tightened guitar string generates better sound than a string that's too lax or loose, a tightened bow delivers a more powerful arrow shot, and a tightened muscle generates more strength or speed. In fact, psychologists distinguish between two types of stress: "distress," bad or unproductive stress, and "eustress," good or productive stress (Selye, 1974, 1975; O'Sullivan, 2010).

Reflection 8.12

Can you think of a situation in which you performed better because you were slightly nervous or experiencing a moderate amount of stress?

Many years of research indicate that a *moderate* or intermediate level of stress improves mental and physical performance (see Figure 8.6). When stress is moderate and manageable, it can generate energy, increase motivation, and focus attention (Halvorson, 2010; Sapolsky, 2004). Remind the students you work with that not all stress is bad; it can work either for them or against them, depending on its level of intensity and how long it continues. They shouldn't expect to eliminate stress entirely, nor should they want to; instead, their goal should be to contain it and maintain it at a level where it's more productive than destructive.

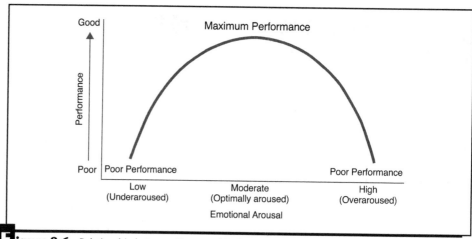

Figure 8.6   Relationship between Stress and Performance

When stress is very intense and chronic (ongoing), it becomes distress, or what's more commonly called *anxiety* (Mayo Clinic Staff, 2015a). Anxiety experienced over an extended period of time jeopardizes our physical health by suppressing the immune system, leaving the body more vulnerable to flu, colds, and other infectious diseases. For example, the immune systems of college students who experience high levels of stress during midterms and finals have been found to produce fewer antibodies, rendering them more susceptible to physical illness (Bosch et al., 2004; Deinzer et al., 2000).

Studies also show that students who experience high levels of academic anxiety are more likely to engage in "surface" approaches to learning that rely on memorization instead of "deep learning" strategies, such as reflecting on and finding meaning in what they're learning (Biggs & Tang, 2011; Ramsden, 2003). Students who experience *test anxiety* also exhibit poorer academic performance because anxious thoughts and feelings (e.g., fear of failure) occupy their mind during exams, reducing concentration and taking up valuable "mental space" that should be devoted to recalling knowledge and thinking critically (Fernández-Castillo & Caurcel, 2014).

Box 8.4 provides a summary of the signs or symptoms of anxiety. If you know students who experience these symptoms for more than a week, or experience them during or around the time of exams and other academic-performance situations (e.g., making public presentations), encourage them to make an appointment with a professional in your campus Counseling Office.

Posttraumatic Stress Disorder (PTSD): A Distinctive Type of Anxiety Disorder

PTSD is a specific type of anxiety disorder that may take place after someone has had a traumatic experience—an emotionally intense, dangerous, or life-threatening event, such as military combat or sexual assault. It's normal to experience intense feelings of anxiety after such events for several weeks or months. However, if these intense feelings do not gradually subside over the passage of time, or if they intensify over time, the person may be experiencing PTSD.

Box 8.4

The Symptoms (Signs) of Anxiety

- **Jitteriness or shaking**—especially the hands
- **Accelerated heart rate or heart palpitations** (irregular heartbeat)
- **Sweating**—especially sweaty (clammy) palms
- **Dry mouth.** Due to decreased production of saliva (which is why nervous speakers may experience "cotton mouth" and repeatedly sip water)
- **Muscle tension.** Tightness in the chest, upper shoulders or neck (hence, the expression "uptight"), or a feeling of tightness (lump) in the throat (from which comes the expression "choking" under pressure)
- **Body aches.** Caused by heightened muscle tension, which can lead to tension headaches, backaches, or chest pain; in some cases, chest tension can be so intense it may feel like the person is having a heart attack, but in reality, it's a panic attack)
- **Weakness and fatigue.** Caused by a sustained state of muscle tension that can be physically exhausting
- **Cold, pale hands or feet.** As reflected in the expressions "white knuckles" and "cold feet"
- **Feeling faint or dizzy.** Due to blood vessels constricting, which reduces oxygen flow to the brain
- **Stomach cramps, indigestion, or queasiness.** Caused by increased secretion of stomach acid (as reflected in the expression, "I feel like I've got butterflies in my stomach")
- **Elimination problems** (e.g., constipation, or diarrhea)
- **Difficulty sleeping.** Having trouble falling asleep, staying asleep, or experiencing interrupted (fitful) sleep
- **Increased susceptibility to colds, flu, and other infections.** Due to suppression of the body's immune system, resulting in lower production of antibodies.

Symptoms of PTSD include the following:

- Constantly feeling tense or "on edge"
- Easily startled
- Difficulty concentrating
- Difficulty sleeping
- Emotional numbness
- Sudden outbursts of anger
- Memory loss for the traumatic experience or for events around the time of the experience
- Avoiding places, events, or objects that are reminders of the traumatic experience
- "Flashbacks"—reliving the traumatic experience along with feelings of fright and physical arousal (e.g., heart palpitation and sweating). Flashbacks can happen suddenly and spontaneously, or they may be triggered by sights, sounds, and dreams that remind the person of the traumatic experience.

If you know any students who are exhibiting any of the above symptoms for three or more months after experiencing a traumatic event, encourage them to seek professional help by contacting the Counseling Center on campus or the PTSD Information Line (802-296-6300) (e-mail: ncptsd@va.gov).

Stress-Management Strategies

When students experience intense and chronic anxiety, they should seek help from a professional therapist. For students experiencing milder forms of stress that may not require professional assistance, suggest they use self-help practices, such as the following stress-management strategies.

Exercise. Counselors and psychotherapists recommend exercise for people experiencing milder forms of anxiety (Johnsgard, 2004). Exercise lowers stress by increasing the release of serotonin in the brain—a mellowing neurochemical (brain chemical) that reduces feelings of tension.

Journaling. Writing about our feelings in a personal journal helps us identify and express the emotions we're experiencing (a form of emotional intelligence). It can also serve as a cathartic outlet for coping with stress (Seaward, 2011).

> *There are thousands of causes for stress, and one antidote to stress is self-expression. That's what happens to me every day. My thoughts get off my chest, down my sleeves, and onto my pad.*
>
> —Garson Kanin, American writer, actor, and film director

Author's Experience   I'm the kind of person who carries the worries of the day with me to bed at night, which really affects my sleep. I'm also the type of person who juggles many balls during the day, which also adds to my stress level. By chance, I discovered a great strategy for managing my stress while I was conducting a conflict-resolution workshop about 15 years ago. During the workshop, I asked the participants to write down in a journal all the stressors they encountered during the day for 30 consecutive days. Then I told them we would come together as a group at the end of the 30 days to identify our stressors.

After the workshop, I decided to do this for myself on a regular basis. Each night before going to bed, I wrote down the categories or sources of stress that I experienced during the day. After 30 days, I was able to recognize patterns in what triggered my stress and devise strategies to combating my stressors. I also noticed that over time, my level of anxiety decreased and the quality of my sleep increased. I still use this strategy whenever I'm under stress or not sleeping well.

— *Aaron Thompson*

Substitute positive thoughts for negative (anxious) thoughts. The part of the human brain involved in thinking (the cortex) has many connections with the part of the brain responsible for emotions (the limbic system) (Goleman, 1995; Zull, 2011). Thus, the brain is wired in such a way that our thoughts can affect our emotions. If our thinking can influence our feelings, then changing how we think can change how we feel, including whether we feel stressed or anxious.

By changing negative, anxiety-producing thoughts to positive, relaxing thoughts, our level of stress or tension can be reduced. For instance, during an exam, if a student sees other students turning in their tests early, they may have negative thoughts like, "They must all be smarter me." The student could stop that anxiety-producing thought and substitute a more positive thought, such as: "They're getting up and getting out because they're giving up." Or, "They're rushing out without taking the time to carefully review their test before turning it in."

One of the keys to substituting positive for negative thoughts is to focus thinking on what we want to happen, not on what we're afraid might happen (Halvorson, 2010). For instance, students' test anxiety can be reduced if they don't focus on (and worry about) how many points they might be losing during an exam, but focus on how many points they're actually earning.

Reflection 8.13

What types of negative (anxiety-producing) thoughts do you find students commonly expressing? Could you recommend positive thoughts they could substitute for these negative thoughts?

Depression

Along with anxiety, depression is the other major emotional problem that afflicts a significant number of people, including college students. As its name implies, when people are depressed, their mood is lowered or pushed down. In short, depression is an emotional state characterized by feelings of sadness accompanied by loss of interest, hope, and energy (Mayo Clinic, 2015b). Research indicates that depression is associated with lower academic performance in college and higher risk of withdrawal from college—even among highly motivated and academically well-prepared students (Eisenberg, Golberstein, & Hunt, 2009).

In contrast to anxiety, which typically involves worrying about something that's currently happening or is about to happen, depression more often involves something that has already happened, particularly a *loss*, such as a lost relationship (e.g., broken romance or death of a family member), or a lost opportunity (e.g., losing a job or not getting into a desired school) (Bowlby, 1980; Price, Choi, & Vinokur, 2002). It's natural and normal for someone to feel dejected after losses such as these. However, if the dejection reaches a point where the person cannot concentrate and complete day-to-day tasks, and if it continues for an extended period of time, that person may be experiencing what psychologists call *clinical depression or depressive disorder*—a serious form of depression for which professional help should be sought. **Box 8.5** provides a summary of symptoms or signs of clinical depression. If you are aware of students experiencing these symptoms for two or more weeks, strongly encourage them to seek help from a professional. You can start by connecting theme to your Counseling Office on campus.

Reflection 8.14

Have you ever been concerned about someone who you thought might be experiencing serious depression?

If yes:

(a) What specific behaviors did the person exhibit that triggered your concern?

(b) What type of help do you think the person needed?

Box 8.5

The Symptoms (Signs) of Clinical Depression

- Feeling very low, down, dejected, sad, or blue
- Low self-esteem and feeling worthless or guilty (e.g., thinking "I'm a failure" or "I'm a loser")
- Loss of energy
- Speaking more slowly and softly than usual
- Stooped posture (e.g., hung head or drawn face)
- Less animation and slower bodily movements
- Decreased sense of humor
- Difficulty finding pleasure, joy, or fun in anything
- Lack of concentration
- Loss of motivation and interest in things previously found to be interesting or important (e.g., loss of interest in school, sudden drop in rate of class attendance, or suddenly not completing class assignments)
- Social withdrawal
- Neglect of physical appearance
- Changes in eating patterns (e.g., eating more or less than usual)
- Changes in sleeping patterns (e.g., sleeping more or less than usual)
- Pessimistic feelings about the future (e.g., expecting failure or feeling helpless or hopeless)
- Suicidal thoughts (e.g., "I can't take it anymore," "People would be better off without me," or "I don't deserve to live")

Note: Suicidal thoughts occur at alarmingly high rates among college students. In one national study of more than 26,000 students at 70 campuses, it was found that 15% of the students surveyed reported that they "seriously considered" suicide and 5% reported that they actually attempted suicide. Only half of the students who had suicidal thoughts sought counseling or treatment (Drum et al., 2009).

If you suspect that a student is experiencing depression, express your concern in a supportive, non-threatening way (e.g., "You don't seem like yourself today." Or, "You seem kind of down, are you okay?). If your concern is confirmed, immediately connect the student to a personal counselor by using the referral strategies described in chapter 3, pp. 87-88.

> There's a difference between feeling despondent or down and being depressed. When psychologists use the word "depression," they are usually referring to clinical depression—a mood state so low that it's interfering with a person's ability to cope with day-to-day tasks, such as getting to school or going to work.

Strategies for Coping with Milder Forms of Depression

Depression can vary in intensity from severe to moderate to mild. Severe forms of depression are often rooted in genetic factors that result in chemical imbalances in the brain (Lohoff, 2010) and often require prescription of psychiatric medication. For milder forms of depression, the coping practices described below may be suggested to students as self-help strategies. Students can use these strategies on their own or in conjunction with help received from a professional.

Continue trying to get things done. When we're feeling down, staying busy and accomplishing things can boost our mood by providing us with a sense of achievement. Helping others less fortunate than ourselves can be a particularly effective way to elevate our mood because it gets us outside ourselves, increases our sense of self-worth, and helps us realize that our issues may be minor compared to the problems faced by others.

> *The best way to cheer yourself up is to try to cheer somebody else up.*
>
> —Samuel Clemens, a.k.a. Mark Twain, writer, lecturer, and humorist

Make a conscious effort to focus on your strengths and accomplishments. Another way to drive away the blues is by keeping track of the positive developments in our lives. We can do this by keeping a "positive events journal" in which we note the good things that happen to us, things we're grateful for, and accomplishments we've achieved. Positive journal entries leave us with an uplifting visible record that can be viewed and reviewed anytime we're feeling down.

Make a determined effort to continue engaging in activities that are fun and enjoyable. When we're down, we stop doing the things that usually bring us up because we're too down to do them. Naturally, this brings us down further. To break this cycle, it's at times when we're emotionally low that we should try even harder to continue doing the things that bring us joy, such as socializing with closest friends and engaging in our favorite recreational activities. (Interestingly, the root of the word "recreation" means to re-create or create again, suggesting that recreational activity can revive, restore, and renew us—both physically and emotionally.)

Engaging in upbeat behavior can cause the mind (mood) to follow suit. You may have heard of the expression, "Put on a happy face." Actually, smiling can be an effective depression-reduction strategy because it produces changes in facial muscles that trigger changes in brain chemistry, which, in turn, elevate our mood (Liebertz, 2005). In contrast, frowning activates a different set of facial muscles that tend to interfere with production of mood-elevating brain chemicals (Myers, 1993).

Intentionally seek out humor and experiences that make you laugh. Laughter can lighten and brighten a dark mood by elevating endorphins—mood-elevating brain chemicals (Yim, 2016). Furthermore, humor improves memory (Nielson, cited in Liebertz, 2005), which can help combat the memory lapses that typically accompany depression.

> *We don't laugh because we're happy; we're happy because we laugh.*
>
> —William James, influential philosopher and psychologist who taught the first psychology course in the United States

Exercise. Studies show that people who exercise regularly report feeling happier (Myers, 1993). Exercise can improve mood by improving self-esteem—which gets a boost from accomplishing a rigorous physical task and improving one's physical self-image. Exercise also elevates mood by elevating the brain's production of endorphins (Craft & Perna, 2004).

Conclusion

In some cases, students can overcome anxiety and depression through personal effort and use of effective coping strategies, particularly if they experience these emotions in mild forms and for short periods of time. However, overcoming more serious and long-lasting episodes of these emotions isn't as simple as people make it out to be—for example, when they insensitively tell others who are experiencing anxiety or depression to: "Just deal with it," "Get over it," or "Snap out of it." More intense forms of anxiety and depression are often triggered by genetic factors and are not completely within a person's control. If you know students who are experiencing these serious emotional challenges, assure them that it's nothing to be embarrassed about or feel reluctant to seek professional help about, and do your best to get them the help they need.

Reflection 8.15

If you thought you were experiencing an episode of anxiety or depression, would you feel comfortable seeking help from a professional? If yes, why? If no, why not? How do you think most students would respond to the above questions?

Internet Resources

For additional information on promoting wellness and holistic development, consult the following Web sites.

Nutrition
www.eatright.org

Sleep
www.sleepfoundation.org

Alcohol and Drugs
www.nida.nih.gov

Abusive Relationships
http://www.byui.edu/counseling-center/self-help/abusive-relationships

References

Abbey, A. (2002). Alcohol-related sexual assault: A common problem among college students. *Journal of Studies on Alcohol, 14,* 118–128.

American Psychiatric Association. (2013). *Diagnostic and statistical manual of mental disorders, DSM-IV-TR* (5th ed.). Washington, DC: Author.

Anxiety and Depression Association of America (ADAA). (2017). *Facts & statistics.* Retrieved from https://adaa.org/about-adaa/press-room/facts-statistics

Bartlett, T. (2002). Freshmen pay, mentally and physically as they adjust to college life. *The Chronicle of Higher Education, 48,* pp. 35-37.

Bergen-Cico, D. (2000). Patterns of substance abuse and attrition among first-year students. *Journal of the First-Year Experience and Students in Transition, 12*(1), 61–75.

Biggs, J., & Tang, C. (2007). *Teaching for quality learning at university* (3rd ed.). Buckingham: SRHE and Open University Press.

Bordes, V., & Arredondo, P. (2005). Mentoring and first-year Latina/o college students. *Journal of Hispanic Higher Education, 4*(2), 114-133.

Bosch, J. A., de Geus, E. J., Ring, C., & Nieuw-Amerongen, A. V. (2004). Academic examinations and immunity: Academic stress or examination stress? *Psychosomatic Medicine, 66*(4), 625-627.

Bowlby, J. (1980). *Attachment and loss: Vol. 3. Loss, sadness, and depression.* New York: Basic Books.

Brown, S. A., Tapert, S. F., Granholm, E., & Delis, D. C. (2000). Neurocognitive functioning of adolescents: Effects of protracted alcohol use. *Alcoholism: Clinical & Experimental Research, 24*(2), 164–171.

Bushman, B. J., & Cooper, H. M. (1990). Effects of alcohol on human aggression: An integrative research review. *Psychological Bulletin, 107*(3), 341–354.

Cail, J., & LaBrie, J. W. (2010). Disparity between the perceived alcohol-related attitudes of parents and peers increases alcohol risk in college students. *Addictive Behaviors, 35*(2), 135–139.

Center for Collegiate Mental Health. (2017, January). *2017 Annual Report.* (Publication No. STA 17-74) Retrieved from https://sites.psu.edu/ccmh/files/2017/01/2016-Annual-Report-FINAL_2016_01_09-1gc2hj6.pdf

Centers for Disease Control & Prevention. (2015a). *Insufficient sleep is a public health problem.* Retrieved from http://www.cdc.gov/features/dssleep/

Centers for Disease Control & Prevention. (2015b). *Teen drivers: Fact sheet.* Retrieved from http://www.cdc.gov/motorvehiclesafety/teen_drivers/

Covey, S. R. (2004). *Seven habits of highly effective people* (3rd ed.). New York: Fireside.

Craft, L. L., & Perna, F. M. (2004). The benefits of exercise for the clinically depressed. *Primary Care Companion to the Journal of Clinical Psychology, 6*(3), 104-111.

Cuseo, J., Thompson, A., Campagna, M., & Fecas, V. (2016). *Thriving in college & beyond: Research-based strategies for academic success and personal development* (4th ed.). Dubuque, IA: Kendall Hunt.

Deinzer, R., Kleineidam C., Stiller–Winkler, R., Idel, H., & Bachg, D. (2000). Prolonged reduction of salivary immunoglobulin A (S-IgA) after a major academic exam. *International Journal of Psychophysiology, 37,* 219–232.

Dement, W. C., & Vaughan, C. (1999). *The promise of sleep.* New York: Delacorte Press.

Dement, W. C., & Vaughan, C. (2000). *The promise of sleep: A pioneer in sleep medicine explores the vital connection between health, happiness, and a good night's sleep.* New York: Dell.

Drum, D. J., Brownson, C., Denmark, A. B., & Smith, S. E. (2009). New data on the nature of suicidal crises in college students: Shifting the paradigm. *Professional Psychology: Research and Practice, 40*(3), 213-222.

Eisenberg, D., Golberstein, E., Hunt, J. (2009). Mental health and academic success in college. *B.E. Journal of Economic Analysis & Policy, 9*(1), 1-40.

Ellenbogen, J. M., Payne, J. D., & Stickgold, R. (2006). The role of sleep in declarative memory consolidation: passive, permissive, active or none? *Current Opinion in Neurobiology, 16*(6), 716-722.

Epstein, L., & Mardon. S. (2007). *The Harvard medical school guide to a good night's sleep.* New York: McGraw Hill.

Fernández-Castillo, A., & Caurcel, M. J. (2014). State test-anxiety, selective attention and concentration in university students. *International Journal of Psychology, 50*(4), 265-271.

Forke, C. M., Myers, R. K., Catallozzi, M., & Schwarz. D. F. (2008). Relationship violence among female and male college undergraduate students. *National Institutes of Health.* Retrieved from http://archpedi.jamanetwork.com/article.aspx?articleid=379815

Freedner, N., Freed, L. H., Yang, Y. W., & Austin, S.B. (2002). Dating violence among gay, lesbian, and bisexual adolescents: Results from a community survey. *Journal of Adolescent Health, 21,* 469-474.

Gallup-Purdue Index Report. (2014). *Great jobs, great lives: A study of more than 30,000 college graduates across the U.S.* Retrieved from https://www.luminafoundation.org/files/resources/galluppurdueindex-report-2014.pdf

Gardiner, L. F. (1994). *Redesigning higher education: Producing dramatic gains in student learning.* Report No. 7. Washington, D. C.: Graduate School of Education and Human Development, The George Washington University.

Goleman, D. (1995). *Emotional intelligence: Why it can matter more than IQ.* New York: Random House.

Goleman, D. (1998). *Working with emotional intelligence.* New York: Bantam.

Gould, J., & Lomax, A. (1993). The evolution of peer education: Where do we go from here? *Journal of American College Health, 45,* 235-240.

Halvorson, H. G. (2010). *Succeed: How we can reach our goals.* New York: Plume.

Harmon, B. V. (2006). A qualitative study of the learning processes and outcomes associated with students who serve as peer mentors. *Journal of The First-Year Experience & Students in Transition, 18*(2), 53-82.

Heath, H. (1977). *Maturity and competence: A transcultural view.* New York: Halsted Press.

Johnsgard, K. W. (2004). *Conquering depression and anxiety through exercise.* New York: Prometheus.

Johnston, L., O'Malley, P. M., Bachman, J., & Schulenberg, J. E. (2006). *Monitoring the future national survey results on drug use, 1975-2005. Volume II: College students and adults ages 19-45* (NIH Publication No. 06-5884). Bethesda, MD: National Institute on Drug Abuse.

Julien, R. M., Advokat, C. D., & Comaty, J. E. (2011). *A primer of drug action.* New York: Worth.

Karjane, H. K., Fisher, B. S., & Cullen F. T. (2005). *Sexual assault on campus: What colleges and universities are doing about it.* Retrieved from https://www.ncjrs.gov/pdffiles1/nij/205521.pdf

Kegan, R. (1994). *In over our heads: The mental demands of modern life.* Cambridge, MA: Harvard University Press.

Kingkade, T. (2014, August 27). "Sleepy college students are worried about their stress levels." *The Huffington Post.* Retrieved from http://www.huffingtonpost.com/2014/08/27/college-students-sleep-stress_n_5723438.html

Kuriyama, K., Mishima, K., Suzuki, H., Aritake, S., & Uchiyama, M. (2008). Sleep accelerates improvement in working memory performance. *The Journal of Neuroscience, 28*(4), 10145-10150.

Lack, L. C., Gradisar, M., Van Someren, E. J. W., Wright, H. R., & Lushington, K. (2008). The relationship between insomnia and body temperatures. *Sleep Medicine Reviews, 12*(4), 307-317.

Leavy, P., Gnong, A., & Ross, L. S. (2009). Femininity, masculinity, and body image issues among college-age women: An in-depth and written interview study of the mind-body dichotomy. *The Qualitative Report, 14*(2), 261-292.

Levitsky D. A., Garay J., Nausbaum M., Neighbors L., & Dellavalle, D. M. (2006). Monitoring weight daily blocks the freshman weight gain: A model for combating the epidemic of obesity. *International Journal of Obesity, 30*(6), 1003-1010.

Li, K-K., Concepcion, R. Y., Hyo, L., Cardinal, B. J., Ebbeck, V., & Woekel, V. (2012). An examination of sex differences in relation to the eating habits and nutrient intakes of university students. *Journal of Nutrition Education and Behavior, 44*(3), 246-250.

Liebertz, C. (2005). A healthy laugh. *Scientific American Mind, 16*(3), 90-91.

Lohoff, F. W. (2010). Overview of the genetics of major depressive disorder. *Current Psychiatry Reports, 12*(6), 539-546.

Malik, S., Sorenson, S. B., & Aneshensel, C. S. (1997). Community and dating violence among adolescents: Perpetration and victimization. *Journal of Adolescent Health, 21*(5), 291-302.

Marczinski, C., Estee, G., & Grant, V. (2009). *Binge drinking in adolescent and college students.* New York: Nova Science Publishers.

Meilman, P. W., & Presley, C. A. (2005). The first-year experience and alcohol use. In M. L. Upcraft, J. N. Gardner, & B. O. Barefoot, & associates, *Challenging and supporting the first-year student: A handbook for improving the first year of college* (pp. 445-468). San Francisco: Jossey-Bass.

Mayo Clinic Staff. (2015a). *Anxiety: Definition.* Retrieved from http://www.mayoclinic.org/diseases-conditions/anxiety/basics/definition/con-20026282

Mayo Clinic Staff. (2015b). *Depression: Definition.* Retrieved from http://www.mayoclinic.org/diseases-conditions/depression/basics/definition/con-20032977

Mayo Clinic Staff. (2017). *Water: How much should you drink every day?* Retrieved from https://www.mayoclinic.org/healthy-lifestyle/nutrition-and-healthy-eating/in-depth/water/art-20044256

Meynen, G. (2010). Free will and mental disorder: Exploring the relationship. *Theoretical Medicine and Bioethics, 31*(6), 429-443.

Mothers Against Drunk Driving. (2015). *Why 21?: Addressing underage drinking.* Retrieved from http://www.madd.org/underage-drinking/why21/

Murray, C. E., & Kardatzke, K. N. (2007). Dating violence among college students: Key issues for college counselors. *Journal of College Counseling, 10*(1), 79-89.

Myers, D. G. (1993). *The pursuit of happiness: Who is happy—and why?* New York: Morrow.

National Center for Victims of Crime (2012). *About sexual assault.* Retrieved from https://www.victimsofcrime.org/our-programs/dna-resource-center/untested-sexual-assault-kits/about-sexual-assault

National Institute of Justice (2008). "Most victims know their attacker." https://www.nij.gov/topics/crime/rape-sexual-violence/campus/Pages/know-attacker.aspx

National Institute of Mental Health. (2014). *What are eating disorders?* Washington, DC: U.S. Department of Health and Human Services. Retrieved from http://www.nimh.nih.gov/health/publications/eating-disorders-new-trifold/index.shtml

National Institutes of Health (2012). "Why is sleep important?" Retrieved from http://www.nhlbi.nih.gov/health/health-topics/topics/sdd/why.

National Institutes of Health (2013). "Sleep on it: How snoozing strengthens memories." Retrieved from https://newsinhealth.nih.gov/issue/apr2013/feature2

NHTSA/FARS & US Census Bureau. (2012). *Underage drunk driving fatalities.* Retrieved from www.centurycouncil.org/drunk-driving/underage-drunk-driving-fatalities

Nutrition Australia. (2015). *Eat a rainbow.* Retrieved from http://www.nutritionaustralia.org/national/resource/eat-rainbow

Ogden, S. K., & Biebers, A. D. (Eds.) (2010). *Psychology of denial.* New York: Nova Science Publishers.

Ottens, A. J., & Hotelling, K. (2001) *Sexual violence on campus: Policies, programs, and perspectives.* New York: Springer Publishing Company, Inc.

O'Sullivan, G. (2010). The relationship between hope, eustress, self-efficacy, and life satisfaction among undergraduates. *Social Indicators Research, 101*(1), 155-172.

Pascarella, E. T., & Terenzini, P. T. (1991). *How college affects students: Findings and insights from twenty years of research.* San Francisco: Jossey-Bass.

Pascarella, E. T., & Terenzini, P. T. (2005). *How college affects students, Volume 2: A third decade of research.* San Francisco: Jossey-Bass.

Penfold, R. B. (2006). *Dragonslippers: This is what an abusive relationship looks like.* New York: Grove/Atlantic.

Price, R. H., Choi, J. N., & Vinokur, A. D. (2002). Links in the chain of adversity following job loss: How financial strain and loss of personal control lead to depression, impaired functioning, and poor health. *Journal of Occupational Health Psychology, 7*(4), 302-312.

Pryor, J. H., De Angelo, L., Palucki-Blake, B., Hurtado, S., & Tran, S. (2012) *The American freshman: National norms fall 2011.* Los Angeles: Higher Education Research Institute, UCLA.

Ramsden, P. (2003). *Learning to teach in higher education* (2nd ed.). London: RoutledgeFalmer.

Rüsch, N., Angermeyer, M. C., & Corrigan, P. W. (2005). Mental illness stigma: Concepts, consequences, and initiatives to reduce stigma. *European Psychiatry, 20*(8), 529-539.

Sanft, M., Jensen, M., & McMurray, E. (2008). *Peer mentor companion.* Boston: Houghton Mifflin.

Sapolsky, R. (2004). *Why zebras don't get ulcers.* New York: W. H. Freeman.

Sax, L. J. (2003, July–August). Our incoming students: What are they like? *About Campus*, pp. 15–20.

Sax, L., Bryant, A. N., & Gilmartin, S. K. (2004). A longitudinal investigation of emotional health among male and female first-year college students. *Journal of The First-Year Experience, 16*(2), 29-65.

Seaward, B. L. (2011). *Managing stress: A creative journal* (4th ed.) Sudbury, MA: Jones & Bartlett.

Selye, H. (1974). *Stress without distress*. Philadelphia: J.B. Lippincott Company

Selye, H. (1975). Confusion and controversy in the stress field. *Journal of Human Stress, 1*(2), 37-44.

Senn, C. Y., Eliasziw, M., Barata, P. C., Thurston, W. E., Newby-Clark, I. R., Radtke, H. L., & Hobden, K. L. (2015). Efficacy of a sexual assault resistance program for university women. *New England Journal of Medicine, 372*, 2326-2335.

Sobell. L. C., & Sobell, M. B. (2013). *Motivational techniques and skills for health/mental health coaching and counseling*. Retrieved from http://www.nova.edu/gsc/forms/mi-techniques-skills.pdf

Tinto, V. (1993). *Leaving college: Rethinking the causes and cures of student attrition* (2nd ed.). Chicago: The University of Chicago Press.

Tinto, V. (2012). *Completing college: Rethinking institutional action*. Chicago: The College of Chicago Press.

Weschsler, H., & Wuethrich, B. (2002). *Dying to drink: Confronting binge drinking on college campuses*. Emmaus, PA: Rodale.

White, A. M., Jamieson-Drake, D. W., & Swartzwelder, H. S. (2002). Prevalence and correlates of alcohol-induced blackouts among college students: Results of an e-mail survey. *Journal of American College Health, 51*(3), 117-131.

Yim, J. (2016). Therapeutic benefits of laughter in mental health: A theoretical review. *Tohoku Journal of Experimental Medicine, 239*(3), 243-249

Zull, J. E. (2011). *From brain to mind: Using neuroscience to guide change in education*. Sterling, CVA: Stylus.

Exercise 8.1 Quote Reflections

Review the sidebar quotes contained in this chapter and select two that you think would be especially valuable to share with the students you lead or mentor.

For each quote, write a short statement explaining why you chose it.

Name _____ Date _____

Exercise 8.2 Holistic Development Self-Assessment

Read through the following skills and attributes listed beneath each of the eight elements of holistic development and place an asterisk (*) next to those you think are particularly important for *college students* to develop and place a checkmark (✓) next to those you think are particularly important for you to develop in your role as a *peer leader.* (You can place both an asterisk and a checkmark next to the same item.)

1. *Intellectual* Development: acquiring a broad base of knowledge, learning how to learn deeply and how to think critically.

Specific Skills and Attributes:
__ Becoming aware of your intellectual abilities, interests, and learning habits
__ Improving your focus of attention and concentration
__ Moving beyond memorization to learning at a deeper level
__ Improving your ability to retain knowledge on a long-term basis
__ Acquiring research skills to access information from a variety of sources and systems
__ Learning how to view issues from multiple angles or perspectives (psychological, social, political, economic, etc.)
__ Responding constructively to differing viewpoints or opposing arguments
__ Critically evaluating ideas in terms of their truth and value
__ Detecting and rejecting persuasion tactics that appeal to emotion rather than reason
__ Thinking creatively and innovatively

Intellectual growth should commence at birth and cease only at death.

—Albert Einstein, Nobel Prize-winning physicist

2. *Emotional* Development: understanding, managing, and expressing emotions.

Specific Skills and Attributes:
__ Dealing with one's emotions in an honest, non-defensive manner
__ Maintaining a healthy balance between emotional control and emotional expression
__ Responding with empathy and sensitivity to emotions experienced by others
__ Using effective stress-management strategies to control anxiety and reduce tension
__ Dealing effectively with depression
__ Managing anger effectively
__ Responding constructively to frustrations and setbacks
__ Dealing effectively with fear of failure and lack of self-confidence
__ Maintaining optimism and enthusiasm
__ Accepting feedback from others in a constructive, non-defensive manner

It's not stress that kills us, it is our reaction to it.

—Hans Selye, Canadian endocrinologist and author of *Stress Without Distress*

3. *Social* **Development:** Improving the quality and depth of interpersonal relationships.

Specific Skills and Attributes:
___ Developing social self-confidence
___ Improving listening and conversational skills
___ Overcoming shyness
___ Relating to others in an open, non-defensive, and non-judgmental manner
___ Forming meaningful and supportive friendships
___ Learning how to resolve interpersonal conflicts
___ Developing greater empathy for others
___ Relating effectively to people from different cultural backgrounds and lifestyles
___ Collaborating effectively with others while working in groups or teams
___ Exerting positive influence on others

Chi rispetta sarà rippetato.
(Respect others and you will be respected.)
—Italian proverb

4. *Ethical* **(Character) Development:** Developing a clear value system for guiding personal decisions, making sound ethical judgments, and demonstrating consistency between personal convictions (beliefs) and personal commitments (actions).

Specific Skills and Attributes:
___ Gaining deep awareness of personal values and ethical priorities
___ Making personal choices and life decisions based on a meaningful value system
___ Developing the capacity to think and act with integrity and authenticity
___ Resisting social pressure to behave in ways that are inconsistent with one's personal values
___ Treating others in a fair and just manner
___ Exercising freedom responsibly without infringing on the rights of others
___ Using information technology and social media in a civil and ethical manner
___ Becoming an engaged and responsible citizen
___ Increasing awareness of and commitment to human rights and social justice
___ Developing the courage to challenge or confront others who violate human rights and obstruct social justice

If you don't stand for something you will fall for anything.
—Malcolm X, African-American Muslim minister, public speaker, and human rights activist

5. *Physical* **Development:** Acquiring knowledge about the human body and how to apply that knowledge to prevent disease, preserve wellness, and promote peak performance.

Specific Skills and Attributes:
___ Becoming self-aware of one's physical condition and state of health
___ Applying knowledge about exercise and fitness to improve physical and mental energy
___ Developing sleep habits that maximize physical and mental well-being
___ Maintaining a healthy balance between work, recreation and relaxation
___ Applying knowledge about nutrition to reduce risk of illness and achieve peak levels of performance
___ Becoming knowledgeable about nutritional imbalances and eating disorders
___ Developing a positive physical self-image

A man too busy to take care of his health is like a mechanic too busy to take care of his tools.
—Spanish proverb

__ Becoming more knowledgeable about the effects of drugs and how they affect the body and mind
__ Gaining a deeper understanding of human sexuality and sexual diversity
__ Knowing how biological differences between the sexes affect male-female communication and relationships

6. **Spiritual Development:** Pondering the "big questions" about the meaning and purpose of life, the origins of human life and the natural world, and the inevitability of death.

Specific Skills and Attributes:
__ Developing a meaningful and purposeful philosophy of life
__ Exploring the unknown or what cannot be completely understood scientifically
__ Appreciating the mysteries associated with the origin of the universe (cosmos)
__ Searching for connections between the self and the larger world
__ Searching for the mystical or supernatural—what transcends the boundaries of the natural world
__ Examining questions relating to death and life after death
__ Exploring questions about the existence of a Supreme Being or higher power
__ Gaining knowledge about different approaches to spirituality and their underlying beliefs or assumptions
__ Understanding the relationship between faith and reason
__ Becoming more aware and accepting of diverse religious beliefs and practices

> *We are not human beings having a spiritual experience. We are spiritual beings having a human experience.*
>
> —Pierre Teilhard de Chardin, French philosopher, geologist, paleontologist, and Jesuit priest

7. *Vocational* **Development:** Exploring career options, finding and pursuing a career path that is congruent with one's interests, talents, and values.

Specific Skills and Attributes:
__ Understanding the relationship between majors and careers
__ Acquiring effective strategies for exploring and identifying career options
__ Discovering career options that are most compatible with one's personal interests, talents, needs, and values
__ Acquiring work experience related to one's career interests
__ Building an effective resumé or portfolio
__ Identifying personal references and acquiring letters of recommendation
__ Implementing effective job-search strategies
__ Writing effective letters of inquiry and letters of application for positions of employment or acceptance to graduate school
__ Acquiring networking skills for connecting with potential employers
__ Developing strategies for performing successfully in job interviews

> *Your work is to discover your work and then with all your heart to give yourself to it.*
>
> —Hindu Siddhartha Prince Gautama Siddharta a.k.a. Buddha, founder of the philosophy and religion of Buddhism

8. *Personal* **Development:** Developing a strong sense of personal identity, a coherent self-concept, and the ability to manage personal affairs and resources.

Specific Skills and Attributes:
__ Discovering one's personal identity. (Answering the question: Who am I?)
__ Finding a sense of purpose and direction in life. (Answering the question: Who will I become?)
__ Developing greater self-respect and self-esteem

__ Increasing self-confidence

__ Developing self-efficacy—belief that the outcomes of life are within one's control and can be influenced by personal initiative and effort

__ Strengthening skills for managing personal resources (e.g., managing time and money)

__ Becoming more independent, self-directed, and self-reliant

__ Setting realistic goals and priorities

__ Developing the self-motivation and self-discipline needed to reach long-term goals

__ Developing the resiliency to overcome obstacles, bounce back from setbacks, and convert setbacks to comebacks

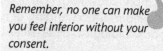

Remember, no one can make you feel inferior without your consent.

—Eleanor Roosevelt, former United Nations diplomat and humanitarian

* Look back at the asterisks and checkmarks you've placed by each of the eight general areas of holistic development. Did you place about the same number in all eight areas, or were there large differences across areas?

* Based on the distribution of asterisks and checkmarks in each area:

(a) Which of the eight areas had the greatest overlap between what you rated as important for student development and also as important for your development as a peer leader? What do you think accounts for this overlap?

(b) Which of the eight areas had the largest *difference* between what you rated as important for student development but not important for your development as a peer leader? What do you think accounts for this difference?

Name _____ Date _____

Exercise 8.3 Wellness Self-Assessment and Self-Improvement

For each aspect of wellness listed below, rate yourself in terms of how close you are to doing what you should be doing.

	Nowhere Close to What I Should Be Doing 1	2	Not Bad but Should Be Better 3	4	Right Where I Should Be 5
Nutrition	1	2	3	4	5
Exercise	1	2	3	4	5
Sleep	1	2	3	4	5
Alcohol and Drugs	1	2	3	4	5

For each area in which there's a gap between where you are now and where you should be, identify the best action step you could take right now to reduce or eliminate this gap.

Do you think the ratings of most college students would be similar to yours? Why?

Exercise 8.4 Case Study: "Drinking to Death—College Partying Gone Wild"

It's estimated that at least 50 college students nationwide die each year as a result of drinking incidents on or near campus. During a single month one fall, three college students died as a result of binge drinking at college parties. The first incident involved an 18-year-old, freshman at a private university who collapsed after drinking a mixture of beer and rum, fell into a coma at his fraternity house, and died three days later. He had a blood-alcohol level of more than .40, which would be equivalent to gulping down about 20 shots in one hour. The second incident involved a student from a public university in the South who died of alcohol poisoning (overdose). The third student died at another public university in the Northeast after an evening of partying and heavy drinking; he accidentally fell off a building in the middle of the night and fell through the roof of a greenhouse. Some colleges in the Northeast now have student volunteers roaming the campus on cold winter nights to make sure that no students freeze to death after passing out from an intense episode of binge drinking.

More recently, a student at a university on the East Coast guzzled an excessive amount of vodka and beer at a fraternity hazing party, staggered around repeatedly during the night, and eventually fell (head first) down a flight of stairs. He died of a fractured skull and damaged spleen.

Listed below are strategies that have been suggested by politicians to stop or reduce the problem of dangerous binge drinking:

1. A state governor announced he was going to launch a series of radio ads designed to discourage underage drinking.
2. A senator filed a bill to toughen penalties for those who violate underage drinking laws, such as producing and using fake identification cards.
3. A group of city council members looked into stiffening penalties for liquor stores that deliver directly to fraternity houses.

(Sources: *Los Angeles Times* and *Chicago Tribune*)

Reflection and Discussion Questions

1. Rank the above-three strategies in terms of how effective you think they'd be for reducing the problem of binge drinking (1 = the most effective strategy, 3 = the least effective).

2. Comparing your highest ranked and lowest ranked choices, why do you think:

   (a) your highest-ranked choice would be most effective?

   (b) your lowest-ranked choice would be least effective?

3. What additional strategies do you think might be effective for reducing dangerous binge-drinking episodes among college students?

Exercise 8.5 Strategy Reflections

Review the strategies recommended for *coping with mild depression* on pp. 258-259. Select two strategies that you think students would be most receptive to learning about and putting into practice.

CHAPTER 9

Leadership for Diversity

Appreciating and Harnessing the Power of Human Differences

Reflection 9.1

When I hear the word "diversity," the first thought that comes to mind is . . .

Chapter Purpose and Preview

This chapter explains what "diversity" truly means and documents how experiencing diversity deepens learning, strengthens critical and creative thinking, and enhances career development. The chapter arms you with specific strategies to help students break down barriers and biases that can block them from developing rewarding relationships with members of diverse groups. It also supplies inclusive leadership practices that you can use to foster collaboration among diverse groups of students and mentor students from diverse backgrounds.

The Importance of Leadership for Diversity

Leadership is challenging under any circumstances, but leadership in the context of diversity is especially challenging because it's harder to feel comfortable, capable and confident when leading, mentoring, and forming relationships with others whose backgrounds and prior experiences are unfamiliar and dissimilar to our own. Research shows that humans display a strong tendency to associate and develop relationships with others with whom they share similar backgrounds, beliefs, and interests. Scholars refer to this phenomenon as the "self-similarity principle" (Uzzi & Dunlap, 2005).

Effective leaders need to resist falling prey to the self-similarity principle and embrace the reality that diversity constitutes the current and future condition of American life. Racial and ethnic minorities now account for almost 37% of the total population—an all-time high. In 2011, for the first time in U.S. history, more than half (50.4%) of all children born in the United States were members of racial and ethnic minority groups (Nhan, 2012). By the middle of the 21st century, minority groups are projected to comprise 57% of the American population and more than 60% of our nation's children (U.S. Census Bureau, 2015). The growing diversity in the America's population is matched by growing diversity in its colleges and universities. In 1960, whites made up almost

> *For many students, regardless of racial background, the higher education environment will be the most racially diverse learning environment they have experienced in their lives.*
>
> —Beverly Daniel Tatum, former president, Spelman College and author of *Why Are All the Black Kids Sitting Together in the Cafeteria*

> *Education, beyond all other devices of human origin, is the great equalizer . . . the balance-wheel of social machinery.*
>
> —Horace Mann, architect of the American public school system, social reformer, and abolitionist

> *We are all brothers and sisters. Each face in the rainbow of color that populates our world is precious and special. Each adds to the rich treasure of humanity.*
>
> —Morris Dees, civil rights leader and co-founder of the Southern Poverty Law Center

95% of the total college population; in 2010, that percentage had decreased to 61.5%. Between 1976 and 2010, the percentage of ethnic minority students in higher education increased from 17% to 40% (National Center for Education Statistics, 2011).

The rising diversity on American campuses is particularly noteworthy when viewed in light of the historical treatment of racial and ethnic minority groups in the United States. In the early 19th century, education was not a right, but a privilege that was available only to those who could afford to attend private schools. That privilege was experienced largely by Protestants of European descent. Later, white immigrants from other cultural backgrounds began migrating to the United States and public education then became mandatory— with the idea that it would acculturate or "Americanize" these new immigrants and obliterate their previous cultural identities (Luhman, 2007). In many states, Americans of color were left out of the educational process altogether or were educated in separate, racially segregated schools with inferior educational facilities. It was not until a groundbreaking Supreme Court ruling (*Brown v Board of Education*, 1954) that the face of education changed for people of color. On that day, the United States Supreme Court ruled that "separate educational facilities are inherently unequal." This decision made it illegal for Kansas and 20 other states to deliver education in segregated classrooms.

Today, a major goal of virtually all American colleges and universities is to ensure that students from diverse backgrounds have the opportunity to enter higher education, benefit from the college experience, and enrich the learning experience of their college classmates. Peer leaders can play a pivotal role in achieving this goal by initiating and facilitating interaction among students from diverse groups.

What is Diversity?

Literally translated, the word "diversity" derives from the Latin *diversus*, meaning "various" or "variety." Thus, human diversity refers to the variety of differences that comprise humanity (the human species). The relationship between humanity and diversity may be likened to the relationship between sunlight and the variety of colors that comprise the visual spectrum. Similar to how sunlight passing through a prism disperses into the variety of colors that comprise the visual spectrum, the human species residing on planet earth is dispersed into a variety of different groups that comprise the human spectrum (humanity). **Figure 9.1** illustrates this metaphorical relationship between diversity and humanity.

As depicted in **Figure 9.1**, human diversity manifests itself in a multiplicity of ways, including differences among people in their national origins, cultural backgrounds, physical characteristics, sexual orientations, and sexual identities. Some dimensions of diversity are easily detectable, some are very subtle, and some are invisible.

Reflection 9.2

Look at the diversity spectrum in Figure 9.1 and look over the list of groups that make up the spectrum. Do you notice any groups missing from the list that should be added, either because they have distinctive characteristics or because they've been targets of prejudice and discrimination?

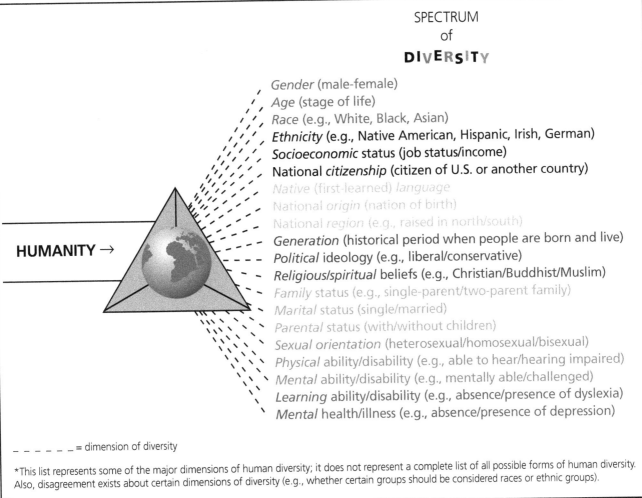

SPECTRUM
of
DIVERSITY

Gender (male-female)
Age (stage of life)
Race (e.g., White, Black, Asian)
Ethnicity (e.g., Native American, Hispanic, Irish, German)
Socioeconomic status (job status/income)
National *citizenship* (citizen of U.S. or another country)
Native (first-learned) *language*
National *origin* (nation of birth)
National *region* (e.g., raised in north/south)
Generation (historical period when people are born and live)
Political ideology (e.g., liberal/conservative)
Religious/spiritual beliefs (e.g., Christian/Buddhist/Muslim)
Family status (e.g., single-parent/two-parent family)
Marital status (single/married)
Parental status (with/without children)
Sexual orientation (heterosexual/homosexual/bisexual)
Physical ability/disability (e.g., able to hear/hearing impaired)
Mental ability/disability (e.g., mentally able/challenged)
Learning ability/disability (e.g., absence/presence of dyslexia)
Mental health/illness (e.g., absence/presence of depression)

HUMANITY →

_ _ _ _ _ _ = dimension of diversity

*This list represents some of the major dimensions of human diversity; it does not represent a complete list of all possible forms of human diversity. Also, disagreement exists about certain dimensions of diversity (e.g., whether certain groups should be considered races or ethnic groups).

© Kendall Hunt

Figure 9.1   Humanity and Diversity

Diversity is a topic that includes discussion of equal rights and social justice for minority groups. However, it's not just a political issue that pertains only to certain groups of people; it's also an *educational* issue—an integral element of the college experience that applies to and enhances the learning, development, and career preparation of *all* students By bringing different perspectives and alternative approaches to *what* is being learned (the content) and *how* it is learned (the process), diversity enriches the quality of the college experience.

Ethnic and cultural diversity is an integral, natural, and normal component of educational experiences for all students.

—National Council for Social Studies

Diversity is a *human* issue that embraces and benefits *all* people; it's not a code word for "some" people. Although one major goal of diversity is to promote appreciation and equitable treatment of particular groups of people who have experienced prejudice and discrimination, it's also a learning experience that enhances the quality of all students' education, career preparation, and leadership potential. (See pp. 289–292.)

Diversity and Humanity

As previously noted, diversity represents variations on the same theme: humanity. Thus, diversity and humanity are interdependent, complementary concepts. To understand human diversity is to understand both our differences and our *similarities*. Diversity appreciation includes valuing the unique experiences of different groups of humans as well as the common (universal) experiences shared by all humans. Members of different ethnic and racial groups may have distinctive cultural or physical characteristics, but members of all ethnic and racial groups live in communities, develop personal relationships, have emotional needs, and undergo life experiences that shape their personal identity. Humans of all races and all cultures also share the same emotions and communicate those emotions with similar facial expressions (see **Figure 9.2**).

Anthropologists have also found that all groups of humans in every corner of the world share the following characteristics: storytelling, dance, music, decorating, adorning the body, socialization of children by elders, a sense of right

Humans all over the world display the same facial expressions when they experience and express certain emotions. See if you can detect the emotions being experienced and expressed by the diverse people in the following picture. (To find the answers, turn your book upside down.)

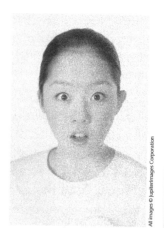

Answers: The emotions shown. Top, left to right: anger, fear, and sadness. Bottom, left to right: disgust, happiness, and surprise.

Figure 9.2

and wrong, supernatural beliefs, and mourning the dead (Pinker, 2000). Although different cultural groups may express these experiences in distinctive ways, they are universal experiences shared by all cultural groups.

Reflection 9.3

In addition to the universal characteristics already mentioned, can you think of any other human characteristic or experience shared by all human groups, no matter what their race or culture happens to be?

You may have heard the question: "We're all human, aren't we?" The answer to this question is "yes and no." Yes, all humans are the same, but not in the same way. A metaphor for making sense of this apparent contradiction is to visualize humanity as a quilt made up of multiple patches representing different group of people, woven together by a common thread: their shared humanity. (See picture below.) The quilt metaphor acknowledges the identity and beauty of all cultures. It differs from the old American "melting pot" metaphor, which viewed cultural differences as something to be melted down and eliminated. It also differs from the old "salad bowl" metaphor that depicted America as a hodgepodge or mishmash of cultures thrown together without any common connection. In contrast, the quilt metaphor suggests that the cultures of different human groups should be recognized, preserved, and valued. Yet, despite the fact that these cultures are different, they come together to form a seamless, unified whole. This blending of diversity and unity is captured in the Latin expression *E pluribus unum* ("Out of many, one")—the motto of the United States—which appears on all its currency.

> *We are all the same, and we are all unique.*
>
> —Georgia Dunston, African-American biologist and research specialist in human genetics

© steven r. hendricks, 2013. Used under license of Shutterstock, Inc.

Author's Experience

I was 12 years old, living in New York City, when I returned home after school one Friday. My mother asked me if anything interesting happened in class that day. I told her that the teacher went around the room asking students what they had for dinner the night before. At that moment, my mother became a bit concerned and nervously asked me: "What did you tell the teacher?" I said: "I told her and the rest of the class that I had pasta last night because my family always eats pasta on Thursdays and Sundays." My mother exploded and fired the following question back at me in a very agitated tone, "Why didn't you tell her we had steak or roast beef?" I was stunned and confused because I didn't understand what I'd done wrong or why I should have hidden the fact that we had eaten pasta. Then it dawned on me: My mom was embarrassed about being an Italian-American. She wanted me to conceal our family's ethnic background to make us sound more "American."

As I grew older, I understood why my mother felt the way she did. She was raised in America's "melting pot" generation—a time when different American ethnic groups were expected to melt down and melt away their ethnicity. They were not to celebrate diversity; they were to eliminate it.

— Joe Cuseo

> *We have become not a melting pot but a beautiful mosaic.*
>
> —Jimmy Carter, 39th president of the United States and winner of the Nobel Peace Prize

> When different human groups are appreciated for both their diversity and commonality, their separate streams merge into a single river carrying the collective strength of humanity.

Diversity and Individuality

When we talk about diverse groups, it's important to keep in mind that individual differences among members within a particular racial or ethnic group are greater than the average difference between groups. Said in another way, there's more variability (individuality) within the same group than between groups. For instance, differences among individuals of the same race with respect to their physical characteristics (e.g., height and weight) and psychological characteristics (e.g., temperament and personality) are greater than any average difference there might be between their racial group and other racial groups (Caplan & Caplan, 2008). Consequently, although it's valuable to learn about differences between different human groups, the substantial differences among individuals within the same racial or ethnic group should not be overlooked or underestimated. We shouldn't assume that individuals who share the same racial or ethnic characteristic share similar personal characteristics.

As you encounter diversity in your college experience and in your leadership role, keep the following key distinctions in mind:

> "I realize that I'm black, but I like to be viewed as a person, and this is everybody's wish.
>
> —Michael Jordan, Hall of Fame basketball player

- **Humanity.** All humans are members of the *same group*—i.e., the human species.
- **Diversity.** All humans are members of *different groups*—e.g., different racial and ethnic groups.
- **Individuality.** Each human is a *unique individual* who differs from other members of any group to which he or she may belong.

> "Every human is, at the same time, like all other humans, like some humans, and like no other human.
>
> —Clyde Kluckhohn, American anthropologist

Cultural Diversity

Culture is the distinctive pattern of beliefs and values learned by a group of people who share the same social heritage and traditions. In short, culture is the whole way in which a group of people has learned to live (Peoples & Bailey, 2011). It includes their style of speaking (language), fashion, food, art and music, as well as their beliefs and values. Box 9.1 contains a summary of the key components of culture that are typically shared by members of the same cultural group.

Reflection 9.4

Look at the components of culture cited in Box 9.1. In your role as a peer leader, which aspect(s) of culture do you think you'll need to be most aware of and sensitive to? Why?

Box 9.1 Key Components of Culture

- **Language:** How members of the culture communicate through written or spoken words, including their particular dialect and their distinctive style of nonverbal communication (body language).
- **Use of Physical Space:** How cultural members arrange themselves with respect to social-spatial distance (e.g., how closely they stand next to each other when having a conversation).
- **Use of Time:** How the culture conceives of, divides up, and uses time (e.g., the speed or pace at which they conduct business).
- **Aesthetics:** How cultural members appreciate and express artistic beauty and creativity (e.g., their style of visual art, culinary art, music, theater, literature, and dance).
- **Family:** The culture's attitudes and habits with respect to family interactions (e.g., customary styles of parenting children and caring for the elderly).
- **Economics:** How the culture meets its members' material needs, and the customary ways in which wealth is acquired and distributed (e.g., its overall level of wealth and the wealth gap between its very wealthy and very poor members).
- **Gender Roles:** The culture's expectations for "appropriate" male and female behavior (e.g., how men and women are expected to dress and whether or not women are allowed to hold the same occupational positions as men).
- **Politics:** How decision-making power is exercised in the culture (e.g., democratically or autocratically).
- **Science and Technology:** The culture's attitude toward, and use of, science and technology (e.g., the degree to which the culture is technologically "advanced").
- **Philosophy:** The culture's ideas and views about wisdom, goodness, truth, and social values (e.g., whether its members place greater value on individual competition or collective collaboration).
- **Spirituality and Religion:** Cultural beliefs about the existence of a supreme being and an afterlife (e.g., its members' predominant faith and belief systems about the supernatural).

A major advantage of culture is that it builds group solidarity by binding its members into a supportive, tight-knit community. Unfortunately, however, culture can not only bind us, it can also blind us from seeing things from different cultural perspectives. Since culture shapes thought and perception, people from the same ethnic (cultural) group run the risk of becoming *ethnocentric*—centered so much on their own culture that they end up viewing the world through just one cultural lens or frame of reference (their own) and fail to consider or appreciate other cultural viewpoints (Colombo, Cullen, & Lisle, 2013).

Optical illusions are a good example of how strongly our particular cultural perspective can influence (and distort) our perceptions. Compare the lengths of the two lines in **Figure 9.3**.

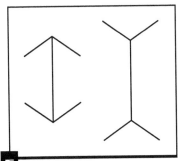

Figure 9.3 Optical Illusion

If you perceive the line on the right as longer than the one on the left, your perception has been shaped by your cultural background. People from Western cultures (such as Americans and Europeans) perceive the line on the right to be longer. However, both lines are actually equal in length. (If you don't believe it, take out a ruler and measure them.) Interestingly, this perceptual error is not made by people from non-Western cultures whose living spaces and architectural structures are predominantly circular (e.g., huts or igloos)—as opposed to the rectangular-shaped buildings with angled corners that characterize Western cultures (Segall, Campbell, & Herskovits, 1966).

The optical illusion depicted in Figure 9.3 is just one of a number of illusions experienced by people in some cultures but not others (Shiraev & Levy, 2013). These cross-cultural differences in susceptibility to optical illusions illustrate how

People whose cultural experiences involve living and working in circular structures would not be fooled by the optical illusion in Figure 9.3.

strongly our cultural experiences can influence and sometimes misinform our perception of reality. People think they're seeing things objectively (as they actually are), but they're actually seeing things subjectively (from their particular cultural perspective).

If our cultural experiences can influence our perception of the physical world, they can certainly shape our perception of the social world. Research in social psychology reveals that the more exposure people have to somebody or something, the more familiar it becomes and the more likely it will be perceived positively and judged favorably. This effect of familiarity is so prevalent and powerful that social psychologists have come to call to it the "familiarity principle"—i.e., what is familiar is perceived to be better or more likeable (Zajonc, 1968, 1970, 2001). Thus, our familiar cultural experiences can bias us toward viewing our culture as being better or more "normal" and acceptable than others. By remaining open to the viewpoints of people from other cultures who perceive the world from vantage points different than our own, we uncover our cultural blind spots, expand our range of perception, and put ourselves in a better position to view the world with greater objectivity and cultural sensitivity.

> *Everyone in the world is not raised like me. There is a whole world out there. I think you need to learn to adapt.*
>
> —Peer leader

Effective leaders reflect on and critically examine their own cultural perspectives and are willing to explore other cultural perspectives. By doing so, they open up themselves (and those they lead) to different experiences, alternative perspectives, and new possibilities.

Ethnic Diversity

An *ethnic group* refers to a group of people who share the same culture. Thus, the term "culture" refers to *what* an ethnic group has in common (e.g., language and traditions) and "ethnic group" refers to the *people* who share the same cultural characteristics—which they have acquired (learned) through shared social experiences. Members of different ethnic groups may still be members of the same racial group—a group of people whose shared physical characteristics have been *inherited*. For instance, white Americans constitute the same racial group, but are members of different ethnic groups (e.g., French, German, Irish); similarly, Asian Americans constitute the same racial group, but are members of different ethnic groups (e.g., Japanese, Chinese, Korean).

European Americans are still the majority ethnic group in the United States; they account for more than 50% of the American population. Native Americans, African Americans, Hispanic Americans, and Asian Americans are considered to be *minority* ethnic groups because each of these groups represents less than 50% of the American population (U.S. Census Bureau, 2015).

Reflection 9.5

Are you a member of, or do you identify with, any particular ethnic group(s)? If yes, what would you say are the key cultural values shared by your ethnic group(s)?

Racial Diversity

A *racial group (race)* is a group of people who share distinctive physical traits—most notably, skin color. The variation in skin color we now see among humans is largely due to biological adaptations that have evolved over thousands of years, beginning at the time when humans first began to migrate to different climatic regions of the world. Currently, the most widely accepted explanation of racial differences among humans is the "Out of Africa" theory. Genetic studies and fossil evidence indicate that all *Homo sapiens* inhabited Africa 150,000-250,000 years ago; over time, some of them migrated from Africa to other parts of the world (Mendez, et al., 2013; Meredith, 2011; Reid & Hetherington, 2010). Those humans who lived and reproduced in hotter regions of the world nearer the equator (e.g., Africa and South America) developed darker skin color that helped them adapt and survive by providing them with better protection from the potentially damaging effects of intense sunlight (Bridgeman, 2003). In contrast, lighter skin tones emerged over time among humans inhabiting colder climates farther from the equator (e.g., Central and Northern Europe). Their lighter skin color contributed to their survival by enabling them to absorb greater amounts of vitamin D from by the less direct sunlight they received in their region of the world (Jablonski & Chaplin, 2002).

Currently, the U.S. Census Bureau categorizes humans into five racial categories (U.S. Census Bureau, 2013b):

- **White:** people whose lineage may be traced to the original humans inhabiting Europe, the Middle East, or North Africa.
- **Black or African American:** people whose lineage may be traced to the original humans inhabiting Africa.
- **American Indian or Alaska Native:** people whose lineage may be traced to the original humans inhabiting North and South America (including Central America) who continue to maintain their tribal affiliation or attachment.
- **Asian:** people whose lineage may be traced to the original humans inhabiting the Far East, Southeast Asia, or the Indian subcontinent, including: Cambodia, China, India, Japan, Korea, Malaysia, Pakistan, the Philippine Islands, Thailand, and Vietnam.
- **Native Hawaiian or Other Pacific Islander:** people whose lineage may be traced to the original humans inhabiting Hawaii, Guam, Samoa, and other Pacific Islands.

It's important to keep in mind that racial categories merely represent classifications that a particular society decides to construct—i.e., race is a socially constructed concept (Anderson & Fienberg, 2000). No identifiable set of genes distinguishes one race from another; in fact, there continues to be disagreement among scholars about what groups of people constitute a human race or whether distinctive races actually exist (Wheelright, 2005). You can't do a blood test or any other type of biological test on a person that will immediately and accurately indicate that person's race. Human societies have simply decided to create social categories called "races" based on certain external differences in peoples' outer physical appearance, particularly the color of their outer layer of skin. Human societies elected to use skin color to categorize themselves, but they could have divided themselves into categories based on eye color (blue, brown, and green), hair color (brown, black, blonde, or red), or body length (tall, short, or mid-sized).

Author's Experience My father stood approximately six feet tall and had straight, light brown hair. His skin color was that of a Western European with a very slight suntan. My mother was from Alabama; she was dark in skin color with high cheekbones and had long curly black hair. In fact, if you didn't know that my father was of African American descent, you would not have thought he was black.

All my life, I've thought of myself as African American and all people who know me think of me as being African American. I've lived half of a century with that as my racial identity. Several years ago, I carefully reviewed records of births and deaths in my family history and discovered that I had less than 50% African lineage. Biologically, I can no longer call myself Black; socially and emotionally, I still am. Clearly, my "race" has been socially constructed, not biologically determined.

— *Aaron Thompson*

Although humans may display diversity in the color or tone of their external layer of skin, the reality is that all members of the human species are remarkably similar at an internal biological level. More than 98% of the genes found in humans are exactly the same, regardless of what their particular racial category may be (Bronfenbrenner, 2005). This large amount of genetic overlap among humans accounts for the fact that all humans are clearly distinguishable from members of other animal species. This tremendous amount of genetic overlap among humans also accounts for why the internal body parts of all humans look the same; and no matter what the color of our outer layer of skin, when it's cut, we all bleed in the same color.

Attempting to categorize people into distinct racial or ethnic groups is more difficult today than at any other time in history because humans of different ethnic and racial groups are increasingly forming cross-ethnic and interracial families. By 2050, the number of Americans who identify themselves as being of two or more races is projected to more than triple, growing to 26.7 million (U.S. Census Bureau, 2013a).

Author's Experience I am "white." I grew up in New Jersey in a predominantly white town. I am married to a "black" woman and we have a racially "mixed" child (Lauren). The town we now live in is mostly, but not exclusively, "white." I'm not sure how people perceive Lauren racially; I've never asked. Her best friend is "white." Her other good friend is "Latina." Another one of her friends is "black." Who is Lauren Metz?

— *Greg Metz*

Reflection 9.6

What race(s) do you consider yourself to be? Would you say you identify strongly with your racial identity, or do you rarely think about it? How do you think the students you lead or mentor would answer these questions?

International Diversity

Adding further to the diversity on college campuses are international students. Since the turn of the century, the number of international students in the United States has grown by 72%. During the 2016-2017 academic year, over a million international students were enrolled on American campuses, more than any other country in the world (Institute of International Education, 2017).

The need for American college students to better understand and appreciate international diversity is highlighted by a study conducted by an anthropologist who went "undercover" to pose as a student in a university residence hall. She found that the biggest complaint international students had about American students was their poor knowledge of other countries and the misconceptions they held about people from different nations (Nathan, 2005). Leadership scholars have also noted that because of increasing economic interdependence among nations and the growing number of multinational organizations (House & Javidan, 2004), future leaders of businesses and organizations need to have a stronger "global leadership mindset"–i.e., greater commitment to gaining knowledge about other nations' cultures and stronger intercultural communication skills (Cabrera & Unruh, 2012). For instance, an effective American business leader in today's global economy should know that American business culture values risk taking and quick business decisions, whereas Middle Eastern countries (e.g., Kuwait and Egypt) value a more conservative approach to decision making, take fewer risks, take longer time to deliberate, and devote more time to relationship building (Northouse, 2016).

Gender Diversity

At one time, all college students were men. In fact, the term college "freshman" literally meant "fresh man" because every new college student was, indeed, a man; at one time, no females enrolled in (or were allowed to enroll in) college. Even as late as 1955, only 25% of college students were female. By 2000, that percentage had jumped to almost 66% (Postsecondary Education Opportunity, 2001). Between 1990 and 2009, the proportion of women enrolling in college increased at a rate almost three times higher than that of men (Kim, 2011). Women now earn the majority of bachelor's, master's, and doctoral degrees granted in the United States (National Center for Education Statistics, 2011). Women also hold almost 40% of all management positions in American organizations (Torpey, 2017).

Sexual Diversity: Gay, Lesbian, Bisexual, and Transgender (GLBT)

Humans experience and express sexuality in different ways. "Sexual diversity" refers to differences in: (a) *sexual orientation*–the gender (male or female) an individual is physically attracted to, and (b) *sexual identity*–the gender an individual identifies with, which can be the same or different than the gender that person was assigned at birth. These two general differences in orientation and identity combine to create a spectrum of sexual diversity that includes:

- *Heterosexual*–males who are sexually attracted to females, and females who are sexually attracted to males

- *Gay*–males who are sexually attracted to males
- *Lesbian*–females who are sexually attracted to females
- *Bisexual*–individuals who are sexually attracted to both males and females
- *Transgender*–individuals who do not identify with the gender they were assigned at birth (transsexuals) and may seek to change their gender surgically.
- *Gender Fluid*–individuals who do not identify with a single gender, but a mix of two genders, sometimes feeling more like a male and other times more like a female. Since their gender identity fluctuates, they typically don't seek to change their gender surgically.

College campuses across the country are increasing their support for GLBT students, creating centers and services that promote their acceptance and adjustment. These campus support services play an important role in combating homophobia and related forms of sexual prejudice on campus, while promoting awareness and tolerance of all forms of sexual orientation and identity. By accepting individuals who span the spectrum of sexual diversity, we acknowledge and appreciate the reality that heterosexuality is just one form of human sexual expression (Dessel, Woodford, & Warren, 2012). This growing acknowledgement is reflected in the Supreme Court's historic decision to legalize same-sex marriage nationwide (Dolan & Romney, 2015).

As a peer leader, you can help promote student awareness and acceptance of sexual diversity. One way to do so is by encouraging your college to invite guest speakers to campus that represent sexually diverse groups. For instance, you could invite a panel of representatives from a chapter of *PFLAG* to campus to promote awareness and tolerance of groups with alternative sexual orientation and lifestyles. PFLAG is an international organization of LBGTQ people and their families and friends with almost 300 chapters in the United States, including at least one in every state. (To locate a chapter of PFLAG in your geographical area, go to: http://www.pflag.org/Find_a_Chapter.68.0.html.) The organization consists of "parents, families and friends of lesbian, gay, bisexual and transgender persons" and their goal is to "celebrate diversity and envision a society that embraces everyone, including those of diverse sexual orientations and gender identities." Trained panelists from this organization speak about their experiences and then field questions from the audience. If you decide to bring members of this organization to campus, you can increase your students' preparation for and engagement with the panel by asking them to bring one or two questions to ask the panelists; you could also share these questions with the panelists in advance of their presentation. After the panel presentation, ask students to reflect on the experience, what they learned from it, and what unanswered questions they may still have.

Reflection 9.7

What diverse groups do you see represented at your college or university? When you first arrived on campus, did you find certain groups that you: (a) didn't expect to see, (b) didn't expect to see in such large numbers, or (c) didn't expect to be so open about their group membership?

The Benefits of Experiencing Diversity

National surveys show that by the end of their first year in college, almost two-thirds of freshmen report "stronger" or "much stronger" knowledge of people from different races and cultures. The majority of first-year students also report becoming more open to experiencing diverse cultures, viewpoints, and values than they were when they started college (HERI, 2013; HERI, 2014). The degree of diversity on college campuses today represents an unprecedented educational opportunity. College students may never again be members of a community that includes so many people from such a wide variety of backgrounds. Encourage your students not to withdraw or insulate themselves from the diversity that surrounds them, but to experience it and reap its benefits.

Remind students that experiencing and appreciating diversity is not just a socially sensitive or "politically correct" thing to do, but an educationally effective thing to do—it enriches the quality of their education and the education of diverse students with whom they interact. Below is a summary of the key benefits of experiencing diversity. Sharing this information with the students you lead and mentor will help motivate them to capitalize on the power of diversity.

> *I am very happy with the diversity here, but it also frightens me. I have never been in a situation where I have met people who are Jewish, Muslim, atheist, born-again, and many more.*
>
> —First-year student (quoted in Erickson, Peters, & Strommer, *Teaching First-Year College Students*)

> *Empirical evidence shows that the actual effects on student development of emphasizing diversity and of student participation in diversity activities are overwhelmingly positive.*
>
> —Alexander Astin, *What Matters in College?*

Diversity Increases Self-Awareness and Self-Knowledge

Interacting with people from diverse backgrounds enables us to compare and contrast our life experiences with others whose experiences differ sharply from our own. Exposure to others with different life experience serves to deepen our understanding of ourselves and how we got to be who we are. By stepping outside ourselves and contrasting our experiences with the experiences of others from different backgrounds, we move beyond ethnocentrism and gain a *comparative perspective*—a reference point that positions us to see more clearly how our particular cultural background has shaped our personal development and personal identity.

A comparative perspective also allows us to gain insight into how our cultural background may have advantaged or disadvantaged us. For instance, learning about cross-cultural differences in access to higher education can raise our awareness of the more limited educational opportunities there are for people in other countries to attend college. By gaining this cross-cultural knowledge, we gain greater appreciation of how advantaged we are in America—where college is available to everyone—regardless of their race, gender, age, social class, or level of academic performance prior to college.

> *It is difficult to see the picture when you are inside the frame.*
>
> —An old saying (author unknown)

> **The more we learn about people different than ourselves, the more we learn about ourselves.**

Diversity Deepens Learning

Research consistently shows that students learn more from students who are different from them than they do from students who are similar to them (Pascarella, 2001; Pascarella & Terenzini, 2005). Learning about different cultures and interacting with people from diverse cultural groups supplies our brain with more varied routes or pathways through which to connect (learn) new ideas. Experiencing diversity also "stretches" the brain beyond its normal "comfort zone," requiring it to work harder to assimilate the unfamiliar. When the brain encounters something unfamiliar, it has to engage in the extra effort of comparing, contrasting, and connecting it to something it already knows (Acredolo & O'Connor, 1991; Nagda, Gurin, & Johnson, 2005). This added expenditure of mental energy results in the brain forming deeper and more durable neurological connections (Willis, 2006).

Simply stated: We learn more deeply from diversity than we do from similarity or familiarity. In contrast, when we restrict the diversity of people with whom we interact (out of habit or prejudice), we limit the breadth and depth of our learning.

Diversity Promotes Higher-Level Thinking

Studies show that college students who have more exposure to diversity—such as enrolling in multicultural courses, participating in diversity programs on campus, and interacting with peers of different races and ethnicities—experience greater gains in:

- thinking *complexity*—the ability to think about all parts of an issue and from multiple perspectives (Association of American Colleges & Universities, 2004; Gurin, 1999),
- *reflective* thinking—the ability to think deeply about personal and global issues (Kitchener, Wood, & Jensen, 2000), and
- *critical* thinking—the ability to evaluate the validity of their own reasoning and the reasoning of others (Gorski, 2009; Pascarella et al., 2001).

> *The nation's future depends upon leaders trained through wide exposure to that robust exchange of ideas which discovers truth out of a multitude of tongues.*
>
> —William J. Brennan, former Supreme Court Justice

These mental benefits of experiencing diversity are likely due to the fact that exposure to perspectives that differ from our own creates *cognitive dissonance*—a state of cognitive (mental) disequilibrium or imbalance. This tension "forces" our minds to deal with different perspectives simultaneously, resulting in thinking that is less simplistic, more nuanced, and more complex (Brookfield, 1987; Gorski, 2009).

Diversity Stimulates Creative Thinking

> *What I look for in musicians is generosity. There is so much to learn from each other and about each other's culture. Great creativity begins with tolerance.*
>
> —Yo-Yo Ma, French-born, Chinese-American virtuoso cellist, composer, and winner of multiple Grammy Awards

In addition to promoting critical thinking, research reveals that diversity enhances creativity (Leung et al., 2008; Maddux & Galinsky, 2009). When ideas are exchanged among people from diverse cultures, a "cross-stimulation" effect is generated in which ideas for people from different cultural backgrounds stimulate the creation of additional ideas (Brown, Dane, & Durham, 1998); these ideas then "cross-fertilize" and give birth to new ideas and solutions for tackling old problems (Harris, 2010). Research also indicates that when people seek out alternative viewpoints and diverse perspectives, it increases their openness to considering different goal options and their willingness to try different goal-achievement strategies (Stoltz, 2014).

In contrast, when diverse cultural perspectives are dismissed or devalued, the variety of lenses through which we can view issues and problems is reduced. This, in turn, reduces our capacity to think creatively because our ideas are less likely to diverge (go in different directions). Instead, they're more likely to converge and merge into the same cultural channel—the one shared by the homogeneous group of people doing the thinking. Thus, segregation not only segregates people socially, it also segregates their ideas and suppresses their collective creativity. This is well illustrated in the book and movie *Hidden Figures*, which documents how a group of bright, talented African-American female mathematicians, initially segregated from their white male coworkers at NASA, were eventually integrated into the work team and made crucial, creative contributions to the successful launching of America's first astronaut (Shetterly, 2017).

> **Drawing on the ideas of people from diverse backgrounds and bouncing our ideas off them stimulates *divergent* (out-of-the-box) thinking, generates *synergy* (multiplication of ideas), and results in *serendipity* (unexpected discoveries of new ideas).**

Diversity Enhances Career Preparation and Career Success

Whatever line of work today's college graduates decide to pursue, they're likely to find themselves working with employers, co-workers, customers, and clients from diverse cultural backgrounds. America's workforce is now more diverse than at any other time in history and will grow ever more diverse throughout the 21st century. By 2050, the proportion of American workers from minority ethnic and racial groups will jump to 55% (U.S. Census Bureau, 2008).

National surveys reveal that policymakers, business leaders, and employers seek college graduates who are more than just "aware" or "tolerant" of diversity. They want graduates who have actual *experience* with diversity and are able to collaborate with diverse co-workers, clients, and customers (Association of American Colleges & Universities, 2002; Education Commission of the States, 1995; Hart Research Associates, 2013).

In addition to the growing domestic diversity within the United States, the current "global economy" requires skills relating to international diversity. The work world is now characterized by increasing economic interdependence among people of different nations, more international trading, multinational corporations, international travel, and instantaneous worldwide communication—due to rapid advances in the Internet (Dryden & Vos, 1999; Friedman, 2005). Even smaller companies and corporations are becoming more international in nature (Brooks, 2009). As a result, employers in all sectors of the economy are seeking job candidates with the following skills and attributes: sensitivity to human differences, ability to understand and relate to people from different cultural backgrounds, international knowledge, and ability to communicate in a second language (Fixman, 1990; National Association of Colleges & Employers, 2014; Office of Research, 1994; Hart Research Associates, 2013).

The benefits that accrue to college students who are exposed to racial and ethnic diversity during their education carry over in the work environment. The improved ability to think critically, to understand issues from different points of view, and to collaborate harmoniously with co-workers from a range of cultural backgrounds all enhance a graduate's ability to contribute to his or her company's growth and productivity.

—Business/Higher Education Forum

Technology and advanced communications have transformed the world into a global community, with business colleagues and competitors as likely to live in India as in Indianapolis. In this environment, people need a deeper understanding of the thinking, motivations, and actions of different cultures, countries and regions.

—Partnership for 21st Century Skills

Author's Experience I was once involved in an informal discussion with a small group of engineering students who were bemoaning the accent of one of their professors. A colleague of mine was part of that discussion group and pointed out that her husband worked in a multinational company which conducted business transactions with clients from China, India, and many other countries. She explained that if her husband complained about his business associates' accents, it would be viewed as cultural insensitivity and professional incompetence. She advised the students, with humor but firmness, to get used to accents because work today takes place on a global game board.

— *Greg Metz*

Increasing diversity, both domestic and international, has made *intercultural competence* an essential 21st century skill (Bennett, 2004; Thompson & Cuseo, 2014). Intercultural competence may be defined as the ability to appreciate and learn from human differences and to interact effectively with people from diverse cultural backgrounds. It includes "knowledge of cultures and cultural practices (one's own and others), complex cognitive skills for decision making in intercultural contexts, social skills to function effectively in diverse groups and personal attributes that include flexibility and openness to new ideas" (Wabash National Study of Liberal Arts Education, 2007).

Reflection 9.8

What intercultural skills do you think you already possess? What intercultural skills do you need to develop further in order to maximize your effectiveness as a peer leader or mentor?

Stereotyping: A Barrier to Diversity

"Stereotype" derives from two roots: *stereo*—to look at in a fixed way, and *type*—to categorize or group together (as in the word "typical"). Thus, to stereotype is to view individuals of the same type (group) in the same (fixed) way. Stereotyping overlooks or disregards individuality; instead, all people with the same group characteristic (e.g., race or gender) are viewed as having the same personal characteristics—as reflected in comments like: "You know how they are; they're all alike."

Stereotypes involve *bias*, which literally means "slant." This bias or slant can tilt toward the positive or the negative. Positive bias results in favorable stereotypes (e.g., "Asians are great in science and math"); negative bias leads to unfavorable stereotypes (e.g., "Asians are nerds who do nothing but study"). While most people would reject such blatant stereotypes, people can and do hold overgeneralized beliefs about members of certain groups. When these overgeneralizations are negative, they malign a group's reputation, rob its members of their individuality, and damage their self-esteem or self-confidence—as is illustrated in the following story.

Author's Experience When I was 6 years old, a 6-year-old girl from a different racial group told me that people of my race could not swim. Since I couldn't swim at that time and she could, I assumed she was correct. I asked a boy (a member of the same racial group as the girl) whether her statement was true. He responded emphatically: "Yes, it's definitely true!" Since I grew up in an area where few other African Americans were around to counteract this belief about my racial group, I continued to buy into this stereotype until I finally took swimming lessons as an adult. After many lessons, I am now a lousy swimmer because I didn't even attempt to swim until I was an adult. Moral of this story: Group stereotypes can limit the confidence and potential of members of the stereotyped group.

— *Aaron Thompson*

Neither males nor females should let gender stereotypes limit their career options.

Gender stereotypes continue to impair women's potential to pursue leadership opportunities. For instance, although significantly more women today hold management positions, they hold a very small percentage of top leadership positions in America's top (Fortune 500) companies (Catalyst, 2014a, 2014b) and they hold fewer political leadership positions in our nation's legislature compared to other nations (Inter-Parliamentary Union, 2014). A key factor contributing to the high-level leadership gap between men and women is the long-held gender stereotype that "women take care and men take charge" (Hoyt & Chemers, 2008). Women continue to be responsible for the majority of child care responsibilities (Belkin, 2008), and if working women take time off from their careers to bear and care for children, this lost work time is often held against them when they are evaluated for advancement to high-level leadership positions (Williams, 2010). Gender bias is compounded by a phenomenon called *homosocial reproduction*—the tendency to replace departing members of an organization with candidates whose characteristics are similar to the departing member or the person doing the hiring (Elliott & Smith, 2004; Kanter, 1977). In elite organizations, males dominate high-level leadership positions, so when it's time to hire or advance another member, their tendency (sometimes unconscious) is to select another male.

Even when female leaders manage to rise to high-level leadership positions, they often encounter a double standard: They're likely to be expected to display traditional, masculine-like leadership traits while still being "feminine" (Eagly & Carli, 2003). For instance, being assertive and task-oriented are considered positive leadership qualities in men, but if women display these traits, they may be viewed as unfeminine and lacking warmth (Ayman & Frame, 2004). "Women are often confronted with cross-pressures: As leaders, they should be masculine and tough, but as women, they should not be 'too manly.' These opposing expectations for women often result in the perception that women are less qualified for elite leadership positions than men" (Northouse, 2016, p. 405). Such gender bias not only limits leadership opportunities for women, it also limits the diversity of the pool of leadership candidates an organization can choose from, which in turn, can limit an organization's overall effectiveness (Nielsen & Huse, 2010). Research has shown that when women are included in leadership positions, it results in higher levels of collective organizational intelligence, innovation, productivity, and ethical behavior (Bernardi, Bosco, & Columb, 2009). Female leaders have been found to receive consistently higher ratings for such leadership behaviors such as gaining the trust of subordinates, noticing and praising their good work, empowering them, and mentoring them (Eagly, Johannesen-Schmidt, & van Engen, 2003).

One element of effective leadership is empowering others to reach their full potential (Kouzes & Posner, 2002). As a peer leader, you should vigorously oppose disempowering, potential-limiting stereotypes. If you witness stereotyping of any sort, step up and take a public stand against it. Your students may not want to hear you "lecture" them on the harms of stereotyping, but you can still gently, but firmly remind them that all of us have some cultural blind spots and we need to make an intentional effort to perceive and treat others as individuals—not as members of a stereotyped group. You can do this by periodically asking yourself and your students the following question when discussing issues that have diversity implications: "How are our cultural traditions and background experiences influencing, and perhaps biasing, our attitude or behavior with respect to this person, topic or issue?"

Reflection 9.9

1. Have you ever been stereotyped based on your appearance or group membership? If so, what was the stereotype and how did it make you feel?

2. Do you think there are certain groups on your campus that may be especially vulnerable to stereotyping? If yes, what are these groups and what type of stereotypes do you think they encounter?

P rejudice

> See that man over there? Yes. Well, I hate him.
> But you don't know him.
> That's why I hate him.
>
> —Gordon Allport, influential social psychologist and author of *The Nature of Prejudice*

If all members of a stereotyped group are judged and evaluated in a negative way, the result is *prejudice*. The word "prejudice" literally means to "pre-judge." Typically, prejudice is negative and involves *stigmatizing*—ascribing inferior or unfavorable traits to people who belong to the same group. Thus, prejudice may be defined as a negative stereotype about a group of people that's formed before the facts are known.

People who hold a group prejudice typically avoid contact with members of that group. This avoidance leaves little or no opportunity for the prejudiced person to have positive experiences with members of the stigmatized group that could contradict or disprove the prejudice. This sets up a vicious cycle whereby the prejudiced person continues to avoid contact with members of the stigmatized group, which, in turn, continues to maintain and reinforce the prejudice.

Once prejudice has been formed, it also remains intact and resistant to change through a psychological process known as *selective perception*—the tendency for biased (prejudiced) people to see what they *expect* to see and fail to see what contradicts their bias (Hugenberg & Bodenhausen, 2003). Have you ever noticed how fans rooting for their favorite sports team tend to focus on and "see" the referees' calls that go against their own team, but don't seem to react (or even notice) the calls that go against the opposing team? This is a classic example of selective perception. In effect, selective perception takes the old adage, "seeing is believing" and makes it "believing is seeing." It leads prejudiced people to continue "seeing" things that are consistent with their prejudicial belief while remaining "blind" to things that refute or contradict it.

Making matters worse, selective perception is often accompanied by *selective memory*—the tendency for prejudiced people to remember information that supports their prejudicial belief and forget information that fails to support it (Judd, Ryan, & Parke, 1991). The two prejudice-preserving processes of selective perception and selective memory work together and often *unconsciously*. As a result, people may not even be aware that they are using these processes and that their use of them is holding their prejudice intact (Baron, Byrne, & Brauscombe, 2008).

> *We see what is behind our eyes.*
>
> —Chinese proverb

Reflection 9.10

Have you ever witnessed selective perception or selective memory—people seeing or recalling what they believe to be true (due to bias), rather than what's actually true? If yes, what bias was involved and how was selective perception or selective memory used to support the bias?

Strategies for Overcoming Stereotypes and Prejudices

People often hold prejudices, stereotypes, or subtle biases without being fully aware that they hold them (Fiarman, 2016). To help students remain aware of unconscious biases, and reduce their risk of developing biases in the first place, share the following strategies with them.

Consciously avoid preoccupation with physical appearances. Don't forget the old proverb: "It's what's inside that counts." Judge others not by the familiarity of their outer features, but by the merits of their inner qualities. Dive beneath the superficial surface of appearances and view people not in terms of how they look, but in terms of who they are and how they act.

> *Stop judging by mere appearances, and make a right judgment.*
>
> —Bible, John 7:24

Form impressions of others on a person-to-person basis, not according to their group membership. This may seem like a very obvious and simple thing to do, but research shows that humans have a natural tendency to perceive individual members of unfamiliar groups as being more alike than individual members of their own group (Taylor, Peplau, & Sears, 2006). We need to remain mindful of this tendency and make a conscious effort to perceive and treat members of unfamiliar groups as unique individuals with distinctive personalities, not in terms of some general (stereotypical) rule of thumb.

> *You can't judge a book by the cover.*
>
> —1962 hit song by Ellas McDaniel, a.k.a. Bo Diddley (Note: a "bo diddley" is a one-stringed African guitar)

Take a stand against prejudice and discrimination by constructively disagreeing with students who make stereotypical statements and prejudicial remarks. By saying nothing, you may avoid conflict, but silence can send others the message that you tacitly agree with the person who made the prejudicial remark. Studies show that when members of the same group observe one of their own members make a prejudicial comment about a member of a different group, prejudice tends to increase among all members of the group whose member made the prejudicial comment—probably due to peer pressure and group conformity (Stangor, Sechrist, & Jost, 2001). In contrast, if the person's prejudicial remark is challenged by a member of his or her own group, particularly a member who is liked and respected by other group members, it reduces the prejudice of the person making the remark as well as similar prejudices held by other members of the group (Baron, Byrne, & Brauscombe, 2008). Thus, by taking a leadership role and challenging a peer who makes prejudicial remarks, you're not only likely to reduce that person's prejudice but also the prejudice of others who hear the remark. Furthermore, when you combat prejudice, you help create a campus culture characterized by higher levels of student satisfaction and student success. Studies show that campus cultures that are hostile toward students from minority groups have lower rates of student satisfaction with their college experience and lower rates of college completion—for both minority and majority students (Cabrera et al., 1999; Eimers & Pike, 1997; Nora & Cabrera, 1996).

> By actively opposing prejudice on campus, you demonstrate leadership qualities and personal character, and you send a clear message to other members of the campus community that valuing diversity is not just the "politically correct" thing to do, it's the morally *right* thing to do.

Reflection 9.11

Would you say your campus climate or culture supports and facilitates intercultural interaction among students from different racial and cultural backgrounds? In your position as a peer leader, is there anything you could do to try to improve your campus climate so that it's more supportive of, or conducive to, intercultural interaction?

P romoting Interaction and Collaboration among Members of Diverse Groups

In a national study of peer leaders, it was found that the best predictor of their level of leadership development in college was the amount of interaction they had with students from different cultural backgrounds (Dugan & Komives, 2007). As a peer leader, you can make this type of intercultural interaction happen by: (a) stepping out of your comfort zone to reach out to students whose backgrounds are different than your own, and (b) creating opportunities for students to associate with other students from diverse backgrounds. If you're able to promote interaction among members of diverse student groups while they're in college, you're also likely to promote their interaction beyond college. Studies show that students who have more cross-racial interactions during college continue to have more cross-racial interactions in their local communities and places of work after they graduate from college (Tatum 2017).

Listed below are specific practices you can use to engage with diverse students and stimulate interaction between members of majority and minority groups.

- Introduce yourself and strike up conversations with students from different cultural groups.
- Encourage students to expand their social networks and broaden the range of people with whom they choose to interact.
- Join up with majority-group students to welcome and interact with minority students, particularly if you sense that majority students are uncomfortable about doing so on their own.
- Intentionally invite students from diverse backgrounds to join your social groups and campus organizations.
- Keep your eye out for student groups who may be feeling left out or isolated and make an intentional attempt to engage them in campus life.
- Bring diverse students together to form study groups or engage in community service projects.
- Host celebrations of group accomplishments, invite members from all student groups and make a special effort to solicit the attendance of students from minority groups.

In addition, you may use the following practices to increase your access to and interaction with members of diverse groups. Share these practices with the students you lead and model these practices for them.

Place yourself in situations and locations on campus where you're likely to experience diversity. Distancing ourselves from diversity ensures we'll never experience it and benefit from it. Research in social psychology confirms what we'd expect: People who regularly find themselves in the same place at the same time are more likely to communicate and form relationships with one another (Latané et al., 1995). Research also shows that if regular contact takes place between members of different racial or ethnic groups, stereotyping is sharply reduced and intercultural friendships are more likely to form (Pettigrew, 1997, 1998; Pettigrew & Tropp, 2006). You can create these conditions by making an intentional attempt to position yourself near diverse students in class, the library, or student café, and by teaming up with them for group discussions, study groups, and group projects. Also, consider spending time at the multicultural center on your campus or become a member of a campus club or organization that is committed to diversity awareness and appreciation (e.g., multicultural or international student club). Putting yourself in these situations will enable you to make regular contact with members of cultural groups other than your own, and by taking the initiative to visit with these groups on "their turf," it sends them a clear message that you value them.

Reflection 9.12

Your comfort level seeking out diversity is likely to depend on how much prior experience you've had with diverse groups. Rate the amount or variety of diversity you have experienced in the following settings:

1. The high school you attended	high	moderate	low
2. The college or university you now attend	high	moderate	low
3. The neighborhood in which you grew up	high	moderate	low

4. Places where you have been employed   high   moderate   low

Which setting had the *most* and the *least* diversity? What do you think accounted for this difference?

Take advantage of social media to "chat" virtually with students from diverse groups. Electronic communication can be a convenient and comfortable way to initiate contact with members of diverse groups with whom you've had little prior experience. Interacting *online* may be a good way to "break the ice" and set up future interaction *in person.*

Engage in co-curricular experiences involving diversity. Studies indicate that student participation in co-curricular experiences relating to diversity improves critical thinking (Pascarella & Terenzini, 2005) and reduces unconscious prejudice (Blair, 2002). Review your student handbook to identify co-curricular programs, student activities, student clubs, and campus organizations that emphasize diversity awareness and intercultural interaction.

If your campus sponsors multicultural or cross-cultural retreats, strongly consider participating in them. A retreat setting provides a comfortable off-campus environment in which personal interaction with diverse students can take place without being distracted by familiar friends and daily routines.

Seek out the views and opinions of classmates from diverse backgrounds. Group discussions among students of different cultures can reduce prejudice and promote intercultural appreciation, but only if each member's cultural identity and perspective is sought out and valued by members of the discussion group (Baron, Byrne, & Brauscombe, 2008). During class discussions, you can demonstrate leadership by seeking out the views and opinions of classmates from diverse backgrounds and ensuring their ideas are heard. After class discussions, you can also ask students from different backgrounds if there were points made or positions taken in class that they would strongly question or challenge, but didn't get the chance or opportunity to do so.

If there's little or no student diversity in your classes, encourage your classmates to approach course topics and issues from diverse perspectives. For instance, you might ask: "If there were international students here, what might they be adding to our discussion?" Or, you could ask: "If members of certain minority groups were here, would they be offering a different viewpoint?"

Be a community builder who identifies similarities and recurring themes across the ideas and experiences of students from diverse backgrounds. Look for common denominators—themes of unity that co-exist or underlie diversity. Individuals from different ethnic and racial groups are likely to have shared experiences as citizens of the same country, persons of the same gender, or members of the same generation. As you discuss issues relating to diversity, look to discover and discuss patterns of unity that traverse or transcend group differences, and use these commonalities to create a sense of community among members of diverse groups.

Diversity-related discussions that focus exclusively on group differences without also attending to intergroup commonalities can actually increase divisiveness between groups and cause members of minority groups to feel further isolated or alienated (Smith, 1997, 2015). To minimize this risk, dig below the surface of group differences and unearth the common ground on which all groups stand. One way to do so is by calling students' attention to the universal experiences that unite different groups under the umbrella of humanity. For instance, before launching students into a discussion of diversity, first discuss the common elements of all cultures (see p. 283), or common components of the human self and human development (described on p. 236). Taking time to raise awareness of what different groups have in common can help defuse feelings of divisiveness and supply a solid foundation on which open and honest discussions of diversity can be built.

If you are given the opportunity to form your own discussion groups and group-project teams, join or create groups of students from diverse backgrounds. You can gain greater exposure to diverse perspectives by intentionally joining or forming learning groups with students who differ in terms of gender, age, race, or ethnicity. Including diversity in your discussion groups not only creates social variety, it also enhances the quality of the group's discussion by allowing members to gain access to and learn from multiple perspectives. For instance, if a group is composed of members who are diverse with respect to age, older students will bring a broad range of practical life experiences to the group discussion that younger students can draw on and learn from, while younger students bring a more contemporary and possibly idealistic perspective that can enrich the discussion.

Intentionally incorporating gender diversity into group discussions can expose the discussants to different learning approaches and ways of understanding issues. Studies show that males are more likely to be "separate knowers"—they tend to "detach" themselves from the concept or issue being discussed so they can analyze it. In contrast, females are more likely to be "connected knowers"—they tend to relate personally to concepts and connect them with their own experiences and the experiences of others. For example, when interpreting a poem, males are more likely to ask: "What techniques can I use to analyze it?" In contrast, females are more likely to ask: "What is the poet trying to say to me?" (Belenky et al., 1986). Both of these learning approaches are valuable, and as a peer leader you can capitalize on the benefits of both approaches by forming gender-diverse discussion groups.

It's also been found that females are more likely to work collaboratively during group discussions, sharing ideas with others and collecting ideas from others; in contrast, males are more likely to adopt a competitive approach and debate the ideas of others (Magolda, 1992). Consistent with these results are studies of females in leadership positions, which reveal that women are more likely to adopt a democratic or participative style of leadership than men (Eagley & Johnson, 1990; van Engen & Willemsen, 2004).

Form and facilitate collaborative learning teams composed of students from diverse backgrounds. A learning *team* is much more than a discussion group. The latter simply discusses (tosses around) ideas. A learning team moves beyond discussion to *collaboration*—its members "co-labor" (work together) to reach the same goal. Research from kindergarten to college indicates that when students collaborate in teams, their academic performance and interpersonal skills are strengthened (Cuseo, 1996). Also, when individuals from different racial groups work collaboratively toward the same goal, racial prejudice decreases and interracial friendships increase (Allport, 1954; Amir, 1969, 1976; Brown et al., 2003;

Box 8.5

Dovidio, Eller, & Hewstone, 2011; Pettigrew & Tropp, 2000). These positive developments may be explained, in part, by the fact that when members of diverse groups join together to form a team, no one is a member of an "out" group ("them"); instead, everybody is a member of the same "in" group ("us") (Pratto et al., 2000; Sidanius et al., 2000).

The physical environment in which teamwork takes place can also influence the nature and quality of the team's work. Teammates are more likely to interact openly and work collaboratively if their work takes place in a friendly, informal environment that's conducive to relationship building. If possible, have the team come together in a living room or a lounge area. Compared to a sterile classroom, these environments supply a warmer atmosphere that's more conducive to collaboration.

After facilitating teamwork, take time to reflect on the experience. The final step in any learning process, whether it be learning from a professor or learning from group discussion, is to step back from the process and thoughtfully review it. Deep learning requires not only effortful action but also thoughtful reflection (Bligh, 2000; Roediger, Dudai, & Fitzpatrick, 2007). As a peer leader, you can reflect on and learn from your experiences leading diverse learning groups by asking yourself (and the team) the following questions:

- What major similarities in viewpoints did all group members share? (What were the common themes?)
- What major differences of opinion were expressed by diverse members of the group? (What were the variations on the themes?)
- Were there particular topics or issues raised during the discussion that provoked intense reactions or emotional responses from certain members of the group?
- Did the group discussion lead any individuals to change their mind about an idea or position they originally held?

Reflection 9.13

In your role or position as a peer leader, will you have opportunities to form diverse discussion groups and learning teams? If yes, what forms or types of diversity could you include on these groups and teams?

Internet Resources

For additional information related to the ideas discussed in this chapter, consult the following websites:

Cross-cultural communication
http://www.pbs.org/ampu/crosscult.html

Combating stereotypes, prejudice, and discrimination
www.tolerance.org

Preservation of human rights worldwide
https://www.amnesty.org/en/

References

Acredolo, C., & O'Connor, J. (1991). On the difficulty of detecting cognitive uncertainty. *Human Development, 34*, 204-223.

Allport, G. W. (1954). *The nature of prejudice.* Cambridge, MA: Addison-Wesley.

Allport, G. W. (1979). *The Nature of prejudice* (3rd ed.). Reading, MA: Addison-Wesley.

Amir, Y. (1969). Contact hypothesis in ethnic relations. *Psychological Bulletin, 71*, 319-342.

Amir, Y. (1976). The role of intergroup contact in change of prejudice and ethnic relations. In P. A. Katz (Ed.), *Towards the elimination of racism* (pp. 245-308). New York: Pergamon Press.

Anderson, M., & Fienberg, S. (2000). Race and ethnicity and the controversy over the U.S. Census. *Current Sociology, 48*(3), 87-110.

Association of American Colleges & Universities (AAC&U). (2002). *Greater expectations: A new vision for learning as a nation goes to college.* Washington, DC: Author.

Association of American Colleges & Universities (AAC&U). (2004). *Our students' best work.* Washington, DC: Author.

Astin, A. W. (1993). *What matters in college?* San Francisco: Jossey-Bass.

Ayman, R., & Frame, M. (2004). Gender stereotypes and leadership. In J. M. Burns, G. R. Goethals, & J. G. Sorenson (Eds.), *Leadership encyclopedia.* Thousand Oaks, CA: SAGE.

Baron, R. A., Brauscombe, N. R , & Byrne, D. R. (2008). *Social psychology* (12th ed.). Hoboken, NJ: Pearson.

Belenky, M. F., Clinchy, B., Goldberger, N. R., & Tarule, J. M. (1986). *Women's ways of knowing: The development of self, voice, and mind.* New York: Basic Books.

Belkin, L. (2008, June 15). When mom and dad share it all. *The New York Times.* Retrieved from http://www.nytimes.com/2008/06/15/magazine/15parenting-t. html?mcubz=1

Bennett, M. J. (2004). From ethnocentrism to ethnorelativism. In J. S. Wurzel (Ed.), *Toward multiculturalism: A reader in multicultural education* (2nd ed.) (pp. 62-78). Newton, MA: Intercultural Resource Corporation.

Bernardi, R. A., Bosco, S. M., & Columb, V. L. (2009). Does female representation on boards of directors associate with the "Most Ethical Companies" list? *Corporate Reputation Review, 12*, 270-280.

Blair, I. V. (2002). The malleability of automatic stereotypes and prejudice. *Personality and Social Psychology Review, 6*(3), 242-261.

Bligh, D. A. (2000). *What's the use of lectures?* San Francisco: Jossey-Bass.

Bridgeman, B. (2003). *Psychology and evolution: The origins of mind.* Thousand Oaks, CA: SAGE.

Bronfenbrenner, U. (Ed.) (2005). *Making human beings human: Bioecological perspectives on human development.* Thousand Oaks, CA: SAGE.

Brookfield, S. D. (1987). *Developing critical thinkers.* San Francisco: Jossey-Bass.

Brooks, I. (2009). *Organizational behavior* (4th ed.). Englewood Cliffs, NJ: Prentice Hall.

Brown, T. D., Dane, F. C., & Durham, M. D. (1998). Perception of race and ethnicity. *Journal of Social Behavior and Personality, 13*(2), 295-306.

Brown, K. T., Brown, T. N., Jackson, J. S., Sellers, R. M., & Manuel, W. J. (2003). Teammates on and off the field? Contact with Black teammates and the racial attitudes of White student athletes. *Journal of Applied Social Psychology, 33*, 1379-1403.

Cabrera, A., Nora, A., Terenzini, P., Pascarella, E., & Hagedorn, L. S. (1999). Campus racial climate and the adjustment of students to college: A comparison between White students and African American students. *The Journal of Higher Education, 70*(2), 134-160.

Cabrera, A., & Unruh, G. (2012). *Being global: How to think, act, and lead in a transformed world.* Boston: Harvard Business Review Press.

Caplan, P. J., & Caplan, J. B. (2009). *Thinking critically about research on sex and gender* (3rd ed.). New York: HarperCollins College Publishers.

Catalyst. (2014a). *Fortune 500 CEO positions held by women*. Retrieved from http://www.catalyst.org/knowledge/fortune-500-ceo-positions-held-women

Catalyst. (2014b). *U.S. women in business*. Retrieved from http://www.catalyst.org/knowledge/us-women-business

Colombo, G., Cullen, R., & Lisle, B. (2013). *Rereading America: Cultural contexts for critical thinking and writing* (9th ed.). Boston: Bedford Books of St. Martin's Press.

Cuseo, J. B. (1996). *Cooperative learning: A pedagogy for addressing contemporary challenges and critical issues in higher education*. Stillwater, OK: New Forums Press.

Dessel, A. (2010). Effects of intergroup dialogue: Public school teachers and sexual orientation prejudice. *Small Group Research, 41*(5), 556-592.

Dolan, M., & Romney, L. (2015, June 27). "Law in California is now a right for all." *Los Angeles Times*, pp. A1 & A8.

Dovidio, J. F., Eller, A., & Hewstone, M. (2011). Improving intergroup relations through direct, extended and other forms of indirect contact. *Group Processes & Intergroup Relations, 14*, 147-160.

Dryden, G., & Vos, J. (1999). *The learning revolution: To change the way the world learns*. Torrance, CA and Auckland, New Zealand: The Learning Web.

Dugan, J. P., & Komives, S. R. (2007). *Developing leadership capacity in college students: Findings from a national study*. A Report from the Multi-Institutional Study of Leadership. College Park, MD: National Clearinghouse for Leadership Programs.

Eagly, A. H., & Carli, L. L. (2003). The female leadership advantage: An evaluation of the evidence. *Leadership Quarterly, 14*, 807-834.

Eagly, A. H., Johannesen-Schmidt, M . C., & van Engen, M. L. (2003). Transformational, transactional, and laissez-faire leadership styles: A meta-analysis comparing women and men. *Psychological Bulletin, 129*(4), 69-91.

Eagly, A. H., & Johnson, B. T. (1990). Gender and leadership style: A meta-analysis. *Psychological Bulletin, 108*, 233-256.

Education Commission of the States. (1995). *Making quality count in undergraduate education*. Denver, CO: ECS Distribution Center.

Eimers, M. T., & Pike, G. R. (1997). Minority and nonminority adjustment to college: Differences or similarities. *Research in Higher Education, 38*(1), 77-97.

Elliott, J. R., & Smith, R. A. (2004). Race, gender, and workplace power. *American Sociological Review, 69*(3), 365-386.

Erickson, B. L., Peters, C. B., & Strommer, D. W. (2006). *Teaching first-year college students*. San Francisco: Jossey-Bass.

Fiarman, S. E. (2016). Unconscious bias: When good intentions aren't enough. *Educational Leadership, 74(3)*, 10-15.

Fixman, C. S. (1990). The foreign language needs of U.S. based corporations. *Annals of the American Academy of Political and Social Science, 511*, 25-46.

Friedman, T. L. (2005). *The world is flat: A brief history of the twenty-first century*. New York: Farrar, Straus & Giroux.

Gorski, P. C. (2009). *Key characteristics of a multicultural curriculum*. Critical Multicultural Pavilion: Multicultural Curriculum Reform (An EdChange Project). Retrieved from www.edchange.org/multicultural/curriculum/characteristics.html

Harris, A. (2010). Leading system transformation. *School Leadership and Management*, 30 (July), 197-207.

Hart Research Associates. (2013). *It takes more than a major: Employer priorities for college learning and student success*. Washington, DC: Author.

HERI (Higher Education Research Institute). (2013). *Your first college year survey 2012*. Los Angeles: Cooperative Institutional Research Program, University of California-Los Angeles.

HERI (Higher Education Research Institute). (2014). *Your first college year survey 2014*. Los Angeles: Cooperative Institutional Research Program, University of California-Los Angeles.

House, R. L., & Javidan, M. (2004). Overview of GLOBE. In R. J. House, P. J. Hanges, M. Javidan, P. W. Dorfman, V. Gupta, & Associates (Eds.), *Culture, leadership, and organizations: The GLOBE study of 62 societies* (pp. 9-28). Thousand Oaks, CA: SAGE.

Hoyt, C. L., & Chemers, M. M. (2008). Social stigma and leadership: A long climb up a slippery ladder. In C. L. Hoyt, G. R. Goethals, & D. R. Forsyth (Eds.), *Leadership at the crossroads: Leadership and psychology* (Vol. 1, pp. 165-180). Westport, CT: Praeger.

Hugenberg, K., & Bodenhausen, G. V. (2003). Facing prejudice: Implicit prejudice and the perception of facial threat. *Psychological Science, 14*, 640-643.

Institute of International Education. (2017). *Open doors report on international education exchange.* New York: Author.

Inter-Parliamentary Union. (2014). *Women in national parliaments.* Retrieved from http://www.ipu.org/wmn-e/classif.htm

Jablonski, N. G., & Chaplin, G. (2002, October). Skin deep. *Scientific American*, 75–81.

Johnson, D., Johnson, R., & Smith, K. (1998). Cooperative learning returns to college: What evidence is there that it works? *Change, 30*, 26-35.

Judd, C. M., Ryan, C. S., & Parke, B. (1991). Accuracy in the judgment of in-group and out-group variability. *Journal of Personality and Social Psychology, 61*, 366-379.

Kanter, R. (1977). *Men and women of the corporation.* New York: Basic Books.

Kouzes, J. M., & Posner, B. Z. (2002). *The leadership challenge: How to get extraordinary things done in organizations* (3rd ed.). San Francisco: Jossey-Bass

Kim, Y. M. (2011). *Minorities in higher education: Twenty-fourth status report, 2011 supplement.* Washington, DC: American Council on Education.

Kitchener, K., Wood, P., & Jensen, L. (2000, August). *Curricular, co-curricular, and institutional influence on real-world problem-solving.* Paper presented at the annual meeting of the American Psychological Association, Boston.

Latané, B., Liu, J. H., Nowak, A., Bonevento, N., & Zheng, L. (1995). Distance matters: Physical space and social impact. *Personality and Social Psychology Bulletin, 21*, 795-805.

Leung, A. K., Maddux, W. W., Galinsky, A. D., & Chie-yue, C. (2008). Multicultural experience enhances creativity: The when and how. *American Psychologist, 63*(3), 169-181.

Luhman, R. (2007). *The sociological outlook.* Lanham, MD: Rowman & Littlefield.

Maddux, W. W., & Galinsky, A. D. (2009). Cultural borders and mental barriers: The relationship between living abroad and creativity. *Journal of Personality and Social Psychology, 96*(5), 1047-1061.

Magolda, M. B. B. (1992). *Knowing and reasoning in college.* San Francisco: Jossey-Bass.

Mendez, F., Krahn, T., Schrack, B., Krahn, A. M., Veeramah, K., Woerner, A., Fomine, F. L. M., Bradman, N., Thomas, M., Karafet, T., & Hammer, M. (2013). An African American paternal lineage adds an extremely ancient root to the human Y chromosome phylogenetic tree. *The American Journal of Human Genetics, 92*, 454-459.

Meredith, M. (2011). *Born in Africa: The quest for the origins of human life.* New York: Public Affairs.

Nagda, B. R., Gurin, P., & Johnson, S. M. (2005). Living, doing and thinking diversity: How does pre-college diversity experience affect first-year students' engagement with college diversity? In R. S. Feldman (Ed.), *Improving the first year of college: Research and practice* (pp. 73-110). Mahwah, NJ: Lawrence Erlbaum.

Nathan, R. (2005). *My freshman year: What a professor learned by becoming a student.* Ithaca, New York: Cornell University Press.

National Association of Colleges & Employers. (2014). *Job Outlook 2014 survey.* Bethlehem, PA: Author.

National Center for Education Statistics. (2011). *Table 317: Bachelor's, master's, and doctor's degrees conferred by degree-granting institutions, by sex of student and discipline division: 2010-11.* Washington, DC: Digest of Education Statistics.

Nhan, D. (2012). "Census: Minorities constitute 37 percent of U.S. population." *National Journal: The Next America-Demographics 2012*. Retrieved from http:www. nationaljournal.com/thenextamerica/demographics/census-minorities-constitute-37-percent-of-u-s-population-20120517

Nielsen, S., & Huse, M. (2010). The contribution of women on boards of directors: Going beyond the surface. *Corporate Governance—An International Review, 18*, 136-148.

Nora, A., & Cabrera, A. (1996). The role of perceptions of prejudice and discrimination on the adjustment of minority college students. *The Journal of Higher Education, 67*(2), 119-148.

Northouse, P. G. (2016). *Leadership: Theory and practice* (7th ed.). Los Angeles: SAGE.

Office of Research. (1994). *What employers expect of college graduates: International knowledge and second language skills.* Washington, DC: Office of Educational Research and Improvement, U.S. Department of Education.

Pascarella, E. T. (2001, November/December). Cognitive growth in college: Surprising and reassuring findings from the National Study of Student Learning. *Change,* 21-27.

Pascarella, E. T., Palmer, B., Moye, M., & Pierson C. (2001). Do diversity experiences influence the development of critical thinking? *Journal of College Student Development, 42*(3), 257-291.

Pascarella, E. T., & Terenzini, P. T. (2005). *How college affects students: A third decade of research* (Vol. 2) San Francisco: Jossey-Bass.

Peoples, J., & Bailey, G. (2011). *Humanity: An introduction to cultural anthropology.* Belmont, CA: Wadsworth, Cengage Learning. Retrieved from http://www.aacu.org/leap/documents/2009-employersurvey.pdf

Pettigrew, T. F. (1997). Generalized intergroup contact effects on prejudice. *Personality and Social Psychology Bulletin, 23,* 173-185.

Pettigrew, T. F. (1998). Intergroup contact theory. *Annual Review of Psychology, 49,* 65-85.

Pettigrew, T. F., & Tropp, L. R. (2000). Does intergroup contact reduce prejudice? Recent meta-analytic findings. In S. Oskamp (Ed.), *Reducing prejudice and discrimination* (pp. 93-114). Mahwah, NJ: Lawrence Erlbaum Associates.

Pettigrew, T. F., & Tropp, L. R. (2006). A meta-analytic test of intergroup contact theory. *Journal of Personality and Social Psychology, 90*(5), 751-783.

Pinker, S. (2000). *The language instinct: The new science of language and mind.* New York: Perennial.

Postsecondary Education Opportunity. (2001, November). *Enrollment rates for females 18 to 34 years, 1950-2000.* Number 113. Washington, DC: Center for the Study of Opportunity in Higher Education.

Pratto, F., Liu, J. H., Levin, S., Sidanius, J., Shih, M., Bachrach, H., & Hegarty, P. (2000). Social dominance orientation and the legitimization of inequality across cultures. *Journal of Cross-Cultural Psychology, 31,* 369-409.

Reid, G. B. R., & Hetherington, R. (2010). *The climate connection: Climate change and modern evolution.* Cambridge, UK: Cambridge University Press.

Roediger, H. L., Dudai, Y., & Fitzpatrick, S. M. (2007). *Science of memory: concepts.* New York: Oxford University Press.

Segall, M. H., Campbell, D. T., & Herskovits, M. J. (1996). *The influence of culture on visual perception.* Indianapolis: Bobbs-Merrill.

Shetterly, M. L. (2017). *Hidden figures: The American dream and the untold story of the black women mathematicians who helped win the space race.* New York: HarperCollins.

Shiraev, E. D., & Levy, D. (2013). *Cross-cultural psychology: Critical thinking and contemporary applications* (5th ed.). Upper Saddle River, NJ: Pearson Education.

Sidanius, J., Levin, S., Liu, H., & Pratto, F. (2000). Social dominance orientation, anti-egalitarianism, and the political psychology of gender: An extension and cross-cultural replication. *European Journal of Social Psychology, 30,* 41-67.

Smith, D. (1997). How diversity influences learning. *Liberal Education, 83*(2), 42-48.

Smith, D. (2015). *Diversity's promise for higher education: Making it work* (2nd ed.). Baltimore, MD: Johns Hopkins University Press.

Stangor, C., Sechrist, G. B., & Jost, J. T. (2001). Changing racial beliefs by providing consensus information. *Personality and Social Psychology Bulletin, 27,* 484-494.

Stoltz, P. G. (2014). *Grit: The new science of what it takes to persevere, flourish, succeed.* San Luis Obispo: Climb Strong Press.

Tatum, B. D. (2017, September 11). "Diverse but segregated." *Los Angeles Times,* p. A11.

Taylor, S. E., Peplau, L. A., & Sears, D. O. (2006). *Social psychology* (12th ed.). Upper Saddle River, NJ: Pearson/Prentice-Hall.

Thompson, A., & Cuseo, J. (2014). *Diversity and the college experience.* Dubuque, IA: Kendall Hunt.

Torpey, E. (2017). *Women in management.* Retrieved from https://www.bls.gov/careeroutlook/2017/data-on-display/women-managers.htm

U.S. Bureau of Labor Statistics. (2013). Table 11: Employed persons by detailed occupation, sex, race, and Hispanic or Latino ethnicity. *Current Population Survey, Annual Averages: Household Data.* Retrieved from http://www.bls.gov/cps/cpsaat11.pdf

U.S. Census Bureau. (2008). *An older and more diverse nation by midcentury.* Retrieved from http://www.census.gov/Press-release/www/releases/archives/population/012496.html

U.S. Census Bureau. (2013a, July 8). *About race.* Retrieved from http://www.census.gov/topics/population/race/about.html

U.S. Census Bureau. (2013b). *Poverty.* Retrieved from http://www.censensus.gov/hhes/www/poverty/data/threshld/

U.S. Census Bureau. (2015, March). *Projections of the Size and Composition of the U.S. Population: 2014 to 2060.* Retrieved from http://www.census.gov/content/dam/Census/library/publications/2015/demo/p25-1143.pdf

Uzzi, B., & Dunlap, S. (2005). How to build your network. *Harvard Business Review, 83*(12), 53-60.

van Engen, M. L., & Willemsen, T. M. (2004). Sex and leadership styles: A meta-analysis of research published in the 1990s. *Psychological Reports, 94,* 3-18.

Wabash National Study of Liberal Arts Education. (2007). *Liberal arts outcomes.* Retrieved from http:www.liberalarts.wabash.edu/ study-overview/

Wheelright, J. (2005, March). Human, study thyself. *Discover,* 39–45.

Williams, J. (2010). *Reshaping the work-family debate: Why men and class matter.* Cambridge, MA: Harvard University Press.

Willis, J. (2006). *Research-based strategies to ignite student learning: Insights from a neurologist and classroom teacher.* Alexandria, VA: ASCD.

Zajonc, R. B. (1970, February). Brainwash: Familiarity breeds comfort. *Psychology Today,* pp. 32-35, 60-62.

Zajonc, R. B. (2001). Mere exposure: A gateway to the subliminal. *Current Directions in Psychological Science, 10,* 224-228.

Exercise 9.1 Quote Reflections

Review the sidebar quotes contained in this chapter and select two that you think would be especially valuable to share with the students you lead or mentor.

For each quote, write a short statement explaining why you chose it.

Name _____ Date _____

Exercise 9.2 Gaining Awareness of Your Group Identities

An individual is likely to be a member of multiple groups at the same time and membership in these overlapping groups can combine to influence that individual's development and personal identity. In the following figure, consider the shaded center circle to be yourself and the six non-shaded circles to be six different groups to which you belong and that you think have influenced your development.

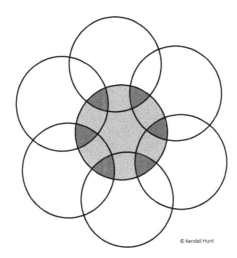

© Kendall Hunt

Fill in the non-shaded circles with the names of groups to which you belong that have had the most influence on your personal development and identity. You can use the diversity spectrum (p. 279) to identify different groups of which you may be a member. Don't feel compelled to fill in all six circles; more important than filling in all the circles is identifying those groups that you think have had the most significant influence on your personal development or identity.

Self-Assessment Questions:

1. Which one of your groups has had the *greatest influence* on your development or identity? Why?

2. Have you ever felt *limited* or *disadvantaged* by being a member of any group(s) to which you belong? Why?

3. Have you experienced *advantages or privileges* as a result of being a member of any group(s) to which you belong? Why?

Exercise 9.3 Hidden Bias Test

Go to www.tolerance.org/activity/test-yourself-hidden-bias and take one or more of the hidden bias tests on this website. These tests assess subtle biases we may have with respect to gender, age, ethnic minority groups, religious denominations, sexual orientations, disabilities, and body weight.

After completing the test, answer the following questions:

1. Do you think your results were accurate or valid?

2. Did the results suggest that you had a bias you weren't unaware of?

3. If your answer to the previous question was "yes," what do you think may account for or contribute to this bias?

4. If your closest family member and best friend took the test, how do you think their results would compare with yours?

Exercise 9.4 Personal Reflections on Diversity

1. On your campus, do you see members of diverse groups interacting with each other frequently, occasionally, or rarely? What factors do you think contribute to and detract from their level of interaction?

2. Identify a group on campus that you think is most isolated or segregated. What might be one thing you could do as a peer leader to help these students become better connected to, or integrated into, the campus community?

3. What group(s) of students on campus do you currently feel least comfortable leading or least prepared to lead? Why do you feel that way and what might you do to increase your level of comfort or preparedness?

4. Think of a time in your life when you felt uncomfortable or unconfident about interacting with people from certain groups, but later became more comfortable and confident.

    (a) What enabled you to gain comfort and confidence?

    (b) As a peer leader, is there anything you could do to facilitate the same growth process for the students you lead and mentor?

Exercise 9.5 Intercultural Interview

1. Find a person on campus from a cultural group with which you've had little previous contact. Ask that person for an interview, and, during the interview, ask the following questions.

   • What does "diversity" mean to you?

   • What prior experiences have affected your current viewpoints or attitudes about diversity?

   • What would you say have been the major influences and turning points in your life?

   • Who would you say are your positive role models, heroes, or sources of inspiration?

   • What societal or national contributions made by your cultural group are you most proud of and think should be acknowledged?

   • What do you hope will never again be said about your cultural group?

2. If you were the interviewee instead of the interviewer, how would you have answered the above questions?

Exercise 9.6 Strategy Reflections

Review the strategies recommended for *promoting interaction and collaboration among members of diverse groups* on p. 297. Select three strategies that you think students would be most receptive to learning about and putting into practice.

CHAPTER 10

Leading Groups

Understanding Group Dynamics and Facilitating Teamwork

Reflection 10.1

Think of a situation in which you were a member of a group that had an effective leader. How did the leader act? How did the leader's actions affect the group? How did the leader's actions affect you as an individual member of the group?

Chapter Purpose and Preview

Leadership can go beyond mentoring individuals on a one-to-one basis to leading groups, both small and large. High-impact leaders understand how groups function and how to transform a group of individuals into a unified, high-performing team. This chapter equips you with specific strategies for building team vision and developing team commitment to that vision. You will also acquire practical strategies for delivering presentations to groups, managing group dynamics, and empowering groups to make consensus-based decisions.

Establishing a Common Vision and Shared Purpose

"If you build it, they will come." This is a quote from the movie *Field of Dreams*, in which an Iowa farmer (played by Kevin Costner) builds a beautiful baseball diamond in the middle of his farm, hoping to attract great (but long dead) baseball players. Of course, nobody believes they will come, but they do! The baseball ghosts from 1919 come to his 1980s farm. Why? Because they have a *passion* for baseball and because the farmer created a place and space where they believed their passion could be played out. In leadership terminology, the farmer (leader) established a vision that attracted a team of followers and enabled them and their leader to make the vision a reality. The farmer carefully prepared the field, made it inviting for the team to participate, reassured skeptics, and persevered in the face of setbacks. And not only did the players come; fans came as well! Although the movie was obviously fictional, it dramatically highlights some of the key qualities of effective group leadership.

> *A dream you dream alone is only a dream. A dream you dream together is reality.*
>
> —John Lennon, founding member of the Beatles

> *People support what they helped create.*
>
> —Komives, Lucas, & McMahon,
> *Exploring Leadership for College Students Who Want to Make a Difference*

When a group has a shared sense of purpose, its members are far more likely to invest their time, energy, and effort to fulfill the group's vision. The best group leaders inspire, encourage, and challenge their group to fulfill its intended purpose. In the words of an old spiritual that became prominent during the U.S. civil rights movement, they empower the group to "keep its eyes on the prize."

As a peer leader, you can play a major role in helping group members create a shared vision, which is vital during the initial stages of a group development. Group members are much more likely to buy into a vision that's been shaped and molded by them rather than imposed on them. Even though group members may not initially know what their ultimate purpose and future direction may be, they should be involved in shaping that purpose and direction. You can start this process by supplying group members with a list or menu of possible group goals, allow them to add goals of their own to the list, and then have them rank the listed goals in terms of their importance or priority. It's especially important to get group members' input early on, but don't stop there; continue to seek their feedback as the group develops.

Once input from group members has been sought and considered, work with your group to create a *vision statement*. What's a vision statement? It's an inspiring statement of:

- The group's primary *purpose* (What are we here for?)
- The group's most deeply held *principles* (What do we stand for?)
- The *end point* of the group's actions (Where are we going?)
- The *essential actions* the group will engage in to achieve its purpose. (How will we get there?)

> *The real key to a successful team is having a firm understanding of the goal of the group, and then knowing how each individual can most effectively contribute to the achievement of this goal.*
>
> —Senior peer leader

A group's vision comes alive in everyday practice when it is "owned" by its members and when it incorporates their interests, needs, priorities, and values. The first step in the process of transforming a group into a team with a shared vision and common goals is to become familiar with the group members as individuals, including the goals and aspirations they have in common (Kouzes & Posner, 2012). (Some of the personal information questions listed in Exercise 1.3 at the end of chapter 1 may be used to facilitate this process.) Once you become familiar with your group members' goals and aspirations, you can help them develop a common group vision by asking members to submit goals to you in writing about what they'd like to accomplish. (For a list of the sequence of steps involved in constructing a group vision statement, see **Box 10.1**.)

Once the group's vision has been established, the next step is to translate the vision into *specific goals* and *objectives* that align with it. Like individuals, groups need clear goals to strive for and work toward. Research based on observations of numerous teams shows that one key characteristic of effective group leaders is that they always keep their team focused on its goals (LaFasto & Larson, 2001). Encourage your group to engage in the process of goal setting that's described in chapter 5, p. 140. Create a "group goals" document, distribute a copy to all group members, post it at all group meetings, and continually refer to it to ensure that your group is on course and moving in the direction of its stated goals.

Reflection 10.2

Think of a group experience you've had in which your group reached (or exceeded) its goals. How did the leader establish the group's purpose and keep the group focused until its goals were achieved?

Constructing a Group Vision Statement: Key Steps

- Become familiar with your group members' personal interests and aspirations, and identify those they have in common.
- Ask group members to submit goals they'd like to see the group achieve or accomplish.
- Create a draft version of a vision statement that synthesizes the group's common interests, aspirations, and goals.
- Distribute the draft and ask for feedback (e.g., invite the group to edit it on a discussion board).
- Construct a final draft of the vision statement and request the group to approve it.
- Place the vision statement in a place where your group regularly meets, or post it on an electronic site that the group frequently visits (e.g., Blackboard or Facebook).
- Have the group periodically review its vision statement and assess how well it's living it.

Note: A vision statement doesn't have to be perfect and permanently set in stone; it can be revised and refined as group members become more familiar with one another and gain greater experience working together. What's most important is that the vision statement be authentic and serve as a living document that the group can refer to, reflect on, and use as a compass to guide its work.

Group Development

Group *performance* is measured by whether or not the group reached its goal (Northouse, 2016). Group *development* refers to its cohesiveness, how well its members work as a unit, and its ability to meet the needs of its individual members (Nadler, 1998). Group development may be viewed as the *process* that leads to positive group *outcomes* (e.g., achievement of the group's goals).

Leading groups will test your confidence, patience, and perseverance. Despite your best intentions and most heartfelt efforts, not every member of the group will immediately jump on board and continue to stay on board for the entire trip. A group's development will have its highs, lows, ebbs, and flows.

Similar to personal development, group development is a maturational process that takes time and emerges in stages. Research suggests that group development typically progresses through the stages listed in **Box 10.2**. A group's movement through these stages may take a linear path—following the order in which are listed in the box, or it make take a more spiral path— moving ahead to the next stage, slipping back temporarily to an earlier stage, and then moving forward again. The total time it takes for groups to progress through all these stages can vary from group to group, and the rate or speed at which groups move through these stages may also vary—some groups spend about the same amount of time at each stage as they progress through them, while other groups may move quickly through some stages and more slowly through others.

Despite the variety of ways in which groups move through their stages of development, it's been found that high-performing groups go through all these stages before reaching their peak level of performance (Tuckman, 1965; Tuckman & Jensen, 1977, 2010).

Box 10.2

Stages of Group Development

Your familiarity with the following stages of group development will allow you to understand how groups evolve and help you determine whether your group is moving in the right direction. Share your knowledge of these stages with the groups you lead; it will help them realize that these are "normal" steps in the process of group development and the achievement of group goals.

Stage 1. Forming

When a group first comes together, participants typically feel a bit anxious because they don't know each other well, are unsure how well they're going to work together, and may not know what's expected of them. As group members progress through this first "forming" stage of development, they begin to grow more comfortable relating to each other and develop a better understanding of the group's purpose and goals.

Stage 2. Storming

As the word suggests, here's where the going can get a little rough. Often this is the make-or-break stage of group development because the group's initial enthusiasm and idealism may be suddenly dampened (or decimated) by early frustrations, disagreements, and setbacks. Results don't come as easily as was first thought. Conflicts emerge, differences of opinion begin to be expressed, the leader's role may be challenged, and the value of the group's work may be questioned. Such conflict may be uncomfortable, but not always unhealthy or unproductive because once the conflict is resolved, it can lead to positive change in group cohesiveness and improvement in group performance (Northouse, 2016).

As group leader, this is the stage where you should: (1) maintain and model optimism, (2) help the group members assess what's happening and remind them that this is a "normal" stage of group development, and (3) make necessary changes to ensure that the group resolves its conflict, learns from it, and remains optimistic about reaching its goals. Studies show that one characteristic of effective leaders is that they maintain and manifest optimism about their group's efforts, especially during trying times (Chemers, Watson, & May, 2000).

> If your group appears to be going nowhere or its members are arguing so much that no work can get accomplished or even started, remember that this is a normal part of the group-development process. Remind yourself and your team that thunderstorms do occur, but the skies will eventually clear.

Stage 3. Norming

This stage represents the "calm after the storm." The group has weathered the tumult of the previous stage, addressed its earlier issues, modified its approach, and begins to make significant progress toward its goals. Group members start to work harmoniously and collaboratively, reaching mutual agreement about the methods they will use to accomplish their goals as well the specific roles each member will play in the process.

Stage 4. Performing

At this stage, the group begins to function in a highly effective and efficient manner. Communication is honest, open, and respectful. All members are actively involved in the group process, individual members execute their specific roles, and each member takes personal responsibility for contributing to the group's work. It's at this stage that co-leaders often emerge to help facilitate the group process and keep the group moving in the right direction.

Stage 5. Retiring/Adjourning

At this advanced stage of group development, the group has bonded to the point where its members chat informally and confer with each other about the group's work on their own time. Following completion of group tasks, members may spend time together socializing and discussing the group's work in more relaxed settings. As group leader, you can capitalize on this stage by arranging optional, informal get-togethers after official meetings. These follow-up activities could simply be social get-togethers that help members bond together as a team. Or, these gatherings may be used as opportunities for members to reflect on their group's work and engage in informal discussions about how to improve it. For instance, as the group's leader, you may ask: "Are we accomplishing what we've set out to do?" If the answer is no or not sure, you can engage them in an informal yet honest discussion about how the group might function more effectively and efficiently. If their answer is yes, ask them what they think is working well and should be continued or accentuated, and acknowledge the group's accomplishments. Research on high-performing groups indicates that one of their practices is engaging in regular rituals to celebrate the accomplishments they've made and the milestones they've reached (Kouzes & Posner, 2012). These celebratory events reinforce the group's vision and further solidify relationships among its members. For instance, you can celebrate group successes by arranging for your group to periodically share meals together or drinks at a local coffee house. Even a short congratulatory e-mail or Facebook post following a successful meeting can be an effective way to validate and appreciate your group's work.

6. Adjourning and Mourning/Grieving

At this stage, the group officially disbands because all its work is done. If group members have been together for an extended period of time, disbanding can sometimes trigger feelings of mourning, grief, or a sense of emptiness and sadness because the group's energy and camaraderie will be missed. As group leader, you can help alleviate their sense of loss by planning a final group celebration activity. This doesn't have to be an expensive or labor-intensive event; it could simply be a modest awards get-together at which all group members are personally recognized for their contributions. Such rituals remind individuals that their contributions made a difference, are worthy of public recognition, and are worth doing again in any future work groups they may join or you may form.

Sources: Tuckman, 1965; Tuckman and Jensen, 1977, 2010.

Facilitating Group Interaction

Facilitation is the process of assisting or improving the progress of improving something. *Group facilitation* is the process of improving group interaction, collaboration, and productivity. Groups typically do not facilitate themselves; they cannot run smoothly without a leader who is attentive to group dynamics and displays group-facilitation skills, such as those discussed below.

Team Building

This is the essential first step in the group-facilitation process. The impact of group work becomes more powerful when it takes place in a social context that's been intentionally designed to promote team cohesiveness and mutual trust. An outstanding leader is able to a transform a group into a *team* with: (a) a common team goal, (b) interdependent (mutually supportive) roles played by teammates, and (c) a strong sense of team identity (Dyer, Dyer, & Dyer, 2007). As a peer leader, you can convert group work into teamwork by intentionally using team-building activities that promote a sense of collective identity. Team-building activities build esprit de corps—a genuine sense of team spirit and supportive connectedness—which enables group members to express their personal viewpoints openly, disagree with each other respectfully, and make decisions collaboratively.

> *For leadership to function well, leaders and followers must be bound by a shared identity and by the quest to use that identity as a blueprint for action.*
>
> —Haslam, Reicher, & Platow, *The New Psychology of Leadership*

The word "compete" comes from the Latin, meaning "to strive together."

> *Taking the time needed to build a sense of community in a group acknowledges that relationships are central to effective leadership [and] builds a strong organization with committed participants who know they matter.*
>
> —Komives, Lucas, & McMahon, *Exploring Leadership for College Students Who Want to Make a Difference*

The following team-building activities may be used to create a sense of collective identity and group cohesiveness:

- Engage teammates in "ice breakers" or "community builders," such as the "Personal Scavenger Hunt." (See Exercise 10.4, p. 349.) The Office of Student Affairs or Student Activities on campus should be able to provide you with a variety of other ice-breakers that could be used for team-building purposes.
- Take a team photo.
- Have the group select a team name and/or a team motto.
- Use team language (e.g., instead of referring to them as a "group, refer to them as a "team"; maximize your use of the words "we" and "us" and minimize use of the words "me" and "you").

Setting Ground Rules and Establishing Group Norms

Once a sense of team identity has been created, the next step in the group-facilitation process is to decide on guidelines for collaboration and teamwork that teammates will abide by. When social-interaction guidelines and ground rules are established "up front," it lays the ground work for group work to run smoothly. Establishing ground rules proactively—before group work begins, is more effective than trying to impose them reactively—after group work has begun and unproductive behavior has taken place.

You can take a proactive approach to group facilitation by first establishing *group norms*—clear, mutually agreed-upon guidelines for group interaction that specify how individuals will communicate and how group members will treat each other during group meetings and discussions. (See **Box 10.3** for a sample list of group norms.) Formulating group norms is consistent with "adaptive leadership" theory (discussed in chapter 2), which posits that an adaptive leader pays close attention to norms that maximize group effectiveness and challenges norms that impair or impede the group's ability to adapt to change (Northouse, 2016).

Group norms work most effectively when team members initially collaborate to create them and subsequently enforce the norms they create. Here are some strategies for getting the process started.

- Ask the group for behaviors they'd like to see all teammates display. For example:
  (a) How would you like to be treated by members of our group?
  (b) What do you expect from other members of our group?
  (c) What would really bother you if a group member were to _____?
- Discuss the above questions with the group. If your group is larger than 10, you may want to start with small-group discussions (3-5) and have the small groups share their ideas with the whole group.
- After all ideas have been discussed, ask the group to identify common viewpoints or recurrent themes that emerged during the discussion.
- Generate a first draft of group norms that pulls together the members' shared viewpoints and distribute the draft to the group for feedback.
- Based on the group's feedback, revise the draft and construct an official list of group norms.
- Once the group's norms have been drawn up and agreed upon, send them to all group members individually via e-mail or whatever mode of communication they prefer. Also print them out on a poster, bring them to group meetings, and place them where all group members cannot help but see them.

- Periodically ask group members to reflect on and discuss how well the group is adhering to its norms. Be specific—go from norm to norm and ask group members for their assessment. (For example, have members rate the group's performance for each norm on a scale of 1-10 and ask them to provide an explanation for each of their ratings.)

Box 10.3

Group Norms: A Sample

1. We arrive at meetings on time (or ahead of time) and all meetings start on time.
2. We are prepared for group meetings by:
   (a) reviewing notes from the previous meeting;
   (b) coming ready to report on tasks we agreed to complete after our previous meeting;
   (c) bringing questions and ideas to discuss at the meeting.
3. During meetings:
   (a) We share air time—no one dominates the conversation.
   (b) Only one member speaks at a time and other members listen actively to the person speaking.
   (c) There are no "side bars"—side conversations while someone else is speaking.
   (d) There is no texting and checking e-mail or Facebook posts.
4. We don't introduce a new topic until discussion of the current topic is complete. (Any issues raised that do not relate directly to the topic under discussion are placed in a "parking lot"—put on hold and not discussed until discussion of the current topic is finished.)
5. When group members express an idea we disagree with:
   (a) We respectfully allow them to express their point of view (e.g., no head shaking while the person is speaking and no interruptions until the person is finished speaking).
   (b) When it's our turn to speak, we first look for and acknowledge points we may agree with before launching into points we disagree with.
   (c) We focus disagreements on ideas, not people—on *what* is being said, not *who* is saying it.

When group norms are well-defined and faithfully followed, group members become more comfortable about expressing their ideas openly and are more likely to focus on the group's agenda, not their personal agenda.

Reflection 10.3

Based on your experience with groups, do you think it will be difficult to get all members of a group to agree on and abide by group norms? If yes, why? If no, why not?

Planning Group Meetings and Activities

When group meetings and activities are planned in a thoughtful manner, group members are more likely to become engaged and group goals are more likely to be achieved. As a group leader, when you take the time and make the effort to plan group meetings carefully, you demonstrate commitment to the group and respect for its members' time and effort. A well-planned meeting should include the following components.

- Communication prior to the meeting that answers the following questions:
  1. When are we meeting?
  2. What are the goals or objectives of the meeting?
  3. What questions or issues will be addressed at the meeting?
  4. How should we prepare for the meeting?
  5. What do we need to bring to the meeting?
  6. What will we be expected to do at the meeting?
- To ensure that all group members receive and remember pre-meeting communications, try to use more than one mode of communication (e.g., face-to-face, e-mail, Facebook, Blackboard discussion board).
- Select a building, room, and seating configuration that will work best for achieving the meeting's purpose. For example, if the goal of the meeting is to discuss and reach consensus on a controversial issue, choose a meeting place that has a warm ambience and is conducive to face-to-face discussion.

Conducting Meetings and Group Activities

Before diving into the work task, engage group members in a social "warm up" activity at the outset of the meeting. For instance, start the meeting with a "check-in"—a short question or prompt that each group member quickly responds to, such as: "What's the best thing that's happened to you since our last meeting?"

- At the start of the meeting, identify the meeting's primary purpose. Always be sure to take time to explain why the meeting is being held and how it relates to the group's purpose or goals.
- Monitor the level of engagement of group members during the meeting. Pay special attention to their nonverbal signals (body language). Are some members visibly detached or disengaged? Are they tuning out? Are they engaging in side conversations unrelated to the task at hand? If there are members who appear to be disengaged, approach them privately and use "I" messages to sensitively express your concern (e.g., "I'm sensing that you're not really into what we're doing"). In some cases, just taking the time to connect personally with a disengaged student is enough to restore or re-ignite that student's engagement. If the group as a whole seems disengaged, bring it to their attention—not in a judgmental or accusatory manner, but as a topic for discussion. You could pose questions such as: "Why is this not working well for us?" or, "What can I do, or what can we do together, to make this work better?"
- At the end of the meeting:
  1. Reserve time to seek input from members whose voices were not heard during the meeting. (These members can elect to pass if they have no input to offer or if they feel their ideas have already been expressed by someone else.)
  2. "Tie it altogether" by asking questions like the following:
     (a) What did we accomplish during this meeting? (This question could be asked while providing group members with index cards on which they could provide their feedback in writing.)
     (b) When will we meet next?
     (c) What should we do individually and collectively to prepare for our next meeting?
  3. Sum up what was accomplished during the meeting. (This practice serves to "wrap up" the just-concluded meeting and "set up" the next meeting.)
- After the meeting, send a follow-up correspondence. Shoot out a text or e-mail requesting feedback about the meeting, thanking members for their con-

tributions to the meeting, and reminding them about any tasks they need to complete before the next meeting.

Making Presentations to Groups

Much of what you do as a group leader will require sitting down with and facilitating group discussion and decision-making, but there may be occasions when you'll stand and deliver presentations to groups. Your ability to present ideas in a clear, confident, and convincing manner will strengthen your leadership performance in college and beyond. Listed below are strategies and practices that you may use to improve the quality of your presentations.

Decide on the purpose or point of your presentation. A presentation usually falls into one of the following two categories, depending on its purpose or objective:

1. *Informative* presentation—provides group members with information that increases their knowledge or supplies them with practical information to help them complete tasks, or
2. *Persuasive* (expository) presentation—persuades (convinces) group members to buy into a particular idea or course of action.

The first step to delivering an effective presentation is to decide what you want your presentation to accomplish and then keep that end goal in mind when determining the points you'll make during your talk. When deciding on whether to include (or exclude) an idea or piece of information in your presentation, always ask yourself: Will this help me achieve the ultimate purpose or goal of my presentation?

Begin with the end in mind.
—Stephen Covey, *The Seven Habits of Highly Effective People*

Reflection 10.4

In your peer leadership role, will it be necessary for you to make public presentations or speeches to groups? If yes, who would comprise your audience and what would be the primary purpose(s) of your presentations?

Create an outline or bulleted list of the major (general) points you're going to make. First, get your major points down on PowerPoint slides or index cards; second, arrange them in an order that provides the smoothest sequence or flow of your ideas—from start to finish.

Use your slides or index cards as retrieval cues ("cue cards") to remember each of the major points you will make during the presentation. Beneath each major point on your slide or index card, list 3-5 sub-points or specific ideas you'd like to make in relation to that general point. Research shows that humans can only keep about four points or bits of information in mind (in their working or short-term memory) at a time (Cowan, 2001).

When delivering your presentation, maximize eye contact with the group. During your talk, it's okay to occasionally look at your index cards and slides and use them as cue cards to help you recall the key points you intend to make; however, you should spend most of your time looking at your audience. PowerPoint presentations have the potential to become deadly boring when the speaker's "presentation" involves looking at and reading slides off a screen, rather than looking at and speaking to the audience. (See **Box 10.4** for summary of top tips for using and not abusing PowerPoint.)

Effective presentations shouldn't be written out entirely in advance and read verbatim (Luotto, Stoll, & Hoglund-Ketttmann, 2001), nor should they be entirely impromptu (improvised) presentations delivered off the top of your head. Instead, effective presentations are *extemporaneous*, meaning that they fall somewhere in-between "winging it" and memorizing it word-for-word. Extemporaneous speaking involves advanced preparation and the use of notes or slides as memory-retrieval cues, allowing you some freedom to ad lib or improvise. If you happen to forget the exact words you planned to use, you can freely substitute different words to make the same point—without stumbling or stressing out—and without your audience even noticing you made any substitutions. The key to extemporaneous speaking is to rehearse and remember your major points, not the exact words you will use to make each and every point. This will ensure your presentation comes across as natural and authentic, not mechanical or robotic.

Box 10.4

Tips for Using (Not Abusing) PowerPoint

- Use the titles of slides as general headings or categories for your major ideas.
- List only 3-5 points (ideas) on each slide.
- List information on your slides as bulleted points, not complete sentences. The more words included on your slides, the more time your audience will spend reading the slides instead of listening to you. You can help keep the focus on *you* (not your slides) by showing only one point on your slide at a time. This will keep the audience members focused on the point you're discussing and prevent them from reading ahead.

The words on your PowerPoint slides do not constitute your entire presentation. They are just memories cues and slide holders for related ideas that you will present and elaborate on during your presentation.

- Use a font size of at least 18 points to ensure that people in the back of the room can read what's printed on each slide.
- Don't use color merely for decorative purposes—which can be a source of distraction, but for educational purposes—as a visual aid to highlight how your points are organized. For example, a dark or bold blue heading may be used to highlight the title of the slide (representing your major point) and a lighter shade of blue may be used for the bulleted sub-points beneath it.
- Incorporate visual images into your presentation. Don't hesitate to use pictures, graphs, cartoons, or other visual illustrations that relate to and reinforce your major points. (As discussed in chapter 7, this practice allows information to be stored in the audience's brain as two different memory traces—verbal and visual—which increases the likelihood it will be retained.)

A presentation is about explaining things to people that go above and beyond what they get in the slides. If it weren't, they might just as well get your slides and read them in the comfort of their own office, home, boat, or bathroom.

—Jesper Johansson, senior security strategist for Microsoft and author of "Death by PowerPoint" (personal blog)

The true "power" of PowerPoint may not be its capacity to project words, but to project visual images that illustrate and illuminate your words.

- If you include words or images on a slide that are not your own, demonstrate academic integrity by noting their source at the bottom of the slide.
- Before going public with your slides, proofread them with the same care as you would a written paper.

Sources: Hedges (2014); Johansson (2005); Moller (2011).

When preparing your presentation, also prepare questions to stimulate interaction and discussion. A presentation doesn't have to be a full-blown lecture in which with the group sits passively and listens to you present information for an extended period of time. Instead of speaking *at* the group, speak *with* the group by including time for them to interact with you and with each other. The following formats may be used to infuse interaction into your presentations.

I think [peer mentor's name] really tried too hard. She talked so much she didn't give us a chance. It was like another lecture.

—First-year student

1. *Shared* Presentation. Before presenting your ideas on the topic, have the group share their ideas first and record their ideas on the board or a flip chart. You could do this quickly by using a strategy known as the *whip*—in rapid-fire fashion, "whip" around the room and have each group member quickly share a word or phrase that comes to mind about the topic you will be discussing. Or, you could employ a procedure called *"background knowledge and interest probes"* that involves asking each group member to jot down what they already know, and what else they would like to know, about the topic you're presenting.

   After group members have shared their ideas, you can begin your presentation by first noting the ideas you were going to present that your group already mentioned (e.g., by underlining or highlighting them). Then present your ideas that were not mentioned by the group. This will result in a "master list"—a composite product representing the *shared knowledge* of the group and the group leader.

2. *Punctuated* Presentation. During your presentation, periodically stop and ask the group to do something with the information you've just presented. This strategy serves to break up or "punctuate" your presentation, which can intercept "attention drift" that typically takes place when listeners do nothing but listen for more than 10 minutes at a time (Bligh, 2000). You can help prevent attention drift by periodically pausing to ask members to react to, or act on, the information you're presenting (e.g., ask them what they agree or disagree with, or how they can apply it).

3. *Post-Presentation* Reflection. After completing your presentation, ask group members to reflect on the major ideas that were presented. They could do this by completing a *one-minute paper*—a short (one-paragraph) written response to a question you ask about what you covered during the presentation. For example, at the end of a presentation you could ask students to write a one-minute paper in response to any of the following questions:
   * What do you think was the most important point or key idea delivered during this presentation?
   * What was the most surprising and/or unexpected idea presented?
   * Were there any puzzling, confusing, or disturbing ideas presented?
   * Was there any idea presented that struck you as something our group should immediately implement or put into practice?

Reflection 10.5

Think about an instructor you've who was particularly good at presenting ideas and engaging students in discussion of those ideas. Did the instructor use any strategies that you might use when making presentations to groups?

Leading and Facilitating Group Discussions

Effective group leaders are able to draw out members and engage them in spirited discussions. Described below are research-based strategies that you could used to increase students' level of involvement and participation in group discussions.

Ask discussion-provoking questions. Effective discussion leaders give careful thought to how they ask questions because the way a question is framed or phrased will affect whether anyone responds to it. All questions are not created equal; certain types of questions are more likely to elicit discussion than others. Research indicates that the following types of questions are most likely to trigger student responses and stimulate group discussions (Cuseo, 2017).

- *Open-ended* questions. These are questions that "open up" the floor to a variety of possible answers and encourage *divergent* thinking—thinking that goes off in different directions instead of converging on one (and only one) "correct" answer. Open-ended questions send the message to students that all answers are welcomed by containing a plural word that calls for a plurality or multiplicity of responses—for example: "What are some approaches (plural) we can take to reach our goal?"
- *Conditionally phrased* questions (e.g., "What *might* be . . . ." "What *could* be . . . ?" "What *may* be . . . ?"). Such tentative phrasing sends a signal to group members that a diversity of answers is possible, encourages creative responses, and reduces fear or embarrassment about not providing "the" correct answer you are "looking for."
- *Focused* questions. These are questions that focus on a specific idea or issue. For instance, if you're facilitating a discussion about the advantages of getting involved in campus life, a focused question might be: "What do you think might account for the point I made about more females getting involved in student clubs and campus organizations than males?" In contrast, an unfocused question would be: "Does anybody have any questions or comments about what I just covered?"

In addition to designing and delivering discussion-provoking questions, you can elevate student involvement in group discussions by using the following strategies.

Have the group respond *nonverbally*. Rather than asking individual students to respond verbally, one at a time, you can ask all group members to respond simultaneously with body language. For example, students could respond by a show of hands to questions like: "How many of you agree with the following statement . . . ?" or "How many of you had an experience similar to . . . ?"

Other ways in which you can engage students nonverbally are by: (a) having them take a position on an issue or course of action by moving to one of four corners in the room—each corner representing a different choice: strongly agree, agree, disagree, strongly disagree; or (b) asking them to take a position along an imaginary line across the room that represents where they stand with respect to a question or issue. For example, you could say: "The center aisle represents middle ground, the far right side of the room represents extreme agreement and the far left side represents extreme disagreement. Where do you stand (literally) on the issue of _____?"

Questions that call for nonverbal responses have the advantage of involving all students, not just students who are the most verbally assertive or outspoken. Nonverbal responses can also be used as a stepping-stone to stimulate verbal discussion. For instance, after students take a position by moving to a place in the room, they could be asked why they chose to occupy that particular place or space. They might also be given the opportunity to move to a different place after hearing others' ideas and then asked why they changed their position (mind).

Have all members jot down their ideas individually before beginning the group discussion. This practice implements the principle of "independent judgments": individuals gather and record their thoughts and opinions independently—before hearing and being influenced by the thoughts and opinions of others (Kahneman, 2011). In contrast, opening up a group discussion without allowing some opportunity for members to engage in independent forethought can result in a discussion that's dominated and biased by the views of more assertive or impulsive group members—who may speak early, steer the discussion in the direction of their ideas, and limit the diversity of viewpoints heard and considered.

One systematic procedure you can use to encourage independent thinking is a strategy called "brain-writing" (Heslin, 2009). Here are its key steps:

1. Ask the group a question and have members write down their responses on an index card.
2. After group members finish writing their responses, ask all members to pass their index cards to the person on their right.
3. Ask them to add another response on the index card they just received, but not to use the response they previously wrote down or a response that's already on the card.
4. Repeat this process until each card gets back to the student who wrote the first response.
5. You can collect the cards and review the ideas generated at a later time, or have the group immediately discuss the responses they see on their cards.

Remember, people can be independent thinkers and team players at the same time. Help them fill both roles.

—Carol Dweck, *Mindset: The New Psychology of Success*

Prior to group discussions, arrange chairs to maximize eye contact among group members. Instead of having chairs arranged in rows and columns, place them in a circle, semi-circle, or horseshoe so that group members make more eye contact with one another. More eye contact between participants should, in turn, result in more interpersonal interaction and dialogue.

Before starting group discussions, first take a moment to tell the group that you need and value their participation and input. First impressions can be powerful and can set the tone for what follows (DeCoster & Claypool, 2004). You can capitalize on the power of the first impression and increase the level of group participation by making a sincere statement at the very outset that warmly invites and encourages student participation.

After asking a question, be sure to wait long enough to give group members a chance to respond. If you don't get an immediate response and you start speaking again, it may send a signal to students that your questions are merely rhetorical—intended to set up your ideas rather than seek out their input. Another advantage of patiently waiting for a response is that it encourages thoughtful reflection and gives less-impulsive group members time to gather their thoughts before speaking.

If your question fails to elicit any response—even after waiting for a fair amount of time—phrase the question in a different way. Lack of response to a question doesn't always mean that the group is disinterested or disengaged; it may have more to do with the nature of question than the nature of the group. The question may have been worded in a way that group members couldn't follow or relate to. Sometimes simply rephrasing the question can reboot the process and get the discussion going.

If dead silence continues for a significant period of time, even after rephrasing your question, consider using a little humor to lighten the moment and make a plea for involvement. You might kiddingly say: "Can someone, anyone, help me out here? The silence is killing me!"

Acknowledge the name of the student who responds. This serves to affirm the student's individuality and shows all members of the group that you remembered the student's name. Moreover, when you refer to group members by name, it strengthens your memory of their names and helps them remember each other's names.

After a group member offers a response, encourage further involvement by asking follow-up questions that call for elaboration on the original response. You could use follow-up questions such as: (1) "Can you provide us with a few more details?" (2) "Can you connect or piggy-back your idea onto an idea that's been previously shared?" or (3) "What do you think might be some action steps we could take with respect to your idea?"

Record ideas expressed by group members on the board or on a flip chart. This practice serves to validate the contributions of individual students and provides a cumulative record of all contributions. This record can later be reviewed and used as a springboard to launch a follow-up discussion (e.g., ask the group if they detect any recurrent themes or patterns across the separate responses).

Whenever possible, deflect or redirect questions directed at you to other members of the group. This practice has the following advantages: (1) it increases the number of individuals who become involved in the group discussion; (2) it encourages group members to become co-leaders with you; and (3) it shows the questioning student how their peers may serve as a valuable resource.

If a student's response to your discussion question is off base or inaccurate, try to praise some aspect of it (e.g., its creativity). If nothing about the student's response can be praised without appearing patronizing, praise the effort (e.g., "Thanks for taking a stab at it."). This practice reinforces the student's willingness to speak up, which should encourage the student to speak up again.

If the discussion veers off track and begins moving in a direction that's irrelevant to the question you asked, use "I" and "we" messages to bring it back on track. For instance, you could say: "I think we've strayed from the original question, haven't we?" This strategy gently reminds the whole group to keep the discussion focused on the point under discussion, and it does so in a way that doesn't single out or embarrass the student who derailed the discussion.

Encourage participation of students who haven't responded by asking for their reaction to the ideas of students who have responded. For instance, you could say: "Let's hear from some folks who haven't spoken yet." You could also ask: "Does anyone else agree with what has already been said?" Or, "Does anyone else want to express a different or opposing point of view?"

Keep an eye out for students who have not contributed verbally, but who display nonverbal signs of interest or thoughtfulness. Look for students whose body language indicates they are reacting to what's being discussed (e.g., smiling, nodding their head, frowning, or raising their eyebrows). Mention that you noticed their nonverbal response and gently invite them to respond verbally by addressing them by name (e.g., "Donna, it seems like this point we're discussing has triggered your interest, would you like to share your thoughts about it?").

Make eye contact with students who have been reluctant to participate and move closer to them when delivering questions. Making eye contact and moving a little closer to students when posing a question can send a subtle but powerful nonverbal signal that you're really interested in hearing from them. There is an art to effective questioning and much of it is created through nonverbal channels. A warm demeanor, a welcoming smile, and inviting body language can spell the difference between a question that evokes an enthusiastic response or dead silence.

If you run out of questions and there's still time remaining in your discussion session, allow group members to take control of the agenda. Ask them, "What's on your mind that you'd like to talk about?" Or, "Is there anything you're curious or concerned about that you'd like for us to discuss as a group?" (Using back-up questions like these at the end of a group session is sometimes referred to as a "sponge activity"—it "soaks up" the session's remaining time in a productive way.)

Reflection 10.6

What would you say are your strengths, or potential strengths, as a discussion leader? What do you think will be your most difficult challenge?

Author's Experience   I've been able to involve students in class discussions by asking them a series of questions about themselves early in the term (see Exercise 1.2, pp. 19-20). I save their responses to these questions and use them throughout the term to involve them in class discussions. I also use the information students provide me about themselves to connect personally with students who are not participating or who seem "detached." If I observe a student who appears to be shy or disengaged, I review the student's information sheet before going to class and try to strike up a conversation with that student about something relating to his or her information sheet. For instance, as students enter the room at the beginning of class, I may stand by the door as they enter. When a quiet or non-participative student is entering, I'll quickly ask that student something relating to his information sheet (e.g., "Paul, are you still running marathons?"). I've found that this little bit of personal attention strengthens non-participating students' personal connection with me and increases their level of subsequent participation in class discussions.

I've shared this strategy with peer leaders on my campus. Many of them said they tried it with the groups they lead and found that it helped them make personal connection with group members and raised the overall level of student participation in group discussions.

— *Joe Cuseo*

Facilitating Large-Group Discussions

Certainly, there are times when large-group discussions and meetings must be held, but they can result in students feeling anonymous and becoming disengaged—particularly students who are shy or reluctant to speak up in large-group settings. As you might expect, there's an inverse relationship between the size of the group and the percentage of group members who become involved in the group discussions; in other words, as the size of the group size increases, the amount of individual participation decreases (Karau & Williams, 1993). Smaller group size allows more individuals to participate, gives them a greater sense of ownership of the group process, and provides them with more opportunities to become co-leaders.

If you're leading a large group (i.e., more than 15 members) and would like to increase student participation in group discussions, it may be useful to break the group into smaller sub-groups to increase each member's level of involvement. A large group can be deconstructed into smaller discussion groups by using any of the following formats developed by educational and social psychologists (Aronson, Wilson, & Akert, 2009; Cuseo, 2002; Kagan, 1994).

1. *Pairs-Share.* This format involves two-member groups. One partner shares his or her ideas while the other listens, then the members switch roles. When students work in pairs, it ensures that both members of the group are involved equally and simultaneously—each one is actively engaged at all times—either speaking to the partner or listening to the partner. (It's hard to hide or get lost in a group of two.)

2. *Pairs-Square.* Students first share their ideas in pairs, then join another pair of students to form a "*square*" (four-member team) and integrate the ideas they previously shared in pairs.

3. *Corners.* This is a four-member group process that involves the following steps:
   - Each corner of the room is designated for a different task (e.g., in each corner, a different component of a general topic is discussed or a different aspect of an event is planned).
   - The large group is divided into four smaller groups, each of which occupies one corner of the room and completes the task designated for that corner. (As the small groups do their work, you circulate among the groups, ensure they're "on task" and provide encouragement, but do not attempt to control or interfere with their independent work.)
   - Each group selects a recorder—who compiles the ideas generated by the group during its small-group discussion, and a spokesperson—who will later share the group's ideas with the large group.
   - All small groups join together as a large group and the spokesperson for each of the small groups shares the group's ideas with the large group.

4. *Jigsaw.* In this format, each member of a small group assumes responsibility for becoming an "expert" on one part or piece of the group task. These experts leave their home group to work with members of other groups who've chosen to be an expert on the same topic or task. After meeting and working with their fellow experts, the experts return to their home teams and integrate their separate parts to complete the whole—like piecing together parts of a jigsaw puzzle. Here's how you can implement this strategy in a step-by-step fashion:

- First, break the large group into 3- or 4-member "home teams" and ask these teams to have each of their members take responsibility for becoming an expert on one component of a topic to be discussed or a task to be completed. For example, if you're planning an event, each member of the small group assumes a different role, such as: organizational expert, public relations expert, financial expert, etc. Encourage group members to assume a role that capitalizes on their personal interests, strengths, or unique perspectives.
- Ask members to leave their home teams to join up with students from other groups who chose to be experts on the same task or topic (e.g., all the public relations experts come together in "expert groups" to share their ideas, as do the financial experts, organizational experts, etc.).
- After meeting in their separate "expert groups," students return to their home team to share what they learned with their teammates and connect their separate parts into an integrated whole.

The jigsaw method works particularly well when a large group is working on a complex task that has multiple parts or components. It allows members of a large group to work less anonymously and more actively in small-group settings, while also giving them more opportunities to take on leadership and co-leadership roles.

> When a group has a common goal and its members have different, yet interdependent, roles, group work is transformed into teamwork.

In addition to the jigsaw method, you can use the practices below to reconstruct a large group after it has been deconstructed into small groups and to coordinate or synthesize the work they completed separately. The following practices are important to consider because studies show that one of the major reasons why large groups and organizations fail to accomplish their goals is their "collective failure to coordinate and synchronize their individual contributions" (Zaccaro, Rittman, & Marks, 2001, p. 451).

- *Plenary Reporters.* After completing a small-group task, one student from each small group plays the role of "plenary reporter" who shares the group's main ideas with the large group. Have each group record its ideas on posters so you can keep track of their ideas and identify recurrent themes (and variations) across ideas generated by different groups.
- *Roving Reporters.* After small groups complete their work, one "roving reporter" from each group makes a succession of visits to each of the other groups to share her team's ideas. The remaining members of her group stay "home" to listen to the ideas presented by roving reporters from other groups.

The role of the stay-home group members is to integrate the roving reporters' ideas with the ideas generated by their own group.

- *Group Rotation.* After small groups complete their work, they rotate clockwise and merge with another small group to share and integrate their separate work. This rotational share-and-integrate process continues until each group has interacted with all other groups. The final step in the process is for each group to create a final product that synthesizes its ideas with the ideas of other groups.

All of the above intergroup-interaction strategies have the following advantages: (1) they enable groups to build on each other's ideas, generating synergy and synthesis; and (2) they enable students in small groups to interact with members of other small groups, creating a sense of large-group solidarity and community.

Developing Co-Leaders

A good indicator that a leader has transformed a group into a *team* is when co-leaders begin to emerge. You can develop co-leaders by voicing confidence in your group members' abilities and distributing leadership responsibilities among them (Kouzes & Posner, 2002).

For example, you can encourage students to take on such co-leadership responsibilities as: choosing and organizing activities, implementing action strategies, and helping less-engaged group members become more engaged. You're likely to find that students will rise to the level of leadership expectations you set for them.

Although you shouldn't turn over leadership responsibility to group members before they're prepared to assume it, you can begin distributing some of your authority by periodically stepping aside and sharing the stage. Here are some strategies for doing so:

- Involve group members in making decisions about what they plan to do and how they plan to do it (the processes or methods they'll use to get the job done).
- Rotate co-leadership among group members by asking different students to help you co-facilitate group discussions on different occasions.
- Use the "jigsaw" or "corners" format (see pp. 334–335). Ask for volunteers to become experts on each component topic or task, and let them know that you're available to answer questions and provide direction. As the process evolves, periodically check with your co-leadership volunteers, ask them how it's going, and sensitively share your perspective about what's going well and what they could do more effectively. It's good to provide them with such coaching, but be sure to give co-leaders enough space to make their own corrections and solve their own problems.
- Recognize the group's achievements and credit those members who took co-leadership roles in helping the group achieve its goals.

Effective leadership is a "we" thing, not a "me" thing.

> *All of us are smarter than any of us.*
> —Douglas Merrill, former Chief Information Officer & Vice President of Engineering at Google

> *Good leaders grow team members... their key job is not doing programs but growing others.*
> —Tim Elmore, founder and president of Growing Leaders, a non-profit organization

> *I'm trying to teach every one of them [my players] to lead. Leadership is about everybody else, not yourself. We've won a lot more games when it has been about everybody else and not about me. When it's about the players first, they play for you.*
> —John Calipari, head basketball coach, University of Kentucky

As a peer leader, you have a central role in setting group goals and directing group activities. Students may need and want you to be out in front, but the key is not to get so far in front that they don't feel consulted, involved, or respected. Effective leaders know when to take charge and lead the way, and when to get out of the way and let others lead the charge. As the group you lead evolves and matures, your role should become less directive and more facilitative. Great leaders eventually do a Houdini act—they disappear!

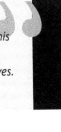

A leader is best when people barely know he exists, when his work is done, his aim fulfilled, they will say: we did it ourselves.

—Lao Tzu

Managing Unproductive and Disruptive Behavior in Groups

Reflection 10.7

What negative or troublesome behaviors have you seen students display in groups? Have you observed a group leader who was particularly adept at handling these negative behaviors? If yes, what practices did the leader employ that you might also employ in your leadership role?

The following strategies, based on research in the fields of human relations and conflict resolution, may be used to handle conflicts or behavioral problems that take place in group settings. You can use these leadership strategies as a group leader, and you can share them with the groups you lead to empower them to handle conflicts on their own.

Focus on the specific behavior causing the problem, not the person's character. Avoid language that targets the person's traits. For instance, if a group member isn't carrying his fair share of the work, don't say, "You're a slacker!" Such broad labels are likely to make the offender feel like he's under attack, put him on the defensive, and increase the likelihood he'll launch a retaliatory counterattack.

Rather than focusing on general traits, focus on the specific behaviors that are causing the problem (e.g., not showing up, showing up late, or not completing tasks). By focusing on behavior, you avoid assassinating the person's character, enable the person to know exactly what actions need to be changed, and increase the likelihood that change will be made. (It's much easier to change behavior than change a personality trait.)

Don't find fault. Find a remedy.

—Henry Ford, creator of the first affordable car, revolutionizing transportation in the United States

Use "I" messages to focus on how the other person's behavior is affecting you and other members of the group. Instead of starting the conversation by focusing on the other person (e.g., "you need to"), "I" messages center on you—what you're experiencing or feeling as a result of the person's behavior (McKay, Davis, & Fanning, 2009). By saying, "I feel angry when . . ." (as opposed to "you make me angry when . . ."), you're taking responsibility for the way you feel, rather than guilt-tripping the individual for making you feel that way. In contrast, a staring with a "you" message (e.g., "You are . . .") is more likely to trigger initial resentment and immediate resistance (Bippus & Young, 2005).

Reflection 10.8

A member of your group isn't carrying his weight on a group project. Create an "I message" for communicating your concern to this student in a non-threatening way.

Conclude your discussion of the problem on a warm, constructive note. Thank the group member for hearing you out and express your confidence that things can be worked out. By ending on a positive note, you let the person know that there are no hard feelings, that you're confident the conflict can be resolved, and that you're optimistic about working well together in the future.

After discussing the problem, if the person makes a positive change in behavior, recognize the person's effort and express your appreciation. Even if your complaint was legitimate and your request justified, the person's effort to accommodate your request shouldn't be taken for granted. Worse yet, don't punish the person with "rubbing it in" comments like: "That's more like it" or, "It's about time!"

Sincerely expressing appreciation for the person's changed behavior isn't only the socially sensitive thing to do, it's also the effective thing to do because it reinforces the positive change in behavior and increases the likelihood that the changed behavior will continue.

Reflection 10.9

Is it hard for you to walk the fine line between being a trusted "friend" and a respected peer "leader" who may need to call out students for disruptive or unproductive behavior? If yes, why? If no, why not?

How do you think you can best provide students with guidance, direction, and discipline without their viewing you as a substitute "parental" authority figure?

A cquiring and Utilizing Group Feedback

To learn *how* to do something well, you need to learn *if* you're doing it well. You can do so by seeking feedback from the groups you lead. This shows group members that their input matters and provides you with information that you can use to continuously improve your leadership performance. It also allows you to stay ahead of the game by anticipating and intercepting problems before they mushroom into full-blown crises. Feedback gathered "after the fact"—after a group problem or crisis has emerged—may come too late to regain the group's energy and enthusiasm.

Just as the students you lead can improve their performance by receiving feedback from you, you can improve your own leadership performance by receiving feedback from them. Make it clear that you're receptive to their input and make an earnest effort to use it productively. You can obtain feedback from your students through various methods, including personal conversations, short surveys, e-mails, and social networking. Rely on whatever methods you think will supply you with the most honest and useful feedback.

A simple way to begin collecting feedback from the groups you lead is by asking open-ended questions such as the following:

- What have been the most effective or productive things we've done thus far? Why?
- What activities haven't worked very well? Why?
- What are some specific things I can do to improve as a group leader?
- What are some specific things we can do to improve as a group?
- Am I helping you make progress toward your goals?
- Do you have any needs or interests that I haven't addressed?
- Do you have any suggestions for me?
- Is there anything I could (or should) be doing that I'm not doing?

You can also get a sense of the pulse of your group at any given time by using more formal procedures, such as: (1) conducting a quick debriefing session at the end of group meetings during which group members provide you with feedback orally or in writing (e.g., on an index card); (2) posting feedback-seeking prompts on an electronic site shared by group members (e.g., "I thought that today's meeting was . . . ."); (3) arranging one-on-one feedback sessions with individual members of the group; and (4) distributing a short group-leadership survey—such as the following:

1	2	3	4
strongly disagree	disagree	agree	strongly agree

My leader:
- is organized
- is approachable
- is available and accessible
- is interested in the group's ideas
- effectively engages different members of the group
- conducts productive meetings
- involves students in decisions and responsibilities
- effectively leads group discussions

If students take the time to supply you with feedback (whether it be positive or negative), express your appreciation and let them know that you'll take their feedback seriously. Reflect on the input they've provided you and share your reflections with the group, noting what you've learned from their feedback and how you plan to use it to make positive changes.

Consider sharing the feedback you receive with fellow peer leaders and ask them to do the same. You can begin by meeting regularly with another student leader or with a small group of leaders whom you respect and trust. In these meetings, discuss your most difficult challenges and most successful practices, and ask them for their ideas about how you could best respond to the feedback you received.

When you're open to receiving feedback from your group, your group becomes more open to receiving feedback from you. Feedback is a two-way street: it should flow from you and to you.

Reflection 10.10

Think of a situation in which you received critical (or even downright negative) feedback. How did you feel? How did you respond? What can you do to increase the likelihood that you'll respond constructively (rather defensively) to feedback you seek and receive from groups you lead?

In addition to seeking feedback from the group about your work as group leader, encourage group members to reflect on and assess their own performance. The following self-assessment questions may be posed to students to increase self-awareness of their performance in groups.

1. For scheduled group meetings, did I:
   (a) attend regularly?
   (b) show-up on time?
   (c) come prepared?
2. Did I participate as much as, more than, or less than other members of my group?
3. Did I do my fair share of the group's work? (Can I honestly say that I "carried my load" or "pulled my own weight?")
4. Did I actively seek out ideas or information from other members of the group?
5. Did I encourage quiet or reluctant teammates to participate?
6. Did I help keep the group stay on track and make progress toward its goal?
7. The strongest skill or greatest contribution I brought to the group was _____.
8. In the future, I could improve my performance as a group member by _____.

Asking questions like these of group members will help them reflect on and improve their performance in group situations.

Internet Resources

For additional information on leading groups, consult the following websites.

Understanding Group Dynamics
https://www.smallgroups.com/articles/2013/group-dynamics.html

Facilitating Group Discussions
https://web.stanford.edu/group/resed/resed/staffresources/RM/training/facilguide.html

Making Presentations to Groups
http://academics.umw.edu/speaking/resources/handouts/planning-a-group-presentation/

Managing Group Conflict
http://extensionpublications.unl.edu/assets/pdf/g2115.pdf

References

Aronson, E., Wilson, T. D., & Akert, R. M. (2009). *Social psychology* (7th ed.). Upper Saddle River, NJ: Pearson/Prentice Hall.

Bippus, A. M., & Young, S. L. (2005). Owning your emotions: Reactions to self- versus other-attributed positive and negative emotions. *Journal of Applied Communication Research, 33*(1), 26-45.

Bligh, D. A. (2000). *What's the use of lectures?* San Francisco: Jossey-Bass.

Chemers, M. M., Watson, C. B., & May, S. (2000). Dispositional affect and leadership effectiveness: A comparison of self-esteem, optimism and efficacy. *Personality and Social Psychology Bulletin, 26*, 267–277.

Covey, S. R. (1990). *Seven habits of highly effective people* (2nd ed.). New York: Fireside.

Cowan, N. (2001). The magical number 4 in short-term memory: A reconsideration of mental storage capacity. *Behavioral and Brain Sciences, 24*, 87–114.

Cuseo, J. B. (2002). *Igniting student involvement, peer interaction, and teamwork: A taxonomy of specific cooperative learning structures and collaborative learning strategies.* Stillwater, OK: New Forums Press.

Cuseo, J. B. (2017, February). *Student engagement: Defining it, distinguishing it, developing it.* Presentation made at the 36th Annual Conference on The First-Year Experience and Students in Transition, Atlanta, GA.

DeCoster, J., & Claypool, H. M. (2004). A meta-analysis of priming effects on impression formation supporting a general model of informational biases. *Personality and Social Psychology Review, 8*(1), 2–27.

Dweck, C. S. (2006). *Mindset: The new psychology of success.* New York: Random House.

Dyer, W. G., Dyer, W. G., & Dyer, J. H. (2007). *Team building: Proven strategies for improving team performance.* San Francisco: Jossey-Bass.

Haslam, S. A., Reicher, S. D., & Platow, M. J. (2011). *The new psychology of leadership: Identity, influence, and power.* New York: Psychology Press.

Hedges, K. (2014). *Six ways to avoid death by PowerPoint.* Retrieved from http://www.forbes.com/sites/work-in-progress/2014/11/14/six-ways-to-avoid-death-by-powerpoint/

Heslin, P. A. (2009). Better than brainstorming? Potential contextual boundary conditions to brainwriting for idea generation in organizations. *Journal of Occupational and Organizational Psychology, 82*, 129-145.

Johansson, J. (2005). *Death by PowerPoint.* Retrieved from http://articles.tech.republic.com5100-22_11-5875608.html

Kagan, S. (1994). *Cooperative learning.* Santa Cruz, CA: Insight Media.

Kahneman, D. (2011). *Thinking, fast and slow.* New York: Farrar, Straus and Giroux.

Kaner, S. (2011). *Facilitator's guide to participatory decision-making.* San Francisco: Jossey-Bass.

Karau, S. J., & Williams, K. D. (1993). Social loafing: A meta-analytic review and theoretical integration. *Journal of Personality and Social Psychology, 65*(4), 681-706.

Komives, S. R., Lucas, N., & McMahon, T. R. (2007). *Exploring leadership: For college students who want to make a difference* (2nd ed.). San Francisco: Jossey-Bass.

Kouzes, J. M., & Posner, B. Z. (2002). *The leadership challenge: How to get extraordinary things done in organizations* (3rd ed.). San Francisco: Jossey-Bass

Kouzes, M. M., & Posner, B. Z. (2008). *The student leadership challenge: Five practices for exemplary leaders.* San Francisco: Jossey-Bass.

Kouzes, M. M., & Posner, B. Z. (2012). *The leadership challenge* (5th ed.). San Francisco: Jossey-Bass.

LaFasto, F. M. J., & Larson, C. E. (2001). *When teams work best: 6,000 team members and leaders tell what it takes to succeed.* Thousand Oaks, CA: SAGE.

Luotto, J. A., Stoll, E. L., & Hoglund-Kettmann, N. (2001). *Communication skills for collaborative learning* (2nd ed.). Dubuque, IA: Kendall/Hunt.

McKay, M., Davis, M., & Fanning, P. (2009). *Messages: The communication skills book* (2nd ed.). Oakland, CA: New Harbinger.

Moller, N. (2011, May 6). *The Ten Commandments of PowerPoint Presentations.* Retrieved from https://avalaunchmedia.com/using-power-point-for-presentations/

Nadler, D. A. (1998). Executive team effectiveness: Teamwork at the top. In D. A. Nadler & J. L. Spencer (Eds.), *Executive teams* (pp. 21-39). San Francisco: Jossey-Bass.

Northouse, P. G. (2016). *Leadership: Theory and practice* (7th ed.). Los Angeles: SAGE.

Tuckman, B. W. (1965). Development sequence in small groups. *Psychological Review, 63*(6), 384-399.

Tuckman, B. W., & Jensen, M. A. C. (1977). Stages of small group development revisited. *Group and Organizational Studies, 2,* 419-427.

Tuckman, B. W., & Jensen, M. A. C. (2010). Stages of small group development revisited. *Group Facilitation: A Research and Applications Journal* (November). International Association of Facilitators (www.iaf-world.org). Retrieved from https://www.staff.science.uu.nl/~daeme101/Stages%20of%20Small-Group%20Development%20Revisted.pdf

Zaccaro, S. J., Rittman, A. L., & Marks, M. A. (2001). Team leadership. *Leadership Quarterly, 12,* 451-483.

Exercise 10.1 Quote Reflections

Review the sidebar quotes contained in this chapter and select two that you think would be especially valuable to share with the students you lead or mentor.

For each quote, write a short statement explaining why you chose it.

Exercise 10.2 Journal Reflections

Provide your top strategy for handling each of the following group-leadership challenges:

1. Students aren't participating enthusiastically in planned activities because they're "too cool for school" or claim that the activities are "boring."

2. Students are questioning why they have to go to scheduled activities.

3. Students are not showing up for meetings or planned events.

4. Only a handful of students are participating in group discussions; not everyone is speaking up or getting involved.

5. Certain students are dominating group discussions.

6. A student is disrupting group discussions by joking around and making sarcastic comments.

7. Students are not responding to messages or staying in touch with their peer leader.

8. The peer leader is not viewed by students as a trusted peer, but more like a supervisor or an authority figure.

9. The peer leader is viewed as just another student—someone without any special expertise, authority, or influence.

Exercise 10.3 Group Goal-Setting

Identify a group that you're now leading or planning to lead and construct a SMART goal for your group. (See chapter 5, p. 140, for key characteristics of a SMART goal.)

Exercise 10.4 Team Building for Large Groups: The Personal Scavenger Hunt

Use this team-building exercise to build an early sense of group trust and cohesiveness in any large group you are currently leading or will be leading. At your first group meeting, ask all group members to write down an interesting or distinctive piece of information about themselves on an index card. Collect the index cards and create a list that contains a personal statement associated with each member of the group. Here are a few statements that were once collected from a group of students:

1. I'm a beach volleyball player who's good in math and would love to take a spontaneous trip to Ireland:_____

2. I'm a computer graphics major who's good at math, loves the arts, and would like to become a cartoonist:_____

3. I'm a former swim instructor, lifeguard, and peer mediator who wants to work with kids—as a child psychologist or teacher:_____

Inform the group that the goal of the exercise is to find each statement on the list that belongs to each member of the group. **Box 10.5** contains specific steps for this personal scavenger-hunt procedure. Print out these directions and hand them out to your group or project them on a screen while your group engages in the exercise. Before having the group actually engage in the exercise, role play it with one member of the group so everyone can literally see what they're about to do.

Box 10.5

The Personal Scavenger-Hunt: A Community Building Exercise

Steps:

1. Pair-up with a classmate. One of you takes the role of questioner who attempts to find your partner's description on the list—by reading one description at a time. The partner assumes the role of respondent who answers either "yes" or "no" to the description read by the questioner. The process continues until the correct "match" is found, at which point the questioner writes down the partner's name next to his or her description.

2. Switch roles (questioner become respondent and vice versa) and follow the same process described in step 1.

3. After both of you find each other's matching descriptions, move on to join another partner, and continue this pairing-up process until you have met and written down the names of every group member next to his or her self-description.

Important Reminders:

• When trying to find your partner's personal statement, don't just randomly go down the list; instead, try to pick a statement that you think is associated with that person. See how good you are at guessing or predicting their interests based on their appearance or behavior. Before beginning the hunt, take a look at the list to get an idea of the different descriptions of the people you'll be looking for.

• When you're asked a question by your partner, you can only say "yes" or "no." Don't tell your partner the statement that relates to you.

• After your partner finds the statement that belongs to you, don't take your partner's sheet and write your name on it. Instead, state your name and have your partner record it; this will help your partner remember your name and self-description.

Exercise 10.5 Oral Communication Self-Assessment

Rate your level of self-confidence about communicating orally in the following situations.

1. Large Groups (e.g., making a presentation to a group of more than 20 students):

    highly anxious   somewhat nervous   fairly relaxed   very relaxed

2. Small Groups (e.g., leading a discussion group of 3–5 students):

    highly anxious   somewhat nervous   fairly relaxed   very relaxed

3. Pairs (e.g., mentoring an individual student):

    highly anxious   somewhat nervous   fairly relaxed   very relaxed

Do your responses to the above questions suggest that you are ready to assume the oral communication responsibilities of your leadership position, or do they suggest that you need to strengthen your social self-confidence and interpersonal communication skills in certain situations?

If there are situations in which you think you need to build your self-confidence and communication skills, what first steps could you take to do so?

Exercise 10.6 Assessing the Quality of Group Work

Below is an assessment instrument you can use to obtain feedback on how well your group is working. Ask members of the group you're leading to complete the instrument, or ask an outside observer (e.g., a fellow peer leader) to observe your group in action and evaluate the group's performance with the instrument. You can also complete the instrument yourself and compare your responses to those provided by group members or an outside observer.

Encourage your group to discuss the results of this assessment and identify strategies for improvement in the areas that received the lowest ratings.

Directions: Each category below contains a pair of statements. Check the statement that you think is the more accurate assessment of our group. (Note: Each pair of statements contains one statement that's considerably more positive than the other.)

Communication within the Group

1.____ Group members displayed a positive attitude (e.g., their nonverbal behavior indicated interest and enthusiasm).

2. ____ Group members' nonverbal behavior suggested they were bored or indifferent.

1. ____ Group members expressed their ideas freely and openly.

2. ____ Group members appeared to be afraid of "rocking the boat" or having their ideas rejected.

1. ____ Group members listened actively to one another.

2. ____ Group members were not fully attentive when other members spoke and often interrupted one another.

1. ____ Group members made sure they understood each other and connected what they said to what others previously said.

2. ____ When a group member spoke, other members appeared to be just waiting for their turn to speak and didn't relate what they said to what was previously said by another member.

Interdependence and Teamwork

1. ____ All members of the group contributed about equally.

2. ____ One or two members seemed to contribute most of the ideas and dominated the discussion.

1. ___ Group members encouraged one another to share ideas.

2. ___ Group members seemed unaware of, or oblivious to, members who were shy and silent.

1. ___ Leadership was displayed by different group members at different times.

2. ___ One member seemed to take charge of the whole group from start to finish.

1. ___ Group members worked together like a team.

2. ___ Group members worked separately or independently, not collaboratively.

Resolving Group Disagreements and Conflict

1. ___ Group members were willing to negotiate and modify their ideas after hearing the ideas of others.

2. ___ Group members tended to cling to their own ideas and stubbornly resisted ideas suggested by others.

1. ___ Group members trusted each other well enough to express disagreements openly.

2. ___ Group members seemed to hold back and appeared uncomfortable about expressing disagreement or creating conflict.

Group Progress and Decision-Making

1. ___ The group was usually able to stay on track and stick to the point being discussed.

2. ___ The group frequently got off track and on tangents.

1. ___ The group was able to keep moving forward toward its goal and effectively handled conflicts or disagreements that took place along the way.

2. ___ The group seemed to get repeatedly bogged down by conflicts or disagreements.

1. ___ The group was able to reach consensus and make decisions that incorporated the ideas of all group members.

2. ___ The group's decisions often reflected or represented the ideas of just a few members, not the group as a whole.

Group Effectiveness

1. ___ The group was productive; it achieved its goal.

2. ___ The group failed to accomplish what it set out to do.

Overall Assessment

The group's greatest strength (what it did most effectively) was:

The group's greatest weakness (what it needed to improve the most) was:

Exercise 10.7 Strategy Reflections

Review the strategies suggested for *leading and facilitating group discussions* on p. 330. Select three strategies that you think would be most important or useful to put into practice.

CHAPTER 11

Organizational Leadership

Leading Student Organizations and Catalyzing Campus-Wide Change

Reflection 11.1

What would you say is the most important change that needs to take place on your campus to improve student enthusiasm for the college experience? In your role as a peer leader, is there anything you could do to help make this change happen?

Chapter Purpose and Preview

Leadership can extend beyond influencing individuals and groups to producing positive change in entire organizations. Leadership in this wider arena requires knowledge of how organizational systems work and how to "work the system" to advance your leadership purpose and cause. This chapter discusses how you can use strategies for leading organizations effectively, employ your positional power ethically, and collect committee input and assessment data to improve organizational performance and mobilize campus-wide change.

Introduction

An effective peer leader goes beyond inspiring and encouraging students to stay in school, get good grades, and graduate. Obviously, helping students succeed in college really matters, but student leaders also have the potential to make positive changes in the organizations of which they are a part, particularly if they take a "big picture" perspective and consider how their work relates to the college or university as a whole. The potential peer leaders have for promoting organizational change is supported by the results of an extensive study of leadership identity development among college students, which revealed that peer leaders' view of the student groups they belonged to, and the groups they led, changed over time. At first, they perceived these groups as a collection of individuals but, eventually, they began to view the groups they led as integral parts of a larger organizational system (Komives et al., 2005).

What Is Organizational Leadership?

A group of 84 scholars, representing more than 60 countries from all regions of the world, agreed that *organizational leadership* is defined as "the ability of an individual to influence, motivate, and enable others to contribute toward the effectiveness and success of the organization of which they are members" (House et al., 2004, p. 15). Compared to group leadership, organizational leadership typically takes place on a wider scale and involves: (1) leading a larger number of constituents (e.g., 20 more), (2) leading a collection of groups rather than a collection of individuals, and (3) interacting with leaders of other groups and organizations (Komives, Lucas, & McMahon, 2007).

Acquiring Organizational Knowledge

Effective organizational leadership requires knowledge and understanding of the larger system in which leadership takes place. According to adaptive leadership theory, effective leaders take a *systems perspective* that views leadership as occurring within the context of a complex interactive system or web of interconnected relationships (Heifetz, Grashow, & Linsky, 2009). The more knowledge a leader has about how this interactive system and web of relationships operates, the more effective that leader becomes.

> **The more you know about how organizational systems run, the more likely you are to get things done.**

Here are some specific steps you can take to gain knowledge about how your campus is organized and operates:

- Familiarize yourself with your college's table of organization (organizational chart); it lays out who the decision makers are, what positions they occupy, and what the chain of decision-making command is (from top to bottom). Learn how the channels of communication work on your campus and how folks positioned "lower" in the organizational hierarchy can communicate with high-ranking decision makers.

  Be mindful and respectful of the chain of command when you have complaints to air or recommendations to make. Go first to the person in charge of the area in which you'd like to see change take place; don't "leap frog" that person and go to someone in a higher position of authority unless or until it's absolutely necessary.

- Review your *Student Handbook* to learn about the mission and purpose of other student organizations on campus.

- Read the campus newspaper to keep up with current issues, events, and opportunities. Many campuses now send out periodic e-newsletters. If your campus does so, make sure you are subscribed to it and read it regularly.

- Immerse yourself in your campus culture by spending time in places on campus where key players (administrators, faculty, student leaders) tend to gather. Introduce yourself to them and, if possible, get to know them. Keep your "ear to the ground" and listen closely to what they're saying. Pay particular attention to discrepancies between student views and the views of faculty, staff, or administrators. One of the key roles of an organizational leader is to understand the culture of the organization at its deeper levels—its underlying beliefs, assumptions, and values (Schein, 2010).

- Make connections between your group or organization and the larger campus system by:
  - (a) Researching and reporting back to members of your group or organization on matters of interest and importance to them (e.g., campus-wide initiatives that affect them individually, other groups to which they belong, and other programs they may be involved with).
  - (b) Representing your group or organization in wider forums (e.g., serve as a member of a college committee composed of leaders from other campus groups or organizations).
  - (c) Interacting with leaders of other campus organizations to explore possible partnerships, share resources, and plan joint projects.

Organizational Mission

A mission typically consists of statements about: (1) what an organization values, (2) how the organization's goals relate to its values, and (3) how the organization attempts to enact its values and reach its goals. As a peer leader, your leadership goals and the goals of the student organization you lead should be consistent with the mission of your college or university. Always keep your organization's mission in sight, do your best to live it in your daily actions, and encourage other members of your organization to do the same.

Reflection 11.2

What is the stated mission (purpose) of your student organization or program? What connection do you see between the mission of your student organization/ program and the mission of your campus?

Organizational Vision

Mission refers to the organization's current purpose and goals. *Vision* refers to what the organization aspires to become in the future. Similar to leading groups, leading organizations involves identifying a vision and engaging organizational members in the process of creating a vision that is shared by and unites all its members. According to the "charismatic theory" of leadership, a great leader is able to connect the personal identities of individuals with the collective identity of the organization (Conger & Kanungo, 1998; DeGroot, Diker, & Cross, 2000). Similarly, a key characteristic of "transformational leaders" is their ability to inspire followers to think about problems in new and creative ways (Avolio et al., 2004). Research on leaders who produce positive organizational change reveals that they are able to create a clear, compelling vision that inspires and energizes members of the organization (Bennis & Nanus, 1985). One simple way to get this process started is by asking your constituents: "What would it take to make this organization great?" (Komives, Lucas, & McMahon, 2007, p. 322).

An organizational vision should be consistent with the campus mission, but it should also reflect your organization's unique identity and future aspirations. Effective leaders create a distinctive "culture" in the organizations they lead that is characterized by shared beliefs and values (Duckworth, 2016). They also enable organizational members to see how their personal aspirations align with the aspirations of their organization. You can start to develop this alignment by asking

A dream you dream alone is only a dream. A dream you dream together is reality.

—John Lennon, founding member of the Beatles

members of your organization: "What are you hoping to get out of this organization?" and "What would you like this organization to do for you?" Use their input to create a shared and inspiring vision for your organization, communicate that vision early and often, and periodically invite open and honest discussion of it. This will ensure that everyone will be able to recall it, articulate it, and live by it.

After creating mission and vision statements for your organization, you can then create a strategic plan that includes its goals, objectives, and core values. These components of a comprehensive strategic plan are summarized in Box 11.1.

Box 11.1

Key Elements of a Strategic Plan

Mission: A concise, overarching statement of the organization's *reason* for existence, its primary *purpose*, and what it's *currently* designed to do. It should be aligned (consistent) with the broader campus mission.

Vision: an ambitious, inspirational statement of what the organization *aspires* to be in the *future*.

Goals: The *broad intentions, aims, or ends* the organization seeks to achieve, which align with and flow from the mission and vision statements. When an organization's goals are met, its mission is fulfilled and its vision becomes more attainable.

Objectives: The *specific* practices and strategies for achieving the organization's goals, which are *actionable* (action-oriented), *manageable* (realistic), and *measurable* (capable of being assessed—either quantitatively or qualitatively).

> *The manager asks how and when; the leader asks what and why.*
>
> —Warren Bennis, former president of the University of Cincinnati, founding chairman of the Leadership Institute at the University of Southern California, and a pioneer in the field of Leadership Studies

> *Some men see things as they are and say, why? I dream things that never were and say, why not?*
>
> —Robert F. Kennedy, former U.S. Senator and Attorney General

Core Values: A list of the organization's *most deeply held beliefs, highest priorities,* and *unwavering commitments.* Core values capture what the organization is passionate about and truly stands for; they serve as the underlying foundation and gold standard for guiding organizational members' conduct, both inside and outside the organization.

Sources: Drucker (1990); Keller (2007); Rowley, Lujan, and Dolence (2001).

Leadership, Power, and Decision Making

If you have a formal leadership title in an organization, you are a "positional leader" and the position you hold supplies you with a certain amount of power or decision-making authority (Komives, Lucas, & McMahon, 2007). To use your decision-making power ethically and effectively, make it clear to those you lead how the decision-making process works in your organization, what legitimate decision-making authority is vested in your leadership position, and how you intend to use your authority. This information is critical information to share with your students because they're likely to have different ideas about what your leadership position empowers you to do and how you should exert that power. Research supports the theory of "implicit leadership" (Lord, Brown, & Frieberg,

1999; Lord & Maher, 1991), which stipulates that an organizational leader is more likely to be accepted and effective when there's a close match between organizational members' implicit (assumed) expectations of how the leader should exercise authority and how the leader does exercise authority (Lord & Emrich, 2001).

There are two major ways in which leaders can use their decision-making power: *authoritarian* (autocratic) and *participative* (democratic). The differences between these two methods of exercising decision-making power are described below.

Authoritarian (Autocratic) Decision Making. Authoritarian or autocratic leaders make decisions on their own—with little or no input from the group they lead. It may sometimes be necessary for a leader to make a decision in this way because there's no time to consult with the group or the group is not available for consultation. There may also be occasions when a leader needs to take charge and make a unilateral decision for the group because it's simply the right or ethical thing to do (Shankman & Allen, 2008).

That being said, authoritarian decision making should be your last resort. This style of decision making shouldn't be used routinely or predominantly because it can result in the leader being perceived as bossy, controlling, or dictatorial (Cherry, 2012). As the old saying goes, "Don't let power go to your head." Whenever and wherever possible, consult with members of your organization and include them in the decision-making process.

If you must use your positional power to make an "executive decision," for your organization, do it by appealing to logic, evidence or ethics, not by pulling a power play. Remember that servant leaders exercise leadership through persuasion, not coercion (Greenleaf, 1977; Greenleaf Center for Servant Leadership, 2016).

> *Positional leaders who make important decisions in an autocratic manner find that they alienate workers and group members, even when they, as leaders, have the authority to make those decisions.*
>
> —Komives, Lucas, & McMahon, *Exploring Leadership: For College Students Who Want to Make a Difference*

Participative (Democratic) Decision Making. In contrast to an authoritarian leader who says, "Here's what we're going to do," a participative leader says, "I offer you this idea for your consideration." A participative leader consults with organizational members, solicits their ideas, and attempts to incorporate their ideas into final decisions (Northouse, 2016). As the leader of your organization, you may have the ultimate authority and the final say. However, you can exercise that authority without being authoritarian or autocratic, but by being an *authoritative* leader who:

- Shares information with followers before making final, binding decisions.
- Consults with followers and allows them to play an advisory role in the decision-making process.
- Carefully considers followers' input and factors their input into your final decision.
- Provides followers with reasons why you may not be able to accept or act on their ideas. (See **Box 11.2** for criteria you could use to judge the quality of ideas and recommendations you receive.)

> *Know the difference between being authoritative and authoritarian. The former represents your responsibility to share the knowledge, wisdom, and experience you possess by virtue of your training and official position. The latter represents the temptation to exploit these very same privileges by imposing your will—on the grounds that you are more powerful [or] older.*
>
> —Robert Nash & Michele Murray, *Helping College Students Find Purpose*

Reflection 11.3

Would you say that the decision-making style of most leaders you've observed has been participative (democratic) or authoritarian (autocratic)? As a peer leader, which of these two decision-making styles would you feel more comfortable using? Why?

Effective peer leaders are facilitators, not dictators. They encourage and support group decisions that are arrived at through thoughtful discussion and respectful listening. They welcome input from their followers by using "*referent power*"—power harnessed through *relationships* formed with members of their own organization and leaders of other organizations that is exercised through collaboration, not command or control (French & Raven, 1959; Raven, 2004).

Some leaders resist collaborative decision making because they fear losing control or authority (Schroeder, 2005). However, research demonstrates that collaborative decision making is more likely to result in decisions that are enthusiastically endorsed and implemented by organizational members because they "own" the decision (Yukl, 2012). Furthermore, when decisions are made collaboratively, they often turn out to be decisions that are more creative and comprehensive because a variety of voices are heard, diverse viewpoints are considered, and multiple options are generated (Kelly, 1994). Over 90% of employers agree that college graduates should have experiences in college that teach them how to solve problems with people whose views are different from their own (Hart Research Associates, 2013). Such diversity serves as a safeguard against "groupthink"—the tendency of like-minded members of a group or organization not to challenge or disagree with each other's ideas, which can lead to their overlooking flaws or biases in their own thinking and reaching decisions that are inaccurate or incomplete (Baron, 2005; Janis, 1982).

Box 11.2 | Criteria for Evaluating Input from Others When Making Leadership Decisions

Effective organizational leaders make decisions after different options have been carefully considered, weighed, and evaluated. Here are some criteria you may use to judge the quality of ideas and recommendations offered to you by members of your organization.

- *Logical Consistency:* Does it make good sense? Does it rest on a premise—an initial statement or observation that's true or reasonable—as opposed to a questionable assumption, and is the conclusion reached or action recommended logically consistent with the premise?
- *Empirical Evidence:* Is the idea backed by factual information, statistical data, or research findings?
- *Feasibility:* Is the idea practical to implement? Will it involve a manageable amount of time and money?
- *Ethicality:* Will implementing the idea be the right, just, or moral thing to do?
- *Impact:* Is it likely that the idea will result in productive change or produce a positive effect?

Another way to evaluate the quality of ideas presented to you is by means of a procedure called "SWOT Analysis." This procedure involves evaluating each of the following aspects of an idea or proposal:

- **S**trengths: What are its *advantages* relative to other ideas that have been proposed?
- **W**eaknesses (or Limitations): What are its *disadvantages* compared to other ideas that have been offered?
- **O**pportunities: Are there other sources or entities that may be used to *increase* the decision's likelihood of being implemented and its potential effectiveness? (For example: Are there opportunities to collaborate with other groups or organizations to make it happen or increase its impact?)
- **T**hreats: What may *interfere* with or block the decision's implementation and impact (e.g., lack of support from other student organizations or campus administrators).

After you have carefully considered the pros, cons, and consequences of different recommendations and are still unable to reach a firm conclusion or decision, consider discussing your options with a neutral "third party," such as another peer leader. Sometimes, just the process of verbalizing your options (along with the pros/cons of each option) with someone you trust and respect can help you make an effective decision.

Reaching Decisions through Group Consensus

Participative leaders empower their followers to make choices and reach decisions in two major ways: by voting or by reaching consensus. Making decisions by voting is simply a matter of majority rule—the option receiving the most votes is the one chosen. Although voting is a participative or democratic decision-making process, it's also a competitive process that pits different options (and voters) against each other, creating winners (the majority) and losers (the minority). In contrast, *consensus* is a collaborative decision-making process in which the group strives to reach a decision that all members support (Hartnett, 2011). Literally, the word "consensus" means to "feel together" and "consent." Juries attempt to reach consensus—a unified group decision—before submitting their final verdict about a defendant's guilt or innocence. (If they cannot reach consensus, the result is a "hung jury.")

Reaching consensus involves considerable discussion about the pros and cons of different options, allows everyone to be heard (including those who oppose the majority's opinion), and minimizes the feeling that some group members have won and others have lost. Seeking consensus is consistent with adaptive leadership theory, which stipulates that adaptive leaders resist the tendency to minimize or shut down minority voices for the sake of the majority (Heifetz, Grashow, & Linsky, 2009; Northouse, 2016). When groups reach consensus, the option chosen may not be everyone's ideal choice or first choice, but it's an option that all members are willing to try (Harnett, 2011; Saint & Lawson, 1994). Said in another way, consensus is reached when all members can say: "This is a decision I can live with." During the process of reaching consensus, members can still express dissent or disagreement and those members who are least enthused about the decision may have their reservations noted in the minutes of the meeting (e.g., "Let the record show that that the following members had concerns about the decision, but were willing to move forward with it.").

You may engage students in consensus-seeking simply by asking the members of your group or organization to give: (a) a thumb-up if they really like the idea, (b) a thumb-down if they can't possibly support it, or (c) a thumb-sideways if they can live with it. If no thumbs-down responses appear (only thumbs-up and thumbs-sideways), consensus has been reached. If thumbs-down responses are given, these respondents get a chance to express their concerns, the idea is shelved, another option is introduced, and the same procedure is followed again until consensus is reached. Other procedures for reaching consensus are described in Box 11.3.

As you might expect, reaching consensus is more time-consuming than simply taking a vote. However, because it's a process that accepts input from all members and generates as much agreement as possible, it has the following major advantages: (1) it promotes strong overall support for the final decision, (2) it fosters collaboration among members during and after the decision-making process, and (3) it contributes to a stronger sense of community among members of the organization (Kaner, 2011). In addition, when students practice consensus building, it prepares them for the type of balanced thinking and collaborative decision-making that will be required of them in their professional and civic roles after college.

Box 11.3

Procedures for Reaching Consensus

Finger Voting

This procedure can be used to reach consensus quickly on a single idea or proposal.
Steps:

1. Members review the proposed idea to be sure they understand what it involves.
2. Each member raises 1-5 fingers depending on how strongly they agree with it (5 = I'm enthusiastic about it; 4 = I'm for it; 3 = I'm not sure yet; 2 = I have reservations about it; 1 = I'm strongly opposed to it).
3. If all members raise 4 or 5 fingers, consensus is achieved. If not, members who raised 1-3 fingers are allowed to express their questions or objections and indicate what modifications would need to be made to the proposal for them to accept it.
4. After everyone's questions and objections have been heard, and their suggested modifications have been made considered, the process is repeated to determine if consensus can be reached on round two.

Nominal Group Process

Steps:

1. Have the group generate a list of options.
2. Ask individual members to pick their top-three options and rank them in order of priority or desirability (3 = highest; 1 = lowest).
3. Add up the total numbers (rankings) for all options and list them on a flip chart or screen.
4. The option that receives the highest average ranking is the one chosen because it's one that all members found acceptable and the one that received an overall ranking as most desirable.

Multi-Voting Technique

Steps:

1. The group generates a list of options.
2. All members vote to accept or reject each option.
3. The options that receive acceptance votes by more than one-half of the members are kept on the list for a second round of voting.
4. On the second round of voting, each member votes to accept no more than half the options listed.
5. The options that receive acceptance votes by more than one-half of the members stay on the list for a third and final round of voting.
6. Each member now votes for only one item. The option receiving the highest number of votes should be acceptable to all members of the group, thus resulting in consensus.

If, after extensive efforts, your group cannot reach consensus, then you may have to step up as leader, thank the organization for its efforts, and do either of two things: (a) call for a formal vote, or (b) make an authoritative decision that best respects and incorporates the ideas shared during the consensus-seeking process.

Facilitating group decision making can be challenging, particularly when leading a large group, which is often the case for leaders of organizations. Although the process can be arduous and may test your patience, research shows that decisions made after well-conducted group discussions are almost always more effective and creative than decisions made individually or autocratically (Gunnarsson, 2010; Hall, 1971; Proctor, 2011). Thus, your first approach to making group and organizational decisions should be to seek consensus. If consensus cannot be reached, go to "Plan B"—make a democratic decision by calling for a vote, or go to "Plan C"—make an authoritative decision by yourself after carefully considering the group's input.

Reflection 11.4

Do members of your organization seem satisfied with the way in which choices and decisions are made? Why? How do members of your organization usually go about making decisions?

D elegating and "Dispersing" Leadership

Great leaders know the difference between taking charge and "taking over." Just as an effective small-group leader develops *co-leaders* within the group, an effective organizational leader becomes a "leader of leaders" by *dispersing* leadership throughout the organization (Bryman, 1996; Gordon, 2010). Always ask yourself: "Who else could do this?" "Who has the drive and determination to do it?" "Who would welcome this challenge and rise to the occasion?"

By dispersing leadership you fulfill one important role of an organizational leader: the recruitment, preparation, and mentoring of future leaders (Gardner, 1990). By preparing future leaders you exhibit a positive character trait that the famous psychologist Erik Erickson referred to as *generativity*—"concern for establishing and guiding the next generation" (Erikson, 1963, p. 267).

> *A community is like a ship; everyone ought to be prepared to take the helm.*
>
> —Henrik Ibsen, acclaimed 19th-century Norwegian playwright and poet

Dispersing leadership and delegating responsibility isn't the same as relegating or "dumping" responsibility on others. It's about building future leaders, not by micromanaging them, but by supporting them, mentoring them, and providing feedback to them that increases their work quality and their leadership potential.

C ommittees

It's noteworthy that the word "committee" derives from the same root as "commitment." A committee composed of committed members has the potential to promote positive organizational change by: (1) creating an inclusive, participative system for reaching shared, team-based decisions; (2) dispersing leadership across different members of the organization; and (3) capitalizing on the collective wisdom of multiple organizational members.

Committees also serve to bring together members of an organization who otherwise would not have the opportunity to come together and share ideas. Creating opportunities to connect with other organizational members improves morale, fosters collaboration, and promotes critical thinking—particularly if the committee is composed of people who take different approaches to solving problems, exploring solutions, and making decisions. (For committee-formation strategies, see Box 11.4.)

Box 11.4

Strategies for Forming Committees

- Include members on the committee who are most likely to be *affected* by the committee's decisions. For example, if the committee's decisions will affect commuter students, at least one commuter student should be represented on the committee.
- Include members on the committee who are best positioned to *implement* the committee's decisions. Things are more likely to get done if the people responsible for doing them are involved in the planning and decision-making process. Try to avoid scenarios in which the decision makers decide what's to be done (the king and queen bees) and others must do all the work to get it done (the worker bees).
- Form committees that represent "cross-functional teams" whose members have different skill sets (e.g., verbal, quantitative, and technological). This practice will enable committee members to combine their diverse talents and generate *synergy*—a powerful effect produced when the contributions of separate members of a group don't just add up, they multiply, resulting in an outcome in which the whole is greater than the sum of its parts (Krajewski, Ritzman, & Malhotra, 2009).
- Periodically invite non-committee members with special knowledge and skills to committee meetings as consultants or advisors. This practice expands the range of expertise available to the committee and is likely to result in decisions that are better informed and balanced.

Purposes and Types of Committees

Before a committee begins its work, all of its members should have a clear understanding of what the committee's purpose is, what type of decisions it has the power to make, and how its work relates to the work of other committees. Listed below are major types of committees and the purposes they serve.

- *Coordinating* Committee: serves as a vehicle for communicating information to its members and coordinating the members' activities.
- *Advisory* Committee: generates recommendations that are forwarded to, and considered by, another person or governing body—which has the authority to accept or reject the committee's recommendations.
- *Decision-Making* Committee: has the authority to make final decisions without the need to have their decisions approved by another committee or someone in a higher position of authority.
- *Review Committee*: receives and reviews reports from other committees and forwards recommendations about the reports it reviews to a higher level of authority for consideration and action.
- *Ad Hoc Committee* (a.k.a. *Task Force* or *Project Team*): focuses on a specific issue or task ("ad hoc" literally means "for this") that it completes within a relative short period of time, after which the committee disbands. (In contrast, a "standing committee" occupies a more permanent place in the college's organizational structure and continues to meet from year to year.)

  Ad hoc committees or task forces may be formed within standing committees to divide up the committee's work. For instance, a large committee may be sub-divided into 3-4-member task forces or project teams, each of which works on a specific issue and then reports its work to the committee at large. After their task or project is completed, these task forces disband. Additional task forces or project teams may be assembled later to tackle different tasks or projects.

  Creating task forces within a committee enables the committee (large group) to operate as a group of small groups. If the size of a committee is very large, task forces are particularly advantageous because they provide opportunities for personalized face-to-face dialogue among committee members, increasing their sense of personal connection with each other and sense of personal accountability to one another. Another advantage of creating specialized task forces is that they may require the involvement of additional students. Thus, forming tasks forces can be an effective way to attract and recruit new members to your organization (Strange & Banning, 2001).

Reflection 11.5

If you were a new student on campus, would you choose to join the organization you're now leading? What would attract students to, and encourage them to become involved with, your organization? What would detract or discourage students from becoming involved with your organization?

M eetings

Scheduling and conducting meetings is one responsibility of an organizational leader. Meetings ensure that the voices of organizational members are heard and provide a place where participative decision making may take place. Although members of an organization will want their voices to be heard and their input considered, they may also gripe if they have to attend too many meetings. To keep the number of meetings manageable, call them only when: (a) you think that in-person discussion is needed to solve an important problem or reach a key decision, and (b) when members or your organization request a meeting to discuss something that's important to them. Time spent at meetings should be devoted mostly to important issues that require meaningful interaction among the participants. Meetings should not be filled with time-consuming announcements or delivery of factual information that could be communicated more efficiently in other ways (e.g., voice or text messages, e-mail, Twitter, or Facebook posts). Meeting time should be reserved for significant issues and high-impact agenda items that require face-to-face discussion and decision making.

The efficiency and effectiveness of meetings are maximized when they are accompanied by two key documents: (a) an *agenda* that identifies the key issues to be addressed at the meeting, and (b) *minutes* that summarizes they key decisions made and actions taken during the meeting.

Setting an Agenda

The term "agenda" literally means "things to be done." As its literal meaning suggests, an agenda identifies actions to be taken and tasks to be accomplished. If possible, circulate an agenda before the committee meets so that members can come to the meeting prepared with their ideas and recommendations. To further encourage action-oriented thinking prior to the meeting, phrase agenda items as problems to be solved or questions to be answered (e.g., "What strategies will we use to _____?" "What position will we take on _____?").

Since an agenda is an action plan, it should identify the actions to be taken and the dates by which those actions will be taken. You can ensure that high-priority actions are handled first by labeling or flagging agenda items in terms of their level of priority (e.g., High—must do immediately; Medium—will do soon; Low—should do eventually). Items are then covered at the meeting in their order of priority (highest-priority item first, next highest-priority item second, etc.). You may also designate the approximate amount of meeting time that will be devoted to each item on the agenda.

Keeping Minutes

"Minutes" represent the written record of a meeting; they typically include a summary of the key points made during discussion of the agenda items, as well as the major decisions made and actions taken with respect to the agenda items. Minutes should include the meeting's place, date, start and stop time, and the names of those in attendance.

One way to determine the success or effectiveness of meetings is by assessing whether the outcomes of the meeting (as captured in the minutes) align with the meeting's agenda items. In other words: Did the meeting solve the problems, resolve the issues, and make the decisions called for by its agenda? Also, do the minutes reflect a clear action plan that specifically stipulates *what* is to be done, *who* will do it, and *when* it will be done?

Save and post the minutes of all your meetings to ensure you have a cumulative record of your organization's work and an observable record of its accomplishments. This will make the work of your organization "transparent"—openly visible to the campus community, showing everyone what your organization is doing and how much it's getting done!

Using Parliamentary Procedure

An agenda and minutes bring order and structure to the meeting's *content—what* is covered at the meeting, but leaders also need to bring structure and order to the meeting's *process—how* the meeting is conducted. One way to run meetings in an orderly manner is by using *parliamentary procedure*—a formal set of operational rules and procedural guidelines designed to conduct meetings in an effective, efficient, and equitable manner. Parliamentary procedure dates back to the original practices used by the United Kingdom's House of Commons of the Parliament (hence the term, "parliamentary" procedure). Parliamentary procedure stipulates that the following sequence of steps be followed at all meetings:

1. Calling to order—the presiding officer (person in charge of running the meeting) calls for the attention of all those present
2. Reading and approval of minutes of the previous meeting
3. Receiving reports from officers and standing committees
4. Receiving reports from ad hoc committees and task forces
5. Taking care of unfinished business
6. Taking care of new business
7. Calling for announcements
8. Adjournment.

Parliamentary procedure also involves rules for debating and reaching group decisions efficiently—by voting and majority rule, while at the same time, ensuring fairness toward the minority—by building in opportunities for their voices to be heard. Probably the most well-known and frequently used form of parliamentary procedure is *Robert's Rules of Order,* originally published in 1876 by Henry

Martyn Robert, a U.S. Army Colonel. Robert observed that people at meetings had very different views about how parliamentary rules were to be applied and their differing views were interfering with the group's ability to reach decisions effectively and efficiently. Thus, he constructed a manual of rules to facilitate the decision-making process that is similar to those currently practiced by the United States House of Representatives. Robert's rules are still commonly used today to conduct organizational meetings and his manual is in its eleventh edition (Robert, 2011). A brief summary of *Robert's Rules of Order* is contained in Box 11.5.

Box 11.5 — Robert's Rules of Order: Practices for Conducting Orderly Meetings

- Members must be recognized by the presiding officer before they may make a "motion"—a proposal of an idea to be discussed and voted on.
- Members must formally state their motions ("I move that . . .) and only one motion can be stated at a time.
- Another member must "second" (agree with) the first motion before it's put "on the floor" for discussion by the assembly.
- After the motion is seconded, the presiding officer restates the motion and opens it up to the assembly for discussion.
- All members have the right to agree or disagree with the motion and suggest amendments (modifications) to it; however, any amendment must first be recognized and restated by the presiding officer before it can be discussed by the assembly.
- No member may speak a second time to a motion (or to an amended notion) until all members who have not yet spoken have had the opportunity to speak.
- Members must not direct remarks, questions, or criticisms at particular individuals; all comments are to be addressed to the presiding officer and the group at large.
- Before voting on a motion, members have the right to seek clarification about what the motion specifically states and what an affirmative ("yes") vote or negative ("no) vote actually means.
- The presiding officer takes the vote and announces the result.

Source: Adapted from *Robert's Rules of Order Newly Revised* (Robert, 2011).

Formal procedures for running meetings, such as *Robert's Rules of Order,* provide structure and order, but they can also restrict spontaneous discussion and inhibit consensus-building. An informal alternative to *Robert's Rules of Order* are guidelines for running meetings that were developed by Jay Hall (1971), a social psychologist who studied group decision-making in a wide variety of situations and organizations. Hall discovered groups reached higher-quality decisions when they used the practices listed below.

- The group tries to avoid using decision-making methods that minimize discussion and consensus-building (e.g., voting, averaging, or bargaining).
- Differences of opinion are viewed as natural and are sought out to ensure that balanced decisions are reached and multiple options are considered.
- When disagreement or debate occurs, members don't adopt the mindset that there will be winners and losers; instead, they look for common ground that's acceptable to both parties.
- Rather than argue at length for their own views, group members state their position as clearly and briefly as possible, allow others to respond, and care-

fully consider others' responses before continuing to argue for their position.

- Members don't change their mind just to prevent conflict and preserve harmony (giving in to get along). Instead, they yield to another position only if they think it's reasonable and acceptable. When agreement comes quickly and easily, the leader makes sure that the decision wasn't reached prematurely and everyone truly agrees with it.

Members of your organization should decide on ground rules they will work best for running its meetings. The key is to establish rules that strike a balance between order—keeping the meeting focused on its agenda, and flexibility—allowing some opportunity for spontaneity and creativity. As the presiding officer, you may have to play the role of traffic cop or court judge. You'll need to decide whether the meeting is veering too far off track and needs to be reeled in, or "go with the flow" and allow discussion to continue even if it's not directly related to the current item on the agenda, particularly if it's a thought-provoking discussion that may lead to productive action. You can also "table" (postpone) the discussion and come back to it at the end of the meeting (e.g., under "new business"), or schedule the discussion as an agenda item for your next meeting.

As the meeting's presiding officer, another key role you play is ensuring that all voices have been heard. You can do this by setting aside some time at the end of each meeting for participants to express orally, or record in writing and submit to you, any ideas they didn't express at the meeting—either because time ran out or because they were reluctant to compete with others for "air time." For instance, before bringing the meeting to a close, you could ask members to provide a written response to the question: "What would you have said at today's meeting if you had the time or opportunity to do so?"

Handling Conflicts during Meetings

Since organizations are complex systems composed of multiple members, differences of opinion are inevitable; at the same time, they're invaluable—particularly if the leader ensures these differing viewpoints are aired openly and respectfully. A heated discussion isn't necessarily a bad thing. It may just mean that the discussants are intensely interested in, and passionate about, the topic being discussed. Spirited, vigorous dialogue can often lead to better decisions and a stronger organization. Don't confuse *conflict* with *controversy*. The former is an intense, often emotionally charged disagreement between two opposing parties that has reached a stalemate; the latter is a healthy, vigorous public debate among parties holding different opinions. Thus, it's important not to squelch controversy; just ensure that it takes place in a civil and courteous manner (Higher Education Research Institute, 1996).

If you detect controversy beginning to merge into conflict, here are three key things you can do: (1) remind the disputants to keep the discussion positive and constructive, (2) give equal time to both parties' arguments and carefully weigh their pros and cons, and (3) look for and point out areas of agreement that may serve as bridges between their opposing positions. When organizational members find themselves immersed in an emotionally intense disagreement, they often overlook rational alternatives that may be agreeable to both parties. Opponents can get so locked into a win-lose mindset, they erect artificial barriers that block discovery of win-win solutions. To help the disagreeing parties break through this winner- vs.-loser mentality, encourage them to think beyond the competitive boundaries of their opposing positions and look for common ground. As the presiding officer, you are well-positioned to serve as an objective "third party" who may detect win-win alternatives that the disputants overlook. By using your leadership position to help disagreeing parties explore and identify bipartisan (two-party) solutions, you not only help resolve disagreements, you model effective problem-solving and consensus-building skills for students to emulate and put into practice themselves.

> *Leadership has a harder job to do than just choose sides. It must bring sides together.*
>
> —Jesse Jackson, American civil rights activist and recipient of the Presidential Medal of Freedom

romoting Organizational Change

Organizational change is the process of improving an organization's policies, programs, or practices to more effectively achieve its mission and goals. Organizational leaders move from promoting change individually ("I can make it happen") to promoting change collectively ("we can make it happen together"). Peer leaders may be in a position to advocate (and agitate) for campus-wide change that benefits both current and future generations of students, particularly if the changes they create are incorporated into the college's organizational structure, policies, and procedures.

Reflection 11.6

If you were to conduct a *campaign* to change something about your campus, what would your change campaign focus on? Who could implement the campaign? What positive change(s) would take place on campus if your campaign proved to be successful?

ssessing Where Campus Change Is Needed

Students often consider peer leaders to be sounding boards for their campus experiences, both positive and negative. This may enable you to gain insight into common sources of student satisfaction and dissatisfaction on your campus. Studies show that dissatisfaction among members of an organization dampens their enthusiasm, lowers their morale, and increases the likelihood they will leave the organization (Harter, Schmidt, & Hayes, 2002). This is also true for members of educational organizations, including students enrolled in colleges and universities (Noel & Levitz, 1995; Strange & Banning, 2001). By asking questions and listening actively, you can identify current and recurrent sources of student dissatisfaction that contribute to college attrition, and propose changes in campus policies or procedures that increase student satisfaction and college completion. In addition to asking students informally about their college experience, you could use more formal and systematic methods for collecting student data, such as the following.

Surveys and Questionnaires. By asking students to rate their level of satisfaction with various campus programs and experiences, you can obtain a sizable amount of quantitative data that can be quickly analyzed and summarized. Here are a few quick tips for improving the quality of any survey or questionnaire you may decide to construct.

- Use a rating scale that includes the following five options:

4	3	0	2	1
Strongly Agree	Agree	Not Sure	Disagree	Strongly Disagree

The "not sure" option will allow students to choose a neutral option if the question is asking them to rate an experience or program they know little or nothing about.

- As illustrated below, leave a space beneath each survey item that allows students to provide a reason or explanation for their rating.

4	3	0	2	1
Strongly Agree	Agree	Not Sure	Disagree	Strongly Disagree

Reason/explanation for rating:

When students supply a written response along with their rating, it helps you understand *why* the rating was given (the reasoning behind the rating).

- In addition to asking students to rate their satisfaction with a program or experience, ask them to rate how *important* that program or experience is to them. You can do this by having students give two ratings for each item on the survey: (1) a rating of how *satisfied* they are with the experience/program, and (2) a rating of how *important* that experience or program is to them. The layout of the survey can be arranged in a way that obtains both of these ratings efficiently by positioning the items to be rated in the middle of the page and placing a "satisfaction" scale and "importance" scale below each item—as illustrated below:

There is a good variety of student activities offered on campus.

Satisfaction

4	3	0	2	1
Strongly Agree	Agree	Not Sure	Disagree	Strongly Disagree

Importance

4	3	0	2	1
Strongly Agree	Agree	Not Sure	Disagree	Strongly Disagree

Items rated high in importance but low in satisfaction may be key targets for campus-change efforts because they represent high-priority student interests or needs that are not being met.

- At the end of the survey, include a section that asks for demographic information, such as the student's: (1) gender, (2) race/ethnicity, (3) residential status (campus resident or commuter), and (4) national citizenship (domestic or international). Collecting demographic information from the survey respondents will enable you to determine how ratings of satisfaction and importance (need) can vary widely across different student groups. Studies show that different groups of students on the same campus often vary in terms of their needs and level of satisfaction with different campus programs or services (Schuh & Upcraft, 2001).
- Before officially distributing the survey, ask some students to complete it, comment on its strengths, and suggest ways in which it could be improved. This practice will not only improve the survey's quality, it will enable you to exhibit participative leadership by giving students opportunity for input.

Focus-Group Interviews. A focus group is a group of people (e.g., 6-8) who meets with a moderator in a relaxed environment to explore the group's perceptions, attitudes, and ideas about a particular topic or issue. In contrast to surveys or questionnaires, which provide information in the form of numerical ratings and written comments, focus groups supply you with verbal (oral) information. When students respond to questions posed to them in person, the qualitative (non-numerical) data generated is often richer and more detailed than data obtained from quantitative surveys.

You can also use a "mixed method" approach by combining focus-group interviews with surveys. For instance, after distributing a survey and summarizing its results, you can conduct focus-group interviews and ask students for their interpretations or explanations of the survey's results. Focus groups can also be conducted before a survey is distributed to gather input about student needs and issues that should be addressed on the survey.

Participants who are chosen for the focus groups should be selected intentionally to create a positive group dynamic and to generate the best possible data. Here are two group-formation strategies that may used to maximize the value of focus groups.

1. *Heterogeneous* group formation. Members included in the group are selected from different student populations (e.g., minority and majority students, males and females, commuters and residents). This group-formation strategy ensures that a balanced blend of student subgroups is included and that diverse perspectives are heard.
2. *Homogeneous* group formation. Members included in the group are selected from the same student population (e.g., the same racial or ethnic group). This grouping procedure allows students to discuss their perceptions and concerns with peers who may have common experiences and with whom they may feel more comfortable expressing their views.

You may also use both of these grouping strategies, or combine them by creating groups that are heterogeneous with respect to one characteristic and homogeneous with respect to another—for example, a focus group composed of students of different races, ethnicities, or gender that have the same academic major or live in the same campus residence.

Open Forums. These are meetings with no set agenda. Instead, topics for discussion are raised by group members spontaneously at the time of the meeting. Open forums work most effectively when ground rules are set before the discussion begins. For instance, ground rules would include reminders to participants that: (1) comments should focus on campus issues, practices, or policies, rather than targeting or blaming particular individuals, and (2) each complaint or criticism mentioned should be followed by a discussion of suggested solutions before another complaint or criticism is raised.

By encouraging students to express their campus concerns openly, you can unearth areas where organizational change is needed. If a number of students cite similar experiences as frustrating or dissatisfying, these may be viewed as "critical incidents" and be introduced as topics for discussion with key college administrators and decision makers.

Suggestion Boxes. Students may express concerns and make recommendations at any time by depositing them in a conveniently located box (actual or electronic). Sometimes, students will be more willing to express their ideas anonymously than publicly.

Higher Education Research. In addition to identifying target areas for organizational change by gathering data from students on your campus, you can also use multi-campus research conducted by college researchers and scholars. National research points strongly to the need for campuses to strive to make changes that enable them to operate less like "complex organizations" and more like "developmental environments" (Strange & Banning, 2001). The differences between these two modes of operation are charted in **Box 11.6**. This chart may be used to identify areas where change is needed on your campus and help you develop change strategies relating to these areas that move your campus closer to becoming a true "developmental environment."

> *Powerful developmental environments are those that exhibit characteristics of dynamic organizations, where individual differences are appreciated, participation is expected, interactions are personal rather than functional, and risk-taking is encouraged.*
>
> —Carney Strange & James Banning,
> *Education by Design: Creating Campus Learning Environments That Work*

Box 11.6

Characteristics of Complex Organizations	Characteristics of Developmental Environments
Emphasize formality and rigid procedural routines	Emphasize procedural flexibility and openness to innovation and creativity
Minimize risk-taking to maximize organizational efficiency	Encourage risk-taking to maximize organizational effectiveness
Minimize discussion of differing viewpoints to avoid conflict or controversy	Welcome multiple perspectives and diverse viewpoints to encourage critical and creative thinking
Centralize decision making, restricting power to a few high-ranking authorities	Decentralize decision making, distributing power throughout the organization
Members' status is differentiated and stratified by their position (level) in the organization's hierarchy	Status differences are minimized and members at all levels of the organization are valued equally
Interpersonal interactions are based on members' formal roles and job duties in the organization	Interpersonal interactions are based on relationships and mentoring

Source: Adapted from Strange (1983) and Strange & Banning (2001).

Strategies for Catalyzing Organizational Change

As a peer leader, you have the potential to use your organizational position to promote positive change on campus, particularly if you devise a strategic plan for change that capitalizes on the varieties of tools and tactics available to you. Described below is a systematic set of strategies for promoting organizational change that includes ideas about *how* to do it, *who* to do it with, and *when* to do it.

The HOW of Change: The Art, Science, and Politics of Persuasion

To ensure that your change message reaches as many members of the campus community as possible, use all *communication modalities* available to you, including social media (e.g., Facebook and Twitter) and campus ecology (e.g., stickers, placards, postings on bulletin boards and kiosks).

Reflection 11.7

On your campus, what forms of *media* for mobilizing change do you think would be most powerful or persuasive?

To increase the likelihood that members of the campus community buy into your change message, use *multiple methods of persuasion*. Listed below are different approaches to persuasion that may be used to get buy-in for your change initiatives.

- *Appeal to Reason (The Rational Approach)*—show how your proposed change "makes sense"—that it's the logically sound thing to do. For example, point out how the change is logically consistent with your university's mission, goals, strategic plan, or most recent accreditation report.
- *Appeal to Evidence (The Empirical Approach)*—show how your proposed change is supported by research, data, and facts. For example, cite student-satisfaction research on your campus and/or national research findings that support the change you're seeking to make.
- *Appeal to Personal Conscience and Ethical Principles* (*The Moral Approach*)— show how the change you're proposing is the right, just, or fair thing to do.
- *Appeal to Self-Interest (The What's-In-It-For-Me Approach)*—show how the change will benefit the people you're trying to persuade (e.g., make their job easier, more satisfying, or more fulfilling). Organizational change research shows that change agents are more likely to gain support for the change they're proposing when they're able to show how the change will advance decision-makers' professional needs or interests (Jenkins, 2011). Effective leaders are socially perceptive; they know what's important to others, what motivates them, and how they're likely to react to change initiatives (Zaccaro et al., 1991).
- *Appeal to Feasibility (The Practical and Manageable Approach)*—show that the change you're proposing can be implemented without the need for lots of money, time, or energy. Remember to take the "path of least resistance" or use the "law of least effort"—i.e., the probability that people will make a change

To catch a fish, you need to think like a fish.

—Old saying suggesting that to get others hooked on your ideas, be aware of how they think, how they operate, and what matters to them is negatively (inversely) related to the amount of time, effort, and energy required to make the change. In other words, by requiring less of them to make change happen, the more likely they are to make the change happen.

The WHO of Change: Finding Partners and Enlisting Allies

Organizational change rarely happens through the efforts of a single individual; it typically takes place through collective and collaborative effort. Think about members of your campus community who can help you ignite and galvanize change. Build coalitions with people on campus who are sympathetic to your cause and willing to support your efforts. In particular, partner with people who bring different change-promoting talents to the table (e.g., "idea" people and "action" people).

Organizational change can be driven by different groups at different levels of the organization's hierarchy. Referred to as "network change," this change process rests on the principle that leadership is distributed throughout the organization and may come from any direction at any time (Allen & Cherrey, 2000). Since organizational change can be put into motion by people at different levels of the organizational hierarchy, you can enlist allies to drive your change campaign from three key directions:

1. Top (support from high-ranking administrators)
    ⇩
    Down

2. Up
    ⇧
    Ground (support from faculty, staff, and students)

3. Side ⇨In (support from middle managers—e.g., department heads and program directors).

Each of the key three vectors for catalyzing organizational change is further described in **Box 11.7.**

The WHEN of Change: Timing Matters

Making change happen depends not only on what you do, how you do it, and who you do it with; it also depends on *when* you do it. It's been said that "timing is everything." That may be an overstatement—it may not be everything—but it's certainly an important thing. Change should be introduced at a time when people are most likely to be receptive to it. Avoid introducing change initiatives at crunch times when people are likely to be stressed out, burnt out, or simply pooped out (e.g., near midterm and finals). Try to initiate change at times during the school year when people are likely to be more relaxed and energized.

Good timing also means "striking when the iron is hot"—at a time when the campus community sees the need for change. This could be a time when the campus has experienced a setback (e.g., a drop in student retention), bad publicity (e.g., a critical article in the campus or local newspaper), or a disturbing campus incident (e.g., hate crime). High-level administrators are likely to be receptive to inventive ideas and change efforts that meet the college's need to address negative developments immediately and prevent their reoccurrence. It's been said that "necessity is the mother of invention." It could also be said that necessity is the mother of change.

Reflection 11.8

Is your campus currently experiencing a serious issue or crisis that could serve as a rallying point for change? If yes, as a peer leader what could you and other peer leaders do to help the campus community make the change needed to address this issue or crisis?

Catalyzing Organizational Change: Three Key Vectors

1. *Top→Down* ("Trickle Down"): Change generated by high-level administrators.
   Research on individuals who've made successful, student-centered change on college campuses reveals that the factor most responsible for their ability to promote change was gaining support from the president or other high-level administrators (Anttonen & Chaskes, 2002). Seeking support from high-ranking campus leaders can provide high-octane fuel for your change efforts because they have the decision-making power and can supply you with needed resources. Their support may also be enlisted by asking them if they would be willing to (a) make a brief appearance at your meetings or rallies (e.g., to provide a welcoming or closing message), and (b) refer to your change effort in their written communications or formal addresses to the campus community (e.g., while giving a speech kicking off the school year or delivering a state-of-the-college report to the campus community).

2. *Ground→Up* ("Bubble Up"): Change catalyzed by peer leaders and the student body.
   "Grassroots" change starts with the "foot soldiers" on the "front line"—those closest to the action (the student experience). Although students may rank lowest on the organizational totem pole, they have informal power because they are the organization's tuition-paying customers and primary constituents. As such, high-level administrators and decision-makers may actually be more attentive to students' requests for change than requests from faculty and staff. A peer leader can "rally the troops," bringing them together to join forces with peer leaders of other student groups and organizations to coordinate their efforts, pool their resources, and create a united front for positive change.

3. *Side→In* ("Across the Middle"): Change driven by department heads and program directors.
   The organizational structure of most colleges and universities tends to be highly decentralized, meaning that there are multiple layers of divisions and departments within the organizational hierarchy (Strange & Banning, 2001). In decentralized organizations, there are many "middle managers" who wield considerable decision-making authority. As such, it's important not to forget to solicit support from these mid-level leaders when initiating change efforts, particularly if the proposed change can affect or be affected by their particular program, department or division.

Internet Resources

For additional information on leading organizations, consult the following websites.

Leadership and Decision-Making Power
www.ccl.org/leadership/pdf/research/roleOfPower.pdf
www.uthscsa.edu/gme/documents/LspasaFunctionofPower.pdf

Conducting Meetings
Strategies for Conducting Meetings
treegroup.info/topics/facilitation_primer.pdf
Summary of Robert's Rules of Order
www.Robertsrules.org

Organizational Development and Change Strategies
http://www.strategies-for-managing-change.com/strategies-for-managing-change.html
https://www.prosci.com/change-management/thought-leadership-library/change-management-process
http://www.orgsync.com (Note: OrgSync is a commercial online system that can be purchased and used by student organizations to manage their programs and events, communicate with students and staff, and track student involvement in campus life. Now a for-profit company, it was originally founded by students and alumni at the University of Texas at Austin for the purpose of improving communication among campus organizations and increasing student involvement in campus life.)

References

Allen, K. E., & Cherrey, C. (2000). *Systemic leadership: Enriching the meaning of our work.* Lanham, MD: University Press of America.

Anttonen, R., & Chaskes, J. (2002). Advocating for first-year students: A study of the micropolitics of leadership and organizational change. *Journal of The First-Year Experience and Students in Transition, 14*(1), 81-96.

Avolio, B. J., Gardner, W. L., Walumbwa, F. O., Luthans, F., & May, D. R. (2004). Unlocking the mask: A look at the processes by which authentic leaders impact follower attitudes and behaviors. *Leadership Quarterly, 15,* 801-823.

Baron, R. S. (2005). So right it's wrong: Groupthink and the ubiquitous nature of polarized group decision making. *Advances in Experimental Social Psychology, 37,* 219-253.

Bennis, W. G., & Nanus, B. (1985). *Leaders: The strategies of taking charge.* New York: Harper & Row.

Bryman, A. (1996). Leadership in organizations. In S. R. Clegg, C. Hardy, & W. R. Nord (Eds.), *Handbook of Organization Studies:* London: SAGE.

Cherry, K. (2012). *What is autocratic leadership?* Retrieved from www.http:psychology.about.com/od/leadershp/f/autocraticleadership.htm

Conger, J. A., & Kanungo, R. N. (1998). *Charismatic leadership in organizations.* Thousand Oaks, CA: SAGE.

DeGroot, T., Diker, D. S., Cross T. C. (2000). A meta-analyses to review organizational outcomes related to charismatic leadership. *Canadian Journal of Administrative Sciences, 17*(4), 356-371.

Drucker, P. F. (1990). *Managing the nonprofit organization: Principles and practices.* New York: HarperCollins.

Duckworth, A. (2016). *Grit: The power of passion and perseverance.* London: Vermillion.

Erikson, E. H. (Ed.). (1963). *Youth: Change and challenge.* New York: Basic Books.

French, J. R. P., & Raven, B. H. (1959). The bases of social power. In D. Cartwright (Ed.), *Studies in social power* (pp. 150-167). Ann Arbor, MI: Institute for Social Research.

Gardner, J. W. (1990*). On leadership.* New York: The Free Press.

Gordon, R. D. (2010). Dispersed leadership: Exploring the impact of antecedent forms of power using a communicative framework. *Management Communication Quarterly, 24*(2), 260-287.

Greenleaf, R. K. (1977). *Servant leadership: A journey into the nature of legitimate power and greatness.* New York: Paulist Press.

Greenleaf Center for Servant Leadership (2016). *What is servant leadership?* Retrieved from https://www.greenleaf.org/what-is-servant-leadership/

Gunnarsson, M. (2010). *Group decision making.* Frederick, MD: Verlag.

Hall, J. (1971). Decisions, decisions, decisions. *Psychology Today, 5* (November), pp. 51-54 & 86-88.

Hartnett, T. (2011). *Consensus-oriented decision making.* Gabriola Island, BC, Canada: New Society Publishers.

Hart Research Associates. (2013). *It takes more than a major: Employer priorities for college learning and student success.* Washington, DC: Association of American College and Universities.

Harter, J. K., Schmidt, F. L., & Hayes, T. (2002). Business unit level relationship between employee satisfaction: A meta-analysis. *Journal of Applied Psychology, 87,* 268-279.

Hartnett, T. (2011). *Consensus-oriented decision making.* Gabriola Island, BC, Canada: New Society Publishers.

Heifetz, R. A., Grashow, A., & Linsky, M. (2009). *The practice of adaptive leadership: Tools and tactics for changing your organization and the word.* Boston: Harvard Business School Press.

Higher Education Research Institute (HERI). (1996). *A social change model of leadership development: Guidebook version III.* Los Angeles: University of California Los Angeles Higher Education Research Institute.

House, R. J., Hanges, P. J., Javidan, N., Dorfman, P. W., & Gupta, V. (Eds.). (2004). *Culture, leadership, and organizations: The GLOBE study of 62 societies.* Thousand Oaks, CA: SAGE.

Janis, I. L. (1982). *Groupthink: Psychological studies of policy decisions and fiascoes* (2nd ed.). Boston: Houghton Mifflin.

Jenkins, D. (2011). *Redesigning community colleges for completion: Lessons from research on high-performance organizations.* (CCRC Working Paper No. 24, Assessment of Evidence Series.) New York: Columbia University, Teachers College, Community College Research Center.

Kaner, S. (2011). *Facilitator's guide to participatory decision-making.* San Francisco: Jossey-Bass

Keller, G. (2007). The emerging third stage in higher education planning. *Planning for Higher Education, 35*(4), 60-64.

Kelly, K. (1994). *Out of control: The new biology of machines, social systems, and the economic world.* Reading, MA: Addison-Wesley.

Komives, S. R., Lucas, N., & McMahon, T. R. (2007). *Exploring leadership: For college students who want to make a difference* (2nd ed.). San Francisco: Jossey-Bass.

Komives, S. R., Owen, J. E., Longerbeam, S., Mainella, F. C., & Osteen, L. (2005). Developing leadership identity: A grounded theory. *Journal of College Student Development, 46,* 593-611.

Krajewski, L. J., Ritzman, L. P., & Malhotra, M. K. (2009). *Operations management: Processes and value chains* (9th ed.). Upper Saddle River, NJ: Pearson.

Lord, R. G., Brown, D. J., & Frieberg, S. J. (1999). Understanding the dynamics of leadership: The role of follower self-concepts in the leader/follower relationship. *Organizational Behavior and Human Decision Processes, 75,* 167-203.

Lord, R. G., & Emrich, C. G. (2001). Thinking outside the box by looking inside the box: Extending the cognitive revolution in leadership research. *Leadership Quarterly, 11*(4), 551-579.

Lord, R., & Maher, K. J. (1991). *Leadership and information processing: Linking perceptions and performance.* Boston: Unwin-Everyman.

Nash, R. J., & Murray, M. C. (2010). *Helping college students find purpose.* San Francisco: Jossey-Bass.

Noel, L., & Levitz, R. (1995). New strategies for difficult times. *Recruitment & Retention in Higher Education, 9*(7), 4-7.

Northouse, P. G. (2016). *Leadership: Theory and practice* (7th ed.). Los Angeles: SAGE.

Proctor, T. (2011). *Creative problem solving: Developing skills for decision making and innovation.* New York: Routledge.

Raven, B. H. (2004). Power, six bases of. In G. R. Goethals, G. J. Sorenson, & J. M. Burns (Eds.), *Encyclopedia of leadership* (pp. 1242-1249). Thousand Oaks, CA: SAGE.

Robert, H. M. (2011). *Robert's rules of order newly revised* (11th ed.). Philadelphia: De Capo Press.

Rowley, D. J., Lujan, H. D., & Dolence, M. G. (2001). *Strategic change in colleges and universities.* San Francisco: Jossey-Bass.

Saint, S., & Lawson, J. R. (1994). *Rules for reaching consensus: A modern approach to decision making.* San Diego: Pfeiffer.

Schein, E. (2004). *Organizational culture and leadership* (3rd ed.). San Francisco: Jossey-Bass.

Schroeder, C. C. (2005). Collaborative partnerships between academic and student affairs. In M. L. Upcraft, J. N. Gardner, & B. O. Barefoot (Eds.), *Challenging and supporting the first-year student: A handbook for improving the first year of college* (pp. 204-220). San Francisco: Jossey-Bass.

Schuh, J. H., & Upcraft, M. L. (2001). *Assessment practice in student affairs.* San Francisco: Jossey-Bass.

Shankman, M. L., & Allen, S. J. (2008). *Emotionally intelligent leadership: A guide for college students.* San Francisco: Jossey-Bass.

Strange, C. C. (1983). Human development theory and administrative practice in student affairs: Ships passing in the daylight? *NASPA Journal, 21,* 2-8.

Strange, C. C., & Banning, J. H. (2001). *Educating by design: Creating campus learning environments that work.* San Francisco: Jossey-Bass.

Zaccaro, S. J., Gilbert, J., Thor, K. K., & Mumford, M. D. (1991). Leadership and social intelligence: Linking social perceptiveness and behavioral flexibility to leader effectiveness. *Leadership Quarterly, 2,* 317-331.

E xercise 11.1 Quote Reflections

Review the sidebar quotes contained in this chapter and select two that you think would be especially valuable to share with the students you lead or mentor.

For each quote, write a short statement explaining why you chose it.

Exercise 11.2 Journal Reflections

1. Based on your prior experience with meetings, what would you say is the most important ground rule for ensuring that meetings run in an orderly and constructive manner?

2. What topics or issues do you think would be the most difficult for members of your organization to reach consensus on? What would be the easiest?

3. If you were to construct a survey to assess students' needs and their sources of campus satisfaction/dissatisfaction, what questions would you include on the survey?

4. If you were to conduct focus-group interviews with students on your campus, what do you think they'd say they were most pleased with and frustrated by?

Exercise 11.3 Organizational Structure and Communication

Locate the Table of Organization (Organizational Chart) that shows the offices/positions on your campus and how communication and decision making flows from top to bottom (the chain of command).

1. To what person or position does your student organization report?

2. Where does that person or position fall in the organizational hierarchy?

3. If you wanted to communicate an idea or concern to the highest authorities on campus, would you go directly to them, or would you first run it by someone at a lower level in the organizational hierarchy?

Exercise 11.4 Forming Committees and Task Forces

Reflect on your organization's purpose, goals, and activities.

1. What standing committees do you think should be formed and should meet regularly to ensure that your organization fulfills its purpose and reaches its goals?

2. What task forces or project teams should be temporarily formed to tackle current challenges or issues?

3. What members of your organization do you think should comprise the above committees and task forces?

Exercise 11.5 SWOT Analysis

Think about the student organization you lead or play a leadership role, and answer the following questions about that organization.

1. **S**trengths: What are your organization's strong points? What's working really well?

2. **W**eaknesses: What are your organization's limitations or areas needing the most improvement?

3. **O**pportunities: What resources or people on campus might your organization capitalize on, or collaborate with, to better achieve its goals?

4. **T**hreats: What aspects of your campus environment, or how it operates, tend to interfere or weaken your organization's effectiveness?

Name _____ Date _____

Exercise 11.6 Strategy Reflections

Review the strategies suggested for *assessing where campus change is needed* on pp. 373-376. Select two strategies that you think would be most relevant to your leadership role or most effective for the organization you lead.

CHAPTER 12

Civic Leadership

Promoting Change at the Local, National, and Global Level

Reflection 12.1

When you hear the word "civic," what's the first thing that comes to mind?

Chapter Purpose and Preview

The mission of colleges and universities goes beyond helping students better themselves to helping students better their communities, their nation, and the world in which they live. You can contribute to this larger mission of higher education by engaging students in change efforts that go beyond the boundaries of your campus. This chapter provides you with peer-leadership strategies for promoting students' civic engagement, community service, participation in local and national elections, and involvement with worthy societal and global causes.

Introduction

A leader's influence can extend beyond individuals to progressively wider social circles that encompass groups, organizations, communities, and society as a whole. (See **Figure 12.1**.)

According to servant leadership theory, leading individuals, groups, and organizations intersects with the larger leadership goal of promoting society's common good (Greenleaf, 1970, 1977; Greenleaf Center for Servant Leadership, 2016). Servant leaders link the purposes and goals of their particular leadership program or organization to the larger purpose of serving their community (Northouse, 2016). When student leaders of different organizations adopt a servant leadership approach, it helps create a college culture of service to others, both within and beyond the campus (Liden et al., 2008).

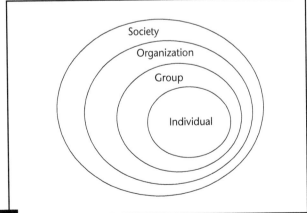

Figure 12.1   Peer Leadership: Circles of Influence

What Is a Community?

Sociologists define *community* as a group of people who share an interpersonal connection, mutual commitment, and collective identity (Bruhn, 2005). Thus, a community refers not only to a group of people who occupy the same geographical place or space, but people who are connected by a shared purpose or common cause. What distinguishes all true communities is that their members move beyond self-interest to benefit the common good. In fact, the word "community" derives from a combination of two Latin roots, meaning "with/together" and "gift."

Communities vary in size, with smaller communities nested within larger communities (Strange & Banning, 2001). As illustrated in **Figure** 12.2, individuals are embedded in a nest of progressively broader communities, ranging from their local community to the global community. When individuals view themselves as being members of a web of intersecting communities, they're more likely to appreciate the common bond that connects them with other humans (their shared humanity) and connects all humans to their shared global environment (planet Earth). These connective bonds enable individuals to experience a stronger sense of connection with the world around them and reduce feelings of personal isolation or alienation (Bellah et al., 1985).

> Skill in the building and rebuilding of community is one of the highest and most essential skills a leader can command.
>
> —J. W. Gardner, former secretary of Health Education and Welfare, U.S. Marine Corps captain, and recipient of the Presidential Medal of Freedom

> Effective communities realize they are not insular but are in a constant, dynamic interaction with the broader environment.
>
> —Komives, Lucas, & McMahon, *Exploring Leadership: For College Students Who Want to Make a Difference*

> Humankind has not woven the web of life. We are but one thread within it. Whatever we do to the web, we do to ourselves. All things are bound together. All things connect.
>
> —Chief Seattle, prominent Native American after whom the city of Seattle was named

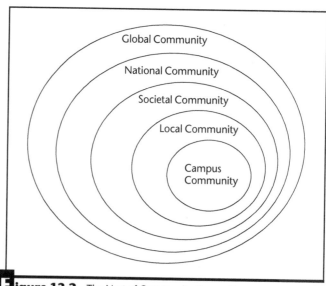

Figure 12.2 The Nest of Community Connections

What Is Civic Engagement?

The word "civic" derives from the same root as "citizen"—a member of a city or community. *Civic engagement* refers to actions that citizens make, either individually or collectively, to promote the welfare of their community (American Psychological Association, 2012). Responsible citizens are involved citizens—they actively participate in their community, attempting to make it the best it can be (Komives, Lucas, & McMahon, 2007). They understand that members of a community are more than a collection of independent parts but are integrated and interdependent elements of a larger whole—whose collective well-being depends on how well its individual members support one another and work to promote the common good (Higher Education Research Institute, 1996; Wagner, 2006).

> To be a good citizen is to work for positive change on behalf of others and the community.
>
> —Higher Education Research Institute, University of California at Los Angeles

What Is Civility?

As its most basic level, civic engagement involves *civility*–showing respect for and sensitivity to the rights of other community members. Civility could be defined as "responsible freedom"–the freedom to exercise individual rights and freedom, but without stepping (or stomping) on the rights and freedom of others (Forni, 2002). Preserving individual freedom is not the same as promoting self-centeredness. The former includes social responsibility and a commitment to the common good; the latter involves thinking and acting in ways that benefit only oneself, without concern for the needs or rights of others.

Civility includes taking action (not looking away) when the rights or needs of other community members are being violated. The quality of life in any community is threatened when any of its members' sense of inclusion or belongingness is threatened (Strange & Banning, 2001). At a national level, if any group of citizens in a democratic country is threatened by prejudice and discrimination, the political stability and viability of democracy itself is threatened. As a peer leader, when you take an active role and challenge prejudice or discrimination displayed by any member of your community, you demonstrate both civic leadership and civic character.

> *The right to do something does not mean that doing it is right.*
> —William Safire, American author, journalist, and presidential speechwriter

> **Civility and democracy go hand-in-hand; when the former is practiced, the latter is protected.**

> *Injustice anywhere is a threat to justice everywhere.*
> —Martin Luther King, Jr., civil rights leader and winner of the Nobel Peace Prize

The Campus Community

The term "university" derives from the Latin, meaning "the whole"; and the term "college" derives from the Latin, meaning "community." Thus, colleges and universities should be places where the ideals of a unified community are valued strongly and practiced vigorously.

In addition to combating campus incivility, you can promote campus community by encouraging students to engage in campus traditions and rituals (or help create them if they don't already exist). Such practices unite students, connecting them both to their campus and to each other (Kuh, 1997; Manning, 2000).

> *For some students, college represents their first opportunity to experience what it is like to live in a real community where we assume responsibility for each other.*
> —David Boren, President of the University of Oklahoma

Reflection 12.2

Does your campus have any long-standing traditions or rituals? If yes, what are they? If no, can you think of any that might be worth starting?

Campus communities become stronger when its members share a common space (Strange & Banning, 2001). You can take a leadership role in this regard by creating or advocating for spaces and places on campus where students can come together to share common interests and experiences. For example, you might seek a place to hold town hall meetings–where student "citizens" come together to discuss common concerns and share ideas for improving the campus community with peer leaders and campus officials. By creating such community-building opportunities, you enable students to practice the type of civic skills expected of citizens in a democratic society.

You can also promote students' civic engagement by encouraging them to participate in college governance, student elections, and student-run political organizations—such as young Democrat and Republican clubs (Bok, 2006). Studies show that when students get involved in student government and other campus organizations while in college, they're more likely to become engaged citizens after college (Verba, Schlozman, & Brady, 1995).

Another way you can foster active student citizenship is by using democratic processes when leading student groups and organizations. (See the participative decision-making processes described in chapter 11, p. 363.)

Lastly, you can strengthen community on your campus by sharing with students, and modeling for students, the six principles of campus community described in **Box 12.1**.

Box 12.1

The Six Principles of Campus Community

1. **An *Educationally Purposeful* Community:** The campus should be a place where faculty and students share academic goals and work together to strengthen the teaching-and-learning process.
2. **An *Open* Community:** The campus should be a place where civility is affirmed, and where freedom of expression and differences of opinion are accepted, protected, and promoted.
3. **A *Just* Community:** The campus should be a place where the sacredness of each person is honored and where diversity is welcomed and appreciated.
4. **A *Disciplined* Community:** The campus should be a place where individuals accept their obligations to the group and where well-defined governance procedures are used to guide members' behavior toward the common good.
5. **A *Caring* Community:** The campus should be a place where the well-being of each member is sensitively supported and where service to others is encouraged. (Caring is the foundation on which the first four principles rest; it's the key to establishing a community place where the feelings and freedoms of all its members are preserved and affirmed.)
6. **A *Celebrative* Community:** The campus should be a place where the heritage of the institution is remembered and where rituals that affirm its heritage and traditions are routinely held and well attended.

Source: Adapted from Boyer (1990).

The Carolinian Creed
—Reprinted by permission of the University of South Carolina

Choosing to join the community obligates each member to a code of civilized behavior.

As a Carolinian . . .

I will practice
personal and academic integrity;

I will respect
the dignity of all persons;

I will respect
the rights and property of others;

I will discourage
bigotry, while striving to learn from
differences in people, ideas and opinions;

I will demonstrate
concern for others, their feelings, and their need for
conditions which support their work and development.

Allegiance to these ideals requires each Carolinian
to refrain from and discourage behaviors which
threaten the freedom and respect every individual
deserves.

The Local Community

In addition to being members of a campus community, college students are members of a *local community*—the neighboring community in which their campus is located. As a peer leader, you can practice civic leadership by encouraging and organizing students' involvement in service to the local community surrounding campus. (Specific strategies for doing so are provided in **Box 12.2**.)

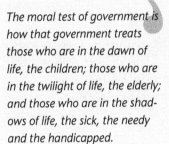

Think globally, act locally.

—Patrick Geddes, Scottish urban planner and social activist

Community Service

One of the most powerful ways that community members can demonstrate civic engagement is by stepping beyond their narrow self-interests to commit personal time and energy to help other members of their community. Volunteers measure their success not only in terms of what they do to serve themselves, but also in terms of what they do to serve others. Their volunteerism shows that they are *humane*—they have compassion for others less fortunate than themselves, and they are *humanitarian*—they have passion for helping others in need—the sick, the poor, the weak, the handicapped, the very young and the very old.

According to "servant leadership theory," effective leaders give back to the community by involving themselves in community affairs and by engaging their followers in community service (Greenleaf, 1970, 1977; Greenleaf Center for Servant Leadership, 2016). Encourage students to serve their community by participating in such volunteer activities as tutoring, working in a soup kitchen, or engaging in community cleanup. Additional target areas for community-service activities are summarized in **Box 12.2**.

The moral test of government is how that government treats those who are in the dawn of life, the children; those who are in the twilight of life, the elderly; and those who are in the shadows of life, the sick, the needy and the handicapped.

—Hubert Humphrey, 38th Vice President of the United States

We make a living by what we get; we make a life by what we give.

—Winston Churchill, English Prime Minister and Nobel Prize-winning author

Box 12.2

Target Areas for Community Service

Community Renewal
   Helping people who have lost their job or their home by supplying food and donating clothing

Disaster Preparedness
   Helping communities prepare for and recover from natural disasters (e.g., hurricanes, floods, and earthquakes)

Education
   Helping to close the learning gap for educationally underprivileged children by tutoring them, reading to them, and organizing book drives

Energy and Environment
   Helping members of the community reduce energy costs and preserve their environmental resources

Health
   Helping community members make healthy lifestyle choices that reduce their risk of illness and improve their quality of life

Hunger
   Feeding hungry families in the community and organizing food drives

Veterans and Military Families
   Supporting injured veterans and their family members

For I was hungry and you gave me food, I was thirsty and you gave me something to drink, I was a stranger and you welcomed me.

—Jesus of Nazareth, *Matthew 25:34-36*

Source: Corporation for National & Community Service (2010).

Author's Experience I've been amazed, delighted, and at times even awe-struck by the service projects that teams of students have created and implemented. I admire the capacity of student leaders to inspire and mobilize fellow students and the spirit and generosity of the countless students who participate. I've seen students gather clothing and other resources for a local needy family of seven children, construct and deliver hundreds of Halloween cards for sick children at a local hospital, assemble and mail "goody bags" for troops overseas, assemble Relay for Life teams, put together dodge ball tournaments to raise money for local charities, and create a video for "Extreme Home Makeover" to rehabilitate a community center in Haiti ravaged by an earthquake.

Students really enjoy participating and making a difference. It just requires some imaginative thinking, some inspiration, some organization and some follow through, but there are so many possibilities. As leaders, you can help turn these possibilities into realities.

— Greg Metz

> *Unless someone like you cares a whole awful lot, nothing is going to get better. It's not.*
>
> —Theodor Seuss Geisel, a.k.a. "Dr. Seuss."

Reflection 12.3

Have you ever been involved in a volunteer (community service) effort that you thought was especially meaningful, gratifying, or rewarding? If you have, what made it such a powerful experience? What or who motivated you to get involved in the first place?

As a peer leader, you can help students engage in community service by keeping them informed about available service opportunities and how to take advantage of them. Many campuses have a centralized office or person that organizes volunteer opportunities and works with various local, regional, and national organizations. (For example, see the Center for Community Engagement at the University of Cincinnati: www.uc.edu/cce.html.) If your campus has such an office, you could organize a visit to it with the students you lead or mentor.

You can also seek leads for volunteer opportunities from campus advisors, student development professionals, and faculty members. Consider creating a website or bulletin board where students receive alerts and updates about community service opportunities. Make it as easy as possible for students to capitalize on these opportunities by including information about who to contact and what specific steps they could take to get started. Social media may also be used as a tool for notification and organization of volunteer projects. The Red Cross uses blogs, Facebook, and Twitter to alert its supporters about emerging community needs and to recruit volunteers (Brionesa et al., 2011). You can use social media for the same purpose.

Another way to engage students in community service is by encouraging them to enroll in service-learning courses, which are designed to integrate service into course work with assignments that get students involved in the community (e.g., research projects that focus on solutions to current social problems or issues in the local community). Especially encourage students to pursue community-service experiences that get them beyond their familiar "comfort zone" and enable them to interact with people different than themselves. Studies show that students benefit most from volunteer experiences that involve interaction with diverse groups of people with whom they've had little or no prior experience (Astin et al., 2000; Gurin et al., 2002; Vogelgesang & Astin, 2000).

As you engage in efforts to promote student involvement in community service, be prepared to encounter some student resistance. You're likely to hear explanations (or excuses) like the following: (a) "I'm too busy with schoolwork." (b) "I have a job." (c) "That's not my thing." Certainly, you don't want to dismiss or minimize students' genuine concerns and special circumstances; however, you can still encourage their involvement by helping them identify the amount of service time and the type of service that, given their circumstances, would still be manageable and valuable. You don't want to come across as preachy or sanctimonious, but you do want to encourage and sensitively challenge students to get involved.

You can also "model the way" by engaging in community service yourself or, better yet, engaging in service with your students and organizing follow-up opportunities for everyone to come together to share their experiences. If students do volunteer, be sure to acknowledge their efforts and recognize their contributions.

Benefits of Community Service

Research indicates that participation in community service deepens student learning and advances students' intellectual development (Gurin et al., 2002; Zlotkowsky, 2002), particularly when students *reflect* on their service experiences and *connect* them to knowledge they've acquired from their college courses and life experiences. When this reflection-and-connection process takes place, a volunteer "activity" is transformed into a *learning* experience.

In addition to experiencing gains in learning, when students volunteer to serve others and contribute to the welfare of their community, they experience gains in self-esteem and self-fulfillment (Astin et al., 2000; Vogelgesang et al., 2002). By helping others, helpers get the feeling that they're doing something meaningful or purposeful with their life. In addition, studies show that people who devote time and energy to helping others are more likely to report higher levels of personal happiness and life satisfaction (Myers, 1993).

Community service is a form of experiential learning that enables students to test out and develop career-relevant skills, such as teamwork, problem-solving, decision-making, intercultural competence, and leadership (Astin et al., 2000; National Association of Colleges & Employers, 2007). Through community service, students may also acquire letters of reference and resumé-building experiences that are relevant to their future career or profession—as illustrated by the following story.

> *I know that being a peer leader will greatly benefit me when I begin my career. What I am even more sure of is what will come at the end of the day: self-pride, respect, knowledge, and contentment. I have made a difference.*
>
> —Peer leader

Author's Experience Students from the Communication Sciences and Speech Disorders Learning Community at the University of Cincinnati made Valentine's cards for the residents of a local nursing home. The students subsequently arranged a visit to the home to present the cards to the residents and mingle with them. Not only did this make the day for the residents, it also gave students in the field of speech and hearing an opportunity to gain career-relevant experience with a population of people with whom they will eventually work: the elderly.

— Greg Metz

Community service also provides students with "real world" experiences they can use to explore and discover careers that best "fit" their interests, needs, and talents. This benefit of community service is highlighted by the experiences of the two students in the following story.

Author's Experience I was once advising two first-year students, Kim and Chris. Kim was thinking about becoming a physical therapist and Chris was thinking about becoming an elementary school teacher. To help Kim get a better idea if physical therapy was the career for her, I suggested that she visit a hospital near campus to inquire about the possibility of doing volunteer work in the physical therapy unit. As it turned out, the hospital needed volunteers; she volunteered and really loved the volunteer work she did in the physical therapy unit. Kim's volunteer experience confirmed for her that a physical therapist is what she wanted to be. Energized by her volunteer experience, she went on to complete a degree in physical therapy and became a physical therapist. Similarly, I suggested to Chris that he test his interest in becoming an elementary school teacher by visiting some local schools to see if they could use a volunteer teacher's aide. One of the schools did need his services, so Chris volunteered as a teacher's aide for ten weeks. About two weeks into his volunteer experience, he came into my office to tell me that the kids were just about driving him crazy and he was no longer interested in becoming a teacher! He finished up his ten-week volunteer commitment, but changed his major from education to communication and ended up working in the broadcasting industry.

Kim and Chris were the first two students that I advised to get involved in volunteer work to test their career interests. Their volunteer experiences proved to be so useful in helping them identify or modify their career path that I continued to encourage all my students to get volunteer experience in the career field they were considering.

— *Joe Cuseo*

Reflection 12.4

Are you optimistic about your capacity to get other students involved in volunteer or community service efforts? Why?

The Societal Community

Besides being members of a local community, we are also members of *society*—a larger group of people organized under the same social system. The larger societal community is stratified into socioeconomic classes (based on income, education, and job status) with unequal levels of social and economic capital. For instance, in the United States, the wealthiest 20% of Americans controls approximately 85% of America's income and the income gap is growing (Silver, 2014). In addition to lower income, groups occupying lower socioeconomic strata also have poorer educational and social-networking opportunities (Feagin & Feagin, 2012). One important way in which you can serve as a civic leader is by engaging students in volunteer experiences designed to help members our societal community who lack educational opportunities and socioeconomic privileges (e.g., tutoring children in poor communities and organizing food drives for the homeless).

Reflection 12.5

Why do you think poverty and homelessness continue to exist in our society? Do you predict that these societal problems will eventually be solved? If no, why not? If yes, what will it take?

The National Community

In addition to being members of society, we are also citizens of a nation. In contrast to nations governed by dictators and autocrats, people living in democratic nations govern themselves by selecting (electing) their own leaders. The term "democracy" derives from the Greek "demos" (people) and "kratos" (rule); thus, literally translated, democracy means "people rule."

The right to vote is one of the distinctive privileges of being a citizen in a democratic nation. This privilege brings with it the responsibility of participating in the nation's governance through the voting process. In a democracy, deciding to vote isn't just a political choice, it's a patriotic act. Disappointingly, American citizens between the ages of 18 and 24 continue to display the lowest voter-turnout rate of any age group that's eligible to vote (Center for Information & Research on Civic Learning and Engagement, 2010). Also disappointing are the results of surveys indicating that first-year college students rank preparation for citizenship and civic engagement among the least important reasons for attending college (Schneider, 2005). As a peer leader, you can take an active role in increasing student awareness of the importance of developing citizenship skills and by urging them to vote in national, state, and local elections. (Box 12.3 supplies you with specific strategies for doing so.)

For democracy to survive and political freedom to thrive, voting citizens in democratic nations need to be well-informed, ask intelligent questions, and make wise choices about whom they elect as leaders and lawmakers (Bishop, 1986; Cheney, 1989). This was the primary reason why America's original colleges (the colonial colleges) were established in the first place—to educate young adults broadly and deeply so they could use their knowledge to make wise decisions about who to elect as leaders of our new nation and prepare to become future leaders themselves (Association of American Colleges & Universities, 2007).

Thus, a successful democracy depends on citizens who can learn deeply and think critically, and use these skills to make discerning decisions about their elected leaders. As a peer leader, you can help students develop deep learning and thinking skills (see chapter 7) and encourage them to apply these skills to the voting process.

> *Most people today think of college primarily as a stepping-stone to well-paid careers but not as a vital means for achieving better government or stronger communities.*
>
> —Derek Bok, President Emeritus and Research Professor, Harvard University

> *Knowledge will forever govern ignorance; and a people who mean to be their own governors [in a democracy] must arm themselves with the power which knowledge gives.*
>
> —James Madison, 4th president of the United States; co-signer of the American Constitution and Bill of Rights

> *If a nation expects to be ignorant and free, it expects what never was or will be."*
>
> —Thomas Jefferson, 3rd president of the United States and principal author of the Declaration of Independence

Reflection 12.6

What would you say to counter students who claim they don't vote because:

(a) "One vote won't really make a difference in the final outcome."

(b) "The political system is rigged and can't really be changed"

Strategies for Encouraging Student Participation in the Voting Process

- Work with the technology department on campus to place the "Rock the Vote" registration tool on your campus websites. (See: www.rockthevote.com)
- Work with the local board of elections to create an on-campus polling location.
- Plan parades to polls and absentee-ballot mailing parties. (See: www.longdisancevoter.org)
- Collect pledges to vote.
- Serve as poll watchers on Election Day and encourage other students to join you.
- Steer students to resources where they can access candidates' stands on key issues (e.g., votesmart.org).
- Help students detect misleading campaign ads by encouraging them to visit such websites as: Factcheck.org, Flackcheck.org, and Politifact.com
- Invite candidates or candidates' advocates to campus for organized debates, discussion forums, or town hall meetings.

Get involved. Don't gripe about things unless you are making an effort to change them. You can make a difference if you dare.

—Richard C. Holbrooke, former Director of the Peace Corps and American Ambassador to the United Nations

"Town hall meetings" are informal public meetings open to everybody in the community; they got that name because these meetings were originally held in the towns of colonial America. At these meetings, all members of the community are able to voice their opinions and pose questions to public figures or elected officials. By getting students involved in town hall meetings and similar public debates, you not only promote their civic engagement, you also help them acquire one of the key skills associated with a college education: seeking out and considering alternative points of view (Bok, 2006).

Source: Adapted from Loeb (2012).

You can also help students get politically involved by engaging them in efforts to raise public awareness about important national issues. Here are some activities you can suggest to, or do with, your students:

Too many people have developed into observers instead of activists . . . they act as if they are spectators instead of citizens."

—Komives, Lucas, & McMahon, *Exploring Leadership: For College Students Who Want to Make a Difference*

- Letter-writing campaigns to political representatives
- Attending meetings on local government or school affairs
- Signing petitions
- Attending political rallies
- Fundraising—gathering money or other resources to help meet a local, regional, national, or international need
- Volunteering for a political party or candidate

Studies show that the above forms of political engagement are declining in America (Bok, 2006; Putnam, 2000). As a civic leader, you can help revive them.

Another way in which you can engage students in the political process is through community organizing and public protest. A good example of this approach was the "Occupy Wall Street" protest movement organized by a group of mostly young Americans who rallied at various public places around the country to call attention to income inequality. They organized sit-ins and protests aimed at financial institutions they considered responsible for widening the income gap in favor of the very wealthy. Their protest movement moved the governor of New York to reverse his initial opposition to renewing the state's "millionaire's tax" and influenced the Los Angeles City Council's decision to pass a "responsible banking" ordinance that required banks to disclose detailed data about their lending practices (Loeb, Astin, & Palmer, 2012). The protest also spawned the creation of a community-organizing group called "Can Kicks Back" whose purpose is to give young Americans a voice in the debate over tax hikes and budget cuts. Part of the protest group's original plan was to send a giant mascot in the shape of a can to at least 500 college campuses—where they hoped to launch chapters and attract the attention of Congress (Puzzanghera, 2012).

A more recent example of the power of community organizing and public protest is the "March for Our Lives" movement led by high school students who organized 800 student-led, gun-control demonstrations across the United States and around the world. The students intend to make gun control a major issue in upcoming elections and have created a website to encourage voting and solicit funding to support political candidates committed to taking action on gun control (Burns & Turkewitz, 2018).

The Global Community

Beyond being citizens of a national community (our country), we are also members of an international community that includes close to 200 nations around the globe (Rosenberg, 2014). In today's internationally interdependent world, citizens of all nations are affected by events in nations other than their own. Traditional boundaries between countries are blurring or disappearing altogether due to increasing international travel, international trading, and the creation of international corporations. In addition, the information-technology explosion is enabling communication to take place between citizens of different nations at a more frequent and rapid rate than any time in world history (Dryden & Vos, 1999; Friedman, 2005; Smith, 1994). The Internet (originally called the "worldwide web") has truly made today's world a "small world after all," and success in it requires an international perspective.

You can encourage students to become active members of this interdependent global community by taking courses that have a global focus (e.g., international relations) and partaking in international experiential-learning opportunities (e.g., study abroad or study travel). Research on students who study abroad indicates that it changes their perspective on the world and promotes: (a) greater appreciation of international and cross-cultural differences, (b) greater interest in world affairs, and (c) greater commitment to peace and international cooperation (Bok, 2006; Kauffmann et al., 1992). Research also shows that students who study abroad experience such personal benefits as increased self-confidence, a stronger sense of independence, and the ability to function effectively in complex or unfamiliar environments (Bok, 2006; Carlson et al., 1990). When students learn about and from people of other nations, they extend their sense of citizenship beyond the boundaries of their own country—they become *cosmopolitan*—a citizen of the world.

As "global citizens" sharing the same planet, we have a collective responsibility to protect Earth's natural resources and the life forms that depend on its natural resources for their current and future survival. Scientists across the globe have reached consensus that man-made pollution is building up levels of carbon dioxide in the atmosphere, causing temperatures to rise (and sometimes fall) around the world (Intergovernmental Council on Climate Change, 2013; IPCC, 2014). These changing temperatures are creating more extreme weather conditions and more frequent natural disasters—such as droughts, wildfires, hurricanes, and dust storms (Joint Science Academies Statement, 2005; National Resources Defense Council, 2005, 2012). Addressing the problem of climate change requires a global perspective and appreciation of how waste emissions generated

> *Treat the Earth well. It was not given to you by your parents. It was loaned to you by your children.*
>
> —Kenyan proverb

by all countries around the world must be held to an environmentally sustainable level in order to preserve the future health of the planet and the health of future generations who will rely on its resources (Daly, 1999; Goodland, 2002). As a peer leader, you can demonstrate leadership by increasing students' global awareness and encouraging them to engage in causes that serve to preserve our shared ecology.

Reflection 12.7

Other than climate change (a.k.a. global warming), could you identify another "global" issue that peer leaders should help raise student awareness of and commitment to?

Conclusion

The well-being of all communities (local, societal, national, and global) rests on its members' collective consciousness, individual commitments, and personal contributions. We have received much from our communities and it is our obligation—our "civic responsibility"—to give back to them. According to Howard Gardner, an internationally acclaimed psychologist, in order for today's young people to thrive in the communities of the future, they will need to demonstrate "ethical" commitment—an understanding of the needs of others, willingness to go beyond narrow self-interest, and take the initiative to get involved in broader societal and global issues (Gardner, 2006).

Internet Resources

For additional information relating to civic engagement and leadership, consult the following websites:

Community Service

www.nationalservice.gov/

This is a nationwide online resource for locating volunteer opportunities in your community and for creating your own opportunities. It's also the website of the *Corporation for National and Community Service*—a federal agency in charge of former President Obama's national call-to-service initiative, "United We Serve."

www.payitforwardfoundation.org/

Website for the *Pay it Forward Foundation*, an organization started by a small group of University of Minnesota students who wanted to find a way for college students to do things to improve their world, both locally and internationally. They created a group called "Students Today, Leaders Forever" (STLF). Their main event each year is a bus trip that students take during spring break to several cities, where they engage in community service projects. They call the event the "Pay It Forward" tour, because it's expected that those they serve will, in turn, "pay it forward" and do the same for other members of their community.

www.ysa.org/ServiceVote
Home page for *Youth Service America*, an organization that improves communities by increasing the number and diversity of young people, ages 5-25, who become engaged in community service, service learning, and community leadership.

www.americorps.gov/
Home of *AmeriCorps*, a governmental organization that addresses critical needs in communities all across America. AmeriCorps is made up of three main programs:
1. *AmeriCorps State and National*, which supports a broad range of local service programs that engage thousands of Americans in intensive service to meet critical community needs.
2. *AmeriCorps Volunteers in Service to America (VISTA)*, a national service program whose purpose is to fight poverty.
3. *AmeriCorps National Civilian Community Corps (NCCC)*— a full-time residential program for 18-24 year olds that's designed to strengthen communities and develop community leaders by involving them in direct, team-based national and community service projects.

www.peacecorps.gov
The Peace Corps originated in 1960, when then-Senator John F. Kennedy challenged students at the University of Michigan to serve their country in the cause of peace by living and working in developing countries. Since then, Peace Corps Volunteers from the United States have served in almost 140 countries, helping their citizens with issues such as AIDS education, information technology, and environmental preservation.

Voting and Political Engagement
www.aascu.org/programs/ADP/
Website of *The American Democracy Project (ADP)*, a multi-campus initiative that focuses on higher education's role in preparing the next generation of informed, engaged citizens in our democracy. The project began in 2003 as an initiative of the American Association of State Colleges and Universities (AASCU) in partnership with *The New York Times*.

www.Compact.org/initiatives/campus-vote-home
Home page for *Campus Compact's* election engagement resources and the *Campus Election Engagement Project*—a related effort led by Paul Loeb (author of *Soul of a Citizen*) who works with Campus Compact to increase student involvement in the voting process.

https://www.rockthevote.org
Website for *Rock the Vote*, an organization that uses music, popular culture, new technologies, and grassroots organizing strategies to motivate and mobilize young people across the country to participate in every election and use their right to vote to promote political and social change.

Community Organizing

www.communitychange.org

Website for the *Center for Community Change*, a national organization whose mission is building the power and capacity of low-income citizens to improve their communities and change political policies that adversely affect their lives.

https://peoplesaction.org

Home page for the *National People's Action (NPA)*, a community organizing group with over 200 organizers who work to unite everyday people in cities, towns, and rural areas to promote economic and racial justice.

References

American Psychological Association (2012). *Civic engagement.* Retrieved October 1, 2012, from www.apa.org/education/undegrad/civic-engagement.aspx

Association of American Colleges & Universities (2007). *College learning for the new global century.* A Report from the National Leadership Council for Liberal Education and America's promise. Washington, DC: Association of American Colleges & Universities.

Astin, A. W., Vogelgesang, L. J., Ikeda, E. K., & Yee, J. A. (2000). *How service-learning affects students.* Los Angeles: Higher Education Research Institute, University of California.

Bellah, R. N., Madsen, R., Sullivan, W. M., Swidler, A., & Tipton, S. M. (1985). *Habits of the heart: Individualism and commitment in American life.* Berkeley: University of California Press.

Bishop, S. (1986). Education for political freedom. *Liberal Education, 72*(4), 322–325.

Bok, D. (2006). *Our underachieving colleges.* Princeton, NJ: Princeton University Press.

Boyer, E. L. (1990). *Campus life: In search of community.* San Francisco: Jossey-Bass.

Brionesa, R. L., Kucha, B., Liu, B. F., & Lin, Y. (2011). Keeping up with the digital age: How the American Red Cross uses social media to build relationships. *Public Relations Review, 37*(1), 37–43.

Bruhn, J. G. (2005). *The sociology of community connections.* New York: Kluwer Academic/Plenum.

Burns, A., & Turkewitz, J. (2018, March 22). Beyond gun control, student marchers aim to upend elections. *The New York Times.* Retrieved from https://www.nytimes.com/2018/03/22/us/politics/march-for-our-lives-gun-control.html

Carlson, J. S., Burn, B. B., Useem, J., & Yachimowicz, D. (1990). *Study abroad: The experience of American undergraduates.* New York: Greenwood Press.

Center for Information & Research on Civic Learning and Engagement (CIRCLE) (2010). *Youth voting.* Retrieved from www.civicyouth.org/quick-facts/youth-voting/

Cheney, L. V. (1989). *50 hours: A core curriculum for college students.* Washington, DC: National Endowment for the Humanities.

Corporation for National & Community Service (2010). *United we serve.* Retrieved from www.serve.gov/toolkits.asp

Daly, H. E. (1999). *Ecological economics and the ecology of economics.* Cheltenham, UK: Edward Elgar Publishing.

Dryden, G., & Vos, J. (1999). *The learning revolution: To change the way the world learns.* Torrance, CA: Learning Web.

Feagin, J., & Feagin, C. (2012). *Racial and ethnic relations* (9th ed.). Saddle River, NJ: Prentice Hall.

Forni, P. M. (2002). *Choosing civility: The twenty-five rules of considerate conduct.* New York: St. Martin's Press.

Friedman, T. L. (2005). *The world is flat: A brief history of the twenty-first century.* New York: Farrar, Straus & Giroux.

Gardner, H. (2006). *Five minds for the future.* Cambridge, MA: Harvard Business School Press.

Goodland, R. (2002). Sustainability: Human, social, economic, and environmental. In T. Munn (Ed.), *Encyclopedia of global environmental change* (pp. 488-489). Hoboken, NJ: Wiley.

Greenleaf, R. K. (1970). *The servant as leader.* Westfield, IN: Greenleaf Center for Servant Leadership.

Greenleaf, R. K. (1977). *Servant leadership: A journey into the nature of legitimate power and greatness.* New York: Paulist Press.

Greenleaf Center for Servant Leadership (2016). *What is servant leadership?* Retrieved from https://www.greenleaf.org/what-is-servant-leadership/

Gurin, P., Dey, E. L., Hurtado, S., & Gurin, G. (2002). Diversity and higher education: Theory and impact on educational outcomes. *Harvard Educational Review, 72,* 330-367.

Higher Education Research Institute (HERI). (1996). *A social change model of leadership development: Guidebook version III.* Los Angeles: University of California Los Angeles Higher Education Research Institute.

Intergovernmental Council on Climate Change. (2013). *Climate change 2013: The physical science basis.* Working Group I Contribution to the Fifth Assessment Report of the Intergovernmental Council on Climate Change. Switzerland: Intergovernmental Panel on Climate Change. Retrieved from http://www. climatechange2013.org/images/uploads/WGI_AR5_SPM_brochure.pdf

IPCC. (2014). *Climate change 2014: Synthesis report.* Contribution of Working Groups I, II and III to the Fifth Assessment Report of the Intergovernmental Panel on Climate Change [Core Writing Team, R. K. Pachauri & L. A. Meyer (Eds.)]. IPCC, Geneva, Switzerland. Retrieved from http://www.ipcc.ch/pdf/assessment-report/ar5/syr/AR5_SYR_FINAL_Front_matters.pdf

Joint Science Academies Statement. (2005). *Global response to climate change.* Retrieved from http://nationalacademies.org/onpi/06072005.pdf

Kaufmann, N. L., Martin, J. M., Weaver, H. D., & Weaver, J. (1992). *Students abroad: Strangers at home: Education for a global society.* Yarmouth, ME: Intercultural Press.

Komives, S. R., Lucas, N., & McMahon, T. R. (2007). *Exploring leadership: For college students who want to make a difference* (2nd ed.). San Francisco: Jossey-Bass.

Kuh, G. D. (1997). Strengthening the ties that bind: Cultural events, traditions, and rituals. In J. N. Gardner & G. Van der Veer (Eds.), *The senior year experience: Facilitating integration, reflection, closure, and transition* (pp. 152-170). San Francisco: Jossey-Bass.

Liden, R. C., Wayne, S. J., Zhao, H., & Henderson, D. (2008). Servant leadership: Development of a multidimensional measure and multi-level assessment. *Leadership Quarterly, 19,* 161-177.

Loeb, P. (2012, March 23). *10 things schools can do this spring to engage their students in the elections.* Retrieved from www.paulloeb.org/College/spring2012.html

Loeb, P., Astin, A., & Palmer, P. J. (2012). *My vote doesn't matter.* Retrieved from www. insidehighered.com/views/2012/09/25/essay-role-college-encouraging-students-vote

Manning, K. (2000). *Rituals, ceremonies, and cultural meaning in higher education.* Westport, CT: Greenwood.

Myers, D. G. (1993). *The pursuit of happiness: Who is happy—and why?* New York: Morrow.

National Association of Colleges & Employers. (2007). *Developing the diverse college-educated work force.* Retrieved from www.naceweb.org/Journal/2007october/Diverse_Work_Force/?...

National Resources Defense Council. (2005). *Global warming: A summary of recent findings on the changing global climate.* Retrieved from http://www.nrdc.org/global/Warming/fgwscience.asp

Northouse, P. G. (2016). *Leadership: Theory and practice* (7th ed.). Los Angeles: SAGE.

Putnam, R. D. (2000). *Bowling alone: The collapse and revival of American community.* New York: Simon & Schuster.

Puzzanghera, J. (2012). Millennial group pushes for debt plan. *Los Angeles Times,* November 13, p. B2.

Rosenberg, M. (2014). *The number of countries in the word.* Retrieved from http://geography.about.com/cs/countries/a/numbercountries.htm

Schneider, C. G. (2005). Liberal education and the civic engagement gap. In A. Kezar, T. C. Chambers, & J. C. Burkhardt (Eds.), *Higher education for the public good: Emerging voices from a national movement* (pp. 127-145). San Francisco: Jossey-Bass.

Silver, D. (2014, January 7). *5 facts about economic inequality.* Pew Research Center. Retrieved from http://www.pewresearch.org/fact-tank/2014/01/07/5-facts-about-economic-inequality/

Smith, R. L. (1994). The world of business. In W. C. Hartel, S. W. Schwartz, S. D. Blume, & J. N. Gardner (Eds.), *Ready for the real world* (pp. 123–135). Belmont, CA: Wadsworth Publishing.

Strange, C. C., & Banning, J. H. (2001). *Educating by design: Creating campus learning environments that work.* San Francisco: Jossey-Bass.

Verba, S., Schlozman, K. L., & Brady, H. E. (1995). *Voice and equity: Civic voluntarism in American politics.* Cambridge, MA: Harvard University Press.

Vogelgesang. L. J., & Astin, A. W. (2000). Comparing the effects of community service and service-learning. *Michigan Journal of Community Service Learning, 7,* 24-34.

Vogelgesang, L. J., Ikeda, E. K., Gilmartin, S. K., & Keup, J. R. (2002). Service-learning and the first-year experience: Outcomes related to learning and persistence. In E. Zlotkowsky (Ed.), *Service-learning and the first-year experience: Preparing students for personal success and civic responsibility* (pp. 27–36; Monograph No. 34). Columbia, SC: University of South Carolina, National Resource Center for the First-Year Experience and Students in Transition.

Wagner, W. (2006). The social change model of leadership: A brief overview. *Concepts & Connections, 15*(1), p. 9.

Zlotkowsky, E. (Ed.). (2002). *Service-learning and the first-year experience: Preparing students for personal success and civic responsibility* (Monograph No. 34). Columbia, SC: University of South Carolina, National Resource Center for the First-Year Experience and Students in Transition.

Exercise 12.1 Quote Reflections

Review the sidebar quotes contained in this chapter and select two that you think would be especially valuable to share with the students you lead or mentor.

For each quote, write a short statement explaining why you chose it.

Exercise 12.2 Journal Reflections

1. When you hear the word "political," what thoughts or images immediately come to mind?

2. When you hear the word "community," what thoughts or images come to mind?

3. On a scale of 1-5 (5 = high, 1 = low), rate your campus in terms of how it embodies the following six principles of a campus community (Boyer, 1990).

   An *educationally purposeful* community: the campus is a place where faculty and students share academic goals and work together to strengthen the teaching-and-learning process.

   Rating ____

   Reason for Rating:

   An *open* community: the campus is a place where civility is affirmed, and where freedom of expression and differences of opinion are accepted, protected, and promoted.

   Rating ____

   Reason for Rating:

   A *just* community: the campus is a place where the sacredness of each person is honored and where diversity is welcomed and appreciated.

   Rating ____

   Reason for Rating:

A *disciplined* community: the campus is a place where individuals accept their obligations to the group and where well-defined governance procedures are used to guide members' behavior toward the common good.

Rating ___

Reason for Rating:

A *caring* community: the campus is a place where the well-being of each member is sensitively supported and where service to others is encouraged.

Rating ___

Reason for Rating:

A *celebrative* community: the campus is a place where the heritage of the institution is remembered and where rituals that affirm its heritage and traditions are routinely held and well attended.

Rating ___

Reason for Rating:

Look back at your ratings and identify the principle of campus community you rated the lowest.

As a peer leader, what could you do to improve your campus with respect to this principle of community?

Exercise 12.3 Getting Students Involved in the Voting Process

1. Go to www.Compact.org/initiatives/campus-vote-home. This is the home page for the *Campus Election Engagement Project*, a nationwide effort to help get students involved in elections.

2. Click on the link titled, "Ten Things Campuses Can Do This Spring to Engage Students in the Elections" and print out the list.

3. Share the list with your students and ask for volunteers to take responsibility for implementing different items on the checklist.

Exercise 12.4 Promoting Political Knowledge and Engagement

1. Go to www.aascu.org/programs/ADP/ This is the site of *The American Democracy Project (ADP),* an initiative of the American Association of State Colleges and Universities (AASCU) whose mission is to prepare the next generation of informed, engaged citizens for our democracy.

2. Click the link titled, "Special Days in Action" (in the side margin) and print out the information associated with each of the special days listed at this link.

3. Share this list with your students and discuss whether any of these action items should be pursued by members of your group or organization.

Exercise 12.5 Identifying and Organizing Local Community Service Opportunities

1. Go to https://www.nationalservice.gov/focus-areas/environmental-stewardship
   This is a nationwide online resource for locating volunteer opportunities in your community.

2. Go to the "Focus Areas" link and click on a category of service (education, veterans, etc.) that is most relevant to your leadership role and the students you lead.

3. From the list of possibilities that come up, choose three that you think would be most appealing to your students.

4. Ask your students to reach agreement about their first choice and contact that organization to discuss ways in which your student group could help advance its cause.

Exercise 12.6 Creating Service Opportunities at the Local, National and International Level

1. Go to www.payitforwardfoundation.org/ This is the website for the Pay it Forward Foundation, an organization started by a small group of University of Minnesota students who wanted to find a way for students to do things to improve their world, both locally and internationally.

2. Click on the "About Us" link and show the video to your students.

3. If any of your students show interest or excitement about getting involved in this organization, ask them to follow-up by contacting the person whose contact information is listed at the end of the video.

4. Have the students who contacted the organization report back to your group about what they learned and whether they think it's an organization that your group should join.

Exercise 12.7 Identifying and Publicizing Service-Learning Courses

Check your college catalog or university bulletin to see if there are any courses offered that integrate community service into students' course work. (If you cannot find any courses listed, check with the office of the Academic Dean or Vice President for Academic Affairs.)

Compile a list of the service-learning courses available on your campus and share it with the students you lead.

Name _____ Date _____

Exercise 12.8 Strategy Reflections

Review the strategies suggested for *encouraging student participation in the voting process* on p. 404. Select two strategies that you'd be most comfortable implementing and think would work most effectively with the students you lead or mentor.

APPENDIX A
Key Campus Resources and Why Students Should Use Them

Below is a description of the key resources offered on most college campuses and the reasons why students should utilize them. The specific names given to these resources may differ from campus to campus, but their purposes are similar, as are their benefits for the students who capitalize on them. Strongly encourage students to take advantage of these resources; they can play a pivotal role in improving students' level of academic performance and their ability to persist to college completion.

Learning Center (a.k.a. Academic Resource Center or Academic Success Center). Students can use this campus resource to strengthen their academic performance in any course or field of study. The individual and group tutoring provided at the Center can help students master difficult course concepts and assignments, and the people working there are professionally trained to help students learn *how to learn*. Just as professors are experts in the subjects they teach, learning resource professionals are experts on how students learn. They have the knowledge and expertise to equip students with effective learning strategies that can be used to handle the unique challenges posed by different subjects and teaching styles. Learning Centers also employ trained peer tutors who can be especially effective learning coaches because (a) they're close in age and experience to the students seeking help, which may enable them to explain concepts in language that's easier for students to understand, and (b) they've recently learned the material that the help-seeking students are currently trying to learn.

Despite the powerful advantages associated with student use of academic support services, these services are typically underused by college students—especially by students who need them the most (Cuseo et al., 2016). Some college students believe that seeking academic help is an admission that they're not smart, self-reliant, or capable of succeeding on their own. Don't let your students buy into this myth. In high school, students may have learned that you only go to a campus office if you're *required* to, or if you've done something wrong. In college, students *choose* to use campus offices to enhance their success by taking advantage of the personalized support these offices and programs provide.

> At colleges where I've taught, the grade-point averages of students who used the Learning Center were higher than the college average, and honors students were more likely to use the Center than other students.
>
> —Joe Cuseo, Professor Emeritus of Psychology

Be sure students know that using academic support services doesn't mean they have a "problem" requiring remedial repair work, or that they're on the brink of failure and need to be put on academic life support. All students benefit from academic support services and using these services is a sign of motivation, resourcefulness, and pursuit of academic excellence.

Writing Center. Writing is an academic skill that students will use in virtually all their courses, freshman through senior year. Thus, when students strengthen their writing skills, they will simultaneously strengthen their college grades. Many college campuses offer specialized support for students seeking to improve their ability to write. Typically referred to as the Writing Center, this is the place on campus where students can receive assistance at any stage of the writing process, whether it be collecting and organizing their ideas, composing a first draft, or proofreading a final draft. Encourage student to take advantage of this resource to improve their writing, which, in turn, will improve their overall academic performance in college as well as their career performance after college.

> *The next best thing to knowing something is knowing where to find it.*
>
> —Dr. Samuel Johnson, English literary figure and original author of the Dictionary of the English Language (1747)

Campus Library. Librarians are professional educators who provide instruction outside of class; students can learn from them just as they can learn from instructors inside of class. Remind students that when they develop research skills for accessing, retrieving, and evaluating information, they're developing lifelong learning skills that can be used throughout college and in their future career.

Academic Advisement. The Academic Advisement Center is the campus resource where students can get help with course selection, educational planning, and choosing or changing a major. Studies show that students who have clarified their educational and career goals are more likely to persist in college and complete their degree (Braxton, Hirschy, & McClendon, 2011; Kuh et al., 2011; Lotkowski, Robbins, & Noeth, 2004). Research also shows that most new students need assistance in clarifying their educational goals, deciding on a college major, and identifying their career options (Cuseo, 2005; Tinto, 2012). Assure first-year students that being undecided about their educational and career goals is nothing to be embarrassed about. However, advise them that they should start thinking about their major and career plans now. Encourage them to connect early and often with an academic advisor to help them think through their educational goals and discover a college major that best complements their interests, talents, and values.

Disability Services (a.k.a. Disability Resource Center). If students have a documented physical or learning disability that's interfering with their performance in college, or if they think they may have a disability, direct them to the Office of Disability Services for assistance and support. Programs and services typically provided by this office include:

- Assessment for learning disabilities,
- Verification of eligibility for disability support services,
- Authorization of academic accommodations for students with disabilities,
- Specialized counseling, advising, and tutoring.

Financial Aid Office. If you know of any students who are concerned about their ability to pay for college, refer them to this office. The process of applying (and reapplying) for financial aid can be complicated and intimidating for students and may sometimes prevent them from capitalizing on the fiscal support that they're eligible to receive. Professional financial aid counselors can walk students through the process and help them find:

- Low-interest student loans,
- Grants or scholarships, and
- Part-time campus employment as a work–study student.

Remind students to check their e-mail regularly for messages from the Financial Aid Office, especially messages pertaining to financial-aid application and renewal deadlines. If they have any doubt about whether they're using the most effective plan to finance their college education, encourage them to make an appointment to see a professional in the Financial Aid Office.

Health or Wellness Center. The Health Center is the campus resource designed to help students develop productive habits for maintaining physical health and attaining optimal wellness. It's also the place where students should be directed to receive medical care for physical illnesses and sexually transmitted diseases.

The transition from high school to college often requires students to take more personal responsibility for decisions that affect their health and well-being, particularly if they're living away from home. Students who develop good health habits are better equipped to cope with college stress and better positioned to achieve peak levels of academic performance.

Career Development Center (a.k.a. Career Center). Students may think their career is light-years away, but they should be reminded that the process of career exploration, planning, and preparation begins in the first year of college. Research indicates that students are more likely to stay in college and graduate from college when they see a connection between their current college experience and their future career goals (Braxton et al., 2011; Kuh et al., 2011; Tinto, 1993). Unfortunately, however, most first-year students are uncertain about their career goals and vocational plans (Gordon & Steele, 2003).

The Career Development Center is the place on campus where students can receive help identifying their future career goals and developing educational plans to reach those goals. The Center is likely to provide personal career counseling, deliver workshops on career exploration and development, and organize career fairs where students can meet professionals working in a variety of career fields.

Personal Counseling Center. Here's where students can get ideas and develop strategies for managing college stress, gaining greater self-awareness, and reaching their full potential. Be sure students realize that personal counselors are professionals who not only deal with mental health issues; they're also professional educators who are able to help students improve their relationships, develop social and emotional intelligence, and reach their full potential.

> **Personal counseling is not just for students experiencing emotional problems. It's for all students who want to enrich their quality of life.**

References

Braxton, J. M., Hirschy, A. S., & McClendon, S. A. (2011). *Understanding and reducing college student departure.* ASHE-ERIC Higher Education Report, Volume 30, Number 3.

Cuseo, J. B. (2005). "Decided," "undecided," and "in transition": Implications for academic advisement, career counseling, and student retention. In R. S. Feldman (Ed.), *Improving the first year of college: Research and practice* (pp. 27–50). Mahwah, NJ: Lawrence Erlbaum.

Cuseo, J. B., & Thompson, A., Campagna, M., & Fecas, V. S. (2016). *Thriving in college & beyond: Research-based strategies for academic success and personal development* (4th ed.). Dubuque, IA: Kendall Hunt.

Gordon, V. N., & Steele, G. E. (2003). Undecided first-year students: A 25-year longitudinal study. *Journal of the First-Year Experience and Students in Transition, 15*(1), 19–38.

Kuh, G. D., (2005). Student engagement in the first year of college. In M. L. Upcraft, J. N. Gardner, B. O. Barefoot, & Associates (Eds.), *Challenging and supporting the first-year student: A handbook for improving the first year of college* (pp. 86-107). San Francisco: Jossey-Bass.

Kuh, G. D., Kinzie, J., Buckley, J. A., Bridges, B. K., & Hayek, J. C. (2011). *Piecing together the student success puzzle: Research, propositions, and recommendations: ASHE Higher Education Report* (Vol. 116). Hoboken, NJ: John Wiley & Sons.

Lotkowski, V. A., Robbins, S. B., & Noeth, R. J. (2004). *The role of academic and non-academic factors in improving student retention.* ACT Policy Report. Retrieved from https://www.act.org/research/policymakers/pdf/college_retention.pdf

Tinto, V. (1993). *Leaving college: Rethinking the causes and cures of student attrition* (2nd ed.). Chicago: The University of Chicago Press.

Tinto, V. (2012). *Completing college: Rethinking institutional action.* Chicago: The University of Chicago Press.

APPENDIX B

Leadership Self-Assessment Instrument

Assessing Your Leadership Skills and Attributes

Effective leaders continually assess how well they are leading and use the results to become better leaders. This self-assessment instrument is designed to help you engage in the process of continuous leadership improvement. It isn't intended to be a test of your leadership competence or potential; it's simply a tool to help you recognize and accentuate your strengths, and identify areas for self-improvement and future growth.

The instrument's 12 sections correspond to the 12 chapters of the book. You could complete the instrument one section at a time—after you've read the corresponding chapter and completed its reflections and exercises. Using the instrument in this way would enable you to get immediate feedback on whether you acquired the leadership knowledge covered in each chapter immediately after completing the chapter. You could also use the instrument to assess your overall leadership development. For example, you could complete the entire instrument *before* and *after* experiencing a leadership development course or program to assess how much you've changed or improved.

Lastly, you may use the instrument as a tool for "360 degree" assessment—a full-circle assessment process that involves not only assessing yourself, but also assessments you receive from your students and your supervisor(s). Comparing your self-assessment with the assessment of other parties can help you uncover personal leadership strengths you may have underestimated and discover leadership weaknesses you may have overlooked.

When answering the items on this instrument, use the following rating scale:

5 = Strongly Agree 4 = Agree 3 = Not Sure 2 = Disagree 1 = Strongly Disagree

1. The Purpose and Power of Peer Leadership

___ 1. I have a clear understanding of what "leadership" means.

___ 2. I have a clear understanding of what "mentoring" means.

___ 3. I'm aware of the different ways in which students benefit from peer leadership.

___ 4. I'm familiar with the concept of "social capital" and how peer leaders can supply it for inexperienced college students.

___ 5. I'm aware of the variety of leadership roles and positions that students hold on college campuses.

___ 6. I have reflected on my decision to become a peer leader and am aware of my reasons for becoming one.

___ 7. My motivation for becoming a peer leader is driven more by a desire to help students succeed and serve my college than to receive social recognition and build my resumé.

___ 8. I've given careful thought to what leadership roles or positions best match my leadership interests and talents.

___ 9. I'm aware of the personal attributes of great leaders and attempt to embody these attributes in my work as a peer leader.

___ 10. I'm aware of my leadership strengths and weaknesses.

___ 11. I seek feedback from others to improve my leadership effectiveness.

___ 12. I'm able to balance the sometimes-conflicting roles of being a "friend" to and "leader" of students.

---

5 = Strongly Agree 4 = Agree 3 = Not Sure 2 = Disagree 1 = Strongly Disagree

2. The Essence of Leadership

___ 1. I'm familiar with leadership theories and research.

___ 2. I use the knowledge that I've acquired from leadership theories and research to guide my leadership practices.

___ 3. I'm aware of the common myths about what makes a great leader.

___ 4. I'm a reliable leader who is accountable to others and can be counted on by others.

___ 5. Students see me as a leader who's neither phony nor hypocritical, but "real" and authentic.

___ 6. I'm an honest and ethical leader.

___ 7. I'm a humble leader who's neither showy nor boastful.

___ 8. I model the behavior I expect students to engage in.

___ 9. I'm an enthusiastic and optimistic leader.

___ 10. I recognize students' accomplishments and achievements.

___ 11. I regularly reflect on my effectiveness as a leader with an eye toward continually improving my leadership skills.

___ 12. I keep a journal or portfolio to track and document my leadership development.

---

5 = Strongly Agree　4 = Agree　3 = Not Sure　2 = Disagree　1 = Strongly Disagree

3. The College Experience

___ 1. I'm aware of the major challenges and adjustments experienced by new students during their first term in college.

___ 2. I can explain to students why college is worth it.

___ 3. I am familiar with the major theories of college student development—i.e., theories about how students adjust to college and what college experiences contribute most to their success.

___ 4. I'm familiar with the major theories of college student retention—i.e., why students remain in college and why they leave.

___ 5. I suggest different ways for students to become actively involved in the college experience, both inside and outside the classroom.

I promote students' social integration into the college community by connecting them with:

___ 6. academic advisors.

___ 7. faculty.

___ 8. student development (student support) professionals.

___ 9. peers.

___ 10. I'm familiar with the support services and resources available to students on my campus.

___ 11. I remind students that the student-support professionals on my campus care about them and can help them succeed.

___ 12. I'm aware of effective referral strategies and use these strategies to connect students with campus services.

---

5 = Strongly Agree   4 = Agree   3 = Not Sure   2 = Disagree   1 = Strongly Disagree

4. Social and Emotional Intelligence

____ 1. I'm familiar with the concepts of social and emotional intelligence and why they are important for effective leadership.

____ 2. I reach out to students and initiate relationships with them.

____ 3. I know the students I lead or mentor by name and refer to them by name.

____ 4. I get to know students on an individual basis by soliciting information about them (e.g., their interests, talents, needs, and values).

____ 5. I show interest in students by asking open-ended questions that encourage them to respond with more than one-word or one-sentence answers.

____ 6. I'm familiar with the concept of "active listening" and use this approach when leading and mentoring others.

____ 7. I gather my thoughts before speaking (rather than while speaking) so I can express my ideas concisely and give others more time to speak.

____ 8. I share my experiences with the students I lead and mentor so they, in turn, become more comfortable sharing their experiences with me.

____ 9. I make a conscious effort to remember information that students share with me and refer to it when I interact with them.

____ 10. I remain positive and optimistic about students, even when they continue to make mistakes or engage in counterproductive behavior.

____ 11. I'm aware of effective problem-solving strategies and use these strategies to help students find their own solutions to problems.

____ 12. If a student is experiencing a crisis, I know how to respond and where to refer that student for help.

---

5 = Strongly Agree   4 = Agree   3 = Not Sure   2 = Disagree   1 = Strongly Disagree

5. Setting Goals and Maintaining Motivation

____ 1. I point out to students the importance of goal setting and future planning.

____ 2. I help students set SMART goals—i.e., goals that are specific, meaningful, actionable, realistic, and time-framed.

___ 3. I am familiar with motivational strategies and share them with students to help them to continue striving toward the goals they've set for themselves.

___ 4. I check with and provide feedback to students on the progress they're making toward their goals.

___ 5. I establish SMART goals for myself as a peer leader.

___ 6. I monitor the progress I'm making toward leadership goals I've set for myself.

___ 7. I help students explore and set career goals.

___ 8. I point out to students that being aware of their personal talents, interests, and values is the first step in the process of identifying a career goal.

___ 9. I help students identify short- and mid-range goals they need to achieve in order to reach their long-term goals.

___10. I remind students to celebrate and reward themselves for reaching their short- and mid-range goals along the path to their long-term goals.

___11. I point out to students that achieving long-term goals requires resiliency—the ability to bounce back from setbacks and convert them into comebacks.

___12. I am familiar with the motivational concepts of self-efficacy, growth mindset, and grit, and can explain to students how these qualities are important for achieving their long-term goals.

_____

5 = Strongly Agree 4 = Agree 3 = Not Sure 2 = Disagree 1 = Strongly Disagree

6. Managing Time and Tasks

___ 1. I can explain to students why time management is critical for college success and why it's a challenging task for students transitioning from high school to college.

___ 2. I suggest to students ways in which they can get course work done during the "free time" they have outside of class.

___ 3. I model effective time-management habits for students to observe and emulate.

___ 4. I encourage students to take advantage of time- and task-management tools, such as portable daily planners and Smartphone apps.

___ 5. I encourage students to construct a time-management plan that includes long-range, mid-range, and short-range tasks.

___ 6. I remind students that an effective time-management plan includes scheduling time for both work and play.

___ 7. I remind students that a good time-management plan builds in some unscheduled time to accommodate unexpected emergencies and opportunities.

___ 8. I alert students to the dangers of procrastination and point out how common it is among college students.

___ 9. I can explain to students why the following belief is a myth: "People work better under the pressure of a last-minute deadline."

___ 10. I can explain to students why the following belief is a myth: "Studying ahead of time is a waste of time because you'll forget it all by test time, so you're better off doing all your studying the night before an exam."

___ 11. I'm aware of specific strategies for combating procrastination and I share these strategies with the students I mentor.

___ 12. I'm aware that some students engage in procrastination for psychological reasons and I know where to refer these students for help.

---

5 = Strongly Agree 4 = Agree 3 = Not Sure 2 = Disagree 1 = Strongly Disagree

7. Becoming a Learning Coach

___ 1. I'm familiar with research on effective learning and memory-improvement strategies.

___ 2. I can explain to students the difference between "deep" and "surface" learning (memorization).

___ 3. I share effective learning strategies with students.

___ 4. I model effective learning strategies for students to observe and emulate.

___ 5. I provide students with feedback on the effectiveness of their learning habits and strategies.

I encourage students to:

___ 6. complete reading assignments on time.

___ 7. take thorough notes in class.

___ 8. review their class notes before the next class session.

___ 9. participate in study groups.

___10. carefully review tests and assignments that have been returned to them and use the results as feedback to improve their future performance.

___11. I can explain to students what critical thinking is and how to demonstrate it.

___12. I remind students that learning effectively is not just a "school thing" but a lifelong skill that they will use beyond college and throughout life.

---

5 = Strongly Agree 4 = Agree 3 = Not Sure 2 = Disagree 1 = Strongly Disagree

8. Holistic Leadership

___ 1. I'm aware of the key dimensions of holistic (whole person) development.

___ 2. I take interest in each student as a "whole person" and provide support in ways that go beyond academics.

___ 3. I can articulate to students the concept of "wellness" and why it's important.

___ 4. I remind students that their eating habits can affect their academic performance and overall well-being.

___ 5. I help students understand how their sleeping habits can affect their academic performance and overall well-being.

___ 6. I'm familiar with the major eating disorders experienced by college students and feel confident that I can recognize students who are experiencing them.

___ 7. I can explain to students what constitutes sexual abuse, sexual assault, and sexual harassment.

___ 8. I can articulate to students the difference between alcohol use and abuse.

___ 9. I'm aware of the telltale signs (symptoms) of substance abuse and know effective strategies for reaching out to students who may be experiencing substance abuse.

___10. I'm familiar with the defense mechanism of "denial" and am aware of strategies for helping students overcome it.

___11. I'm aware of the telltale signs (symptoms) of anxiety and can recommend effective stress-management strategies for students experiencing mild or moderate anxiety.

___12. I'm familiar with the telltale signs (symptoms) of depression and can provide students with self-help strategies for coping with mild or moderate depression.

5 = Strongly Agree   4 = Agree   3 = Not Sure   2 = Disagree   1 = Strongly Disagree

9. Leadership for Diversity

____ 1. I know what diversity means and am familiar with its major forms or varieties.

____ 2. I'm aware of the major benefits of experiencing diversity and share them with the students I lead and mentor.

____ 3. I'm familiar with the concept of "ethnocentrism" and explain to students how it can bias their perceptions and beliefs about other cultures.

____ 4. I'm familiar with concept of "privilege" and inform students how it can advantage certain groups of people.

____ 5. I make intentional attempts to welcome students from diverse backgrounds to campus and to the groups and organizations I lead.

____ 6. I reach out to students from minority groups who appear to be isolated, segregated, or marginalized.

____ 7. I encourage students to learn from and about different cultures and to seek out interaction with students from diverse cultures.

____ 8. I initiate discussions of diversity among students I lead.

____ 9. I intentionally form discussion groups and learning teams composed of students from diverse backgrounds.

____ 10. I can explain what stereotyping means and provide students with strategies to guard against it.

____ 11. I can explain what prejudice and discrimination mean and supply students with strategies for guarding against them.

____ 12. I'm willing to challenge students who make prejudicial remarks or engage in discriminatory behavior.

---

5 = Strongly Agree   4 = Agree   3 = Not Sure   2 = Disagree   1 = Strongly Disagree

10. Leading Groups

____ 1. I help the groups I lead to create a vision, set goals, and stay focused on their goals.

____ 2. I'm familiar with research on group dynamics and group development.

____ 3. I use team-building activities to create solidarity and a sense of team identity among groups I lead.

___ 4. I collaborate with members of groups I lead to establish ground rules (norms) about how they should treat and interact with one another.

___ 5. I am familiar with effective public speaking and oral communication strategies and use them when making presentations to groups I lead.

___ 6. I know how to frame or phrase questions in ways that are most effective for eliciting responses from group members and stimulating group discussions.

___ 7. I am comfortable leading and facilitating discussion groups.

___ 8. I encourage members of groups I lead to become co-leaders.

___ 9. I'm able to manage unproductive or disruptive behavior that students display in group situations.

___10. I seek feedback from others on my group-facilitation skills.

___11. I encourage members of the groups I lead to reflect on, discuss, and assess how well they're performing as a team.

___12. I organize events to recognize and celebrate group accomplishments.

---

5 = Strongly Agree 4 = Agree 3 = Not Sure 2 = Disagree 1 = Strongly Disagree

11. Organizational Leadership

___ 1. I'm familiar with my college or university's table of organization (organizational chart) and its decision-making "chain of command."

___ 2. I periodically review the mission and vision of my student organization with other members to ensure we're doing what we say we do and being what we aspire to be.

___ 3. I'm aware of the mission of my college or university, and can articulate how the mission of my student organization relates to it.

___ 4. Whenever possible, I use a participative (democratic) decision-making process with members of my student organization.

___ 5. I'm familiar with the concept of consensus and with strategies for reaching consensus.

___ 6. I understand the difference between an authoritative and authoritarian style of decision-making.

___ 7. I distribute leadership across my organization by delegating responsibility to different groups and individuals.

___ 8. I'm aware of the purpose of committees and task forces, and I use them effectively to help my organization accomplish its mission and goals.

___ 9. I establish procedural rules to ensure that my organizational meetings are run in an orderly and efficient manner.

___ 10. At meetings I lead, we set an agenda and keep minutes.

___ 11. I'm willing to question and respectfully challenge campus processes, policies, and practices that are unfair to students or are interfering with the quality of their education.

___ 12. I am familiar with strategies for promoting campus-wide change.

---

5 = Strongly Agree 4 = Agree 3 = Not Sure 2 = Disagree 1 = Strongly Disagree

12. Civic Leadership

___ 1. I can articulate to students what a "community" is and the different types of communities to which they belong.

___ 2. I'm aware of the principles that embody an ideal campus community and encourage students to put them into practice.

___ 3. I am willing to confront students who display campus incivility, inside or outside the classroom.

___ 4. I can explain to students what civic engagement means and why it's important.

___ 5. I can articulate to students the benefits of engaging in community service.

___ 6. I alert students to community-service opportunities.

___ 7. I help organize community-service projects.

___ 8. I engage in community service with the students I lead and mentor.

___ 9. I encourage students to take on leadership roles in community-service projects.

___ 10. I urge students to vote in campus, local, and national elections.

___ 11. I encourage students to become engaged in political efforts aimed at solving societal problems (e.g., poverty and homelessness).

___ 12. I encourage students to become engaged in political efforts that address important global issues (e.g., human rights violations and environmental sustainability).

INDEX

CPSIA information can be obtained
at www.ICGtesting.com
Printed in the USA
FSHW020255270521
81866FS